Penn Quarter

Capitol Hill

PENN
QUARTER

THE
MALL

CAPITOL
HILL

Washington Channel

The Mall

| 0 meters | 750 |
| 0 yards | 750 |

Anacostia River

EYEWITNESS TRAVEL

WASHINGTON, DC

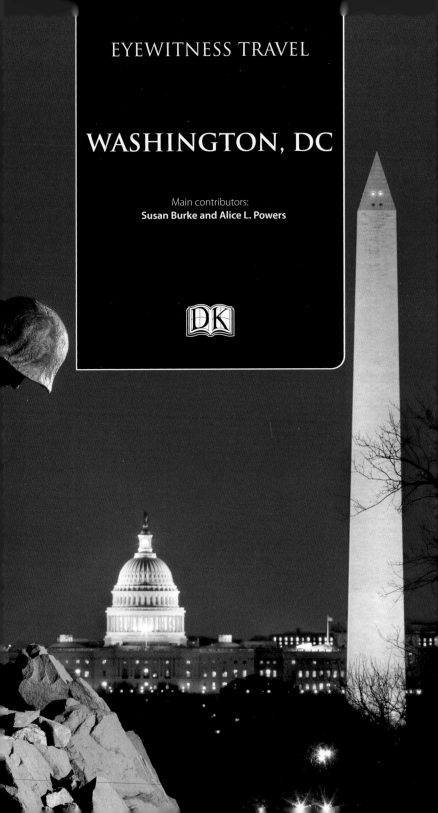

EYEWITNESS TRAVEL

WASHINGTON, DC

Main contributors:
Susan Burke and Alice L. Powers

DK

LONDON, NEW YORK,
MELBOURNE, MUNICH AND DELHI
www.dk.com

Project Editor Claire Folkard
Art Editors Tim Mann, Simon J.M. Oon
Senior Editor Helen Townsend
Editors Emily Anderson, Felicity Crowe
US Editor Mary Sutherland
Designers Gillian Andrews, Eli Estaugh,
Elly King, Rebecca Milner
DTP Designers Sam Borland, Maite Lantaron
Picture Researchers Brigitte Arora, Katherine Mesquita
Production Mel Allsop

Contributors
Susan Burke, Alice L. Powers, Jennifer Quasha, Kem Sawyer

Photographers
Philippe Dewet, Kim Sayer, Giles Stokoe, Scott Suchman

Illustrators
Stephen Conlin, Gary Cross, Richard Draper, Chris Orr & Associates, Mel Pickering,
Robbie Polley, John Woodcock

Printed and bound by L. Rex Printing Company Limited, China

First American Edition, 2000
14 15 16 17 10 9 8 7 6 5 4 3 2 1

Published in the United States by
DK Publishing, 375 Hudson Street,
New York, New York 10014

**Reprinted with revisions 2002, 2003, 2004, 2005, 2006, 2008,
2009, 2010, 2011, 2012, 2013, 2014**

Copyright © 2000, 2014 Dorling Kindersley Limited, London
A Penguin Random House Company

Published in the UK by Dorling Kindersley Limited.

A catalog record for this book is available from the Library of Congress.

ISSN 1542-1554
ISBN 978-1-46541-056-6

Floors are referred to throughout in accordance with
American usage; ie the "first floor" is at ground level.

MIX
Paper from
responsible sources
FSC™ C018179
www.fsc.org

**The information in this
DK Eyewitness Travel Guide is checked annually.**
Every effort has been made to ensure that this book is as up-to-date as possible
at the time of going to press. Some details, however, such as telephone numbers,
opening hours, prices, gallery hanging arrangements and travel information are
liable to change. The publishers cannot accept responsibility for any consequences
arising from the use of this book, nor for any material on third party websites, and
cannot guarantee that any website address in this book will be a suitable source of
travel information. We value the views and suggestions of our readers very highly.
Please write to: Publisher, DK Eyewitness Travel Guides, Dorling Kindersley,
80 Strand, London, WC2R 0RL, UK, or email: travelguides@dk.com.

Front cover main image: The United States Capitol

◄ Iwo Jima Statue, with the Washington Monument and the United States Capitol in the background

Contents

Fountain in Dumbarton Oaks

Introducing
Washington, DC

View toward the Lincoln Memorial from
Arlington National Cemetery

Columns from the US Capitol building, now in the National Arboretum

Quirky decor at Acadiana restaurant

Washington, DC Area by Area

Map seller outside the National Gallery
of Art on the Mall

Travelers' Needs

The George, a boutique hotel

Survival Guide

Monticello, home of Thomas Jefferson
in Charlottesville, Virginia

HOW TO USE THIS GUIDE

This guide helps you to get the most from your stay in Washington, DC. It provides detailed practical information and expert recommendations. *Introducing Washington, DC* maps the city and the region, sets it in its historical and cultural context, and gives an overview of the main attractions. *Washington, DC Area by Area* is the main sightseeing section, giving detailed information on all the major sights, with photographs, illustrations and maps. *Farther Afield* looks at sights outside the city center, and *Beyond Washington, DC* explores other places within easy reach of the city. Carefully researched suggestions for restaurants, hotels, entertainment, and shopping are found in the *Travelers' Needs* section, while the *Survival Guide* contains useful advice on everything from changing money to traveling on Washington's Metrorail system.

Washinton, DC Area by Area

The center of Washington has been divided into five sightseeing areas. Each section opens with a portrait of the area, summing up its character and history and listing all of the sights to be covered. Sights are numbered and clearly located on an *Area Map*. After this comes a large-scale *Street-by-Street Map* focusing on the most interesting part of the area. Finding your way about the area section is made easy by a numbering system. This refers to the order in which the sights are described on the pages that complete the section.

Color-coding on each page makes the area easy to find in the book.

Recommended restaurants in the area are listed and plotted on the map.

A locator map shows you where you are in relation to surrounding areas. The area of the *Street-by-Street Map* is highlighted.

Numbered circles pinpoint all the listed sights on the area map. The Octagon Museum, for example, is ❽

1 Area Map
For easy reference, the sights in each area are numbered and located on an area map. To help the visitor, the map also shows Metrorail stations.

Octagon Museum ❽ is shown on this map as well.

Stars indicate the sights that no visitor should miss.

A suggested route for a walk takes in the most attractive and interesting streets in the area.

2 Street-by-Street Map
This gives a bird's-eye view of the heart of each sightseeing area. The numbering of the sights ties in with the area map and the fuller descriptions on the pages that follow.

Washington, DC at a Glance

Each map in this section concentrates on a specific theme: *Museums and Galleries in Washington, DC* and *Monuments and Memorials in Washington, DC*. The top sights are shown on the map.

Each sightseeing area is color-coded.

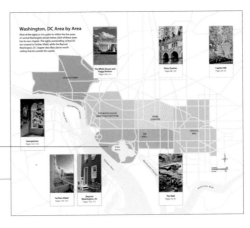

Practical Information lists all the information you need to visit every sight, including a map reference to the *Street Finder* at the back of the book.

Numbers refer to each sight's position on the area map and its place in the chapter.

3 Detailed information on each sight
All important sights in each area are described in depth in this section. They are listed in order, following the numbering on the *Area Map*. Practical information on opening hours, telephone numbers, websites, admission charges, and facilities available for each sight is given. The key to the symbols used can be found on the back flap.

The Visitors' Checklist provides the practical information you will need to plan your visit.

Stars indicate the most interesting architectural details of the building, and the most important works of art or exhibits on view inside.

The façade of each major sight is shown to help you spot it quickly.

Numbered circles point out key features of the sight listed in a key.

4 Washington, DC's major sights
These are given two or more full pages in the sightseeing area in which they are found. Historic buildings are dissected to reveal their interiors; and museums and galleries have colour-coded floor plans to help you find important exhibits.

INTRODUCING WASHINGTON, DC

GREAT DAYS IN WASHINGTON, DC

Washington boasts not only world-renowned works of art and majestic monuments, but picturesque neighborhoods and beautiful gardens. Here are itineraries for some of the best of the attractions and unexpected treasures, arranged first under themes and then by length of stay. All the sights can be reached on foot or by public transportation. Feel free to dip into the itineraries as you wish. Price guides on pages 10–11 show the daily cost for two adults or for a family of two adults and two children including lunch.

The White House, the Presidential residence

Monumental City

Two adults allow at least $40

- Lincoln Memorial
- World War II Memorial
- Corcoran Gallery of Art
- The White House

Morning
Start your day at the **Lincoln Memorial** (see pp86–7), six blocks south of the Foggy Bottom Metro stop. Inside, on the north and south walls, you will find inscriptions of President Lincoln's **Gettysburg Address** (see p165). In front of the memorial, to the left of the Reflecting Pool, is the moving **Vietnam Veterans Memorial** (see p85). Engraved on black granite are the names of Americans who died in the war. Then make your way through the shady Constitution Gardens back to the Reflecting Pool. To the right is the **Korean War Veterans Memorial** (see p85) and nearby is the **World War II Memorial** (see p84). Here you can see the Freedom Wall, its inscriptions, and the bas-reliefs showing the US at war. After this memorial, move on to 17th Street where there are several historic buildings including the **Organization of American States** and the **Daughters of the American Revolution** (see p116). Drop into the **Corcoran Gallery of Art**, one of the country's first art galleries (see p115). Have lunch here, or head to a café near Pennsylvania Avenue.

Afternoon
Stroll down Pennsylvania Avenue, passing the red brick Renwick Gallery, Blair House (where presidential guests stay), and **The White House** (see pp110–11). Walk around the White House to the Visitor Center at 1450 Pennsylvania Avenue. Afterwards, visit the **US National Archives** (see p92) to see historic documents including the *Declaration of Independence* and the *Bill of Rights*. End your day with a tour of **Ford's Theater** (see p98) where Lincoln was shot, followed by a meal in **Chinatown** (see pp98–9) or **Penn Quarter** (see pp88–105).

Black History

Two adults allow at least $20

- Frederick Douglass House
- Mary McLeod Bethune Site
- U Street landmarks
- African American Civil War Museum and Memorial

Morning
If traveling by car, spend the morning at the **Frederick Douglass House**, an estate in Anacostia (see p147). Douglass was a fugitive slave who became a famous abolitionist. Almost all of the furnishings here are original (look out for the walking stick collection). Cross the river to **The Shaw Neighborhood** (see p143) with its lovely Victorian houses, where prominent African-Americans lived in the 1940s. Visit the **Mary McLeod Bethune Council House** (see p142), home of the civil rights leader and founder of the National Council of Negro Women.

Lunch at **Ben's Chili Bowl** (see p189) on U Street, a place that was once the Minnehaha silent movie theater.

Lincoln Theatre, the venue for many of Duke Ellington's performances

◀ An 1801 aquatint view of Washington

Georgetown's pretty gardens and houses, a delightful neighborhood to stroll through

Afternoon
Stroll along U Street, once known as Black Broadway. Audiences went wild when Duke Ellington performed at the **Lincoln Theatre** *(see p142)*. He lived nearby at numbers 1805 and 1816 13th Street. Visit the **African American Civil War Museum and Memorial**, honoring black soldiers *(see p135)*. End the day in style in Georgetown with dinner and jazz at **Blues Alley** *(see pp198–9)*.

Art and Shopping

Two Adults allow at least $35

- **National Gallery of Art**
- **Lunch on the Mall**
- **Georgetown Shopping**
- **Washington Harbor**

Morning
To experience the full scope of art covered at the **National Gallery of Art** *(see pp60–63)*, visit both the West Building (13th–19th century European and American art) and the East Building (modern and contemporary art). Don't miss the Matisse Cut-Outs in the tower of the East Building. Have a coffee break at the Espresso Bar on the Concourse level. Outside, in the Garden Court (north side of East Building), find the Andy Goldsworthy installation entitled *Roof*, a

study of domes. Wander through the enchanting Sculpture Garden to the Pavilion Café, a charming spot for lunch.

Afternoon
Now head to cobblestoned **Georgetown** *(see pp122–9)*. You could take the 90-minute walk *(see pp150–51)*, but if shopping is your ultimate goal, go to M Street or Wisconsin Avenue for numerous galleries and shops and a range of stylish goods – lamps, Italian ceramics, prints and cutting-edge fashion. To finish, have tea in the Garden Terrace at the **Four Seasons Hotel** *(see p179)*, or have a drink at **Washington Harbor** while watching the boats *(see p124)*, then stroll through the Georgetown waterfront park next to the harbor.

A Family Day

Family of Four allow at least $55

- **Visit the National Zoo**
- **National Air and Space Museum**
- **Washington Monument**

Morning
Start early at the **National Zoo** *(see pp140–41)*, checking at its Visitor Center for feeding times, talks, and training sessions (entry is free). See Clouded

Leopards and Giant Pandas on the Asia Trail and the Sumatran Tigers in Great Cats. At the Great Ape House orangutans scale a 400-ft (130-m) "O Line." Have lunch at the Mane Restaurant or at one of the snack bars.

Afternoon
Go by metro to the **National Air and Space Museum** *(see pp66–7)*. Discover facts such as the cruising speed of the *Spirit of St. Louis*, or the reason Skylab was covered with a coating of gold. Catch a film at the IMAX theatre, where you can experience flying without leaving the ground. Then head for the **Washington Monument** *(see p80)* and take the elevator to the top for the spectacular view (advance booking required). Finish off at the **Kennedy Center** *(see pp120–21)* in Foggy Bottom, for free entertainment on the Millennium Stage at 6pm.

Washington Monument, for a fabulous view of the city

The Martin Luther King, Jr. memorial, surrounded by cherry blossom

2 days in Washington, DC

- Marvel at the White House
- Watch first-class entertainment at the Kennedy Center
- Discover great paintings at the National Gallery of Art

Day 1

Morning Start the day with a roam around the nation's legislative heart, the **US Capitol** *(pp52–3)*, admiring its Neo-Classical architecture. Then stroll the grand mile-long **National Mall** *(pp56–87)*, lined on either side with an amazing choice of museums. Stop at the **National Museum of American History** *(pp76–9)* to see the First Ladies exhibition, the flag that inspired the national anthem, and Abraham Lincoln's top hat. Afterward, join the line for the elevator taking you to the top of the city's tallest landmark, the **Washington Monument** *(p80)*.

Afternoon Marvel at one of the world's most recognizable homes, the **White House** *(pp110–13)*, residence of the US president, then take a virtual tour at the **White House Visitor Center** *(p113)*. End the day with a show at the legendary **Kennedy Center** *(pp120–1)*, renowned for its music, theater, and ballet productions.

Day 2

Morning While away a few hours exploring the trove of great painting at the **National Gallery of Art** *(pp60–3)*. Then head to

the **National Air & Space Museum** *(pp64–7)*, which showcases exhibits ranging from the Wright brothers' first airplane to the latest space rockets.

Afternoon Walk along **Tidal Basin** *(p81)*, which is particularly pretty when the cherry trees are in blossom. Take in the striking monuments honoring past presidents, including the **Jefferson Memorial** *(p81)* and **Franklin D. Roosevelt Memorial** *(pp86–7)*. A short distance from here is the awe-inspiring **Lincoln Memorial** *(p87)*, which looms large over the Reflecting Pool. Make your way to the **Smithsonian Museum of American Art & National Portrait Gallery** *(pp100–103)*, which houses portraits of all the American presidents.

3 days in Washington, DC

- Learn about the nation's history at the many memorials
- Shop along Wisconsin Avenue in Georgetown
- Enjoy the view from the Washington Monument

Day 1

Morning Stroll the scenic **Tidal Basin** *(p81)*, passing the **Jefferson Memorial** *(p81)*, **Franklin D. Roosevelt Memorial** *(pp86–7)*, and the statue of civil rights leader **Martin Luther King, Jr.** *(p85)*. Visit the imposing **Lincoln Memorial** *(p87)*, and then spend time exploring the

poignant **Vietnam Veterans Memorial** *(p85)* and **World War II Memorial** *(p84)*. Next, ascend the **Washington Monument** *(p80)*, for far-reaching views.

Afternoon Stand in awe of the **White House** *(pp110–13)* and explore the **White House Visitor Center** *(p113)* for a chance to see the rooms where history is made. Nearby, the **Smithsonian Museum of American Art & National Portrait Gallery** *(pp100–103)* tells the nation's story through paintings and photos. End the day with an evening show at the infamous **Ford's Theatre** *(p98)*, the scene of Abraham Lincoln's assassination.

A view of the Jefferson Memorial from across Tidal Basin

Day 2

Morning After a tour of the soaring Rotunda and statuary hall of the **US Capitol** *(pp52–3)*, witness history in action at the **US Supreme Court** *(p50)*. Then stop at the impressive **Library of Congress** *(pp48–9)* to admire the stunning Great Hall and Main Reading Room. For something different, head to the **National Gallery of Art** *(pp60–3)*, which houses a remarkable collection of painting and sculpture.

Afternoon Explore the riveting **Newseum** *(p95)*, documenting events from the past and present in both print and digital formats. Then pop into the enormous **National Museum of Natural History** *(pp72–3)*. The Dinosaur Hall and Ocean Hall are a must. Wind down after a busy day with a performance at the **Kennedy Center** *(pp120–1)*.

Day 3

Morning Head to the **National Mall** (pp56–87) for a variety of world-class museums. Highlights include the **National Air & Space Museum** (pp64–7), the **National Museum of American History** (pp76–9), and the **Hirshhorn Museum** (pp68–9) for modern art.

Afternoon Visit the city's most historic quarter, **Georgetown** (pp122–9), to meander its pretty streets lined with Federal townhouses and browse the shops on **Wisconsin Avenue** (pp124–5). Follow with a tour of the splendid **Dumbarton Oaks** estate (p129), and then dine at one of the riverside restaurants at **Washington Harbor** (p124).

5 days in Washington, DC

- Visit George Washington's estate at Mount Vernon
- Pay your respects at Arlington Cemetery
- Explore the portraits at the Smithsonian Museum

Day 1

Morning See American history in the making at the **US Capitol** (pp52–3), and then take in some culture at the **National Gallery of Art** (pp60–3). Ride the elevator to the top of the **Washington Monument** (p80) for magnificent views of the city and the **World War II Memorial** (p84).

Afternoon A walk along **Tidal Basin** (p81) will lead you to the **Jefferson Memorial** (p81), **Franklin D. Roosevelt Memorial** (pp86–7), and **Lincoln Memorial** (p87). Look out for the statue of civil rights leader **Martin Luther King, Jr.** (p85) en route. Nearby is the **Vietnam Veterans Memorial** (p85). After, head to the **Smithsonian Museum of American Art & National Portrait Gallery** (pp100–3), which displays portraits of all the US presidents.

Day 2

Morning Admire the rooms of the **White House** (pp110–13) at the **White House Visitor Center**

(p113), then see it for real. Nearby, the **Corcoran Gallery** (p115) has fine modern and African-American art alongside European and American masterworks.

Afternoon Discover **Dumbarton Oaks** estate (p129) for a leisurely walk in the circular garden. Then continue to **Georgetown** (p122–9), to look around its shops on **Wisconsin Avenue** (pp124–5). Afterward, take a stroll along the historic **Chesapeake and Ohio Canal** (pp124–5) towpath. Round off the day with a show at the **Kennedy Center** (pp120–1).

Day 3

Morning Visit the stately quarters of the nation's tribunal, the **US Supreme Court** (p50), and marvel at the colossal reading rooms in the **Library of Congress** (pp48–9). The historic treasures of the **National Archives** (p92–3), including the original Declaration of Independence and the US Constitution and Bill of Rights, are worth a closer look.

Afternoon Watch history come to life in the newsreels of the **Newseum** (p95). Next, pick between the **National Museum of American History** (pp76–9), the **National Air & Space Museum** (pp64–7), or the **Hirshhorn Museum** (pp68–9), which line the **National Mall** (pp56–87). Later, visit **Ford's Theatre** (p98) and explore the trendy restaurants in the **Penn Quarter** (pp86–105).

Day 4

Morning Immerse yourself at the heart-rending **United States Holocaust Memorial Museum**

A pretty, tree-lined street in Washington's historic quarter, Georgetown

(pp82–3). Then, for something lighter, see the Hall of Mammals and the Dinosaur Hall at the **National Museum of Natural History** (pp72–3).

Afternoon Head out for a tour of the magnificent **Washington National Cathedral** (pp144–5). At night, choose one of the ethnic restaurants in **Adams-Morgan** (p139) or dine in one of the restaurants at lively **Washington Harbor** (p124).

Day 5

Morning Spend the morning at **Mount Vernon** (pp162–3), George Washington's beautiful riverside estate, and tour the mansion, grounds, and gardens.

Afternoon Take a moving trip to **Arlington National Cemetery** (pp132–3) for the tombs of John F. Kennedy and the nation's war heroes. Follow this with a visit to **Old Town Alexandria** (pp160–61), whose streets are lined with boutiques, restaurants, and historic sights aplenty.

The impressive Neo-Classical architecture of the US Capitol

Putting Washington, DC on the Map

Washington, DC is situated near the East Coast of North America, surrounded by the state of Maryland and separated from Virginia by the Potomac River. It covers an area of 108 sq km (67 sq miles) and has a population of 600,000. As the capital of the United States, and seat of federal government, the city is a major focus of American life. It is a very popular tourist destination, attracting millions of visitors each year. The beautiful countryside of Maryland and Virginia is also easily reached from the capital city.

Greater Washington, DC

The city of Washington was created not only as a new capital for the United States but also as the seat of government, independent from the other states. It was laid out in a diamond-shaped area with a grid system of roads. One side of the square was lost after land was ceded back to Virginia in 1846. Although the city has sprawled beyond its original limits, officially the District of Columbia remains within the boundaries indicated. Washington is an easy city to get around, with an efficient modern metro system.

MARYLAND

BETHESDA

Dulles International Airport

VIENNA

FALLS CHURCH

ARLINGTON

FAIRFAX

VIRGINIA

ALEXANDRIA

Key

Central Washington
Built-up area
Freeway
Major road
Train line
Metro line/station
State border

0 kilometers 2.5
0 miles 2.5

For additional map symbols see back flap

THE HISTORY OF WASHINGTON, DC

Native Americans settled in what is now the District of Columbia as long as 6,000 years ago. Archeologists have discovered traces of three villages in the area; the largest was called Nacotchtanke. Its people, the Anacostines, settled along the Potomac River and a smaller tributary now named the Anacostia River.

English Settlement

In December 1606 Captain John Smith of the Virginia Company, under the charge of King James I of England, set sail from England for the New World. Five months later he arrived in the Chesapeake Bay and founded the Jamestown colony. A skilled cartographer, Smith was soon sailing up the Potomac River. In 1608 he came to the area that would later become Washington.

The English settlers who followed supported themselves through the fur trade, and later cultivated tobacco and corn (maize). The marriage in 1614 between John Rolfe, one of the settlers, and Pocahontas, daughter of the Indian chief Powhatan, kept the peace between the English and the Indians for eight years. Struggles over land ownership between the English and the Powhatan Indians, whose ancestors had lived there for centuries, led to massacres in 1622. The English finally defeated the Indians in 1644, and a formal peace agreement was made in 1646.

The first Africans arrived in the region on board a Dutch ship in 1619 and worked as indentured servants on plantations. They were given food and lodging as payment for serving for a fixed number of years. However, within the next 40 years the practice changed so that blacks were purchased for life, and their children became the property of their master. As the number of plantations grew, so did the number of slaves.

In the late 1600s another group of settlers, this time Irish-Scottish, led by Captain Robert Troop, established themselves here. Along the Potomac River two ports, George Town (later known as Georgetown) and Alexandria, soon became profitable centers of commerce. Here planters had their crops inspected, stored, and shipped. In both towns streets were laid out in rectangular patterns. With rich soil, plentiful land, abundant labor, and good transportation, the region rapidly grew in prosperity.

1607 Captain John Smith founds Jamestown settlement in Virginia

Captain John Smith (1580–1631)

1751 George Town is established

1619 The first Africans arrive in American colonies

| 1600 | 1650 | 1700 | 1750 |

1646 The Indians and the English reach a peace agreement in the Tidewater and Potomac region

1748 Tobacco merchants granted land for the town of Alexandria

1634 Lord Baltimore founds Catholic colony in Maryland

◀ George Washington by Rembrandt Peale, painted 1824–5

Revolutionary Years

Some 100 years after the first settlers arrived, frustration over British rule began to grow, both in the Potomac region and elsewhere in the 13 American colonies. In 1775, the colonies began their struggle for independence. On April 19, shots were fired at Lexington, Massachusetts by American colonists who wanted "no taxation without representation," thus beginning the War of Independence.

On July 4, 1776, the Declaration of Independence was issued as colonists attempted to sever ties with Britain. Revolt led to revolution, and the newly formed United States won an important victory at Saratoga, New York in 1777. The French came to the aid of the Americans and finally, on October 19, 1781, the British, led by Lord Cornwallis, surrendered at Yorktown, Virginia. This ended the war and assured the independence of the United States. The peace treaty was signed in Paris on September 3, 1783. Britain agreed to boundaries giving the US all territory to the south of what is now Canada, north of Florida, and west to the Mississippi River.

The Continental Congress, a legislative body of representatives from the newly formed states, appointed a committee to draft the country's first constitution. The result was the Articles of Confederation, which established a union of the newly created states but provided the central government with little power. This later gave way to a stronger form of government, created by the delegates of the Federal Constitutional Convention in Philadelphia in May, 1787. George Washington was unanimously chosen to be president. He took office on April 30, 1789.

Meeting in New York of first delegates of Congress to discuss location for a new capital city

A New City

The Constitution of the United States, ratified in 1788, allowed for the creation of a seat of government, not to exceed 10 square miles, which would be ruled by the United States Congress. This area was to be independent and not part of any state. At the first meeting of Congress in New York City in 1789, a dispute arose between northern and southern delegates over where the capital should be located. Secretary of the Treasury Alexander Hamilton and Secretary of State Thomas Jefferson worked out an agreement whereby the debts incurred by northern states during the Revolution would be taken over by the government, and in return the capital would be located in

1781 The British surrender at Yorktown

1783 The US and Britain sign the Treaty of Paris

1787 The Federal Constitutional Convention meets in Philadelphia

1793 President Washington lays the Capitol's cornerstone

1775 | **1780** | **1785** | **1790**

1775 The first battles of the American Revolution are fought at Lexington and Concord

Articles of Confederation

1789 Delegates gather in New York City to discuss a location for the capital

1791 President Washington obtains land for the capital city

1792 Construction begins on the President's House (later the White House)

the south. George Washington chose an area that incorporated land from both Maryland and Virginia, and included the towns of Alexandria and Georgetown. It was to be known as the city of Washington. At Suter's Tavern in Georgetown, Washington convinced local residents to sell their land for £25 an acre. He chose a surveyor, Andrew Ellicott, and his assistant Benjamin Banneker, a free African-American, to lay out the streets and lots. Washington also invited Major Pierre Charles L'Enfant to create a grand design for the new capital city (see p69).

Ellicott's engraved map of 1792, based on L'Enfant's plan

In 1800 the government was moved to Washington. President John Adams and his wife Abigail took up residence in the new President's House, designed by James Hoban, which was later renamed the White House by Theodore Roosevelt. The city remained empty of residents for many years while the building works took place.

War of 1812

Tension with Britain over restrictions on trade and freedom of the seas began to escalate during James Madison's administration. On June 18, 1812, the US declared war on Britain. In August 1814, British troops reached Washington and officers at the Capitol fled, taking the Declaration of Independence and the Constitution with them. First Lady Dolley Madison escaped from the White House with Gilbert Stuart's portrait of George Washington. On August 24, the British defeated the Americans at Bladensburg, a suburb of Washington. They set fire to the War Department, the Treasury, the Capitol, and the White House. Only a night of heavy rain prevented the city's destruction. The Treaty of Ghent, which finally ended the war, was signed on February 17, 1815 in the Octagon.

The British attack on Washington, DC in August 1814

1802 Robert Brent appointed first mayor of Washington

1814 The British set fire to Washington

1812 US declares war on Britain

1815 President Madison signs the Treaty of Ghent with Britain

| 1800 | 1805 | 1810 | 1815 |

1800 The seat of government is transferred from Philadelphia to Washington

1804 President Jefferson initiates the Lewis and Clark expedition which resulted in the discovery of America's West Coast

The signing of the Treaty of Ghent

The Baltimore and Ohio Railroad's "Tom Thumb" locomotive racing a horse-drawn car

Rebirth

With the end of the War of 1812 came a period of renewed optimism and economic prosperity in Washington. Washingtonians wanted to make their city a bustling commercial capital. They planned to build the Chesapeake and Ohio Canal to connect Washington to the Ohio River Valley and thus open trade with the west. Construction on the Baltimore and Ohio Railroad line also got under way. As the population grew, new hotels and boarding-houses, home to many of the nation's congressmen, opened up. Newspapers, such as the *National Intelligencer,* flourished.

In 1829, James Smithson, an Englishman, bequeathed a collection of minerals, books, and $500,000 in gold to the United States, and the Smithsonian Institution was born.

Construction began on three important government buildings, each designed by Robert Mills (1781–1855): the Treasury Building, the Patent Office, and the General Post Office building. Also at this time, the Washington National Monument Society, led by George Watterston, chose a 600-ft (183-m) obelisk to become the Washington Monument, again designed by the architect Robert Mills.

Slavery Divides the City

Racial tension was beginning to increase around this time, and in 1835 it erupted into what was later known as the Snow Riot. After the attempted murder of the widow of architect William Thornton, a botany teacher from the North was arrested for inciting blacks because plant specimens had been found wrapped in the pages of an abolitionist newspaper. A riot ensued, and in the course of the fighting a school for black children was destroyed as well as the interior of a restaurant owned by Beverly Snow, a free black. As a result, and to the anger of many people, black and white, laws were passed denying free blacks licenses to run saloons or eating places.

Nothing has been more divisive in Washington's history than the issue of slavery. Many Washingtonians were slaveholders; others became ardent abolitionists. The homes of several abolitionists and free blacks, as well as black churches, were used as hiding places for fugitive slaves. On an April night in 1848, 77 slaves attempted to escape the city, and boarded a small schooner on the Potomac River. But the following night they were captured and brought back to Washington, where they

1828 President John Quincy Adams breaks ground for the Chesapeake and Ohio Canal

James Smithson
(1765–1829)

1844 The invention of the telegraph speeds the distribution of news from Washington

1825

1830

1835

1840

1829 James Smithson leaves a fortune worth more than $500,000 to the United States

1835 Baltimore and Ohio Railroad links Washington and Baltimore. Racial tension leads to the Snow Riot

1846 Constructio the Smithsonian C begins. Alexand retroceded to Vir

1827 The Washington Abolition Society is organized

were sold at auction. The incident served only to heighten the tension between pro-slavery and anti-slavery groups. Slavery was abolished in Washington in 1862.

The Civil War

In 1860, following the election of President Abraham Lincoln, several southern states seceded from the Union in objection to Lincoln's stand against slavery. Shots were fired on Fort Sumter in Charleston, South Carolina on April 12, 1861, and the Civil War began. By the summer, 50,000 volunteers arrived in Washington to join the Army of the Potomac under General George B. McClellan. Washington suddenly found itself in the business of housing, feeding, and clothing the troops, as well as caring for the wounded. Buildings and churches became makeshift hospitals. Many people came to nurse the wounded, including author Louisa May Alcott and poet Walt Whitman.

Thousands of northerners came to help the war effort. They were joined by hordes of black people heading north to escape

Black residents of Washington celebrating the abolition of slavery in the District of Columbia

slavery, so that by 1864 the population of Washington had doubled that of 1860, reaching 140,000.

After skirmishes on July 12, 1864, witnessed by Lincoln himself at Fort Stevens, the Confederates retreated. By March 1865 the end of the war appeared to be close at hand. Parades, speeches, and band concerts followed Confederate General Robert E. Lee's surrender on April 9, 1865. Yet the celebratory mood was short-lived. Disturbed by the Union Army's victory, John Wilkes Booth assassinated President Lincoln at Ford's Theatre during the third act of *Our American Cousin* on April 14, 1865. Lincoln was taken to the house of tailor William Petersen, across the street from the theater, where he died the next morning (see p98).

Victory parade through Washington, DC to celebrate the end of the Civil War in April 1865

1851 Major expansion of the Capitol begins

1859 Senate wing of the Capitol is completed

1857 House of Representatives wing of the Capitol is completed

1861 Civil War begins when shots are fired on Fort Sumter, South Carolina

1862 Slavery is abolished in the District of Columbia

1850	1855	1860	1865

1848 77 slaves attempt to escape from Washington by schooner. Ground is broken for the Washington Monument

1863 The Emancipation Proclamation is issued

1865 General Robert E. Lee surrenders to the Union. President Lincoln is assassinated

President Lincoln

1860 President Abraham Lincoln elected

Post Civil War

The Freedmen's Bureau was created to help provide African Americans with housing, food, education, and employment. In 1867 General Oliver Otis Howard, commissioner of the bureau, used $500,000 of the bureau's funds to purchase land to establish a university for African Americans. He was president of this institution, later named Howard University, from 1869 to 1873.

On February 21, 1871, a new "territorial government" was formed to unite Georgetown, the city of Washington, and the County of Washington into the District of Columbia. A governor and a board of public works were appointed by President Ulysses S. Grant. Alexander "Boss" Shepherd, a member of the board of public works, paved streets, installed streetlights, laid sidewalks, planned parks, and designed an advanced sewerage system. But the District's debts rose uncontrollably. As a result, Congress quickly tightened its reins and established home rule. It took over some of the District's debts, and appointed three commissioners to work within a set budget.

Washington became a city of contrasts, attracting both rich and poor. One of the most distinguished literati in the city was Henry Adams, best known for his autobiographical work, *The Education of Henry Adams*. He lived on Lafayette Square next door to John Hay, Secretary of State and also a man of letters. One of Washington's most prominent African Americans, Frederick Douglass, lived at Cedar Hill, across the river in Anacostia. Born a slave in Maryland, he escaped north to freedom where he started an abolitionist newspaper. During the Civil War he became an adviser to President Lincoln.

Many lived well, including the growing middle class, which moved to the new suburbs of Mount Pleasant and LeDroit Park, yet a large number of the poor made their home in Washington's hidden alleys.

The Library of Congress under construction

A New Century

In 1901 Senator James McMillan of Michigan spearheaded a plan to improve the design of Washington by partaking in the "city beautiful" movement, in vogue at the time. L'Enfant's plan was finally completed, and the Mall between the Washington Monument and the US Capitol was laid out. Architects Daniel Burnham, Charles F. McKim, and others planned the building of a memorial to honor President Abraham Lincoln.

1867 Howard University is established

1877 Frederick Douglass moves to Cedar Hill. First issue of the *Washington Post*

1884 Washington Monument is completed

1901 Senator James McMillan spearheads "city beautiful" movement

1889 Construction on the Library of Congress begins

| 1860 | 1870 | 1880 | 1890 |

1871 Territorial government is formed

1878 First telephone service in Washington becomes a municipal corporation

1897 First automobile in the District of Columbia

Oliver Otis Howard (1830–1909)

1899 The Height of Buildings Act puts vertical limitations on all construction in DC

Suffragettes demanding a hearing for imprisoned leader Alice Paul

restaurants. It became home to many successful musicians and writers; Duke Ellington and the opera star Madame Evanti lived here, as did poets Langston Hughes and Paul Dunbar. Alain Locke, a professor of philosophy at Howard, and Jean Toomer, author of *Cane*, were also residents.

When the US entered World War I in 1917, growing numbers of women came to Washington to fill the posts vacated by men. Suffragists took to the streets to campaign for the right to vote. The National Women's Party, led by Alice Paul, picketed the White House to urge President Wilson to endorse a constitutional amendment to give women the vote.

African Americans in Washington were not only banned from voting but also faced discrimination in housing and education. After a local black battalion was excluded from a World War I victory parade, tension mounted. On July 20, 1919, riots erupted on the streets and did not stop for four days. Although discrimination continued, the 1920s were a period of commercial, artistic, and literary success for the black community. The area around U Street and Howard University attracted small businesses, theaters, nightclubs, and

Roosevelt Ushers in a New Deal

Following the stock market crash of 1929, federal workers received salary cuts, and many other Washingtonians lost their jobs. As a result, President Roosevelt created the "New Deal," an ambitious public works program to reduce unemployment. People were paid to do a range of tasks, from planting trees on the Mall to completing some of the city's edifices, such as the Supreme Court, the government office buildings of the Federal Triangle, and the National Gallery of Art.

Roosevelt's wife, Eleanor, was a champion of the poor and a tireless reformer. In 1939, when Marian Anderson, the African American singer, was denied permission by the Daughters of the American Revolution to perform at Constitution Hall, Eleanor Roosevelt arranged for her to sing at the Lincoln Memorial instead, to a crowd of 75,000.

President Franklin D. Roosevelt with First Lady Eleanor

1906 Teddy Roosevelt's daughter, Alice, is married in the White House

1908 Opening of Union Station, designed by Daniel Burnham

1918 Washington celebrates Armistice Day

1919 Race riots continue for four days

Marian Anderson (1897–1993)

1910	1920	1930	1940

1917 US enters World War I

1920 The 19th amendment, granting suffrage to women, is ratified

1929 The Great Depression begins

1933 New Negro Alliance is formed to improve the status of blacks

1939 Marian Anderson performs at the Lincoln Memorial

After the US entered World War II in December 1941, Washington's population soared. Women from all across the country arrived in the capital, eager to take on government jobs while the men were overseas. They faced housing shortages, and long lines as they waited to use rationing coupons for food and services. The city also offered a respite for soldiers on leave. Actress Helen Hayes, a native Washingtonian, opened the Stage Door Canteen where celebrities provided food and entertainment.

Soldiers on patrol after the death of Martin Luther King, Jr.

The Civil Rights Movement

In 1953 the Supreme Court's ruling in the Thompson Restaurant case made it illegal for public places to discriminate against blacks. With the passage of other anti-discrimination laws, life in Washington began to change. In 1954, the recreation department ended its public segregation. In the same year, on May 17, the Supreme Court ruled that "separate educational facilities are inherently unequal."

On August 28, 1963, more than 200,000 people arrived in the capital for the "March on Washington" to support civil rights. From the steps of the Lincoln Memorial, Marian

John F. Kennedy, Jr. salutes his father's casket at Arlington Cemetery in 1963

Anderson sang again and Reverend Martin Luther King, Jr. shared his dream in words that would echo for generations (see p93).

In November 1963, the nation was stunned by the assassination of President John F. Kennedy in Dallas, Texas. An eternal flame was lit at his funeral in Arlington Cemetery by his widow, Jaqueline. Five years later, on April 4, 1968, Martin Luther King was shot. Killed at the age of 39, he is revered as a hero and a martyr.

The opening of the Kennedy Center for Performing Arts in 1971 indicated the growing international character of the city. Several art museums with impressive collections (the East Wing of the National Gallery of Art, the Hirshhorn, the National Museum of American Art, and the National Portrait Gallery) also opened to enrich the city's cultural life. The construction of the Metro helped alleviate traffic problems. The embassies, the foreign banking community (the World Bank, the International Monetary Fund, and the Inter-American Development Bank), and the increasing number of immigrants, provided a cosmopolitan flavor.

1940 First plane lands at National Airport	**1973** Washingtonians gain the right to elect a mayor
1945 The first atomic bomb is dropped on Hiroshima, ending World War II	**1963** Martin Luther King gives "I Have a Dream" speech	**1969** 250,000 anti-Vietnam War protesters march	**1976** Metro opens. National Air and Space Museum opens

1940 **1950** **1960** **1970**

1941 The National Gallery of Art opens. After Japan attacks Pearl Harbor, the US enters World War II

1964 Washington residents vote in a presidential election for the first time

1974 President Richard Nixon resigns following criminal investigation

1978 Marion Barry elected mayor for the first of four terms.

Dr. Martin Luther King, Jr. (1929–68)

1982 Dedication of the Vietnam Veterans Memorial, designed by Maya Ying Lin

Home Rule

Residents of the District of Columbia have never been given full representation in American politics, as they have no congressman. (Until the 23rd Amendment of 1961 they could not even vote for president – the 1964 election was the first in which they took part.) In 1967, with people clamoring for a greater say in local government, President Lyndon Johnson replaced the system of three commissioners, set up by Congress in 1871, with an appointed mayor and a city council with greater responsibility in policy and budget issues. The result was the city's first elected mayor in over 100 years, Walter E. Washington. Residents were permitted to elect a non-voting delegate to Congress in 1971, and the Home Rule Act of 1973 allowed the people to elect both mayor and city council.

In 1978 Marion Barry succeeded as mayor. Born in Mississippi and raised in Tennessee, he came to Washington in 1965 to work for civil rights. He was the city's mayor for 16 of the next 20 years, but toward the end of his tenure, a large deficit and dissatisfaction with city politics developed. Middle-class families, both white and black, continued to flee the increasingly crime-ridden city for the safety of the suburbs. In 1995 Congress stripped the mayor

Walter E. Washington campaigning for re-election

of much of his power and appointed a five-person "financial control board" to oversee the city's affairs. The election in 1998 was won by Anthony Williams, an outsider who offered a fresh outlook and financial stability. Congress returned to the mayor much of the authority it had taken away. Within months of taking his new office it appeared that Mayor Williams was turning the city around. The budget was operating with a surplus, the population had stabilized, and unemployment was down.

A new administration under Adrian Fenty, elected in 2006, transformed the city's image. No longer dubbed the crime capital of the US, Washington, DC has once again become a mecca for tourists and a safer, cleaner place for its residents. In 2010, Fenty was defeated by moderate democrat Vincent Gray.

In 2009 Barack Obama became the first African-American president in US history – a momentous occasion.

Fireworks lighting the Washington Monument during the 2000 celebrations

1993 Opening of the US Holocaust Memorial Museum

President Bill Clinton (1946–)

2005 George W. Bush inaugurated for a second term as US president

2011 Rare 5.8 magnitude earthquake hits DC

2012 Barack Obama re-elected for a second term as president

1990 **2000** **2010** **2020**

2001 September 11 Terrorist attack on the Pentagon

2010 Vincent Gray elected mayor

2009 Barack Obama becomes the first African-American elected president

The American Presidents

The presidents of the United States have come from all walks of life; at least two were born in a log cabin – Abraham Lincoln and Andrew Jackson. Others, such as Franklin D. Roosevelt and John F. Kennedy, came from privileged backgrounds. Millard Fillmore attended a one-room schoolroom and Jimmy Carter raised peanuts. Many, including Ulysses S. Grant and Dwight D. Eisenhower, were military men, who won public popularity for their great achievements in battle.

Benjamin Harrison
(1889–93)

Chester A. Arthur
(1881–5)

Millard Fillmore
(1850–53)

Zachary Taylor
(1849–50)

Franklin Pierce
(1853–7)

James K. Polk
(1845–9)

W.H. Harrison
(1841)

Rutherford B. Hayes
(1877–81)

George Washington
(1789–97) was a
Revolutionary War general.
He was unanimously chosen
to be the first president of
the United States.

James Madison
(1809–17), known as the
Father of the Constitution,
was co-author of the
Federalist Papers.

**Andrew
Johnson**
(1865–9)

| 1775 | 1800 | 1825 | 1850 | 1875 |

| 1775 | 1800 | 1825 | 1850 | 1875 |

John Adams
(1797–1801), a lawyer
and historian, was the
first president to live in
the White
House.

James Monroe
(1817–25)

**John Quincy
Adams** (1825–9)

John Tyler
(1841–5)

**James A.
Garfield**
(1881)

Martin Van Buren
(1837-41)

**Ulysses S.
Grant**
(1869–77)

**Grover
Cleveland**
(1885–9)

Thomas Jefferson
(1801–9), architect,
inventor, landscape
designer, diplomat,
and historian, was
the quintessential
Renaissance man.

**James
Buchanan**
(1857–61)

Andrew Jackson
(1829–37) defeated the
British at the Battle of
New Orleans in the War
of 1812.

Abraham Lincoln
(1861–5) won the
epithet, the Great
Emancipator, for his
role in the abolition
of slavery. He led the
Union through the
Civil War.

**Grov
Clevela
(1893–**

William M
(1897

Key to Timeline

- Federalist
- Democratic Republican
- Whig
- Republican
- Democrat

Woodrow Wilson
(1913–21) led the country through World War I and paved the way for the League of Nations.

Harry S. Truman
(1945–53) made the decision to drop the atomic bombs on Hiroshima and Nagasaki in 1945.

John F. Kennedy (1961–3) was one of the most popular presidents. He sent the first astronaut into space, started the Peace Corps, and created the Arms Control and Disarmament Agency. His assassination rocked the nation.

Franklin D. Roosevelt
(1933–45) started the New Deal, a reform and relief program, during the Great Depression. He was elected to four terms.

Richard Nixon
(1969–74) opened up China and sent the first men to the moon. He resigned after the Watergate scandal (see p119).

Jimmy Carter (1977–81)

George Bush
(1989–93)

George W. Bush
(2001–09)

| 1900 | 1925 | 1950 | 1975 | 2000 | 2025 |

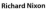

| 1900 | 1925 | 1950 | 1975 | 2000 | 2025 |

William H. Taft
(1909–13)

Dwight D. Eisenhower
(1953–61)

William J. Clinton
(1993–2001)

Herbert Hoover
(1929–33)

Gerald Ford
(1974–7)

Calvin Coolidge
(1923–9)

Ronald Reagan (1981–9), a one-time movie actor and popular president, cut taxes, increased military spending, and reduced government programs.

Warren Harding
(1921–3)

Lyndon B. Johnson
(1963–9) escalated the Vietnam conflict, resulting in widespread protests.

Barack Obama (2009–), a senator from Illinois, is the first African-American president in the history of the US.

Theodore Roosevelt
(1901–9) created many national parks and oversaw the construction of the Panama Canal.

The Role of the First Lady

In the 19th century, the First Lady acted primarily as hostess and "behind-the-scenes" adviser. Later, when Eleanor Roosevelt held her own press conferences, the role of First Lady changed greatly. Jackie Kennedy gave support to the arts, Rosalynn Carter attended Cabinet meetings, Barbara Bush promoted literacy, and Hillary Clinton ran her own political campaign. Michelle Obama follows in this vein, campaigning for charitable causes, including the prevention of childhood obesity.

Eleanor Roosevelt at a press conference in the 1930s

How the Federal Government Works

In September 1787, the Constitution of the United States of America was signed *(see p93)*. It was created as "the supreme Law of the Land," to ensure that it would take precedence over state laws. The powers of the federal government were separated into three distinct areas: the legislative branch to enact the laws, the executive branch to enforce them, and the judicial branch to interpret them. No one branch, however, was to exert too much authority, and the system of checks and balances was instituted. Provisions were made for amending the Constitution, and by December 1791 the first ten amendments, called the Bill of Rights, were ratified.

Checks and Balances

The system of checks and balances means that no one branch of government can abuse its power.

The Executive Branch: The President can recommend and veto legislation and call a special session of Congress. The President appoints judges to the courts and can grant pardons for federal offenses.

The Judicial Branch: The Supreme Court interprets laws and treaties and can declare an act unconstitutional. The Chief Justice presides at an impeachment trial of the President.

The Legislative Branch: Congress can override a presidential veto of a bill with a two-thirds majority. Presidential appointments and treaties must be approved by the Senate. Congress also oversees the jurisdiction of the courts and can impeach and try the President and federal judges.

The Senate, sitting in session in the US Capitol.

The Executive Branch

The President, together with the Vice President, is elected for a four-year term. The President suggests, approves, and vetoes legislation. The Executive also develops foreign policy and directs relations with other countries, serves as Commander-in-Chief of the armed forces, and appoints ambassadors. Secretaries to the Cabinet, composed of various heads of departments, meet regularly to advise the President on policy issues. Several agencies and councils, such as the National Security Council and the Office of Management and Budget, help determine the executive agenda.

Seal of the President

Ulysses S. Grant served as the US President from 1869 to 1877.

EXECUTIVE BRANCH

PRESIDENT

VICE PRESIDENT

CABINET

Henry A. Wallace served as Vice President under Franklin D. Roosevelt from 1941 to 1945.

The White House is the official residence of the US President.

Madeleine Albright, the first woman to serve as Secretary of State, was appointed in 1997.

The Judicial Branch

The Supreme Court and other federal courts determine the constitutionality of federal, state, and local laws. They hear cases relating to controversies between states and those affecting ambassadors or citizens of different states. They also try cases on appeal. The Supreme Court consists of nine justices appointed for life by the President.

The Supreme Court is the highest court in the United States and is the last stop in issues of constitutionality.

JUDICIAL BRANCH

Thurgood Marshall was the first African American to be a Supreme Court Justice. He held the position from 1967 to 1991.

9 SUPREME COURT JUSTICES

OF WHOM ONE IS CHIEF SUPREME COURT JUSTICE

Earl Warren was Supreme Court Justice from 1953 to 1969. He wrote the unanimous opinion in Brown v. Board of Education (1954). *(See p50).*

Oliver Wendell Holmes, Supreme Court Justice from 1902 to 1932, was a strong advocate of free speech.

The Legislative Branch

The Congress of the United States consists of two bodies, the House of Representatives and the Senate. Representatives to the House are elected by the voters in each state for a two-year term. The number of Representatives for each state is determined by the state's population. The Senate is composed of two Senators from each state, elected for six-year terms. Congress regulates commerce and is empowered to levy taxes and declare war. This branch also makes the laws: bills discussed, written, and revised in legislative committees must be passed first by the House and by the Senate before being approved by the President.

Daniel Webster served both in the House of Representatives (1813–17) and in the Senate (1822–41).

LEGISLATIVE BRANCH

HOUSE OF REPRESENTATIVES

SENATE

Sam Rayburn was a popular and distinguished Speaker of the House.

Edward Kennedy, leader of the United States' most famous political family, served in the Senate from 1962 until his death in 2009.

The US Capitol is home to both the House of Representatives and the Senate.

WASHINGTON, DC AT A GLANCE

Washington is more than just the political capital of the United States. It is also the home of the Smithsonian Institution, and as such is the cultural focus of America. Its many superb museums and galleries have something to offer everyone. Always one of the most popular sights, the president's official residence, the White House, attracts millions of visitors each year. Equally popular is the National Air and Space Museum, which draws vast numbers of visitors to its awe-inspiring displays of air and spacecraft. Also of particular interest are Washington's many monuments and memorials. The huge Washington Monument, honoring the first US president, dominates the city skyline. In contrast, the war memorials, dedicated to the thousands of soldiers who died in battle, are quietly poignant.

Washington's Top Ten Attractions

The White House *See pp104–13*

National Air and Space Museum
See pp64–7

Vietnam Veterans Memorial
See p85

National Gallery of Art
See pp60–63

Kennedy Center
See pp120–21

Washington National Cathedral *See pp144–5*

Arlington National Cemetery
See pp132–3

Washington Monument
See p80

Lincoln Memorial
See p86

US Capitol
See pp52–3

◀ Statue of General Grant in front of the United States Capitol

Museums and Galleries in Washington, DC

Few cities can claim to have as many museums and galleries in such a concentrated area as Washington. The Mall forms the main focus because it is lined with museums. Most of these are part of the Smithsonian Institution *(see p74)*, which is funded by the government. They cover a wide range of exhibits, from great works of art to space shuttles, to mementos of major events in American history. Admission to most of the museums and galleries is free.

National Museum of American History
This statue of a toga-clad George Washington is one of millions of artifacts in this museum of American history *(see pp76–9)*.

Georgetown

The White House and Foggy Bottom

Corcoran Gallery of Art
This Beaux Arts building houses a collection of American and European art and sculpture, including some of the best works by US artists of the 19th and 20th centuries *(see p115)*.

Potomac River

Tidal Basin

US Holocaust Memorial Museum
Photographs, videos, and re-created concentration camp barracks bring to life the brutality of the Holocaust and illustrate the terrible fate of Jews and others in World War II Nazi Germany *(see pp82–3)*.

**Smithsonian American Art Museum
and the National Portrait Gallery**
This Neo-Classical building houses the world's
largest collection of American paintings, sculpture,
photographs, and crafts *(see pp100–3)*.

National Museum of Natural History
A huge African elephant is the focal point
of the building's main foyer. The museum's
fascinating exhibits trace the evolution of
animals and explain the creation of gems
and minerals *(see pp72–3)*.

Penn
Quarter

The Mall

Capitol Hill

National Gallery of Art
The futuristic East Building
houses the 20th-century art
in this collection, while the
1930s West Building is home
to older works *(see pp56–63)*.

| 0 meters | 500 |
| 0 yards | 500 |

National Air and Space Museum
Washington's most popular museum
has exhibits from aviation and space
history, including the Wright Brothers'
first airborne plane and the Apollo 14
space module *(see pp64–7)*.

Monuments and Memorials in Washington, DC

As the political center of the United States, and home of its president, Washington has a great number of monuments and memorials honoring America's key figures and historic events. The most well-known among these are the Washington Monument and the Lincoln Memorial – sights of great interest to all who visit the city. For those who wish to remember the countless men and women who lost their lives fighting for their nation, there are poignant monuments, set in tranquil parks, where visitors can reflect in peace.

Korean War Veterans Memorial
Created in 1995, the 19 stainless steel, larger than life-size statues of this memorial recall the thousands who died in the Korean War *(see p85)*.

Georgetown

Lincoln Memorial
This emotive and inspirational marble figure has often been the focus of civil rights protests *(see p87)*.

The White House and Foggy Bottom

0 meters 500
0 yards 500

Potomac River

Iwo Jima Statue (US Marine Corps Memorial)
This iconic memorial depicts US Marines capturing the Japanese island of Iwo Jima at the end of World War II *(see p136)*.

Vietnam Veterans Memorial
Visitors to this dramatic memorial are confronted by a sobering list of names on the V-shaped granite walls *(see p85)*.

Martin Luther King, Jr. Memorial
Surrounded by cherry blossom trees and including an inscription on the wall, this is the first memorial on the Mall to an African-American *(see p85)*.

Washington Monument
One of the most enduring images of Washington, this 555-ft (170-m) marble obelisk can be seen from all over the city. Built in two stages, the monument was finally completed in 1884 *(see p80)*.

Penn Quarter

Capitol Hill

The Mall

Jefferson Memorial
This Neo-Classical building houses a bronze statue of President Jefferson, the key player in America's struggle for independence *(see p81)*.

Franklin D. Roosevelt Memorial
This vast memorial, in the form of a 7-acre park, includes statuary, waterfalls, and ornamental gardens *(see pp86–7)*.

WASHINGTON, DC THROUGH THE YEAR

A wide variety of events takes place in Washington, DC all through the year. In late March or early April, when the famous cherry blossoms bloom, the city really comes to life. Parades and outdoor festivals begin, and continue through the summer as more and more people come to explore the DC area in June, July, and August. The White House is a focus for many visitors, and it plays host to annual events such as the Easter Egg Roll in the spring and the Garden Tours in the spring and fall. Some of the more popular events are listed below; for further details on these and other events in the city, contact the Destination DC tourist office *(see p207)*.

Spring

The air is clear in springtime in Washington, DC, with crisp mornings and warm, balmy days. The cherry tree blossoms surrounding the Tidal Basin are world famous and should not be missed, although the area does get very busy. Memorial Day is a big event in DC; it marks the official beginning of summer, and is celebrated in many ways.

March

Washington Home and Garden Show, Walter E. Washington DC Convention Center, 801 Mount Vernon Place, NW (7th St and New York Ave, NW). **Tel** (202) 249-4039. A vast array of garden items.
St. Patrick's Day *(Sun before Mar 17)*, Constitution Ave, NW. Parade celebrating Irish culture. There are also celebrations in Old Town Alexandria.
Cherry Blossom Kite Festival *(last Sat)*, Washington

Monument. **Tel** (202) 633-1000. Kite designers fly their best models and compete for prizes.

April

National Cherry Blossom Festival *(late Mar–early Apr)*, Constitution Ave, NW. **Tel** 1-877-442-5666. Parade and concerts to celebrate the blooming of Washington's famous trees.
White House Egg Roll *(Easter Mon)*, White House Lawn. www.whitehouse.gov/easteregg roll. Children's races with eggs.
White House Spring Garden Tours *(second weekend)*, White House gardens. **Tel** (202) 456-7041. Tour of the Jacqueline Kennedy Garden and more.
Thomas Jefferson's Birthday *(Apr 13)*, Jefferson Memorial. **Tel** (202) 426-6821. Military drills, speeches, and wreath-laying.
Shakespeare's Birthday Celebration *(end of Apr)*, Folger Shakespeare Library, 201 E Capitol St, SE. **Tel** (202) 544-4600. A day of music, plays, food, and children's events.

Mother-and-daughter team in the Easter Egg Roll at the White House

May

Flower Mart *(first Fri & Sat)*, Washington National Cathedral. **Tel** (202) 537-6200. Flower booths, music, and crafts.
Memorial Day Weekend Concert *(last Sun)*, West Lawn of Capitol. **Tel** (202) 619-7222. National Symphony Orchestra performs. **Memorial Day** *(last Mon)*, Arlington National Cemetery. **Tel** (703) 607-8000. US Navy Memorial. **Tel** (202) 737-2300. Vietnam Veterans Memorial. **Tel** (202) 619-7222. Wreath-laying, speeches, and music to honor war veterans.
Memorial Day Jazz Festival *(last Mon)*, Old Town Alexandria. **Tel** (703) 746-5592. Live, big-band jazz music.
Twilight Tattoo Military Pageant *(7pm every Wed, May & Jun)*, Fort McNair. **Tel** (202) 685-2888. Military parade presenting the history of the US Army.

Cherry tree blossoms surrounding Jefferson Memorial at the Tidal Basin

Average Daily Hours of Sunshine

Sunshine Chart
The amount of sunshine in Washington does not vary greatly – even in winter half the days will enjoy blue skies. In summer the sunshine is at its most persistent, although it is best to be prepared for the occasional rainstorm. The chart gives the number of days per month with little or no cloud.

Summer

In June, July, and August, visitors come to Washington, DC from far and wide. The streets and parks are packed with people enjoying the sunshine. Many attractions become overcrowded, so it is important to call ahead and make reservations at this time of year.

The summer months can also be extremely hot and humid; even so, parades and outdoor fairs are usually very popular. Independence Day on July 4 is particularly exciting, with a parade during the day and fireworks at night.

June
Taste of Georgetown *(second Sat)*, Wisconsin Ave, NW. **Tel** (202) 298-9222. Washington's finest restaurants showcase their talents.
Smithsonian Festival of American Folklife *(late Jun–early Jul)*, The Mall. **Tel** (202) 633-6440. A huge celebration of folk culture, including music, dance, games, and food.
Capitol Pride *(mid-Jun)*, Pennsylvania Ave, NW. Street festival and parade celebrating the gay communities of DC.
DC Caribbean Carnival *(last Sat in Jun)*, Georgia Ave, NW. A colorful parade of more than 3,000 masqueraders, plus food, dance, and music.

July
Independence Day *(Jul 4)*, Constitution Ave & US Capitol, other areas. Concert on west front of the Capitol. A parade along Constitution Avenue,

Fireworks over Washington, DC on the Fourth of July

with fireworks from the base of the Washington Monument. Other areas such as Old Town Alexandria and Mount Vernon have parades and fireworks.
Bastille Day *(Jul 14)*. A celebration involving food, music, and dance. Events are held in the French Embassy and selected cafés and restaurants.
Mary McLeod Bethune Celebration *(Jul 10)*, Bethune Statue, Lincoln Park, E Capitol St, SE, between 11th St & 13th St. **Tel** (202) 673-2402. Memorial wreath-laying, gospel music, and speeches.

Capital Fringe Festival *(Jul)*, venues all over the city. Modeled on Edinburgh's Fringe festival, the focus is on theater, dance, puppetry, and the spoken word. Film and visual arts also feature.
Screen on the Green *(Beginning at dusk: Mon evening Jul–Aug)*, The Mall. **Tel** 1-877-262-5866. A Washington summer tradition. Classic movies are shown on giant screens.

August
Shakespeare Free for All *(mid-Aug)*, Sidney Harmon Hall, 610 F St, NW. www.shakespearetheatre.org. Nightly performances by the Shakespeare Theater Company, free of charge.
Arlington County Fair *(mid-Aug)*, Thomas Jefferson Center, Arlington, VA. **Tel** (703) 829-7471. www.arlingtoncountyfair.us. Food, crafts, music, and fairground rides.
National Frisbee Festival *(late Aug)*, Washington Monument. **Tel** (202) 619-7222. A weekend celebrating the game of Frisbee, including a free Frisbee contest for champions and amateurs alike.

A frenzy of Frisbee throwing at Washington's National Frisbee Festival

Average Monthly Rainfall

Rainfall Chart
It is impossible to escape the rain completely in Washington. The heaviest rainfall occurs during May through August, when it can come as a welcome break from the humidity. Rainfall tails off in September and October and reaches its lowest ebb in late winter. It rarely lingers for long in the city.

A school band performing in front of the Lincoln Memorial

Fall

With the air turning cooler, Labor Day (the first Monday in September) bids goodbye to the summer. The fall (autumn) season covers September, October, and November in Washington, when the temperatures steadily drop. A particularly enjoyable event at this time of year is Halloween, when children dress up as their favorite creatures or characters to go trick-or-treating.

Halloween Jack-O'-Lantern

September

Labor Day Weekend Concert *(Sun before Labor Day)*, West Lawn of the US Capitol. **Tel** (202) 619-7222. National Symphony Orchestra performs a concert.
Fiesta DC *(Sep)*, Columbia Heights neighborhood. A celebration of Latino culture.
International Children's Festival, Wolf Trap Park, Vienna, VA. **Tel** (703) 255-1900.

Musical and dance performances are held from around the world.
National Book Fair *(Sep)*, National Mall. **Tel** (202) 707-5000. A two-day event where more than 80 award-winning authors, illustrators, and poets talk about their books and participate in book signing.
Adams-Morgan Day Festival *(second Sun)*. Giant street party with music, food, and crafts.
Colonial Market and Fair, Mount Vernon, VA. **Tel** (703) 780-2000. Craft demonstrations and 18th-century entertainment.

October

Columbus Day *(second Mon)*, Columbus Memorial, Union Station. **Tel** (202) 289-1908. Speeches and wreath-laying in honour of the man who discovered America.
White House Fall Garden Tours *(mid-Oct)*. **Tel** (202) 456-7041. A chance to walk the grounds of the President's home.
Boo at the Zoo *(end Oct)*,

Washington National Zoo. **Tel** (202) 397-7328, or buy tickets at the zoo. Halloween celebration for children.
Halloween *(Oct 31)*. Young people trick-or-treating, dressed as ghosts, clowns, and witches. Dupont Circle and Georgetown are popular areas.

November

Veterans Day Ceremonies *(Nov 11)*, Arlington National Cemetery. **Tel** (703) 607-8000. Services, parades, and wreath-layings take place at various memorials around the city, commemorating United States military personnel who died in war. There are special Veterans Day ceremonies also at the Vietnam Veterans Memorial. **Tel** (202) 426-6841, and at the US Navy Memorial **Tel** (202) 737-2300).
Kennedy Center Holiday Festival *(late Nov–New Year's Eve)*. **Tel** (202) 467-4600. Musicals, ballet, and classical concerts for the holiday season.

Military guard on Veterans Day in Arlington National Cemetery

Average Monthly Temperature

Temperature Chart
Washington's climate varies greatly. In winter the air is bitterly cold, with temperatures rising little above freezing. In July and August, however, it becomes very hot and extremely humid. The best time to visit the city is in the spring or fall, when the weather is pleasantly mild and the air is clear.

Winter

Temperatures can plummet below freezing during the winter months of December, January, and February. Hence the city is generally quieter at this time of year, making it a good time to see the most popular sights. Over the Christmas period, Washington becomes busy again with festive events to get people into the holiday spirit. Decorations are visible across the city, and many places offer Christmas tours.

Toward the end of winter, a number of famous birthdays are celebrated, including those of Martin Luther King, Jr. and Presidents Abraham Lincoln and George Washington.

December

National Christmas Tree Lighting *(mid-Dec)*, Ellipse south of the White House. www.thenationaltree.org. The President turns on the lights on the National Christmas tree (advance tickets only).

Washington National Cathedral Christmas Services *(throughout Dec)*. **Tel** (202) 537-6200. Holiday celebrations with festive music.

Christmas at Mount Vernon *(weekends late Nov–mid-Dec)*, Mount Vernon, VA. **Tel** (703) 780-2000. Experience an 18th-century Christmas.

January

Robert E. Lee's Birthday *(mid-Jan)*. Tours of the Lee-Fendall house in Alexandria. **Tel** (703) 548-1789.

Martin Luther King, Jr.'s Birthday *(third Mon)*. Commemorative events.

Restaurant week *(mid-Jan)*. Many of Washington's top restaurants offer prix fixe lunch or dinner specials.

Febuary

Chinese New Year *(first two weeks)*, N St, Chinatown. **Tel** *(202) 789-7000*. Parades, dancing, and live music.

African American History Month *(throughout Feb)*. Various events are held across the city:

contact the Smithsonian (**Tel** (202) 633-1000) and the National Park Service (**Tel** (202) 619-7222).

George Washington's Birthday Parade *(around Feb 15)*, Old Town Alexandria, VA. **Tel** (703) 838-4200.

Abraham Lincoln's Birthday, *(Feb 12)*, Lincoln Memorial. **Tel** (202) 619-7222. Wreath-laying ceremony followed by a reading of the Gettysburg Address.

Girl Scouts watching George Washington's Birthday Parade

Federal Holidays

New Year's Day (Jan 1)

Martin Luther King, Jr.'s Birthday (3rd Mon in Jan)

Presidents' Day (3rd Mon in Feb)

Easter Monday (Mar or Apr)

Memorial Day (last Mon in May)

Independence Day (Jul 4)

Labor Day (1st Mon in Sep)

Columbus Day (2nd Mon in Oct)

Veterans Day (Nov 11)

Thanksgiving (4th Thu in Nov)

Christmas Day (Dec 25)

The National Christmas tree outside a snow-covered White House

WASHINGTON, DC AREA BY AREA

CAPITOL HILL

Soon after the Constitution was ratified in 1788, America's seat of government began to take root on Capitol Hill. The site was chosen in 1791 from 10 acres that were ceded by the state of Maryland. Pierre L'Enfant *(see p21)* chose a hill on the east side of the area as the foundation for the Capitol building and the center of the new city.

In more than 200 years, Capitol Hill has developed into a bustling microcosm of modern America. Symbols of the country's cultural development are everywhere, from its federal buildings to its centers of commerce, shops, and restaurants, as well as its multicultural residential areas.

The Capitol Hill area is frequented by the most powerful people in the United States. While access to official government buildings is strictly controlled for reasons of security, ordinary citizens may still find members of Congress greeting tour groups in the halls of the Capitol or dining at local restaurants.

Sights at a Glance

Historic Buildings
1 *Library of Congress pp48–9*
2 Folger Shakespeare Library
3 US Supreme Court
4 Sewall-Belmont House
5 *United States Capitol pp52–3*
13 Union Station

Museums and Galleries
14 National Postal Museum

Market
12 Eastern Market

Monuments and Memorials
6 Robert A. Taft Memorial
7 National Japanese American Memorial
8 Ulysses S. Grant Memorial

Parks and Gardens
9 US Botanic Garden
10 Bartholdi Park and Fountain

Church
11 Ebenezer United Methodist Church

Restaurants *see p183*
1 Acqua Al 2
2 Banana Café
3 Belga Café
4 Bistro Bis
5 Bullfeathers
6 Cava Mezze
7 Dubliner
8 Ethiopic
9 Five Guys
10 Good Stuff Eatery
11 Market Lunch
12 The Monocle
13 Montmartre
14 Sonoma
15 Tortilla Coast
16 Toscana Café
17 Tunnicliff's
18 We, the Pizza

See also Street Finder map 4

| 0 meters | 500 |
| 0 yards | 500 |

◀ United States Capitol with cherry blossom in foreground

For keys to symbols *see back flap*

Street-by-Street: Capitol Hill

The cityscape extending from the Capitol is an impressive combination of grand classical architecture and stretches of grassy open spaces. There are no skyscrapers here, only the immense marble halls and columns that distinguish many of the government buildings. The bustle and excitement around the US Capitol and US Supreme Court contrast with the calm that can be found by the reflecting pool or in a quiet residential street. Many of the small touches that make the city special can be found in this area, such as the antique lighting fixtures on Second Street, the brilliant bursts of flowers along the sidewalks, or the brightly painted façades of houses on Third Street near the Folger Shakespeare Library.

5 ★ US Capitol
The famous dome of the nation's seat of government is one of the largest in the world.

6 Robert A. Taft Memorial
A statue of Taft (1889–1953) stands in front of the bell tower that was erected to honor his principles and achievements.

Ulysses S. Grant Memorial
General Grant (1822–85), the Union leader in the American Civil War, is the central figure in a remarkable group of bronze equestrian statuary.

8 US Botanic Garden
Established in 1820, the Botanic Garden contains thousands of exotic and domestic plants.

4 Sewall-Belmont House
A life-size statue of the French martyr Joan of Arc (a replica of a French sculpture) graces this 18th-century house that serves as the headquarters of the National Women's Party.

0 meters   150
0 yards   150

Locator Map
See Street Finder map 4

Key
— Suggested route

Senate Offices

VUE NE

MARYLAND AVENUE NE

1ST STREET NE

2ND STREET NE

EAST CAPITOL STREET

2ND STREET SE

1ST STREET SE

INDEPENDENCE AVENUE SE

3 US Supreme Court
The highest court in the land has been housed since 1935 in this classical marble building designed by Cass Gilbert .

1 ★ Library of Congress
Thomas Jefferson sold his personal book collection to the Library of Congress after the British had burned the Capitol, which housed the Library, using the books as kindling.

THE TRAGEDIE OF IVLIVS CÆSAR

2 Folger Shakespeare Library
A tribute to the Bard's works and times, the library also doubles as a museum displaying Elizabethan treasures.

● Library of Congress

Congress first established a reference library in the US Capitol in 1800. When the Capitol was burned in 1814, Thomas Jefferson offered his own collection as a replacement, his belief in a universality of knowledge becoming the foundation for the Library's acquisition policy. In 1897 the Library of Congress moved to an Italian Renaissance-style building designed by John L. Smithmeyer and Paul J. Pelz. The main building, the Thomas Jefferson Building, is a marvel of art and architecture, with its paintings, mosaics, and exhibitions, such as Creating the United States and Thomas Jefferson's Library. The Library of Congress has the world's largest collection of books, with over 650 miles (1,050 km) of bookshelves housing 35 million volumes.

Front façade of the Jefferson Building

★ **Main Reading Room**
Eight huge marble columns and 10-ft (3-m) high female figures personifying aspects of human endeavor dwarf the reading desks in this room. The domed ceiling soars 160 ft (49 m) above the reading room floor.

African & Middle Eastern Reading Room
This is one of 10 reading rooms in the Jefferson Building where visitors can use books from the Library's collections.

KEY

① Exhibition Area

② Asian Reading Room

Mosaic of Minerva
This beautiful marble mosaic figure of Minerva of Peace, created by Elihu Vedder, dominates the staircase landing near the Visitors' Gallery, overlooking the Main Reading Room.

★ **Gutenberg Bible**
The 15th-century Gutenberg Bible was the first book printed using movable metal type. This is one of only three perfect vellum copies.

Main Entrance

Neptune Fountain
The bronze statue of Neptune, the Roman god of the sea, forms a striking feature at the front of the Jefferson Building.

★ **Great Hall**
Splendid marble arches and columns, grand staircases, imposing bronze statues, stained-glass skylights, mosaics, and murals all combine to create a magnificent entrance hall.

❷ Folger Shakespeare Library

201 E Capitol St, SE. **Map** 4 F4.
Tel (202) 544-4600. Ⓜ Capitol South.
Open 10am–5pm Mon–Sat. **Closed**
Federal hols. 🎭 ♿ Tickets for plays,
concerts, and readings available from
box office. 🔗 **folger.edu**

Inspired by Shakespeare's own era, this library and museum celebrate the works and times of the Elizabethan playwright.

The research library was a gift to the American people in 1932 from Henry Clay Folger who, as a student in 1874, began to collect Shakespeare's works. Folger also funded the construction of this edifice, built specifically to house his collection. It contains 310,000 Elizabethan books and manuscripts, as well as the world's largest collection of Shakespeare's writings, including a third of the surviving copies of the 1623 First Folio (first editions of Shakespeare's works). One of these first editions is displayed in the oak-paneled Great Hall, along with books and engravings.

The Folger hosts many cultural events. For example, there are regular performances of Shakespeare's plays in the library's 250-seat reconstruction of an Elizabethan theater. There is also an annual series of poetry readings, as well as numerous lectures and talks throughout the year. The Folger Consort early music ensemble, performs concerts of 12th- to 20th-century music.

In the grounds of the library,

The impressive Neo-Classical façade of the US Supreme Court

the Elizabethan Garden has plants and flowers that are featured in Shakespeare's plays. Shakespeare's birthday is celebrated every April with jugglers, music, theater shows, and a tour of the library.

❸ US Supreme Court

1st St between E Capitol St and
Maryland Ave, NE. **Map** 4 E4.
Tel (202) 479-3000. Ⓜ Capitol South.
Open 9am–4:30pm Mon–Fri.
Closed Federal hols. 🏛 📷 ♿
Lectures. 🔗 **supremecourtus.gov**

The Supreme Court forms the judicial and third branch of the US government *(see pp30–31)*. It was established in 1787 at the Philadelphia Constitutional Convention and provides the last stop in the disposition of the nation's legal disputes and issues of constitutionality. Groundbreaking cases settled here include *Brown v. Board of Education*, which abolished racial segregation in schools, and *Miranda v. Arizona*, which declared crime suspects were

entitled to a lawyer before being interrogated. The Court is charged to guarantee "Equal Justice Under Law," the motto emblazoned over the entrance.

As recently as 1929 the Supreme Court was still meeting in various sections of the US Capitol building. Then, at Chief Justice William Howard Taft's urging, Congress authorized a separate building to be constructed. The result was a magnificent Corinthian edifice, designed by Cass Gilbert, that opened in 1935. Sculptures depicting the allegorical figures of the Contemplation of Justice and the Guardian of the Law stand beside the steps while on the pediment above the entrance are figures of Taft (far left) and John Marshall, the fourth Chief Justice (far right).

Visitors can watch the court in session Monday to Wednesday from October to April. Admission is on a first-come, first-served basis. When court is not in session, public lectures on the Supreme Court are held every hour on the half-hour in the Courtroom (contact for confirmation).

The Great Hall in the Folger Shakespeare Library

Hallway of the 18th-century
Sewall-Belmont House

❹ Sewall-Belmont House

2nd St and Constitution Ave, NE.
Map 4 E4. **Tel** (202) 546-1210.
Ⓜ Capitol South, Union Station.
Open noon–5pm Wed–Sun. **Closed**
Federal hols. Donations welcome.
🅿 ⓦ sewallbelmont.org

Robert Sewall, the original owner
of this charming 18th-century
house, rented it out to Albert
Gallatin, the Treasury Secretary
under President Thomas
Jefferson, in the early 1800s. It
was here Gallatin entertained a
number of wealthy contributors
whose financial backing brought
about the Louisiana Purchase in
1803, which doubled the size of
the United States. During
the British invasion in 1814,
the house was the only site in
Washington to resist the attack.
While the US Capitol was burning,
American soldiers took refuge in
the house from where they fired
upon the British.

The National Women's Party,
who won the right to vote
for American women in 1920,
bought the house in 1929 with
the help of feminist divorcee
Alva Vanderbilt Belmont.
Today, the house is still the
headquarters of the Party,
and visitors can admire the
period furnishings and suffragist
artifacts. The desk on which
the, as yet unratified, Equal
Rights Amendment of 1923
was written by Alice Paul,
leader of the Party, is here.

❺ US Capitol

See pp52–3.

❻ Robert A. Taft Memorial

Constitution Ave and 1st St,
NW. **Map** 4 E4. Ⓜ Union
Station. ♿

This statue of Ohio senator
Robert A. Taft (1889–1953)
stands in a park opposite
the US Capitol. The
statue itself, by
sculptor Wheeler
Williams, is dwarfed
by a vast, white bell tower
(the Carillon), that rises up
behind the figure of the
politician. The memorial,
designed by Douglas W. Orr,
was erected in 1959 as
a "tribute to the honesty,
indomitable courage, and
high principles of free
government symbolized by
his life." The son of President
William Howard Taft, Robert
Taft was a Republican, famous
for sponsoring the Taft-Hartley
Act, the regulator of collective
bargaining between labor
and management.

❼ National Japanese American Memorial

Louisiana and New Jersey Avenues at
D St, NW. **Map** 4 E3. Ⓜ Union Station.

This memorial, designed by
Davis Buckley, commemorates
the story of the 120,000
Japanese Americans interned
during World War II and the
more than 800 Japanese

Statue of
Robert Taft

Americans who died in
military service. The names of
these servicemen are
carved upon a curving
granite wall, while etched
on the top are the names
of the ten detention
camps where Japanese
American civilians were
confined. An 18-foot
long aluminum gong
may be rung by visitors,
serving as a call to
reflection and
remembrance.

❽ Ulysses S. Grant Memorial

Union Square, west side of US
Capitol in front of Reflecting Pool.
Map 4 E4. Ⓜ Capitol South, Union
Station. **Open** Visitor center:
9am–5pm daily. ♿

This dramatic memorial
was sculpted by Henry
Merwin Shrady and dedicated
in 1922. With its 13 horses,
it is one of the world's most
complex equestrian statues.
The bronze groupings
around General Grant
provide a graphic depiction
of the suffering of the
Civil War. In the artillery
group, horses and soldiers
pulling a cannon are urged
on by their mounted leader.
The infantry group storms
into the heat of battle, where
a horse and rider have already
fallen under the charge.

Shrady worked on the
sculpture for 20 years, using
soldiers in training for his
models. He died two weeks
before it was dedicated.

The artillery group in the Ulysses S. Grant Civil War Memorial

❺ United States Capitol

The US Capitol is one of the world's best-known symbols of democracy. The center of America's legislative process for 200 years, its Neo-Classical architecture reflects the democratic principles of ancient Greece and Rome. The cornerstone was laid by George Washington in 1793, and by 1800 the Capitol was occupied. The British burned it down in the War of 1812, but restoration began in 1815. Many architectural and artistic features, such as the Statue of Freedom and Brumidi's murals, were added later. An impressive Capitol Visitor Center, located below the East Plaza, offers improved visitor access and facilities.

★ **The Rotunda**
Completed in 1865, the 180-ft (55-m) high Rotunda is capped by *The Apotheosis of Washington*, a fresco by Constantino Brumidi.

KEY

① **The House Chamber**

② **The Hall of Columns** is lined with statues of notable Americans.

③ **The crypt with central star** denotes the city's division into quadrants.

④ **The Senate Chamber** has been the home of the US Senate since 1859.

⑤ **The Brumidi Corridors** are lined with the frescoes, bronzework, and paintings of Italian artist Constantino Brumidi (1805–80).

⑥ **The Columbus Doors**, created by Randolph Rogers, are solid bronze and depict Christopher Columbus's life and his discovery of America, a theme echoed throughout the works of art in the Capitol.

★ **National Statuary Hall**
In 1864 Congress invited each state to contribute two statues of prominent citizens to stand in this hall.

The Dome
Currently undergoing a two-year restoration, the cast iron dome was designed by Thomas U. Walter.

Old Senate Chamber
Occupied by the Senate until 1859, this chamber was subsequently home to the Supreme Court for 75 years.

★ Main Entrance/ Capitol Visitor Center
Carved on the pediment are Classical female representations of America, flanked by figures of Justice and Hope. Guided tours start from the Capitol Visitor Center, located below the East Plaza.

US Capitol
Not only representative of the legislative heart of Washington, the Capitol marks the precise center of the city. The city's four quadrants radiate out from the middle of the building.

❾ US Botanic Garden

1st St and Independence Ave, SW. Entrance: 100 Maryland Ave, SW. **Map** 4 D4. **Tel** (202) 225-8333. Ⓜ Federal Center SW. **Open** 10am–5pm daily. Ⓖ Ⓦ **usbg.gov**

The 80-ft (24-m) tall Palm House is the centerpiece of the Botanic Garden Conservatory. The appearance of the 1933 building has been preserved but modernized, creating a spacious venue for the collection of tropical and subtropical plants, and the comprehensive fern and orchid collections. Other specialties are plants native to deserts in the Old and New Worlds, plants of economic and healing value, and endangered plants rescued through an international trade program.

The Botanic Garden was originally established to cultivate plants that could be beneficial to the American people. The garden was revitalized in 1842, when the Wilkes Expedition to the South Seas brought back an assortment of plants from around the world, some of which are still on display.

A National Garden of plants native to the mid-Atlantic region was created on 3 acres (1 ha) of land west of the Conservatory. It includes a Water Garden, a Rose Garden, and a terraced lawn. Visitors can dial (202) 730-9303 from their cell phones for an audio tour as they walk through.

❿ Bartholdi Park and Fountain

Independence Ave and 1st St, SW. **Map** 4 D4. Ⓜ Federal Center SW. Ⓖ Ⓦ **usbg.gov/bartholdi-park**

The graceful fountain that dominates this jewel of a park was created by Frédéric August Bartholdi (sculptor of the Statue of Liberty) for the 1876 Centennial. Originally lit by gas, it was converted to electric lighting in 1881 and became a nighttime attraction. Made of cast iron, the symmetrical fountain is decorated with figures of nymphs and tritons.

The elegant Bartholdi Fountain, surrounded by miniature gardens

Surrounding the fountain are tiny model gardens, planted to inspire the urban gardener. They are themed, and include Therapeutic, Romantic, and Heritage plants, such as Virginia sneezeweed, sweet william, and wild oats.

⓫ Ebenezer United Methodist Church

4th St and D St, SE. **Tel** (202) 544-1636. **Map** 4 F5. Ⓜ Eastern Market. **Open** 10am–2pm Tue–Fri. **Closed** Federal hols.

Ebenezer Church, established in 1819, was the first black church to serve Methodists in Washington. Attendance grew rapidly, and a new church, Little Ebenezer, was built to take the overflow. After the Emancipation Proclamation in 1863 *(see p23)*, Congress decreed that black children should receive public education. In 1864, Little Ebenezer became the District of Columbia's first school for black children. The number of members steadily increased and another church was built in 1868, but this was badly damaged by a storm in 1896. The replacement church, which was constructed in 1897 and is still here today, is Ebenezer United Methodist Church. A model of Little Ebenezer stands next to it.

⓬ Eastern Market

7th St and C St, SE. **Map** 4 F4. Ⓜ Eastern Market. **Open** 7am–7pm Tue–Fri, 7am–6pm Sat, 9am–5pm Sun. **Closed** Jan 1, Jul 4, Thanksgiving, Dec 25 & 26. Ⓖ at West end. Ⓦ **easternmarket-dc.org**

This block-long market hall has been a fixture in Capitol Hill since 1871, and the provisions sold today still have an Old World flavor. Big beefsteaks and fresh pigs' feet are plentiful, along with gourmet sausages and cheeses from all over the world. The aroma of fresh bread, roasted chicken, and flowers pervades the hall. On Friday afternoons

The redbrick, late-19th-century Ebenezer United Methodist Church

Flowers for sale on the sidewalk outside the Eastern Market

and Saturdays, the covered stalls outside are filled with crafts and farmers' produce, while on Sundays they host a flea market. The markets draw large crowds.

Eastern Market was designed by local architect Adolph Cluss. It is one of the few public markets left in Washington, and the only one that is still used for its original purpose.

❸ Union Station

50 Massachusetts Ave, NE. **Map** 4 E3.
Tel (202) 289-1908. Ⓜ Union Station.
Open daily. 🚹 🚻 🚪 ♿
Ⓦ unionstationdc.com

When Union Station opened in 1908, its fine Beaux Arts design (by Daniel H. Burnham) set a standard that influenced architecture in Washington for 40 years. The elegantly proportioned white granite structure, its three main archways modeled on the Arch of Constantine in Rome, was the largest train station in the world. For half a century, Union Station was a major transportation hub, but as air travel became increasingly popular, passenger trains went into decline.

By the late 1950s, the size of the station outweighed the number of passsengers it served. For two decades, the railroad authorities and Congress debated its fate. Finally, in 1981, a joint public and private venture set out to restore the building.

Union Station reopened in 1988, and today is the second most visited tourist attraction in Washington. Its 96-ft (29-m) barrel-vaulted ceiling has been covered with 22-carat gold leaf. There are around 100 specialty shops and a food court to visit, and the Main Hall hosts cultural and civic events throughout the year. The building still serves its original purpose as a station, however, and over 100 trains pass through daily.

Vintage stamp depicting Benjamin Franklin

❹ National Postal Museum

2 Massachusetts Ave, NE. **Map** 4 E3.
Tel (202) 633-5555. Ⓜ Union Station.
Open 10am–5:30pm daily.
Closed Dec 25. 🚹 🚻 ♿
Ⓦ postalmuseum.si.edu

Opened by the Smithsonian in 1990, this fascinating museum is housed in the former City Post Office building. Exhibits include a stagecoach and a postal rail car, showing how mail traveled before modern airmail.

"Mail Call", a permanent exhibition, explores the history of the military postal system. The Philatelic Gallery displays one of the best stamp collections in the world. "Binding the Nation" explains the history of the mail from the pre-Revolutionary era to the end of the 19th century. Other exhibits illustrate how the mail system works and how a stamp is created.

At postcard kiosks, you can address a postcard electronically, see the route it will take to its destination, and drop it in a mailbox on the spot.

Columbus Memorial, sculpted by Lorado Taft, in front of Union Station

THE MALL

In L'Enfant's original plan for the new capital of the United States, the Mall was conceived as a grand boulevard lined with diplomatic residences of elegant, Parisian architecture. L'Enfant's plan was never fully realized, but it is nevertheless a moving sight – this grand, tree-lined expanse is bordered on either side by the Smithsonian museums and features the Capitol at its eastern end and the Washington Monument at its western end. This dramatic formal version of the Mall did not materialize until after World War II. Until then the space was used for everything from a zoo to a railroad terminal to a wood yard.

The Mall forms a vital part of the history of the United States. Innumerable demonstrators have gathered at the Lincoln Memorial and marched to the US Capitol. The Pope said Mass, African-American soprano Marian Anderson sang at the request of first lady Eleanor Roosevelt, and Dr. Martin Luther King, Jr. delivered his famous "I have a dream" speech here. Every year on the Fourth of July (Independence Day), America's birthday party is held on the Mall, with a fireworks display. On summer evenings, teams of locals play softball and soccer on its fields.

Sights at a Glance

Museums and Galleries
1. National Gallery of Art pp60–63
2. National Air and Space Museum pp64–7
3. Hirshhorn Museum
4. Arts and Industries Building
5. National Museum of African Art
6. National Museum of the American Indian
7. National Museum of Natural History pp72–3
8. Smithsonian Castle
9. Arthur M. Sackler Gallery
10. Freer Gallery of Art
11. National Museum of American History pp76–8
12. Washington Monument
13. United States Holocaust Memorial Museum pp82–3

Official Buildings
14. Bureau of Engraving and Printing

Monuments and Memorials
15. Jefferson Memorial
17. World War II Memorial
18. Vietnam Veterans Memorial
19. Korean War Veterans Memorial
20. Martin Luther King, Jr. Memorial
21. Franklin D. Roosevelt Memorial
22. Lincoln Memorial

Parks and Gardens
16. Tidal Basin

☐ Restaurants see p184
1. The Atrium Café
2. Cascade Café
3. CityZen
4. Mitistam Café
5. Pavilion Café

See also Street Finder map 3, 4

0 meters 500
0 yards 500

◀ America by Air Gallery, National Air and Space Museum   For keys to symbols see back flap

Street-by-Street: The Mall

This 1-mile (1.5-km) boulevard between the Capitol and the Washington Monument is the city's cultural heart; the many different museums of the Smithsonian Institution can be found along this green strip. At the northeast corner of the Mall is the National Gallery of Art. Directly opposite is one of the most popular museums in the world – the National Air and Space Museum, a soaring construction of steel and glass. Both the National Museum of American History and the National Museum of Natural History, on the north side of the Mall, also draw huge numbers of visitors.

❼ ★ National Museum of Natural History
The central Rotunda was designed in the Neoclassical style and opened to the public in 1910.

❽ Smithsonian Castle
The main information center for all Smithsonian activities, this building once housed the basis of the collections found in numerous museums along the Mall.

❾ Arthur M. Sackler Gallery
This extensive collection of Asian art was donated to the nation by New Yorker Arthur Sackler.

⓫ ★ National Museum of American History
From George Washington's uniform to this electric streetcar, US history is documented here.

Washington Monument

❿ Freer Gallery of Art
Asian art, including this 13th-century Chinese silk painting, is a highlight, in addition to a superb Whistler collection.

❺ National Museum of African Art
Founded in 1965 and situated underground, this museum houses a comprehensive collection of ancient and modern African art.

12TH STREET

MADISON DRIVE N

JEFFERSON DRIVE SW

❶ ★ National Gallery of Art
This superb gallery houses paintings and other works of art, such as this terracotta bust of Lorenzo de' Medici, that chronicle the history of art from the Middle Ages to the 20th century.

0 meters 100
0 yards 100

Locator Map
See Street Finder maps 3 & 4

Sculpture Garden

National Gallery of Art, West Building

CONSTITUTION AVENUE NW

7TH STREET NW

MADISON DRIVE NW

US Capitol

National Gallery of Art, East Building

Key

— Suggested route

❸ Hirshhorn Museum
An unusual addition to the Mall, this cylindrical museum houses contemporary art. Only a small selection of the 18,000 works it holds is on display at any one time.

7TH STREET NW

INDEPENDENCE AVENUE SW

❷ ★ National Air and Space Museum
The clean, modern design of the National Air and Space Museum echoes the technological advances in aviation illustrated by the spectacular exhibits inside.

❹ Arts and Industries Building
This masterpiece of Victorian architecture was originally built to contain exhibits from the Centennial Exposition in Philadelphia.

❶ National Gallery of Art

In the 1920s, American financier and statesman Andrew Mellon began collecting art with the intention of establishing a new art museum in Washington. In 1936 he offered his collection to the country and offered also to provide a building for the new National Gallery of Art. Designed by architect John Russell Pope, the Neoclassical building was opened in 1941. Other collectors followed Mellon's example and donated their collections to the Gallery, and by the 1960s it had outgrown the West Building. I.M. Pei designed the innovative East Building, which was opened in 1978. The building was paid for by Andrew Mellon's son and daughter.

★ Ginevra de' Benci
This depiction of a thoughtful young Florentine girl by Leonardo da Vinci (c.1474) is his only painting in the US.

The Alba Madonna
Painted c.1510 by Raphael, this work is considered one of the major achievements of the Renaissance.

★ Woman with a Parasol – Mme Monet and her Son
(1875) This painting by Claude Monet of his wife hangs in the West Building.

West Garden Court

Micro Gallery

Sculpture Garden

Ground Floor

Key to Floor Plan

- ☐ 13th–15th-century Italian
- ☐ 15th–16th-century Netherlands and Germany
- ☐ 16th-century Italian and Spanish
- ☐ 17th-century Dutch and Flemish
- ☐ 17th–18th-century Spanish, Italian, and French
- ☐ 18th–19th-century Spanish and French
- ☐ 19th-century French
- ☐ American paintings
- ☐ British paintings
- ☐ Sculpture, Decorative Arts, Drawings and Prints
- ☐ Special exhibitions
- ☐ Non-exhibition space

Portrait of a Young Man and His Tutor
This charming work by French artist Nicolas de Largilliere (1656–1746) was painted in 1685.

Main Floor

East Garden Court

Founders Room

VISITORS' CHECKLIST

Practical Information
West Building Constitution Ave between 4th St & 7th St, NW; East Building 4th St between Madison Drive and Constitution Ave, NW. **Map** 4 D4.
Tel (202) 737-4215.
w nga.gov
Open 10am–5pm Mon–Sat, 11am–6pm Sun. **Closed** Jan 1, Dec 25. call (202) 842-6247.
Children's activities: call (202) 789-3030 or (202) 842-6176.

Transport
M Archives/Navy Memorial, Judiciary Sq., Smithsonian.
32, 34, 36, 70.

Gallery Guide

The National Gallery of Art is divided into two main buildings. The West Building, shown here, features European paintings and sculptures from the 13th to the 19th centuries, including American works, a substantial Impressionist collection, and Sculpture Gallery. The East Building features modern art. An underground concourse connects the two buildings.

East Building

Concourse Level

Mother and Pearl of Silver: The Andalusian
(c.1888–1900) James McNeill Whistler's portrait of his sister-in-law evokes a sombre, Spanish mood.

Mall Entrance

★ Calder Mobile
The giant mobile that hangs in the middle of the central court-yard of the East Building was one of Alexander Calder's last commissions, completed in 1976.

Exploring the National Gallery of Art

The National Gallery's West and East Buildings are an unusual pair. The West Building, designed by John Russell Pope, is stately and Classical, with matching wings flanking its rotunda. Built of Tennessee marble, it forms a majestic presence on the Mall. Its collection is devoted to Western art from the 13th to the early 20th century. The East Building, completed in 1978, occupies a trapezoidal plot of land adjacent to the West Building. The triangular East Building is as audacious as the West one is conservative, but together they are harmonious. The interior of the East Building is a huge, fluid space, with galleries on either side housing works of modern art. The Sculpture Garden, adjacent to the West Building, has a fountain area that becomes an ice rink in winter.

Detail of *Christ Cleansing the Temple* (c.1570), by El Greco

Giotto's *Madonna and Child*, painted between 1320 and 1330

13th- to 15th-Century Italian Art

The Italian galleries house paintings from the 13th to 15th centuries. The earlier pre-Renaissance works of primarily religious themes illustrate a decidedly Byzantine influence.

The Florentine artist Giotto's *Madonna and Child* (c.1320–30) shows the transition to the Classical painting of the Renaissance. *Adoration of the Magi*, painted around 1480 by Botticelli, portrays a serene Madonna and Child surrounded by worshipers in the Italian countryside. Around the same date Pietro Perugino painted *The Crucifixion with the Virgin, St. John, St. Jerome and St. Mary Magdalene*. Andrew Mellon bought the triptych from the Hermitage Gallery in Leningrad. Raphael's *The Alba Madonna* of

1510 was called by one writer "the supreme compositional achievement of Renaissance painting." Leonardo da Vinci's *Ginevra de' Benci* (c.1474–8) is thought to be the first ever "psychological" portrait (depicting emotion) to be painted.

16th-Century Italian Art

This collection includes works by Tintoretto, Titian, and Raphael. The 1500s were the height of Italian Classicism. Raphael's *St. George and the Dragon* (c.1506) typifies the perfection of technique for which this school of artists is known. Jacopo Tintoretto's *Christ at the Sea of Galilee* (c.1575/1580) portrays Christ standing on the shore while his disciples are on a storm-tossed fishing boat. The emotional intensity of the painting and the role of nature in it made Tintoretto one of the greatest of the Venetian artists.

17th- to 18th-Century Spanish, Italian, and French Art

Among the 17th- and 18th-century European works are Jean-Honoré Fragonard's *Diana and Endymion* (c.1753–6), which was heavily influenced by Fragonard's mentor, François Boucher. El Greco's *Christ Cleansing the Temple* (pre-1570) demonstrates the influence of the 16th-century Italian schools. El Greco ("The Greek") signed his real name, Domenikos Theotokopoulos, to the panel.

17th-Century Dutch and Flemish Art

This collection holds a number of Old Masters including works by Rubens, Van Dyck, and Rembrandt. An example of Rembrandt's self-portraits is on display, which he painted in oils in 1659, ten years before his death.

Oil painting, *Diana and Endymion* (c.1753), by Jean-Honoré Fragonard

Several paintings by Rubens in this section testify to his genius, among them *Daniel in the Lions' Den* (c.1615). This depicts the Old Testament prophet, Daniel, thanking God for his help during his night spent surrounded by lions. In 1617, Rubens exchanged this work for antique marbles owned by a British diplomat. Rubens also painted *Deborah Kip, Wife of Sir Balthasar Gerbier, and her Children* (1629–30). Not a conventional family portrait, the mother and her four children seem withdrawn and pensive, suggesting unhappiness and perhaps even foreboding tragedy. Van Dyck painted Rubens's first wife, *Isabella Brant* (c.1621) toward the end of her life. Although she is smiling, her eyes reveal an inner melancholy.

19th-Century French Art

This is one of the best Impressionist collections outside Paris. Works on display include Paul Cézanne's *The Artist's Father Reading "L'Evénement"* (1866), Auguste Renoir's *A Girl with a Watering Can* (1876), *Four Dancers* (c.1899) by Edgar Degas, and Claude Monet's *Woman with a Parasol – Madame Monet and Her Son* (1875) and *Palazzo da Mula, Venice* (1908). Post-Impressionist works include Seurat's pointillist *The Lighthouse at Honfleur* (c.1886), in which thousands of dots are used to create the image, and Van Gogh's *Self Portrait*. The latter was painted in St Rémy in 1889 when he was staying in an asylum and shows his mastery at capturing character and emotion. Toulouse-Lautrec's painting, *Quadrille at the Moulin Rouge* (1892), depicts a dancer provocatively raising her skirts above her ankles.

Geometric skylights in the plaza from the West Building to the East Building

American Painting

This important collection of American artists shows evidence of European influence, but in themes that are resolutely American. James McNeill Whistler's *Mother of Pearl and Silver: The Andalusian* (1888–1900) has a European sophistication. Mary Cassatt left America for exile in Europe and was heavily influenced by the Impressionists, especially Degas. *Boating Party* (1893–4) is an example of one of her recurrent themes: mother and child. *Children Playing on a Beach* (1884) is also a good example of her child paintings, and *Miss Mary Ellison* of her portraiture. Winslow Homer's *Breezing Up (A Fair Wind)* (1873–6) is a masterpiece by the American

Miss Mary Ellison by Mary Cassatt (1880)

Realist. His painting is a charming depiction of three small boys and a fisherman.

Modern and Contemporary Art

The enormous East Building houses modern and contemporary art. I.M. Pei's "H"-shaped building contains a vast atrium which is edged by four balconies and adjacent galleries. Architecturally, this space provides a dramatic focus and spatial orientation for visitors to the East Building.

Centered in the atrium is *Untitled*, a vast red, blue, and black creation by Alexander Calder. It was commissioned in 1972 for the opening of the museum in 1978. At the entrance to the East Building is Henry Moore's bronze sculpture *Knife Edge Mirror Two Piece* (1977–8).

Also in the East Building are a research center for schools, offices for the curators, a library, and a large collection of drawings and prints.

Both the East and West buildings also host traveling exhibits. These are not limited to modern art, but have included the art of ancient Japan, American Impressionists, and the sketches of Leonardo da Vinci. The East Building's galleries are surprisingly intimate.

Sculpture Garden

Located across the street from the West Building at 7th Street, the elegant Sculpture Garden holds 17 sculptures. The late 20th-century works include pieces by Louise Bourgeois, Roy Lichtenstein, and Joan Miró. Although different, the sculptures do not compete with each other because they are spread out. Transformed into an ice rink in winter and a venue for free jazz concerts in summer, the garden functions both as an outdoor gallery and as a pleasant oasis within the city. The pavilion houses a year-round café.

❷ National Air and Space Museum

The Smithsonian's National Air and Space Museum opened in 1976. The soaring architecture of the building on the Mall, designed by Hellmuth, Obata, and Kassabaum, is well suited to the airplanes, rockets, balloons, and space capsules of aviation and space flight. A second site, the Steven F. Udvar-Hazy Center, located near Dulles International Airport, opened in 2003 to celebrate the 100th anniversary of the Wright brothers' first powered flight. The museum is the largest air and space museum complex in the world and is home to the retired Discovery space shuttle.

Apollo to the Moon
Full of artifacts, this exhibit tells the story of how the United States put a man on the moon.

★ **Spirit of St. Louis**
At the age of 25, pilot Charles Lindbergh made the first solo transatlantic flight in this plane, landing in France on May 21, 1927.

Restaurants

Skylab Orbital Workshop
This was an orbiting workshop for sets of three-person crews, who conducted research experiments.

Lockheed Martin IMAX® Theater

Key to Floor Plan
- Milestones of Flight
- Exploring the Moon
- Aviation in World Wars I and II
- The Space Race Barron Hilton
- Pioneers of Flight
- Other exhibitions
- Explore the Universe
- Temporary exhibition space
- Wright Brothers
- Developments in Flight

Mall Entrance

★ **Apollo 11 Command Module**
This module carried astronauts Buzz Aldrin, Neil Armstrong, and Michael Collins on their historic mission to the moon in July 1969, when Neil Armstrong took his famous first steps.

★ **1903 Wright Flyer**
This exhibit, along with others in the Wright Brothers and the Invention of the Aerial Age gallery, show the accomplishments of Orville and Wilbur Wright.

VISITORS' CHECKLIST

Practical Information
National Mall, Independence Ave at 6th St, SW. **Map** 4 D4.
Tel (202) 633-2214.
W nasm.si.edu
Open 10am–5:30pm daily (to 7:30pm in summer).
Closed Dec 25. 📷 10:15am, 1pm. 🚻 📷 📷 📷

Transport
Ⓜ Smithsonian.
🚌 32, 34, 36, 52.

Albert Einstein Planetarium

Supermarine Spitfire MK. VII
With more than 20,351 Spitfires built, these planes saw service on every major front and successfully defended England against Germany in WWII.

Second Floor

★ **Amelia Earhart's Red Vega**
Amelia Earhart was the first woman to make a solo transatlantic flight. She succeeded in her red Lockheed Vega, five years after Charles Lindbergh.

America by Air
Located near the museum store, this exhibit outlines the fascinating history of America's airline industry and its effect on the nation and the world.

Flight simulators

Milestones of Flight
Many of the firsts in both aviation and space travel are on display in this gallery.

First Floor

Gallery Guide
The first floor houses many themed displays, as well as the Lockheed Martin IMAX® theater and the Museum Store. The lofty second-floor ceilings show exhibits and models demonstrating the history of flight from the early days to the space age.

Exploring the National Air and Space Museum

The National Air and Space Museum on the Mall has a massive exhibition space of 23 galleries. The most visited museum in the world, it has to cope not only with millions of visitors but also with the range and sheer size of its artifacts, which include hundreds of rockets, planes, and spacecraft. In 2003 the museum opened a sister exhibition space: a huge new state-of-the art facility, the Steven F. Udvar-Hazy Center, located near Dulles Airport. Now with two sites, more of NASM's historic collections are on display for the public to enjoy.

The Boeing F4B Navy fighter

Milestones of Flight

Entering the National Air and Space Museum from the Mall entrance, first stop is the soaring **Milestones of Flight** gallery, which gives an overview of the history of flight. The exhibits in this room are some of the major firsts in aviation and space technology, as they helped to realize man's ambition to take to the air.

The gallery is vast, designed to accommodate the large aircraft – many of which are suspended from the ceiling – and spacecraft. Some of these pioneering machines are surprisingly small, however. Charles Lindbergh's *Spirit of St. Louis*, the first aircraft to cross the Atlantic with a solo pilot, was designed with the fuel tanks ahead of the cockpit so Lindbergh had to use a periscope to look directly ahead. John Glenn's Mercury spacecraft, *Friendship 7*, in which he orbited the earth, is smaller than a sports car.

Near the entrance to the gallery is a moon rock – a symbol of man's exploration of

space. Also in this gallery is the *Apollo 11 Command Module*, which carried the first men to walk on the moon. The Wright brothers' *Flyer* (in gallery 209) was the first plane to sustain powered flight on December 17, 1903, at Kitty Hawk, North Carolina.

Developments in Flight

Travelers now take flying for granted – it is safe, fast, and, for many, routine. The National Air and Space Museum, however, displays machines and gadgets

from an era when flight was new and daring. The **Pioneers of Flight** gallery celebrates the men and women who have challenged the physical and psychological barriers faced when leaving the earth. Adventurer Cal Rogers was the first to fly across the United States, but it was not non-stop. In 1911 he flew from coast to coast in less than 30 days, with almost 70 landings. His early biplane is one of the exhibits. (Twelve years later, a Fokker T-2 made the trip in less than 27 hours.)

Amelia Earhart was the first woman to fly the Atlantic, just five years after Charles Lindbergh. Her red Lockheed Vega is displayed. Close by is *Tingmissartoq*, a Lockheed Sirius seaplane belonging to Charles Lindbergh. Its unusual name is Inuit for "one who flies like a bird." Some of the greatest strides in aviation were made in the period between the two world wars, celebrated in the **Golden Age of Flight** gallery. The public's intense interest in flight resulted in races, exhibitions, and adventurous exploration. Here a visitor can see planes equipped with skis for landing on snow, with short wings for racing, and a "staggerwing" plane on which the lower wing was placed ahead of the upper.

The propeller-driven Douglas DC-3 aircraft in the America by Air gallery

Rockets on display in the Space Race gallery

The F4B Navy fighter, used by US Marine Corps squadrons, was developed between the world wars and is on display in the **Sea-Air Operations** gallery. Flight then progressed from propeller propulsion to jets. The **Jet Aviation** gallery has the first operational jet fighter, the German Messerschmitt Me 262A. *Lulu Belle*, the prototype of the first US fighter jet, was used in the Korean War of 1950–53.

America by Air traces the development of commercial air-travel, from the air mail age to the "glass cockpit," and beyond. This is a fun, family-friendly gallery with hands-on exhibits.

Aviation in World Wars I and II

One of the most popular parts of the museum is the **World War II Aviation** gallery, which has planes from the Allied and the Axis air forces. Nearby is an example of the Japanese Mitsubishi A6M5 Zero Model 52, which was a light, highly maneuverable fighter plane.

The maneuverability of the Messerschmitt Bf 109 made it Germany's most successful fighter. It was matched, and in some areas surpassed, by the Supermarine Spitfire of the Royal Air Force, which helped to win control of the skies over Britain in 1940–41.

The Space Race

The animosity that grew between the United States and the Soviet Union after World War II manifested itself in the Space Race. America was taken by surprise when the Soviets launched *Sputnik 1* on October 4, 1957. The US attempt to launch their first satellite proved spectacular failure when the *Vanguard* crashed in December 1957. The satellite is on display here.

In 1961, Soviet cosmonaut Yuri Gagarin became the first man to orbit the earth. The Americans countered with Alan Shepard's manned space flight in *Freedom 7* later the same year. The first space walk was from the *Gemini IV* capsule by American astronaut Edward H. White in 1965.

On July 20, 1969, the race reached a climax when the world watched as Neil Armstrong walked on the moon. His original spacesuit from the Apollo 11 mission is on display. Other exhibits from the Space Race include the *Skylab 4* command module, and *Gemini 7*, a two-person spacecraft that successfully orbited the earth in 1965.

Gemini IV capsule

The Space Hall gallery shows the result of the final détente between the superpowers with the Apollo-Soyuz Test Project. This was a purposefully collaborative space mission meant to symbolize a new era of cooperation. It was the last Apollo flight. When the American *Apollo* module docked alongside the Soviet *Soyuz* spacecraft in 1975, it was the start of the end of the Space Race.

Progress in Air and Space Technology

Mankind's fascination with flight is in part a desire to see the earth from a great distance and also to get closer to other planets. In the Independence Avenue lobby is artist Robert T. McCall's interpretation of the birth of the universe, the planets, and astronauts reaching the moon.

The Hubble Telescope, launched from the *Discovery* shuttle in April 1990, provides pictures of extremely distant astronomical objects. Launched in 1964, the *Ranger* lunar probe also took high-quality pictures of the moon, and then transmitted them to Cape Canaveral.

Moving Beyond Earth gives an insight into recent human spaceflight and future possibilities. A space shuttle model and other launch vehicle models, as well as astronaut gear, are on display. Visitors can also experience aspects of spaceflight through interactive computer kiosks.

The spacesuit worn by Apollo astronauts in 1969

Fountain in the central plaza of the Hirshhorn Museum

❸ Hirshhorn Museum

Independence Ave and 7th St, SW.
Map 3 C4. **Tel** (202) 633-1000.
Ⓜ Smithsonian, L'Enfant Plaza.
Open 10am–5:30pm daily (Sculpture Garden: 7:30am–dusk).
Closed Dec 25. 🎫 ♿ 📷 ⛵
ⓦ hirshhorn.si.edu

When the Hirshhorn Museum was still in its planning stages, S. Dillon Ripley, then Secretary of the Smithsonian Institution, told the planning board that the building should be "controversial in every way" so that it would be fit to house contemporary works of art.

The Hirshhorn certainly fulfilled its architectural mission. It has been variously described as a doughnut or a flying saucer, but it is actually a four-story, not-quite-symmetrical cylinder. It is also home to one of the greatest collections of modern art in the United States.

The museum's benefactor, Joseph H. Hirshhorn, was an eccentric, flamboyant immigrant from Latvia who amassed a collection of 6,000 pieces of contemporary art. Since the museum opened in 1974, the Smithsonian has built on Hirshhorn's original donation, and the collection now consists of 3,000 pieces of sculpture, 4,000 drawings and photographs, and approximately 5,000 paintings. The works of art are arranged chronologically. The main, lower floor displays newly acquired work. It is also home to the "Black Box," a space dedicated to film, video, and other digital works by emerging international artists. The second floor hosts temporary exhibitions, of which there are at least three a year. These are usually arranged thematically, or as tributes to individual artists, such as Lucien Freud, Alberto Giacometti, or Francis Bacon. The third floor houses the permanent collection, which includes works by artists such as Alexander Calder, Arshile Gorky, Willem de Kooning, and John Singer Sargent. In addition, visitors should not miss the outdoor sculpture garden, across the street from the museum. It includes pieces by Alexander Calder, Auguste Rodin, Henri Matisse, and many others.

The outdoor Full Circle Café, located in the plaza at the center of the building, makes a pleasant spot in which to enjoy lunch during the summer months.

❹ Arts and Industries Building

900 Jefferson Drive, SW. **Map** 3 C4.
Tel (202) 633-1000. Ⓜ Smithsonian.
Closed to the public. ♿ 📷
ⓦ si.edu

The ornate, vast galleries and the airy rotunda of the splendid Victorian Arts and Industries Building were designed by Montgomery Meigs, architect of the National Building Museum (see p105). The Arts and Industries Building was extraordinary because of its expanse of open space and abundance of natural light.

The museum served a wide-ranging variety of functions after its completion on March 4, 1881. In its opening year, it was the site of President James A. Garfield's inaugural ball; it also displayed artifacts from Philadelphia's 1876 Centennial Exposition, including a complete steam train; later, it was home to a collection of the First Ladies' gowns, as well as Lindbergh's famous airplane the *Spirit of St. Louis*, before these exhibits were moved to other Smithsonian museums on the Mall. A working carousel is located in front of the building, on the Mall (closed in winter).

Arts and Industries Building's fountain

Concerns over its deteriorating condition led to the building's closure in 2004. However, it has since been allocated $25 million for renovation work and is due to reopen in late-2014.

The Hirshhorn Museum's sculpture garden, a green space in which to contemplate pieces by Calder, Rodin, Matisse, and others

Tribal masks at the National Museum of African Art

❺ National Museum of African Art

950 Independence Ave, SW. **Map** 3 C4.
Tel (202) 633-4600. Ⓜ Smithsonian.
Open 10am–5:30pm daily.
Closed Dec 25. 🔲 🕭 🏛 🖼
🌐 nmafa.si.edu

Washington's National Museum of African Art is one of the most peaceful spots on the Mall. Perhaps because it is mostly underground, with a relatively low above-ground presence, it is often missed by visitors. The entrance pavilion, situated in the Enid A. Haupt Garden directly in front of the Smithsonian Castle, leads to three subterranean floors, where the museum shares space with the adjacent Ripley Center and the Arthur M. Sackler Gallery (see pp74–5).

The museum was founded in 1964 by Warren Robbins, a former officer in the American Foreign Service (he was a cultural attaché and public affairs officer), and was the first museum in the US to concentrate entirely on the art and culture of the African continent. It was first situated in the home of Frederick Douglass (see p147), on Capitol Hill. For several years Robbins had to finance the museum himself, gradually acquiring more space in the form of a collection of town houses near the original building. Eventually financial support was forthcoming as

the importance of the collection was recognized. The Smithsonian Institution acquired Robbins' collection in 1979, and the works were finally moved to their current home on the Mall in 1987.

The 9,000-piece permanent collection includes both modern and ancient art from Africa, although the majority of pieces date from the 19th and 20th centuries. Traditional African art of bronze, ceramics, and gold are on display, along with an extensive collection of masks. There is also a display of *kente* cloth from Ghana – brightly colored and patterned cloth used to adorn clothing as a symbol of African nationalism. The Eliot Elisofon Photographic Archives (Eliot Elisofon was a famous photographer for *Life* magazine) contain 300,000 prints and some 120,000 ft of edited and unedited film footage, as well

A Benin bronze head at the NMAA

as videos and documentaries on African art and culture. The museum now also holds 525 pieces of the Walt Disney-Tishman African Art Collection. The Warren M. Robbins Library has approximately 32,000 books in its collection, mainly on African art, history, and culture. The library, however, also has children's literature and videos. It is open to the public by appointment only.

To display its vast archive of exhibits, the museum runs a rolling program of themed exhibitions. It also hosts performing arts events featuring dance, music, and the spoken word. Year-round there is a full calendar of educational tours, lectures, and workshops, including many for children. At the bi-monthly Music of Africa workshop, children over six can play African musical instruments and learn about different rhythms and playing techniques.

History of the Mall

In September, 1789, French-born Pierre L'Enfant (1754–1825) was invited by George Washington to design the capital of the new United States. While the rest of the city developed, the area planned by L'Enfant to be the Grand Avenue, running west from the Capitol, remained swampy and undeveloped. In 1850, landscape gardener Andrew Jackson Downing was employed to develop the land in accordance with L'Enfant's plans. However, the money ran out, and the work was abandoned. At the end of the Civil War in 1865, President Lincoln, eager that building in the city should progress, instructed that work on the area should begin again, and the Mall began to take on the park-like appearance it has today. The addition of many museums and memorials in the latter half of the 20th century established the Mall as the cultural heart of Washington.

Aerial view, showing the Mall stretching down from the Capitol

❻ National Museum of the American Indian

Built from Minnesota Kasota limestone, the National Museum of the American Indian was established in collaboration with Native American communities throughout the western hemisphere. It is the only national museum dedicated to the Native peoples of the Americas, and is the eighteenth museum of the Smithsonian Institution. The original collections of artifacts were assembled by George Gustav Heye (1874–1957), a wealthy New Yorker, at the turn of the 20th century. The exhibitions showcase the spiritual and daily lives of diverse peoples and encourage visitors to look beyond stereotypes.

★ Our Peoples
American Indians, including the Blackfeet and Kiowa, tell their own stories and histories, focusing on both the destruction of their culture and their resilience.

George Heye (1874–1957)
Collector and world traveler George Gustav Heye and his wife, Thea, accompanied a Zuni delegation in New York c.1923.

★ Lelawi Theater
In this circular theater a spectacular multimedia presentation is shown every 15 minutes. "Who We Are" highlights the diversity of American Indian life from the Arctic, to the Northwest Coast, to Bolivia.

★ Our Universes
Eight groups of American Indians, from the Santa Clara Pueblo in New Mexico to the Lakota in South Dakota, share their world views, philosophies of creation, and spiritual relationship with nature.

Window on Collections: Many Hands, Many Voices
Over 3,500 objects are on display, including dolls, beaded objects, and artwork.

Exterior of Museum
The museum's curvilinear limestone exterior gives it a natural, weathered effect. It is set in a landscape of flowing water, hardwood forest, meadowland, and croplands, to reflect the American Indian's connection to the land.

Window on Collections
Interactive technology allows for a self-guided tour of the exhibits. Shown here is a peace medal that once belonged to Powder Face, an Arapaho.

th Floor

Resource Center

3rd Floor

Key to Floor Plan
- ☐ Our Peoples
- ☐ Window on Collections
- ☐ Our Universes
- ☐ Lelawi Theater
- ☐ Education classrooms
- ▨ Contemporary Gallery
- ☐ Our Lives

Gallery Guide
Begin your visit with the "Who We Are" multimedia presentation at the Lelawi Theater (4th floor). The three permanent exhibitions on this level are "Our Universes," "Our Peoples," and "Window on Collections," while "Our Lives" is on the 3rd floor. On the ground level is a shop and the Mitsitam café.

Our Lives
Examines the lives and identities of Native Americans and the consequences of legal policies that determine who is an American Indian. Here Fritz Scholder (b.1937) explores "nativeness" in this work *The American Indian*.

❼ National Museum of Natural History

Second Floor

The National Museum of Natural History, which opened in 1910, preserves artifacts from the earth's diverse cultures and collects samples of fossils and living creatures from land and sea. Visiting the museum is a vast undertaking, so sample the best of the exhibits and leave the rest for return visits. The O. Orkin Insect Zoo, with its giant hissing cockroaches and large leaf-cutter ant colony, is popular with children, while the Dinosaur Hall delights young and old. The stunning Hall of Mammals displays 274 specimens, and looks at how they adapted to changes in habitat and climate over millions of years.

★ O. Orkin Insect Zoo
This popular exhibit explores the lives and habitats of the single largest animal group on earth and features many live specimens.

Butterflies and Plants: Partners in Evolution
This permanent exhibition, which includes live butterflies, innovatively combines traditional and experiential learning.

First Floor

The Kenneth E. Behring Family Hall of Mammals
has 22,500 sq ft (2,090 sq m) of displays explaining the diversity of mammals.

African Elephant
The massive African Bush Elephant is one of the highlights of the museum. It is the centerpiece of the Rotunda and creates an impressive sight as visitors enter the museum.

Gallery Guide

The first floor's main exhibitions feature mammals and marine life from different continents. Dinosaurs and myriad cultural exhibits are also displayed on this level. The Gems and Minerals collection and the O. Orkin Insect Zoo are on the second floor.

★ **Hope Diamond**
At 45.52 carats, the Hope Diamond is the largest deep blue diamond in the world and is famed for its stunning clarity and color. It is more than one billion years old and once belonged to King Louis XIV of France in the 17th century.

The Johnson IMAX® Theater

Key to Floor Plan

- African Cultures and Ice Age
- Bones, Egyptian Mummies, and the Insect Zoo
- Discovery Room
- Fossils, Dinosaurs, and Early Life
- Geology, Gems, and Minerals
- Human Origins
- Kenneth E. Behring Family Hall of Mammals
- Ocean Hall
- Rotunda
- Special Exhibition space
- Non-exhibition space

Easter Island Stone Head
Originally erected by the hundreds on Easter Island in the South Pacific, these huge stone statues were built in memory of the dead.

Ice Age Mammals, such as the saber-toothed cat and the woolly mammoth, flourished between about 1.6 million and 10,000 years ago.

Ground Floor

A cast of a nest of dinosaur eggs sheds light on the life of *Maiasaura,* a kind of duckbilled dinosaur, who lived around 70 million years ago.

★ **Dinosaur Hall**
Featuring reconstructions of fossils that lived up to 230 million years ago, including this skeleton of *Triceratops horridus,* the Dinosaur Hall is one of the most popular areas of the museum.

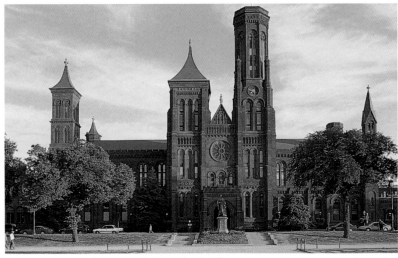

The elegant Victorian façade of the Smithsonian Castle, viewed from the Mall

❽ Smithsonian Castle

1000 Jefferson Drive, SW. **Map** 3 C4.
Tel 633-1000. Ⓜ Smithsonian.
Open 8:30am–5:30pm daily.
Closed Dec 25. ⬚ ⬚ ⬚ W.si.edu

This ornate Victorian edifice served as the first home of the Smithsonian Institution, and was also home to the first Secretary of the Smithsonian, Joseph Henry, and his family. A statue of Henry stands in front of the building.

Constructed of red sandstone in 1855, the Castle was designed by James Renwick, architect of the Renwick Gallery

The tomb of James Smithson

(see p115) and St Patrick's Cathedral in New York. It is an outstanding example of the Gothic Revival style. Inspired also by 12th-century Norman architecture, the Castle has nine towers and an elaborate cornice. Today it is the seat of the Smithsonian administration and houses its Information Center. Visitors can visit the Crypt Room and see the tomb of James Smithson, who bequeathed his fortune to the United States. The South Tower Room was the first children's room in a Washington museum. The ceiling and colorful wall stencils that decorate the room

were restored in 1987.

Outside the castle is the Smithsonian rose garden, filled with beautiful hybrid tea roses. The garden was a later addition that now connects the Castle to the equally ornate Arts and Industries Building (see p68).

❾ Arthur M. Sackler Gallery

1050 Independence Ave, SW.
Map 3 C4. **Tel** 633-1000.
Ⓜ Smithsonian. **Open** 10am–5:30pm daily. **Closed** Dec 25. ⬚ 12:15pm.
⬚ ⬚ ⬚ W asia.si.edu

Dr. Arthur M. Sackler, a New York physician, started collecting Asian art in the 1950s. In 1982, he donated more than

James Smithson (1765–1829)

Although he never once visited the United States, James Smithson, English scientist and philanthropist, and illegitimate son of the first Duke of Northumberland, left his entire fortune of half a million dollars to "found at Washington, under the name of the Smithsonian Institution, an establishment for the increase and diffusion of knowledge among men." However, this was only if his nephew and heir were to die childless. This did happen and hence, in 1836, Smithson's fortune passed to the government of the United States, which did not quite know what to do with such a vast bequest. For 11 years Congress debated various proposals, finally agreeing to set up a government-run foundation that would administer all national museums. The first Smithson-funded collection was shown at the Smithsonian Castle in 1855.

James Smithson

10th-century Indian sculpture of the goddess Parvati in the Arthur M. Sackler Gallery

1,000 artifacts, along with $4 million in funds, to the Smithsonian Institution to establish this museum. The Japanese and Korean governments also contributed $1 million each toward the cost of constructing the building, and the museum was completed in 1987.

The entrance is a small pavilion at ground level that leads down to two subterranean floors of exhibits. The Sackler's 3,000-piece collection is particularly rich in Chinese works, and highlights include a stunning display of Chinese bronzes and jades, some dating back to 4000 BC. There are also 7th-century ceramics from the Ming dynasty and an extensive range of sculpture from India and southeast Asia.

Over the years the gallery has built on Arthur Sackler's original collection. In 1987 it acquired the impressive Vever Collection from collector Henri Vever, which includes such items as Islamic books from the 11th to the 19th centuries, 19th- and 20th-century Japanese prints, Indian, Chinese, and Japanese paintings, and modern photography. The gallery also hosts international traveling exhibitions of Asian art from museums such as the Louvre in Paris.

The Sackler is one of two underground museums in this area; the other is the National Museum of African Art (see p69), which is part of the same complex. The Sackler is also connected by underground exhibition space to the Freer Gallery of Art. The two galleries share a director and administrative staff as well as the Meyer Auditorium, which hosts dance performances, films, and chamber music concerts. There is also a research library in the Sackler devoted to Asian art.

⑩ Freer Gallery of Art

Jefferson Drive and 12th Street, SW. **Map 3** C4. **Tel** 633-1000. Ⓜ Smithsonian. **Open** 10am–5:30pm daily. **Closed** Dec 25. ♿ 🅿 Ⓦ asia.si.edu

The Freer Gallery of Art is named after Charles Lang Freer, a railroad magnate who donated his collection of 9,000 pieces of American and Asian art to the Smithsonian, and funded the building of a museum to house the works. Freer died in 1919 before the building's completion. When the gallery opened in 1923 it became the first Smithsonian museum of art.

Detail of a screen by Thomas Wilmer Dewing

Constructed as a single-story building in the Italian Renaissance style, the Freer has an attractive courtyard with a fountain at its center. There are 19 galleries, most with skylights that illuminate a superb collection of Asian and American art. Since Freer's original donation, the museum has tripled its holdings. In the Asian Art collection are examples of Chinese, Japanese, and Korean art, including sculpture, ceramics, folding screens, and paintings. The gallery also has a fine selection of Buddhist sculpture, and painting and calligraphy from India.

There is a select collection of American art in the Freer as well, most of which shows Asian influences. Works by the artists Childe Hassam (1859–1935), John Singer Sargent (1865–1925), and Thomas Wilmer Dewing (1851–1938) are all on display. The most astonishing room in the museum is James McNeill Whistler's "The Peacock Room." Whistler (1834–1903) was a friend of Freer's who encouraged his art collecting. Whistler painted a dining room for Frederick Leyland in London, but Leyland found that it was not to his taste. Freer purchased the room in 1904; it was later moved to Washington and installed here after his death. In contrast to the subtle elegance of the other rooms, this room is a riot of blues, greens, and golds. Whistler's painted peacocks cover the walls and ceiling.

The attractive courtyard of the Freer Gallery of Art

⓫ National Museum of American History

The National Museum of American History preserves a collection of artifacts from the nation's past. Among the 3 million holdings are the First Ladies' gowns, a 280-ton steam locomotive, the National Quilt Collection, and the original Star-Spangled Banner that flew over Fort McHenry in 1814. The museum's west wing will be under renovation until 2015. Some galleries may be closed and exhibits may be moved around.

Second Floor

★ The First Ladies
Always a popular exhibition, this is a selection of gowns worn by America's First Ladies, such as this floral chine dress worn by Frances Cleveland, a fashion icon in the late 1800s.

Mall Entrance

★ Star-Spangled Banner
This flag is the symbol of America. It inspired Francis Scott Key to write the lyrics that became the US national anthem. Visitors can view the flag through a window wall.

Key to Floor Plan

- ☐ Transportation and Technology
- ☐ Science and Innovation
- ☐ American Ideals
- ☐ American Lives
- ☐ American Wars and Politics
- ☐ Entertainment, Sports and Music
- ☐ Non exhibition space

On the Water: Stories from Maritime America
Visitors can explore the history of maritime America through documents, objects, stories, audiovisual programs and interactive exhibits.

Lincoln's Top Hat
Lincoln was wearing this hat when he was assassinated on April 14,1865 while at Ford's Theatre. It has a molded paper base that is embedded with shaved fur fibers.

Third Floor

★ **The Price of Freedom: Americans at War**
A fascinating look at the ways in which wars have shaped American history, from the Colonial era to the present day, including this famous painting by Louis M. D. Guillaume, *The Surrender of the Arm of Northern Virginia* (1867).

Constitution Avenue Entrance

On the Water: Stories from Maritime America

★ **America on the Move**
This first floor exhibition allows visitors to travel back in time through the history of transport in America, including this famous Ford Model T, bicycles, trains, and more.

First Floor

Gallery Guide

The first floor features the transportation and science exhibits. Highlights of the second floor include the Star-Spangled Banner. The third floor offers an eclectic selection including the American Presidency: A Glorious Burden, The First Ladies exhibit, and military displays.

Exploring the National Museum of American History

The collections at the National Museum of American History are very diverse. Whether you head straight for the First Ladies' gowns or spend time viewing the collections of money, medals, musical instruments, and presidential artifacts, planning is the key to a successful visit. The museum is gradually being transformed with the continuing renovation of the 120,000 sq ft (11,148 sq m) west exhibition wing. The center core and east wing remain open to the public.

The museum's modern façade on Madison Drive

First Floor

Stories on Money explores the museum's collection of American coinage and currency. The exhibition "America's Money" examines the changes from Colonial America to the Gold Rush, and the present day, focusing on the renaissance of American coinage.

"The Power of Liberty" exhibit features an array of coins from the United States and around the world, depicting Liberty and the female freedom movement. The exhibition consists of 1.5 million objects, including a Colonial shilling from 1690 and a unique $20 gold coin from 1849.

America on the Move is the museum's largest single exhibition and tells the story of how trains, streetcars, and automobiles have shaped American lives. Exhibits include the locomotive that pulled Franklin D. Roosevelt's funeral train, a 40-ft (12-m) section of pavement from the legendary Route 66, a 1903 Winton, Ford's *Model T*, and a Hot Rod.

On the Water: Stories from Maritime America is an 8,000-sq-ft (743-sq-m) exhibition

chartering American maritime history and exploring life and work on the nation's waterways. The exhibits on display build on the Smithsonian's unparalleled National Watercraft Collection of rigged ship models, patent models, documents and images to bring the sights, sounds, and stories from the oceans, inland rivers, and coastal communities to museum visitors.

The maritime influence on American history is one of the most compelling chapters in the national story. Maritime trade established major cities, created connections between

people and places and opened the continent. From 18th-century sailing ships, 19th-century steamboats and fishing craft to today's mega containerships, America's maritime connections are shown through interactive displays, documents and film.

Elsewhere on the first floor visitors can explore **Lighting a Revolution**, which looks at electricity and electrical invention in the 20th century, and illuminates the differences in the process of invention between Thomas Edison's time and our own.

For those with an interest in all things mechanical, the **Power Machinery Hall** is a must. This exhibition features examples of the machines that made America a world leader in industrial production, and contains models and actual examples of engines, turbines, pumps, and more. Perhaps the most famous machine of all is the **John Bull Locomotive** in the East Wing, the oldest operative self-propelled locomotive in the world. The **Invention at Play** is a family-orientated exhibit exploring the similarities between the way children and adults play, and the impact play has on invention. Visitors can also "meet" the inventors.

Second Floor

American Stories showcases the historic and cultural journey of American history through more than 100 objects from the museum's vast collection including, Dorothy's ruby

1950 Buick Super sedan displayed in America on the Move

The kitchen of 16 Elm Street, rebuilt in the museum as it was in the 1940s

slippers, the rarely displayed walking stick used by Benjamin Franklin, Abraham Lincoln's gold pocket watch, Muhammad Ali's boxing gloves, and a fragment of Plymouth rock.

Through a chrono-logical look at the people, inventions, issues, and events that shaped the American experience, American Stories serves as an introduction to American history.

The West Wing also contains **Within These Walls...** This exhibition tells the story of American history through the domestic lives of the families who lived at 16 Elm Street in Ipswich, Massachusetts, from the mid-1760s to 1945. This extraordinary house saw American colonists forging a new way of living, the birth of a revolution, community activists united against slavery, a family on the home front in World War II, and more.

Communities in a Changing Nation: The Promise of 19th-Century America takes a look at America's history through the lives of different communities – industrial workers in Bridgeport, Connecticut; Jewish immigrants in Cincinnati, Ohio; and slaves and free blacks in South Carolina. Through hundreds of photographs, objects, and illustrations, visitors can learn about the challenges and successes that made up the lives of these different groups of people.

In the East Wing of the second floor, visitors can see the **Star-Spangled Banner** that flew over Fort McHenry in 1814 and inspired Francis Scott Key to write the lyrics that was later to become the national anthem. Also on the second floor is the **National Museum of African-American History and Culture Gallery**, exploring the role of visual images in the fight for civil rights and racial justice.

Teddy Bear, dating from 1903

Third Floor

One of the museum's most popular exhibits, where fashion meets history: **The First Ladies** is a collection of gowns worn by some of the nation's most iconic presidential wives. The collection includes Michelle Obama's white chiffon gown worn to the 2009 inaugural ball. It was made by a relatively unknown designer, Jason Wu.

The largest exhibition on this floor is **The Price of Freedom: Americans at War** in the East Wing. It explores the nation's military history, from the French and Indian War in the 1750s to recent conflicts in Afghanistan and Iraq. The exhibition features a restored Vietnam-era Huey helicopter, uniforms from the Civil War, a World War II jeep, and General Colin Powell's battle dress uniform from Operation Desert Storm.

The gunboat *Philadelphia* is located on the third floor. Sunk by the British in 1776, the 54-ft (16-m), 29-ton timber boat rested on the bottom of Lake Champlain until it was found and recovered in 1935.

The **American Presidency: A Glorious Burden** displays over 400 objects that represent the lives and office of the presi-dency. Artifacts include the portable desk on which Thomas Jefferson wrote the Declaration of Independence, and the top hat worn by President Lincoln the night he was shot.

Also here is a delightful teddy bear. The name of the bear was inspired by President Theodore "Teddy" Roosevelt, who, while out hunting one day, refused to shoot a bear cub that had been captured for him. A cartoon appeared in the *Washington Post* the next day, which inspired the production of a range of bears, named Teddy Bears.

Office of War information poster

⑫ Washington Monument

Constructed of 36,000 pieces of marble and granite, the Washington Monument remains one of the most recognizable monuments in the capital. Funds for this tribute to the first president of the United States initially came from individual citizens. A design by Robert Mills was chosen, and construction began in 1848. When the money ran out, the building work stopped for 25 years. Then, in 1876, President Ulysses S. Grant approved an act authorizing the completion of the project. (A slight change in the color of stone marks the point where construction resumed.) The Monument has 897 steps to the top. The earthquake of August 2011 caused damage to the Monument, which is currently closed for renovation.

Viewing window

Elevator taking visitors to top

The two-tone stonework indicates the point at which construction stopped in 1858 and then began again in 1876.

The Original Design
Although the original design included a circular colonnade around the monument, lack of funds prohibited its construction.

The Marble Capstone
The capstone weighs 3,300 pounds (2,000 kg) and is topped by an aluminum pyramid. Restoration of the monument was carried out in 1934 as part of President Roosevelt's Public Works Project (see p25).

Commemorative stones inside the monument are donations from individuals, societies, states, and nations.

50 flagpoles surrounding the monument represent each state

View of the Monument The gleaming white stone of the restored monument makes it clearly visible from almost all over the city. The views from the top of the monument across Washington are stunning.

The foundation of the monument is more than 36 ft (10 meters) deep. The width of the base of the shaft is 55 ft (17 meters).

The colonnaded, domed Jefferson Memorial, housing the bronze statue

⑬ United States Holocaust Memorial Museum

See pp82–3.

⑭ Bureau of Engraving and Printing

14th and C St, SW. **Map** 3 B5.
Tel 1-877-874-4114. Ⓜ Smithsonian.
🕒 8:30am–3:30pm Mon–Fri (Apr–Aug: 8:30am–7:30pm). **Closed** Week after Christmas, Federal hols. ♿ 📷
🌐 **moneyfactory.gov**

Until 1863, individual banks were responsible for printing American money. A shortage of coins and the need to finance the Civil War led to the production of standardized bank notes, and the Bureau of Engraving and Printing was founded. Initially housed in the basement of the Treasury Building (*see p114*), the bureau was moved to its present location in 1914. It prints over $140 billion a year, as well as stamps, federal documents, and White House invitations. Coins are not minted here, but in a federal facility in Philadelphia.

The 40-minute tour includes a short film, and a walk through the building to view the printing processes and checks for defects. Also on display are bills that are out of circulation, counterfeit money, and a special $100,000 bill. The Visitor Center has a gift shop, videos, and exhibits.

⑮ Jefferson Memorial

South bank of the Tidal Basin.
Map 3 B5. **Tel** (202) 426-6841.
Ⓜ Smithsonian. **Open** 24 hours daily.
Closed Dec 25. Interpretive talks & Interpretive tours: 10am–11pm hourly. ♿ 📷 🌐 **nps.gov/thje**

Thomas Jefferson (*see p168*) was a political philosopher, architect, musician, book collector, scientist, horticulturist, diplomat, inventor and the third American president, from 1801 to 1809. He also played a significant part in drafting the Declaration of Independence in 1776.

The idea for the memorial came from President Franklin Delano Roosevelt, who felt that Jefferson was as important as Lincoln. Designed by John Russell Pope, this Neo-Classical memorial was dedicated in 1943 and covers an area of 2.5 acres (1 ha). At the time, metal was strictly rationed

Statue of Jefferson

so the standing statue of Jefferson had to be cast in plaster. After World War II, the statue was recast in bronze and the plaster version was moved.

Etched on the walls of the memorial are Jefferson's words from the Declaration of Independence and other writings. The statue of Jefferson is 19 ft (6 m) high and weighs 10,000 lb. It shows him looking towards the White House.

⑯ Tidal Basin

Boathouse: 1501 Maine Ave, SW.
Map 2 F5 & 3 A5. Ⓜ Smithsonian.
Paddle-boats: **Tel** (202) 479-2426.
Open Mar–Oct: 10am–6pm. ♿
🌐 **tidalbasinpaddleboats.com**

The Tidal Basin was built in 1897 to catch the overflow from the Potomac River and prevent flooding. In 1912, hundreds of cherry trees, given by the Japanese government, were planted along the shores of the man-made lake. However, during the two weeks when the cherry trees bloom (between mid-March and mid-April) chaos reigns around the Tidal Basin. The area is filled with cars and busloads of people photographing the sight. The only way to avoid this gridlock is to see the blossoms at dawn. The Tidal Basin reverts to a relatively quiet park after the blossoms have fallen and the hordes depart. Paddle-boats can be rented from the boathouse on Maine Avenue.

The banks of the Tidal Basin, with Jefferson Memorial in the distance

⓭ United States Holocaust Memorial Museum

The US Holocaust Memorial Museum, opened in 1993, bears witness to the systematic persecution and murder in Europe of six million Jews and others deemed undesirable by the Third Reich, including homosexuals and the disabled. The exhibition space ranges from the intentionally claustrophobic to the soaringly majestic. The museum contains 2,500 photographs, 1,000 artifacts, 53 video monitors, and 30 interactive stations that contain graphic and emotionally disturbing images of violence, forcing visitors to confront the horror of the Holocaust. While Daniel's Story is suitable for children of eight years and up, the permanent exhibition is not recommended for the under 12s.

★ Hall of Remembrance
The Hall of Remembrance houses an eternal flame that pays homage to the victims of the Holocaust.

★ Daniel's Story
This exhibit, aimed at children between the ages of eight and 12, tells the history of the Holocaust from the point of view of an eight-year-old Jewish boy in 1930s Germany.

Key to Floor Plan

- ☐ Concourse Level
- ☐ First Floor
- ☐ Second Floor
- ☐ Third Floor
- ☐ Fourth Floor

Second Floor

First Fl

14th Street Entrance

★ Hall of Witness
The soaring central atrium features the Hall of Witness. The Museum aims to preserve the memory of those who died.

The Nazi Assault
On April 1, 1933 the boycott announced by the National Socialist party began. This placard at the Jewish Tietz store in Berlin reads, "Germans, defend yourselves! Do not buy from Jews."

Fourth Floor
Documenting the early years of the Nazi regime, these exhibits expose the ruthless and methodical persecution of the Jews.

Third Floor
The third floor permanent exhibits are devoted to the "Final Solution," the killing of 11 million "undesirable" people. Artifacts include a boxcar used to carry prisoners to the concentration camps.

Children's Tile Wall
Children painted over 3,000 tiles on this memorial to commemorate the lives of the one-and-a-half million children murdered in the Holocaust.

Concourse Level

Gallery Guide

The Holocaust Museum is meant to be experienced, not just seen. Starting from the top, footage, artifacts, photographs, and testimonies of survivors can be seen from the fourth to the second floors. The first floor has an interactive display, and the Concourse Level houses the Children's Tile Wall.

The National WWII Memorial looking west towards the Lincoln Memorial

⓲ National WWII Memorial

17th St, NW, between Constitution Ave & Independence Ave. **Map** 2 E5. **Tel** (202) 426-6841. Ⓜ Smithsonian or Federal Triangle. **Open** 9:30am–11:30pm daily. **Closed** Dec 25. ♿ Ⓦ nps.gov/nwwm The online Registry of Remembrances: Ⓦ wwiimemorial.com

Sixteen million Americans served in World War II, and of them, 400,000 died. The 4,000 gold stars, the "Field of Stars," on the Freedom Wall commemorate these war dead, and in front of the wall is the inscription: "Here We Mark the Price of Freedom." Millions more ordinary citizens contributed in some way to the war effort. The National World War II Memorial on the National Mall honors their service and sacrifice.

The establishment of the memorial, however, was not without controversy as to both location and scale. After a bill was first introduced in 1987 it took a further six years before the legislation made its way through Congress. President Clinton signed the bill into law on May 25, 1993 and then there followed a great debate over where it should be located. The Rainbow Pool site was chosen in October 1995 with the condition that the east-west vista from the Washington Monument to the Lincoln Memorial be preserved. Further delays followed because the Commission of Fine Arts criticized the mass and scale of the initial plans and asked that further consideration be given to preserving the vista. Work finally began in 2001.

Design and construction was awarded to the firm of Leo A. Daly, and the design architect

Ceremonial entrance shield

was Friedrich St. Florian (former dean of Rhode Island School of Design).

Two 43-ft (13-m) pavilions stand on either side of the Rainbow Pool, marking the north and south entrances, and represent the Atlantic and Pacific theaters of war. Fifty-six granite pillars, one for each of the country's states and territories during that time, are adorned with bronze wreaths of oak leaves and wheat, which symbolize the nation's agricultural and industrial strength. Bas-relief panels created by sculptor Ray Kaskey line both sides of the 17th St entrance. They depict the many contributions Americans made to the war effort: from enlistment and embarkation to the Normandy landings, from Rosie the Riveter to medics in the field.

Words spoken by presidents and generals are inscribed throughout the memorial, including these by General Douglas MacArthur marking the war's end: "Today the guns are silent…The skies no longer rain death – the seas bear only commerce – men everywhere walk upright in the sunlight. The entire world is quietly at peace."

The memorial was officially opened to the public in April 2004 and on May 29 some 150,000 people, many of them veterans, joined in the dedication ceremony.

The Freedom Wall lined with 4,000 stars commemorating the US war dead

⑱ Vietnam Veterans Memorial

21st St & Constitution Ave, NW.
Map 2 E4. **Tel** (202) 426-6841.
Ⓜ Smithsonian. **Open** 24 hours daily.
🕐 10am–11pm daily on the hour.
♿ Ⓦ nps.gov/vive

Maya Lin, a 21-year-old student at Yale University, submitted a design for the proposed Vietnam Veterans Memorial as part of her architecture course. One of 1,421 entries, Maya Lin's design was simple – two triangular black walls sinking into the earth at an angle of 125 degrees, one end pointing to the Lincoln Memorial, the other to the Washington Monument. On the walls would be inscribed the names of more than 58,000 Americans who died in the Vietnam War, in chronological order, from the first in 1959 to the last in 1975.

Lin received only a B grade on the course, but she won the competition. Her design has become one of the most moving monuments on the Mall. Veterans and their families leave tokens of remembrance – soft toys, poems, pictures, and flowers – at the site of the fallen soldier's name.

To mollify those opposed to the abstract memorial, a statue of three soldiers, sculpted by Frederick Hart, was added in 1984. Further lobbying led to the Vietnam Women's Memorial, erected close by in 1993.

⑲ Korean War Veterans Memorial

21st St & Independence Ave, SW.
Map 2 E5. **Tel** (202) 426-6841.
Ⓜ Smithsonian, Foggy Bottom.
Open 24 hours daily. ♿
Ⓦ nps.gov/kwvm

The Korean War Veterans Memorial is a controversial tribute to a controversial war. Although 1.5 million Americans served in the conflict, war was never officially declared. It is often known as "The Forgotten War." Intense debate preceded the selection of the memorial's design. On July 27, 1995, the 42nd anniversary of the armistice that ended the war, the memorial was dedicated.

Nineteen larger-than-life stainless steel statues, a squad on patrol, are depicted moving towards the American flag as their symbolic objective. Their ponchos are a

The Vietnam Women's Memorial

Names on the wall at the Vietnam Veterans Memorial

reminder of the war's notoriously miserable weather conditions. On the south side is a polished black granite wall etched with the images of more than 2,400 veterans. An inscription above the Pool of Remembrance reads: "Our nation honors her sons and daughters who answered the call to defend a country they never knew and a people they never met."

⑳ Martin Luther King, Jr. Memorial

1964 Independence Ave, SW.
Map 2 E5. **Tel** (202) 483-3373.
Ⓜ Smithsonian, Foggy Bottom.
Open 9am–10pm daily. ♿
Ⓦ mlkmemorial.org

Set among the famous cherry blossom trees of the Tidal Basin (see p81) is the Martin Luther King, Jr. Memorial. The Mall's first memorial to an African-American, dedicated on August 26, 2011, commemorates the life and work of Dr. King. Designed by Chinese sculptor Lei Yixin, the memorial consists of two massive stone tablets – one features excerpts from King's speeches, while the other shows the figure of Martin Luther King emerging from the stone. The choice of a non-American sculptor proved controversial, as did King's somewhat stern expression.

The poignant statues of the Korean War Veterans Memorial

㉑ Franklin D. Roosevelt Memorial

Franklin Roosevelt once told Supreme Court Justice Felix Frankfurter, "If they are to put up any memorial to me, I should like it to be placed in the center of that green plot in front of the Archives Building. I should like it to consist of a block about the size of this," pointing to his desk. It took more than 50 years for a fitting monument to be erected, but Roosevelt's request for modesty was not heeded. Opened in 1997, this memorial is a mammoth park of four granite open-air rooms, one for each of Roosevelt's terms, with statuary and waterfalls. The president, a polio sufferer, is portrayed in a chair, with his dog Fala by his side.

The statue of Roosevelt by Neil Estern, is one of the memorial's most controversial elements as it shows the disabled president sitting in a wheelchair hidden by his Navy cape.

A relief of Roosevelt's funeral cortège was carved into the granite wall by artist Leonard Baskin. It depicts the coffin on a horse-drawn cart, followed by the crowds of mourners walking behind.

KEY

① **The fourth room** honors Roosevelt's life and legacy. A statue of his wife, Eleanor, stands in this room.

② **Third room**

③ **Second room**

④ **The first room** commemorates FDR's first term and includes a bas-relief of his inaugural parade.

⑤ **The Visitor Center** includes an information area and a bookstore. The wheelchair that FDR used after he had polio is also on display.

Dramatic waterfalls cascade into a series of pools in the fourth room. The water reflects the peace that Roosevelt was so keen to achieve before his death.

VISITORS' CHECKLIST

Practical Information
West Basin Drive, SW. **Map** 3 A5.
Tel (202) 426-6841.
W nps.gov/fdrm
Open 24 hours daily.
Closed Dec 25. 🚻 📷
Interpretive programs and talks.

Transport
Ⓜ Smithsonian and 25-minute
walk. 🚌 13.

***Breadline*, a sculpture of figures** waiting in the breadline, by George Segal, recalls the hard times of the Great Depression, during which Roosevelt was elected and reelected three times.

President Roosevelt initiated the New Deal in the 1930s to create jobs and provide immediate relief during the Great Depression: "…treating the task as we would treat the emergency of war."

㉒ Lincoln Memorial

Constitution Ave, between French & Bacon Drives. **Map** 2 E5. **Tel** (202) 426-6841. Ⓜ Smithsonian, Foggy Bottom, and 20-minute walk. **Open** 24 hours daily. 🚻 📷 Call (202) 747-3420 to listen to interpretive programs. **W** nps.gov/linc

Many proposals were made for a memorial to President Abraham Lincoln. One of the least promising was for a monument on a swampy piece of land to the west of the Washington Monument. Yet this was to become one of the most awe-inspiring sights in Washington. Looming over the Reflecting Pool is the seated figure of Lincoln in his Neo-Classical "temple" with 36 Doric columns, one for each state at the time of Lincoln's death.

Before the monument could be built in 1914, the site had to be drained. Solid concrete piers were poured for the foundation so that the building could be anchored in bedrock. Architect Henry Bacon realized that the original 10-ft (3-m) statue by Daniel Chester French would be dwarfed inside the building, so it was nearly doubled in size. As a result, it had to be carved from 28 blocks of white marble.

Engraved on the south wall is Lincoln's Gettysburg Address *(see p165)*. Above it is a mural painted by Jules Guerin depicting the angel of truth freeing a slave. Dr. Martin Luther King, Jr.'s famous address, "I Have a Dream" *(see p99)*, was given from the steps of the memorial.

Lincoln Memorial, reflected in the still waters of the pool

PENN QUARTER

Bordered by the Capitol to the east and the White House to the west, Washington's Penn Quarter was the heart of the city at the start of the 20th century. F Street, the city's first paved road, bustled with shops, bars, newspaper offices, and churches, as well as horses and carriages. Penn Quarter was also an important residential neighborhood. The upper classes kept elegant homes, while middle-class merchants lived above their shops. By the 1950s suburbia had lured people away, and in the 1980s Penn Quarter was a mixture of boarded-up buildings and discount shops. The 1990s saw a dramatic change and the beginnings of regeneration, as the Verizon Center attracted new restaurants and stores.

Sights at a Glance

Museums and Galleries
5 Newseum
13 National Museum of Women in the Arts
14 Carnegie Library Building
18 Smithsonian American Art Museum and the National Portrait Gallery pp100–103
19 International Spy Museum
22 National Building Museum

Statues and Fountains
1 Mellon Fountain
8 Benjamin Franklin Statue

Aquarium
10 National Aquarium

Historic and Official Buildings
2 National Archives
6 Ronald Reagan Building
7 Old Post Office
11 Willard Hotel
12 National Theatre
15 Ford's Theatre
16 Martin Luther King Memorial Library
20 Verizon Center

Districts, Streets, and Squares
4 Pennsylvania Avenue
9 Freedom Plaza
17 Chinatown

Memorials
3 US Navy Memorial
21 National Law Enforcement Officers' Memorial

0 meters   500
0 yards   500

See also Street Finder map 3, 4

Restaurants see pp184–5
1 Acadiana
2 Austin Grill
3 Brasserie Beck
4 Carmines
5 Chipotle
6 District Chophouse & Brewery
7 District of Pi
8 Fogo de Chao
9 Full Kee
10 Graffiato
11 Jaleo
12 Luke's Lobster
13 Merzi
14 Oceanaire
15 Old Ebbitt Grill
16 Oyamel
17 Paul Bakery
18 Poste
19 Proof
20 Rasika
21 Rosa Mexicano
22 The Source
23 Teaism
24 Zaytinya

◀ The flag-festooned Old Post Office

For keys to symbols see back flap

Street-by-Street: Penn Quarter

By the mid-20th century, Pennsylvania Avenue, the main route for presidential inaugural parades, had become tawdry and run down. It is now a grand boulevard worthy of L'Enfant's original vision. Pennsylvania Avenue links the White House to the US Capitol and is home to some of the city's main sights. Opposite the US Navy Memorial is the US National Archives, housing original copies of the Constitution and the Declaration of Independence. To the east are the Mellon Fountain and the National Gallery of Art. The Ronald Reagan Building was the site of the 1999 NATO summit.

❹ ★ Pennsylvania Avenue
Part of L'Enfant's original plan for the city, Pennsylvania Avenue was the first main street to be laid out in Washington. The thoroughfare reflects the architect's grandiose plans.

❽ Benjamin Franklin Statue
This inventor, statesman, writer, publisher, and man of genius is remembered as "printer, philosopher, philanthropist, patriot".

FBI Building

11TH STREET NW

PENNSYLVANIA AVENUE N W

12TH STREET NW

10TH STREET NW

CONSTITUTION AVENUE NW

Interstate Commerce Commission

❻ Ronald Reagan Building
Built in 1997, this impressive edifice echoes the Classical Revival architecture of other buildings in the Federal Triangle.

❼ Old Post Office
This majestic granite building was completed in 1899 and was the city's first skyscraper. The elegant clock tower measures 315 ft (96 m) in height.

3 **US Navy Memorial**
The memorial at Market Square contains a huge etching of the world surrounded by low granite walls.

Locator Map
See Street Finder Maps 3 & 4

Key

— Suggested route

Commission on the Arts

6TH STREET NW

7TH STREET NW

9TH STREET NW

PENNSYLVANIA AVENUE NW

CONSTITUTION AVENUE NW

| 0 meters | 100 |
| 0 yards | 100 |

Federal Trade Commission

Justice Department

★ US National Archives
The Rotunda houses the National Archives' most precious documents, known as the "Charters of Freedom," including the Bill of Rights. A copy of England's Magna Carta is also on display.

1 **Mellon Fountain**
Located by the National Gallery of Art's West Building, this fountain is named after Andrew Mellon, an industrialist and art collector who founded the gallery in the 1930s.

The cascading water of the Classical-style Mellon Fountain

❶ Mellon Fountain

Constitution Ave & Pennsylvania Ave, NW. **Map** 4 D4. Ⓜ Archives-Navy Memorial.

Situated opposite the National Gallery of Art *(see pp60–63)*, this fountain commemorates the man who endowed the gallery with its collection. Andrew Mellon was Secretary of the Treasury and a financier and industrialist. At his death, his friends donated $300,000 to build the fountain, which was dedicated on May 9, 1952.

The three bronze basins with their cascades of water were inspired by a fountain seen in a public square in Genoa, Italy. On the bottom of the largest basin, the signs of the Zodiac are engraved in bas-relief. The Classical lines of the fountain echo the architectural style of the National Gallery of Art West Building.

❷ National Archives

7000 Constitution Ave, between 7th St & 9th St, NW. **Map** 3 D3. **Tel** 1-866-272-6272.
Ⓜ Archives-Navy Memorial/Penn Quarter. **Open** Mar 15–Labor Day: 10am–7pm daily; Sep–Mar: 10am–5:30pm daily. **Closed** Sun, Thanksgiving, Dec 25. 📷 📹 ♿
Ⓦ **archives.gov**

In the 1930s, Congress recognized the need to preserve the country's paper records before they deteriorated, were lost or were destroyed. The National Archives building, created for this purpose, was designed by John Russell Pope, architect of the National Gallery of Art and the Jefferson Memorial; it opened in 1934. This impressive library houses the most important historical and legal documents in the United States.

On display are all four pages of the *Constitution of the United States*, as well as the *Declaration of Independence*, the *Bill of Rights*, and a 1297 copy of the *Magna Carta*, which is on indefinite loan from Ross Perot.

Also in the National Archives are millions of documents, photographs, motion picture film, and sound recordings going back over two centuries. There is enough material, in fact, to fill around 250,000 filing cabinets. The National Archives and Records Administration (NARA) acataloging, managing, and conserving all this material. Much of the Archives' information is now stored on computer. A permanent exhibition, "Public Vaults," offers people an interactive opportunity to explore a representative sample of the Archives' vast collection. The National Archives is of great importance as a research center. The Central Research Room is reserved for scholars, who can order copies of rare documents for study purposes. Copies of military records, immigration papers, slave transit documents, death certificates, and tax information are also available.

Statue outside the US National Archives

The impressive Neoclassical façade of the National Archives Building

The Constitution of the United States

In 1787, delegates from the 13 original American states convened in the city of Philadelphia to redraft the Articles of Confederation *(see p20)*. It soon became clear that an entirely new document was required, rather than a revised one. Weeks of debate grew into months, as delegates drafted the framework for a new country. Cooperation and compromise finally led to the creation of the Constitution, a document that outlines the powers of the central government and the makeup of Congress. One of the main issues, how to elect the representatives, was finally determined to be by direct voting by the people. Once signed, the new Constitution was sent to the states for review. Federalists and anti-Federalists debated fervently over its content in pamphlets, speeches, and articles. In the end, the majority of states ratified the Constitution, giving up some of their power in "order to form a more perfect union."

The Preamble of the Constitution of the United States

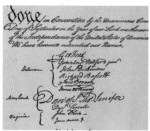

Signatures on the US Constitution

Signing of the Constitution

After many months of debate by the delegates to the Federal Convention, the Constitution was completed and signed by 39 of the 55 state delegates on September 17, 1787, at Assembly Hall in Philadelphia. The oldest delegate was 81-year-old Benjamin Franklin. James Madison, another signatory, played a major role in achieving the ratification of the new Constitution during the two years after it was signed.

James Madison

The Constitution Today

The seven articles of the Constitution (of which the first three lay out the principles of government; see pp30–31) still determine the laws of the United States today. In addition there are Amendments. The first ten form the Bill of Rights, which includes such famous issues as the right to bear arms and the freedom of religion and of speech.

Swearing Allegiance
The pledge of allegiance to the flag was written in 1892 to mark the 400th anniversary of Columbus's discovery of America. Today it is recited daily by schoolchildren and by immigrants taking up American citizenship.

Public Demonstration
Citizens demonstrate their right to free speech by protesting against the Persian Gulf War.

A view down tree-lined Pennsylvania Avenue toward the US Capitol

❸ US Navy Memorial

Market Square, Pennsylvania Ave between 7th St & 9th St, NW. **Map** 3 C3. Ⓜ Archives-Navy Memorial/Penn Quarter. ♿ Naval Heritage Center: 701 Pennsylvania Ave, NW. **Tel** (202) 737-2300. **Open** 9:30am–5pm daily. **Closed** Jan 1, Thanksgiving, Dec 25. 🖼 🆆 navymemorial.org

The memorial to the US Navy centers on the statue of a single sailor. Sculpted in bronze by Stanley Bleifeld in 1990, the figure provides a poignant tribute to the men and women who have served the US Navy.

The sculpture stands on a vast map of the world – the outlines of the countries are laid into the ground and protected by low walls. Four waterfalls and a group of flagpoles complete the memorial. There are free summer concerts by military bands in the square. Behind the memorial is the **Naval Heritage Center**, with historical exhibits and portraits of famous naval personnel, including John F. Kennedy. A free film "At Sea," is shown daily at noon.

The lone sailor of the US Navy Memorial

❹ Pennsylvania Avenue

Pennsylvania Ave. **Map** 3 A2 to 4 D4. Ⓜ Federal Triangle, Archives-Navy Memorial.

When architect and urban designer Pierre L'Enfant drew up his plans in 1789 for the capital city of the new United States, he imagined a grand boulevard running through the center of the city, from the presidential palace to the legislative building. For the first 200 years of its history, however, Pennsylvania Avenue fell sadly short of L'Enfant's dreams. In the early 19th century it was simply a muddy footpath through the woods. Paved in 1833, it became part of a neighborhood of boarding houses, shops, and hotels.

During the Civil War, the area deteriorated quickly into "saloons, gambling dens, lodging houses, quick-lunch rooms, cheap-jack shops, and catch penny amusement places" according to the *Works Progress Administration Guide to Washington*. When President John F. Kennedy's inaugural parade processed down Pennsylvania Avenue in 1961, Kennedy took one look at "America's Main Street" with its shambles of peep shows, pawn shops, and liquor stores and said, "It's a disgrace – fix it." This command by Kennedy provided the impetus to re-evaluate the future of Pennsylvania Avenue.

Almost 15 years later, Congress established the Pennsylvania Avenue Development Corporation – a public and private partnership that developed a comprehensive

Presidential Inaugural Parades

The tradition of inaugural parades to mark a new president's coming-to-office started in 1809, when the military accompanied President James Madison from his Virginia home to Washington, DC. The first parade to include floats was held in 1841 for President William Henry Harrison. In 1985, freezing weather forced Ronald Reagan's inaugural ceremony indoors to the Capitol Rotunda. A record crowd of approximately 1.8 million attended the 2009 parade for Barack Obama. The Army Band traditionally leads the procession down Pennsylvania Avenue from the US Capitol to the White House.

President Franklin D. Roosevelt's third inaugural parade in 1941

The multistory building housing the Newseum

plan of revitalization. Today, Pennsylvania Avenue is a clean, tree-lined street. Parks, memorials, shops, theaters, hotels, museums, and assorted government buildings border the street on either side, providing a suitably grand and formal setting for all future presidential inaugural parades.

❺ Newseum

555 Pennsylvania Ave, NW. **Map** 4 F4. **Tel** 888-639-7386. **M** Archives-Navy Memorial. **Open** 9am–5pm daily. **Closed** Jan 1, Thanksgiving, Dec 25. ♿ 🅿 📷 ✏ **W** newseum.org

This award-winning interactive news and media museum is housed in a beautiful building with a balcony that affords splendid views of the city. The Newseum features seven levels, 14 galleries, and 15 theaters that explore how and why news is made. The galleries span five centuries of news history and include up-to-the-second technology and hands-on exhibits. The gallery of Pulitzer Prize-winning photographs is one of the highlights. Among the iconic images on display are the 1945 photograph documenting the raising of the US flag after the Battle of Iwo Jima and a 1969 photograph portraying the execution of a prisoner in Saigon, Vietnam. Other galleries deal with the history of the Berlin Wall and the events of 9/11. There is also an interactive newsroom where visitors can play the role of a reporter or broadcaster, and a moving memorial to journalists

who have lost their lives in the line of duty. On the front of the building is an inscription of the First Amendment listing the five freedoms – religion, speech, press, assembly, and petition.

Sculpture from the Oscar Straus Memorial Fountain

❻ Ronald Reagan Building

1300 Pennsylvania Ave, NW. **Map** 3 B3. **Tel** (202) 312-1300. **M** Federal Triangle. **Open** 5am–2am daily. **Closed** Federal hols. 🕐 11am Mon, Wed & Fri from 14th St entrance (to book ahead call 312-1647). Visitor Center: **Tel** 289-8317. ✏ 📷 ♿ **W** itcdc.com

The Ronald Reagan Building is a modern 3.1 million sq ft limestone structure that is Classical in appearance on the

outside and modern on the inside. Completed in 1997, it was the most expensive federal building project ever undertaken. Designed by Pei Cobb Freed & Partners, architects of the US Holocaust Memorial Museum (see pp82–3) and the National Gallery of Art's East Wing, the building houses a mix of federal, trade, and public spaces. It is named after President Ronald Reagan, who authorized the construction in the late 1980s.

On the east end of the atrium is the largest neon sculpture in North America – "Route Zenith," a creation of Keith Sonnier. Outside the building is the Oscar Straus Memorial Fountain, with sculpture by Adolph Alexander Weinman.

In summer the four-acre Woodrow Wilson Plaza, graced by sculptures by such artists as Martin Puryear and Stephen Rodin, is the venue for free concerts from noon to 1:30pm every weekday.

The building is the home of the Washington DC Visitor Information Center due to its location in the heart of the capital. The Center provides tour information and tickets to shows and events.

Mock-Classical entrance to the immense Ronald Reagan Building

Food court in the spectacular galleried hall of the Old Post Office

❼ Old Post Office

1100 Pennsylvania Ave, NW. **Map** 3 C3. **Tel** (202) 289-4224. Ⓜ Federal Triangle.**Open** Mar–Aug: 9am–8pm Mon–Sat, 10am–6pm Sun; Sep–Feb: 9am–5pm Mon–Sat, 10am–6pm Sun. **Closed** Jan 1, Thanksgiving, Dec 25. 📷 tower only (call 606-8691). ♿ 🖥 📷 🌐 oldpostofficedc.com

Built in 1899, the Old Post Office was Washington's first skyscraper. Soaring 12 stories above the city, it was a fireproof model of modern engineering with a steel frame covered in granite. The huge interior had 3,900 electric lights and its own generator, the first one to be used in the city. Its fanciful Romanesque architecture was fashionable at the time it was built, and the breathtaking hall, with its glass roof and balconies, remains a spectacular mixture of light, color, and gleaming metal.

In the 15 years following its construction, the Post Office became an object of controversy. Its turrets and arches, once praised by critics, were derided. The *New York Times* newspaper said the building looked like "a cross between a cathedral and a cotton mill." Government planners thought the Post Office building clashed with the Neo-Classical architecture that dominated the rest of

Washington. When the postal system moved its offices in 1934, there seemed to be no reason to keep the architectural relic. Only a lack of funds during the Great Depression of the 1930s *(see p25)* prevented the Old Post Office from being torn down.

The building was occupied intermittently by various government agencies until the mid-1960s, when its decrepit condition again drew a chorus in favor of demolition. A Washington preservation group, Don't Tear It Down, promoted the historical significance of the Old Post Office, and it was spared once more.

The renovated building housed a complex of shops and restaurants, commonly known as the Old Post Office Pavilion, until its purchase in 2013 by business magnate Donald Trump, who is renovating the area once again. It is scheduled to reopen in 2016.

❽ Benjamin Franklin Statue

Pennsylvania Ave & 10th St, NW. **Map** 3 C3. Ⓜ Federal Triangle.

Donated by publisher Stilson Hutchins (1839–1912), it was unveiled by Benjamin Franklin's great-granddaughter in 1889. The words "Printer, Philosopher, Patriot, Philanthropist" are inscribed on the four sides of

the statue's pedestal in tribute to this man of diverse talents. Postmaster general, writer, and scientist, Benjamin Franklin was also a key member of the committee that drafted the 1776 Declaration of Independence. As a diplomat to the court of Louis XVI of France, he went to Versailles in 1777 to gain support for the American cause of independence from Britain. Franklin returned to France in 1783 to negotiate the Treaty of Paris that ended the American Revolution *(see p20)*.

❾ Freedom Plaza

Pennsylvania Ave between 13th St & 14th St, NW. **Map** 3 B3. Ⓜ Federal Triangle, Metro Center.

Freedom Plaza was conceived as part of a Pennsylvania Avenue redevelopment plan in the mid-1970s. Designed by Robert Venturi and Denise Scott Brown, and completed in 1980, the plaza displays Pierre L'Enfant's original plan for Washington in black and white stone embedded in the ground. Around the edge are engraved quotations about the new city from Walt Whitman and President Wilson, among others.

Freedom Plaza provides a dramatic entry to Pennsylvania Avenue *(see pp94–5)*. On the north side of the plaza, where

The large-scale reproduction of L'Enfant's city plans, Freedom Plaza

Pennsylvania Avenue leads into E Street, are the **Warner Theatre** and the **National Theatre**. South of the plaza is the Beaux Arts **District Building** (housing government employees). The Freedom Plaza is a popular site for festivals and political protests.

❿ National Aquarium

Commerce Building, 14th St & Constitution Ave, NW. **Map** 3 B3. **Tel** (202) 482-2825. Ⓜ Federal Triangle. **Open** 9am–5pm daily. **Closed** Thanksgiving, Dec 25. 🐟 🖾 Ⓚ Ⓦ nationalaquarium.org

Originally located in 1873 at Woods Hole, Massachusetts (a major center for marine biology), the National Aquarium was moved to Washington in 1888 in order to make it more accessible. Since 1931 it has been located in the US Department of Commerce Building, and today the aquarium is home to around 1,200 specimens and 200 different species.

Green Turtle at the National Aquarium

The Aquarium has a wide range of freshwater and saltwater fish on display, such as nurse sharks, piranhas, and moray eels, and also a number of reptiles and various species of amphibians, all displayed in simulated "natural environments." There are daily public feedings of the sharks and piranhas at 2pm, as well as talks.

⓫ Willard Hotel

1401 Pennsylvania Ave, NW. **Map** 3 B3. **Tel** (202) 628-9100, 800-827-1747. Ⓜ Metro Center. Ⓚ Ⓦ intercontinental.com

There has been a hotel on this site since 1816. Originally called Tennison's, the hotel was housed in six adjacent two-story buildings. Refurbished in 1847, it was managed by hotel keeper Henry Willard, who gave his name to the hotel in 1850. Many famous people stayed

here during the Civil War (1861–65), including the writer Nathaniel Hawthorne, who was covering the conflict for a magazine, and Julia Ward Howe who wrote the popular Civil War standard *The Battle Hymn of the Republic*. The word "lobbyist" is said to have been coined because it was known by those seeking favors that President Ulysses S. Grant went to the hotel's lobby to smoke his after-dinner cigar.

The present 330-room building, designed by the architect of New York's Plaza Hotel, Henry Hardenbergh, was completed in 1904. It was the most fashionable place to stay in the city until the end of World War II, when the surrounding neighborhood fell into decline. For 20 years it was boarded up and faced demolition. A coalition, formed of preserva-tionists and the Pennsylvania Avenue Development Corporation, worked to restore the Beaux Arts building, and it finally reopened in renewed splendor in 1986.

No other hotel can rival the Willard's grand lobby, with its 35 different kinds of marble, polished wood, and petal-shaped concierge station. There is a style café, a bar, and a restaurant called The Willard Room.

Façade of the National Theatre on E Street

⓬ National Theatre

1321 Pennsylvania Ave, NW. **Map** 3 B3. **Tel** (202) 628-6161, 800-447-7400. Ⓜ Metro Center, Federal Triangle. Ⓚ Ⓦ nationaltheatre.org

The present National Theatre is the sixth theater to occupy this Pennsylvania Avenue site and the oldest cultural institution in the city. The first four theaters burned down, and the fifth one was replaced by the current building in 1922. The National Theatre hosts Broadway-bound productions and touring groups. The National is known as an "actor's theater" because of its excellent acoustics (even a whisper on stage can be heard in the top balcony). It is haunted by the ghost of 19th-century actor John McCullough, murdered by a fellow actor and buried under the stage. There are free per-formances for children every Saturday at 9:30am and 11am.

Peacock Alley, one of the Willard Hotel's luxuriously decorated corridors

⓭ National Museum of Women in the Arts

1250 New York Ave, NW. **Map** 3 C3.
Tel (202) 783-5000, 800-222-7270.
Ⓜ Metro Center. **Open** 10am–5pm
Mon–Sat, noon–5pm Sun.
Closed Jan 1, Thanksgiving, Dec 25.
📷 for groups (call 783-7996). 🅿 ♿
🖥 📷 Ⓦ nmwa.org

Impressive exterior of the National Museum of Women in the Arts

This museum of women's art houses works that span five centuries, from the Renaissance to the present day. The collection was started in the 1960s by Wilhelmina Holladay and her husband, who gathered paintings, sculpture, and photography from all over the world.

The museum operated out of the Holladays' private residence for several years, until it acquired a more permanent home in this Renaissance Revival landmark building, formerly a Masonic Temple. The collection has as its highlights masterpieces by female American artists. Some of the outstanding works on display from the 19th century include *The Bath* (1891) by Mary Cassatt and *The Cage* (1885) by Berthe Morisot. Among the works by 20th-century artists are Elizabeth Cutlett's *Singing their Songs* (1992) and *Self-Portrait Between the Curtains, Dedication to Trotsky* (1937) by Mexican artist Frida Kahlo. The museum shop sells a range of gifts, also created by women.

⓮ Carnegie Library Building

801 K St (Mount Vernon Sq), NW.
Map 3 C2. **Tel** (202) 393-1420.
Ⓜ Gallery Place–Chinatown, Mt
Vernon Sq. Kiplinger Research Library:
Tel 383-1829. **Open** 10am–5pm Tue–
Sat. **Closed** Jan 1, Jul 4, Thanksgiving,
Dec 25. ♿ 🖥 📷 Ⓦ historydc.org

The Carnegie Library Building was once Washington's central library. It hosts various events and exhibitions, and in 2003 the Washington Historical Society moved its headquarters to the building and the City Museum of Washington, DC was created.

The state-of-the-art Kiplinger Research Library and Reading Room houses extensive collections of historic materials, including rare publications, prints, maps, photographs, manuscripts, and memorabilia. There are also lectures, workshops, and videos. Washington Perspectives, an overview exhibit, features a giant map of the city set into the floor.

Painting of John Wilkes Booth poised to shoot Abraham Lincoln

⓯ Ford's Theatre

511 10th St between E St & F St, NW.
Map 3 C3. **Tel** (202) 426-6924.
Ⓜ Gallery Place–Chinatown, Metro
Center. **Open** 9am–5pm daily (except
matinee or rehearsal days – call
ahead). ♿ Petersen House:
Closed Dec 25. **Open** 9:30am–5:30pm
daily with free timed ticket. **Closed**
Dec 25. 📷 Ⓦ fordstheatre.org

John T. Ford, a theatrical producer, built this small jewel of a theater in 1863. Washington was a Civil War boomtown, and the theater, located in the thriving business district, enjoyed great popularity. The fate of the theater was sealed, however, on April 14, 1865, when President Abraham Lincoln was shot here by John Wilkes Booth while watching a performance. Across the road from the theater, **Petersen House**, where the wounded president died the next morning, has been preserved as a museum.

After the tragedy, people stopped patronizing the theater, and Ford was forced to sell the building to the federal government a year later. It was left to spiral into decay for nearly a century until the government decided to restore it to its original splendor.

The theater now stages small productions. The Presidential Box is permanently decorated in Lincoln's honor.

Exterior of Ford's Theatre, site of the shooting of President Lincoln

⓰ Martin Luther King Memorial Library

901 G St at 9th St, NW. **Map** 3 C3.
Tel (202) 727-0321. Ⓜ Gallery Place–
Chinatown, Metro Center. **Open** noon–
9pm Mon–Tue, 9:30am–5:30pm Wed–
Sat, 1–5pm Sun. **Closed** Federal hols.
♿ Ⓦ dclibrary.org/mlk

Washington's Martin Luther
King Memorial Library is the
only example of the Modernist
architecture of Ludwig Mies
van der Rohe in the city.
A prominent figure in 20th-
century design, van der Rohe
finalized his plans for the library
shortly before his death in
1969. It was named in honor of
Dr. Martin Luther King Jr.
at the request of the library's
trustees when it opened in
1972, replacing the small and
out-dated Carnegie Library as
the city's central public library.

Architecturally, the building
is a classic example of van der
Rohe's theory of "less is more."
It is an austere, simple box
shape with a recessed entrance
lobby. Inside, there is a mural
depicting the life of Dr. Martin
Luther King Jr., the leader of the
Civil Rights Movement, painted
by artist Don Miller.

The library sponsors concerts
and readings, as well as a
program of children's events.

The "Friendship Archway" spanning H Street in the heart of Chinatown

⓱ Chinatown

5th St to 8th St & H St to I St,
NW. **Map** 3 C3 & 4 D3. Ⓜ Gallery
Place-Chinatown.

The small area in Washington
known as Chinatown covers
just six square blocks. Formed
around 1930, it has never been
very large and today houses
about 500 Chinese residents.
The area was reinvigorated
with the arrival of the adjacent
Verizon Center (see p104) in
1997. H Street is particularly
lively, with many shops and a
selection of good restaurants.

The "Friendship Archway," a
dramatic gateway over H Street
at the junction with 7th Street,
marks the center of the
Chinatown area. Built in
1986, it was paid for by
Washington's sister city,
Beijing, as a token of esteem,
and is based on the
architecture of the Qing
Dynasty (1649–1911). Its seven
roofs, topped by 300 painted
dragons, are balanced on a
steel and concrete base,
making it the largest single-
span Chinese arch in the
world. It is lit up at night.

During the Chinese New
Year celebrations in late
January or early Febuary, the
area comes alive with parades,
dragon dances, and live
musical performances (see p61).

Dr. Martin Luther King, Jr.

A charismatic speaker and proponent of Mahatma
Gandhi's theories of non-violence, Dr. Martin Luther
King, Jr. was a black Baptist minister and leader of the
civil rights movement in the United States.

Born in Atlanta, Georgia in 1929, King's career in
civil rights began with the 1955 Montgomery, Alabama
bus boycott – a protest of the city's segregated transit
system. The movement escalated to protests at schools,
restaurants, and hotels that did not admit blacks. King's
methods of non-violence were often met with police
dogs and brutal tactics.

The culmination of the movement was the March on
Washington on August 28, 1963, when 200,000 people
gathered at the Lincoln Memorial in support of civil
rights. The highlight of this event was King's "I Have a
Dream" speech, calling for support of the movement. A
direct result was the passing by Congress of the civil
rights legislation in 1964, and King was awarded the
Nobel Peace Prize the same year. In 1968 he was
assassinated in Memphis, Tennessee, triggering riots in
100 American cities, including Washington.

Dr. King speaking at the Lincoln Memorial

⑱ Smithsonian American Art Museum and the National Portrait Gallery

Nowhere in Washington is the city's penchant to copy Greek and Roman architecture more obvious than in the former US Patent Office Building, now the home of the Smithsonian American Art Museum and the National Portrait Gallery (NPG). The wonderfully ornate 1836 building was converted into the twin museums in 1968. The American Art Museum contains a permanent collection of works by more than 7,000 American artists. The NPG is America's family album, featuring paintings, photographs, and sculptures of thousands of famous Americans.

Façade of the building, housing the main entrance to both galleries

★ Achelous and Hercules

This painting (1947) by Thomas Hart Benton (1889–1975) is a mythological analogy of early American life. Interpreted in many ways, it is widely accepted that Hercules is man taming the wild, then enjoying the results of his labors.

KEY

① **An African-American** is depicted climbing over a fence to the idealized equality of America.

② **Hercules** tries to capture the bull.

③ **Achelous**, the river god, appears as a bull being wrestled by Hercules, representing the struggle of the American people.

④ **Hercules** is about to break off the bull's horn.

⑤ **The horn** is transformed into a cornucopia, or horn of plenty, symbolizing America as a land of abundance and opportunity.

⑥ **The man** working in the field represents the people of America, enjoying the fruits of the land after laboring.

★ **Among the Sierra Nevada, California**
Albert Bierstadt painted this Western landscape in 1867–8. He was later criticized by some for not offering a topographically correct view of the West

Mary Cassatt
This portrait by Edgar Degas, painted c.1882, depicts his fellow artist Mary Cassatt playing cards.

John Singleton Copley
This self- portrait of the artist, who was largely known for his depictions of others, was painted c.1780.

"Casey" Stengel
This bronze sculpture of the baseball great was created by Rhoda Sherbell in 1981 from a 1965 cast.

VISITORS' CHECKLIST

Practical Information
Smithsonian American Art Museum: 8th St & F St, NW.
Map 3 C3.
Tel (202) 633-7970.
W americanart.si.edu
Open 11:30am–7pm daily.

National Portrait Gallery:
8th St & F St, NW.
Map 3 C3.
Tel (202) 633-8300.
W npg.si.edu
Open 11:30am–7pm daily.

Transport
M Gallery Place-Chinatown.

★ Manhattan
This 1932 oil painting by Georgia O'Keeffe was created for an exhibition at New York's Museum of Modern Art. It portrays her vision of the city's architectural landscape.

Old Bear, a Medicine Man
This vibrant painting by George Caitlin dates from 1832. Native Americans were a popular choice of subject matter for this artist.

In the Garden
This charming depiction of the poet Celia Thaxter is by the artist Childe Hassam and was painted in 1892.

Exploring the Smithsonian American Art Museum

The Smithsonian American Art Museum was established in 1829 and is the first federal art collection. It began with gifts from private collections and art organizations that existed in Washington, DC before a bequest from British scientist James Smithson enabled the foundation of the Smithsonian Institution "for the increase and diffusion of knowledge" in 1846. The museum is a center for America's cultural heritage, with more than 42,000 artworks spanning 300 years.

19th- and Early 20th-Century Art

Some of the highlights in this collection from the last two centuries are the Thomas Moran Western landscapes and those of Albert Bierstadt. This subject matter can be seen in *Among the Sierra Nevada, California* (1867–8), Bierstadt's evocative depiction of the landscape.

Many of the American artists such as Albert Pinkham Ryder, Winslow Homer, and John Singer Sargent, were contemporaries to the Impressionists. Homer's *High Cliffs, Coast of Maine* (1894) is a dramatic meeting of land and sea. Seascapes were also a popular subject for Ryder. *Jonah*, painted c.1885, illustrates the Bible story of Jonah and the whale, depicting Jonah floundering in the sea during a storm, overlooked by God.

The museum holds hundreds of paintings of Native Americans, many of them works by George Caitlin. This was also a popular subject for Charles Bird King and John Mix Stanley. American Impressionists are also well represented in the museum, including Mary Cassatt, William Merritt Chase, John Henry Twachtman, and Childe Hassam. Hassam's paintings, inspired by the French Impressionists, are refreshing yet tranquil. The calm seascape of *The South Ledges, Appledore* (1913) is typical of his style.

American Modernists

The enormous canvases of the Modernists provide a dramatic contrast to the landscapes and portraits of the 19th and 20th centuries. Franz Kline's black slashes on a white canvas in *Merce C* (1961), which was inspired by his involvement with dancer Merce Cunningham, are the antithesis of the delicacy of the Impressionists. Kenneth Noland's geometrical compositions resemble firing targets. Other Modernists here include Georgia O'Keeffe, Robert Rauschenberg, and David Hockney.

American Folk Art

The collection of American folk art includes some truly amazing pieces of work, created from a wide range of materials. James Hampton's *Throne of the Third Heaven of the Nations' Millennium General Assembly* (c.1950–64) is one of the star pieces in the collection.

Robert Rauschenberg's *Reservoir* (1961), mixed media on canvas

Contemporary Art

Roy Lichtenstein's 6.5-ton (5,900-kg) sculpture *Modern Head* (1989) greets visitors at the main entrance to the museum, and reflects the Smithsonian's dedication to the acquisition of modern and contemporary works. Inside are works by Jenny Holzer, Nam June Paik, and Edward Kienholz, among others. Karen LaMonte's *Reclining Dress Impression with Drapery* (2009) is a glorious, almost luminous, life-size sculpture in rippling cast glass.

Luce Foundation Center

The three-story Luce Foundation Center for American Art holds about 3,300 artworks from the museum's collection. The items on display include paintings and sculptures, contemporary craft objects, folk art, and jewelry.

Throne of the Third Heaven of the Nations' Millennium General Assembly by James Hampton

Exploring the National Portrait Gallery

The National Portrait Gallery keeps generations of remarkable Americans in the company of their fellow citizens. The gallery's mission is to collect and display images of "men and women who have made significant contributions to the history, development and culture of the people of the United States." Through the visual and performing arts, the lives of leaders such as George Washington and Martin Luther King, Jr., artists such as George Gershwin and Mary Cassatt, and activists such as Rosa Parks and Sequoyah are celebrated.

Ronald Reagan, an oil on canvas by Henry C. Casselli, Jr. painted in 1989

Overview of the Collection

The National Portrait Gallery illuminates America's family album, magnificently combining history, biography, and art in its collections. The portraits are fascinating not only because they reveal their subjects but also because they illustrate the times in which they were produced. There are more than 20,000 images in the permanent collection, which includes paintings, photographs, sculptures, etchings, and drawings. Both heroes and villains are represented. Portraits taken from life sittings are favored by the gallery.

Portrait of Pocahontas by an unidentified artist

country's religious or cultural history. Athletes include the famous baseball player Babe Ruth and baseball manager Casey Stengel. Among figures from the world of entertainment are portraits of actresses Judy Garland, Tallulah Bankhead, and Mary Pickford. John Wayne also features among the Hollywood stars, as do Buster Keaton, Clark Gable, and James Cagney. There are also bronze busts of the poet T.S. Eliot and the humorist Will Rogers. Religious leaders, business magnates, pioneers in women's rights and civil rights (such as Dr. Martin Luther King, Jr.), explorers, and scientists are portrayed in a whole range of media, including oils, clay, and bronze. There are also many photographic portraits, including some of Marilyn Monroe, which were taken during a morale-boosting visit the actress made to soldiers during the Korean War.

The Great Hall

The third-floor Great Hall is a crazy quilt of tiles and ceiling medallions. A frieze showing the evolution of technology in America also runs around the room. Once a display area for new inventions, it is a reminder of the building's past as the Patent Office.

20th-Century Americans

The National Portrait Gallery's collection is not limited to the political history of the country. There is also a large collection of portraits of American people notable for their achievements in the arts, sports, or in the

America's presidents

In 1857, Congress commissioned George Peter Alexander Healy to paint portraits of the presidents. The chronologically ordered portrayal of all of the country's leaders remains the heart of the National Portrait Gallery's exhibitions.

Two portraits of George and Martha Washington are featured prominently in the Portrait Gallery. The most famous portrait of George Washington is Gilbert Stuart's "Landsdowne", painted from life in 1796. Abraham Lincoln posed for photographer Alexander Gardener several months before he was assassinated *(see p98)*.

The exhibition also features modern-day presidents, such as Bill Clinton and George W. Bush. Shepard Fairey's iconic portrait of Barack Obama, an image seen throughout the latter's presidential campaign, is also here.

Diana Ross and The Supremes, photographed by Bruce Davidson in 1965

The unique and innovative International Spy Museum

⑲ International Spy Museum

800 F St, NW. **Map** 3 C3. **Tel** (202) 393-7798, EYE-SPY-U. Ⓜ Gallery Place-Chinatown, Metro Center. **Open** Apr–Oct: 9am–7pm; Nov–Mar: 10am–6pm. **Closed** Jan 1, Thanksgiving, Dec 25. 🖼 ♿ 📷 🛍 group tours by reservation. Ⓦ **spymuseum.org**

The Spy Museum is the first museum in the world devoted to international espionage. Its huge collection includes the German Enigma cipher machine from World War II, a Soviet shoe transmitter, a wristwatch camera, and a lipstick pistol, displayed in a variety of themed exhibits. A visit to the museum begins with a film on the real life of a spy, revealing what motivates people to enter this clandestine world. The "School for Spies" exhibit displays over 200 artifacts used by spies to disguise and protect themselves during operations. "The Secret History of Histories" traces the art of spying from biblical times

World War II cipher machine, essential for breaking enemy codes

to the early 20th century. "Spies Among Us" examines the making and breaking of codes during World War II. Other permanent exhibits such as "Weapons of Mass Disruption" explore technology and cyber attacks, while "War of the Spies" looks at espionage from the Cold War to the present day, featuring spy planes, listening and tracking devices, and the lives of spies, such as Aldrich Ames and Robert Hanssen.

⑳ Verizon Center

601 F St, NW. **Map** 4 D3. **Tel** (202) 628-3200. Ⓜ Gallery Place-Chinatown. Team Store: **Open** 10am–5:30pm daily (later on event days). 📷 for National Sports Gallery. ♿ ♿ 🖼 Ⓦ **verizoncenter.com**

Opened in 1997, the Verizon Center is a sports and entertainment complex that houses many shops and restaurants.

The 20,000-seat Verizon stadium is the home of Washington's basketball teams, the Wizards (men's team), Georgetown Hoyas, and the Mystics (women's), as well as the ice hockey team, the Capitals. The presence of the complex has revived the surrounding area beyond recognition. Half of the arena's seats are below ground level, in a vast but harmonious structure. It hosts rock concerts as well as sports events and exhibitions.

Penn Quarter Renaissance

During the 1990s, Washington's Penn Quarter was transformed from a derelict historic area to prime real estate. The construction of the Verizon Center and renewed appreciation for the restoration of dilapidated Victorian buildings helped to accelerate this process. As a result of losing its shabby image, Penn Quarter also lost many of the artists who carved studios out of the high-ceilinged, low-rent spaces, but their influence can still be seen in the large number of art galleries and exhibitions in the area. Some of the non-profit organizations and small businesses that leased offices in the big, aging buildings were forced to relocate due to an increase in rent. Soaring prices also closed a number of traditional Chinese restaurants around the Verizon Center, which have been replaced by upscale eateries. Today Penn Quarter is a safer area for those on foot, with a buzzing selection of nightly activities available, including sports events, theater shows, concerts, and lively restaurants.

A contemporary office building linking two Victorian façades on 7th Street

Majestic lion statue alongside a marble wall at the police memorial

㉑ National Law Enforcement Officers Memorial

E St, NW, between 4th St & 5th St, NW. **Map** 4 D3. **Tel** (202) 737-3400. Ⓜ Judiciary Square. Visitor Center: 605 E St, NW. **Open** 9am–5pm Mon–Fri, 10am–5pm Sat, noon–5pm Sun. **Closed** Jan 1, Thanksgiving, Dec 25. Ⓐ Ⓚ Ⓟ Ⓦ nleomf.org

Dedicated by President George Bush in 1991, the National Law Enforcement Officers Memorial honors the 18,600 police officers who have been killed since the first known death in 1792. Spread over three acres in the center of Judiciary Square, the memorial's flower-lined pathways are spectacular in springtime. The names of the fallen officers are inscribed on marble walls. Each path is guarded by a statue of an adult lion shielding its cubs, symbolic of the US police force's protective role.

㉒ National Building Museum

401 F St at 4th St, NW. **Map** 4 D3. **Tel** (202) 272-2448. Ⓜ Judiciary Square, Gallery Place-Chinatown. **Open** 10am–5pm Mon–Sat, 11am–5pm Sun. **Closed** Jan 1, Thanksgiving, Dec 25. Ⓐ Ⓒ Ⓚ Ⓑ Ⓟ Ⓦ nbm.org

It is fitting that the National Building Museum, dedicated to the building trade, should be housed in the architecturally audacious former Pension Bureau building. Civil War General Montgomery C. Meigs saw Michelangelo's Palazzo Farnese on a trip to Rome and decided to duplicate it as a Washington office building, albeit twice as big and in red brick as opposed to the stone masonry of the Rome original.

Completed in 1887, the building is topped by a dramatic terracotta frieze of the Civil War measuring 3 ft (1 m) in height. The daring exterior of the building is matched by its flamboyant interior. The vast concourse, measuring 316 ft by 116 ft (96 m by 35 m), is lined with balconies containing exhibitions. The roof is supported by huge columns, constructed of brick, plastered, and faux-painted to give the appearance of marble. The Great Hall has been the impressive venue for many presidential balls.

In 1926 the Pension Bureau relocated to different offices, and there was a move to demolish Meigs' building. Instead it was occupied by various government agencies for a time and was even used as a courthouse for a while.

The building was eventually restored, and in 1985 opened in renewed splendor as the National Building Museum. A privately owned collection, the museum has a display on the architectural history of the city – "Washington: Symbol and City." It includes an excellent illustration of Pierre L'Enfant's original plans for the capital, as well as other photographs, models, and interactive exhibits demonstrating how the city grew and changed. The temporary exhibits in the museum often highlight controversial issues in design and architecture. There is a small café in the courtyard, and a gift shop. For children under six, the "Building Zone" offers some hands-on fun including giant lego blocks, bulldozers, and a playhouse.

Ornamental plinth in the grounds of the museum

The splendid, colonnaded Great Hall in the National Building Museum

THE WHITE HOUSE AND FOGGY BOTTOM

The official residence of the President, the White House is one of the most distinguished buildings in DC and was first inhabited in 1800. Although burned by the British during the War of 1812, most of today's building remains as it was planned. Other buildings surrounding the White House are worth a visit, such as the Daughters of the American Revolution building and the Corcoran Gallery. East of the White House is the Foggy Bottom area, which was built on swampland. Notable edifices here include the Kennedy Center, the State Department building, and the notorious Watergate Complex, focus of the 1970s Nixon scandal.

Sights at a Glance

Galleries

5 Renwick Gallery
7 Corcoran Gallery of Art

Squares

3 Lafayette Square
17 Washington Circle

Historic Buildings

4 Hay-Adams Hotel
6 Eisenhower Old Executive Office Building
8 Octagon Museum
9 Daughters of the American Revolution
15 George Washington University
18 Watergate Complex

Official Buildings

1 *The White House pp110–13*
2 Treasury Building
10 Organization of the American States
11 Department of the Interior

12 Federal Reserve Building
13 National Academy of Sciences
14 State Department

Performing Arts Center

19 *Kennedy Center pp120–21*

Church

16 St. Mary's Episcopal Church

See also Street Finder map 2, 3

| 0 meters | 500 |
| 0 yards | 500 |

Restaurants *see pp185–7*

1 Ancora
2 Aroma
3 Bayou
4 Blue Duck Tavern
5 The Bombay Club
6 City Bites
7 Cone E. Island
8 Firefly
9 Founding Farmers
10 Georgia Brown's
11 Johnny Rockets
12 Marcel's
13 McFadden's
14 One Fish, Two Fish
15 Potbelly Sandwich Shop
16 The Public Bar
17 Rasika West End
18 Roof Terrace Restaurant
19 Vidalia
20 Westend Bistro

◀ The south portico of The White House

For keys to symbols *see back flap*

Street-by-Street: Around The White House

The area surrounding the White House is filled with grand architecture and political history, and the vistas from the Ellipse lawn are breathtaking. It is worth spending a day exploring the area and seeing some of its buildings, such as the Treasury Building with its statue of Alexander Hamilton (the first Secretary of the Treasury) and the Eisenhower Old Executive Office Building. The buildings of the Daughters of the American Revolution and the OAS both offer the visitor an insight into the pride the nation takes in its past.

6 Eisenhower Old Executive Office Building
Although it was poorly received on its completion in 1888, this attractive building now houses staff of the Executive branch.

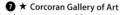

5 Renwick Gallery
The gallery is part of the Smithsonian American Art Museum. The inscription above the entrance of the building reads "Dedicated to Art."

8 Octagon Museum
At one time James Madison's home, this building has had a varied history functioning as a hospital and a school, among other things.

7 ★ Corcoran Gallery of Art
A treasure trove of fine art, the Corcoran Gallery counts works by Rembrandt, Monet, Picasso, and de Kooning among its many exhibits.

9 DAR Building
This beautiful Neoclassical building is one of three founded by the historical organization, the Daughters of the American Revolution.

Key

— Suggested route

10 OAS Building
The central statue of Queen Isabella of Spain stands in front of this Spanish Colonial-style mansion. Built in 1910, it houses the Organization of American States.

H STREET

JACKSON PLACE

NEW YORK AVENUE

STATE P

E STREET

D STREET

C STREE

CONSTITUTION AV

❹ Hay-Adams Hotel
Formed by the joining of two town houses, this luxurious hotel has been the scene of political activity since it opened in the 1920s.

Locator Map
See Street Finder map 2 & 3

❸ Lafayette Square
Named after the Marquis de Lafayette, a Revolutionary War hero, this leafy square has at its center this statue of Andrew Jackson, the seventh president, sculpted by Clark Mills.

❷ ★ Treasury Building
Widely regarded as the most impressive Neoclassical structure in the city, this building took over 60 years to complete.

❶ ★ The White House
One of the most famous sights in Washington, DC, this has been the President's official residence since the 1800s.

0 meters 100
0 yards 100

❶ The White House

In 1791 George Washington chose this site as the location for the new President's House. Irish-born architect James Hoban was selected to design the building, known as the Executive Mansion. In 1800, President and Mrs. John Adams became the first occupants, even though the building was not yet completed. Burned by the British in 1814, the restored edifice was occupied again in 1817, by James Monroe. In 1901, President Theodore Roosevelt changed the official name of the building to the White House and in 1902 ordered the West Wing to be built. The East Wing was added in 1942 on the instruction of President Franklin D. Roosevelt, completing the building as it is today.

The White House
The official residence of the US president for over 200 years, the White House façade is familiar to millions of people around the world

★ State Dining Room
Able to seat as many as 140 people, the State Dining Room was enlarged in 1902. A portrait of President Abraham Lincoln, by George P.A. Healy, hangs above the mantel.

KEY

① **The West Terrace** leads to the West Wing and the Oval Office, the President's official office.

② **The Stonework** has been painted over and over to maintain the building's white façade.

③ **Blue Room**

④ **The Green Room** was first used by Thomas Jefferson as a dining room.

⑤ **Treaty Room**

⑥ **The East Room** is used for large gatherings, such as concerts and press conferences.

⑦ **The East Terrace** leads to the East Wing.

★ Red Room
One of three reception rooms on the state floor, the Red Room is furnished in red in the Empire Style (1810–30).

Lincoln Bedroom
President Lincoln used this room as his Cabinet Room. Today it is used as a guest bedroom furnished in Lincoln-era decor.

VISITORS' CHECKLIST

Practical Information
The White House: 1600 Pennsylvania Ave, NW. **Map** 3 B3.
W **whitehouse.gov**
Open 7:30–10am Tue–Sat only for groups with congressional or embassy appointments. Contact Visitor Center for information. **Closed** federal hols and official functions. 📷 obligatory; call (202) 456-7041 for more information.

White House Visitor Center: 1450 Pennsylvania Ave, NW.
Tel (202) 208-1631.
W **nps.gov/whho**
Open 7:30am–4pm daily.
Closed Jan 1, Thanksgiving, Dec 25. 📷 ♿ 📷

Transport
M Federal Triangle.

★ **The Vermeil Room**
This yellow room houses six paintings of first ladies, including this portrait of Eleanor Roosevelt by Douglas Chandor.

Diplomatic Reception
This room is used to welcome friends and ambassadors. It is elegantly furnished in the Federal Period style (1790–1820).

White House Architects

After selecting the site, George Washington held a design competition to find an architect to build the residence where the US president would live. In 1792 James Hoban, an Irish-born architect, was chosen for the task. It is from Hoban's original drawings that the White House was initially built and all subsequent changes grew. In 1902 President Teddy Roosevelt hired the New York architectural firm of McKim, Mead, and White to check the structural condition of the building and refurbish areas as necessary. The White House underwent further renovations and refurbishments during the administrations of Truman and Kennedy.

James Hoban, architect of the White House

Exploring the White House

The rooms in the White House are beautifully decorated in period styles and filled with valuable antique furniture, china, and silverware. Hanging on their walls are some of America's most treasured paintings, including portraits of past presidents and first ladies. Those not lucky enough to be granted permission to tour the White House can experience a virtual tour at the White House Visitor Center.

The Library

Originally used as a laundry area, this room was turned into a "gentleman's ante-room" at the request of President Theodore Roosevelt in 1902. In 1935 it was remodeled into a library. Furnished in 1962 in the style of the late Federal period (1800–1820), the library was redecorated in 1962, and then again in 1976. It had its latest update in 2006 when it was painted in classic cream and red tones. Today, it is often used for media tapings.

Portraits of four native-American chiefs, painted by Charles Bird King, are displayed in the library. The chandelier was crafted in the early 1800s and was originally owned by the family of James Fenimore Cooper, author of *The Last of the Mohicans.*

The Vermeil Room

The Vermeil Room is named after the collection of vermeil, or gilded silver, that is on display in the cabinets. On show are 18th-, 19th-, and 20th-century tableware, including pieces crafted by English Regency silversmith Paul Storr (1771–1836) and French Empire silversmith Jean-Baptiste Claude Odiot (1763–1850). The collection was bequeathed to the White House in 1958 by Margaret Thompson Biddle.

Several portraits of first ladies hang on the walls: Elizabeth Shoumatoff's painting of Claudia (Lady Bird) Johnson, Aaron Shikler's portrait of Jacqueline Kennedy in her New York apartment, and an unusual painting of Eleanor Roosevelt, caught in various moods, by Douglas Chandor. Also on display are portraits of Lou Hoover, Mamie Eisenhower, Pat Nixon, and Nancy Reagan.

The China Room

Edith Wilson created this room in 1917 to display examples of tableware used in the White House. Today it is used as a reception room. The rich red color scheme is suggested by the stunning portrait of Grace Coolidge, painted in 1924 by Howard Chandler Christy. The Indo-Isfahan rug dates from the early 20th century.

The Blue Room

President James Monroe chose the French Empire-style decor for this magnificent, oval-shaped room in 1817. The Classically inspired furniture and accompanying motifs, such as urns, acanthus leaves, and imperial eagles, typify the style. The settee and seven chairs were created by Parisian cabinetmaker, Pierre-Antoine Bellangé.

A portrait of Thomas Jefferson by Rembrandt Peale, dating from 1800, hangs in this elegant room, along with a portrait of President John Adams, painted in 1793 by artist John Trumball. The Blue Room has always been used as a reception room, except for a brief period during the John Adams administration.

The Red Room

This room was decorated in the Empire style by Jacqueline Kennedy in 1962 and was refurbished in 1971, and again in 2000. Much of the wooden furniture in the room, including the beautiful inlaid round table, was created by cabinetmaker Charles-Honoré Lannuier in his New York workshop. Above the mantel hangs a portrait of Angelica Singleton Van Buren, the daughter-in-law of President Martin Van Buren, which was painted by Henry Inman in 1842. The room is used as a parlor or sitting room; it has also been used for small dinner parties.

The State Dining Room

As a result of the growing nation and its international standing, the size of official dinners in the White House increased. Finally in 1902 the architects McKim, Mead, and White were called in to enlarge the State Dining Room. The plaster and paneling was modeled on the style of 18th-century Neo-Classical English houses. The mahogany dining table was created in 1997. The pieces of French

The red and cream color scheme of the China Room

giltware on the table were bought by President Monroe in 1817.

The dining room was re-decorated in 1998, when the Queen Anne-style chairs, which date from 1902, were reupholstered.

The Lincoln Bedroom

Used today as the guest room for the friends and family of the President, the Lincoln Bedroom is decorated in the American Victorian style, dating from around 1860. Used by Lincoln as an office and cabinet room, this room became the Lincoln Bedroom when President Truman decided to fill it with furniture from Lincoln's era. In the center is a 6 ft- (1.8 m-) wide rosewood bed with an 8 ft- (2.5 m-) high headboard. The portrait of General Andrew Jackson next to the bed is said to have been one of President Lincoln's favorites.

The Treaty Room

Beginning with Andrew Johnson's presidency in 1865, the Treaty Room served as the Cabinet Room for 10 presidential Administrations. The room contains many Victorian pieces bought by President Ulysses S. Grant, including the original table used by the Cabinet. The cut-glass chandelier that hangs here was made in Birmingham, England around 1850. The

The White House Visitor Center

The White House Visitor Center has interesting exhibits about the history of the White House and its decor, as well as royal gifts on display. There are also seasonal lectures by renowned speakers on

aspects of history in and out of the White House. The Center has a monthly Living History program with actors portraying historic figures. The gift shop carries an extensive range, including the annual White House Christmas ornament. Tours of the state rooms of the White House are extremely limited at this time. Guided tours can only be booked by special arrangement through a member of Congress or, if a non-US citizen, through an embassy. Requests need to be made at least 30 days in advance.

Façade of the White House Visitor Center

chandelier has 20 arms, each one fitted with a frosted glass globe.

The East Wing

The East Wing houses offices rather than ceremonial rooms. The walls of the Lobby are adorned with portraits of presidents. Both the East Landing and the East Colonnade, which fronts the East Terrace, look out onto the Jacqueline Kennedy Garden. The Terrace, which links the East Wing to the Residence, houses the White House movie theater. It was once Theodore Roosevelt's coatroom.

The interior of the Oval Office, located in the West Wing

The West Wing

In 1902, the West Wing was built by the architectural firm McKim, Mead, and White for a total cost of $65,196. In this wing, the former Fish Room was renamed the Roosevelt Room by President Nixon, in honor of presidents Theodore and Franklin Roosevelt who created this wing. Their portraits still hang in the room.

Also in the West Wing are the Cabinet Room, where government officials meet with the president, and the Oval Office, added in 1909, where the president meets with visiting heads of state. Over the years, many presidents have personalized this room in some way.

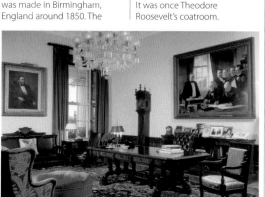

The Victorian-era interior of the Treaty Room

The colonnaded portico of the Neo-Classical Treasury Building

❷ Treasury Building

15th St & Pennsylvania Ave, NW.
Map 3 B3. **Tel** (202) 622-2000. M
McPherson Square. Tours for US
citizens only, by appointment through
congressman. **treasury.gov**

The site of this massive, four-story Greek Revival building, home to the Department of the Treasury, was chosen by President Andrew Jackson. The grand, sandstone-and-granite edifice was designed by architect Robert Mills, who also designed the Washington Monument *(see p80)*. A statue of Alexander Hamilton, the first Secretary of the Treasury, stands in front of the southern entrance to the building.

The official guided tour, shows visitors the restored historic rooms, including the 1864 burglar-proof vault, the Andrew Johnson suite (Johnson's temporary office after the assassination of President Lincoln in 1865), and the marble Cash Room.

Between 1863 and 1880, US currency was printed in the basement, and during the Civil War it was used as storage space for food and arms. Today, the building is home to the Department of the Treasury, which manages the government's finances and protects US financial systems.

❸ Lafayette Square

Map 2 F3 & 3 B3. M Farragut West,
McPherson Square. **nps.gov**

Set behind the White House is Lafayette Square, named after the Marquis de Lafayette (1757–1834), a hero of the American Revolutionary War *(see p21)*. Due to its proximity to the White House, this public park is often the scene of peaceful demonstrations. It is home to 19th-century former mansions and the historic church of St. John's (the "Church of the Presidents"), built in 1816 by Benjamin Latrobe, who designed Decatur House, 748 Jackson Place, which was home to famous figures such as Henry Clay and Martin

Liberty Bell beside the Treasury

Van Buren, and is open to the public. In the center of the Square is a huge statue of President Andrew Jackson (1767–1845) seated on a horse. Cast in bronze by Clark Mills, it was the first equestrian statue of its size to be built in the US and was dedicated in 1853.

At each of the square's four corners stand statues of men who took part in America's struggle for liberty. The southeast corner has the bronze figure of French compatriot Lafayette. In the southwest corner is a statue of another Frenchman, Jean-Baptiste Donatien de Vimeur, Comte de Rochambeau (1725–1807). This was a gift from France to the American people and accepted by Theodore Roosevelt in 1902. A statue of Polish general, Thaddeus Kosciuszko (1746–1817), who fought with the American colonists in the Revolutionary War, stands in the northeast corner. Baron von Steuben (1730–94), a German officer and George Washington's aide at the Battle of Valley Forge, is honored at the northwest end.

❹ Hay-Adams Hotel

1 Lafayette Square, NW. **Map** 2 F3
& 3 B3. **Tel** (202) 638-6600, 1-800-424-5054. M Farragut North, Farragut
West. **hayadams.com**

Situated close to the White House, the historic Hay-Adams Hotel is an Italian Renaissance landmark in Washington. Its plush interior is adorned with European and Oriental antiques.

It was originally two adjacent houses, built by Henry Hobson Richardson in 1885, belonging to statesman and author John Hay and diplomat and historian Henry Adams. A popular hotel since its conversion in 1927 by developer Harry Wardman, the exclusive Hay-Adams remains one of Washington's top establishments *(see p179)*, well situated for all the major sights. Afternoon tea and drinks are available in the Lafayette Restaurant.

Federal-style 19th-century houses overlooking tranquil Lafayette Square

❺ Renwick Gallery

Pennsylvania Ave at 17th St, NW.
Map 2 F3 & 3 A3. **Tel** (202) 633-1000.
Ⓜ Farragut West. **Open** 10am–
5:30pm daily. **Closed** Dec 25. 📷 🚻 ♿
📷 🆆 americanart.si.edu

Forming part of the Smithsonian
American Art Museum *(see p102)*,
this red-brick building was
designed and constructed by
James Renwick Jr. in 1858. It
originally housed the art collection
of William Wilson Corcoran until
this was moved to the current
Corcoran Gallery of Art in 1897.

The building was later bought
by the Smithsonian. Refurbished
and renamed, the Renwick
Gallery opened in 1972, primarily
to conserve and display the
Smithsonian's collection of 20th-
century and contemporary
American arts, crafts, and design.

The museum is currently closed
for a two-year renovation and
refitting of the interior, including
a bold re-imagining of the Grand
Salon as a digital display space,
with state-of-the-art projection
and audio systems that create
extraordinary effects.

❻ Eisenhower Old Executive Office Building

17th St at Pennsylvania Ave, NW.
Map 2 F4 & 3 A3. Ⓜ Farragut West.
Closed to the public. 📷 Sat.
Call (202) 395-5895 to book. ♿
🆆 nps.gov

Formerly known simply as the
Old Executive Office Building,
this structure stands on the
West side of the White House.

Imposing façade of Eisenhower Old
Executive Office Building

The magnificent Renwick Gallery, a fine example of French Empire style

It was once the home of the War,
Navy, and State Departments.
Built over 17 years between
1871 and 1888 by Alfred B.
Mullett, its exuberant French
Second Empire design, which
was inspired by the 1852
expansion of the Louvre in Paris,
generated much criticism at the
time.

The building has long been the
site of historic events, such as
the meeting between Secretary of
State Cordell Hull and the
Japanese after the bombing of
Pearl Harbor.

Lion statue guarding the
Corcoran Gallery

Today the building houses
government agencies, including
the White House Office, the
Office of the Vice President, and
the National Security Council.

❼ Corcoran Gallery of Art

500 17th St, NW. **Map** 2 F4 & 3 A3.
Tel (202) 639-1700. Ⓜ Farragut West,
Farragut North. **Open** 10am–5pm
Wed–Sun (to 9pm Thu, except
Thanksgiving). **Closed** Jan 1, Dec 25.
📷 📷 ♿ 📷 🚻 ♿
🆆 corcoran.org

One of the first fine art museums
in the country, the Corcoran
Gallery of Art opened in 1874.
It outgrew its original home
(what is now the Renwick Gallery
building) and moved to this
massive edifice designed in 1897
by Ernest Flagg. A privately

funded art collection, the
Corcoran was founded by
William Wilson Corcoran – a
banker whose main interest
was American art. Many of
the European works in the
collection were added
in 1925 by art collector
and US senator
William A. Clark.

The Corcoran
Gallery of Art is
filled with works
by European and
American masters
that span the
centuries. These
include 16th- and
17th-century works,
19th- century French
Impressionist paintings by
Monet and Renoir, and other
19th-century works by Eakins,
Homer, and Hassam. The gallery
also contains the largest
collection of paintings by Jean-
Baptiste Camille Corot outside
France. There is a fine collection
of modern and African-American
art, which includes sculpture,
paintings, textiles, and photographs, as well as a permanent
collection highlighting modern
and contemporary art since
1945 with artists such as Rob
Fischer and Andy Warhol.

Within the building is the
only accredited art school in
Washington. A café within the
beautiful atrium serves a selection of delicious soups, cakes
and drinks. The Corcoran also
has a shop selling an excellent
selection of books, postcards,
and other items.

❽ Octagon Museum

1799 New York Ave, NW. **Map** 2 F4
& 3 A3. **Tel** (202) 626-7312.
Ⓜ Farragut West and Farragut North.
Open by appointment. **Closed** Jan 1,
Thanksgiving, Dec 25. 🎫 📷 1–4pm
Thu & Fri. ♿ (first floor only).
ⓦ **theoctagon.org**

Actually hexagonal in shape,
the Octagon is a three-story
red-brick building, designed
in the late-Federal style by Dr.
William Thornton (1759–1828),
first architect of the US Capitol.
The Octagon was completed
in 1801 for Colonel John Tayloe
III, a rich plantation owner from
Richmond County, Virginia, and
a friend of George Washington.

When the White House was
burned in the War of 1812
against Britain *(see p21),*
President James Madison and
his wife, Dolley, lived here from
1814 to 1815. The Treaty of
Ghent that ended the war was
signed by Madison on the
second floor of the house on
February 17, 1815.

In the early 1900s, the building was taken over by the
American Institute of Architects.
The American Architectural
Foundation, established in 1970,
set up a museum of architecture
in the Octagon. The building has
been restored to its historically
accurate 1815 appearance, and
has some original furnishings
and fine architectural features,
such as a circular entrance hall.
Ongoing restoration work and
private events cause occasional
suspension of tours (check
website or call ahead).

The circular main entrance to the attractive
Octagon Museum

South portico of the DAR Memorial Continental Hall

❾ Daughters of the American Revolution

1776 D St, NW. **Map** 2 F4 & 3 A3.
Tel (202) 628-1776. Ⓜ Farragut West.
Open 9:30am–4pm Mon–Fri,
9am–5pm Sat. **Closed** 1 week in Jul,
Federal hols. 📷 9am–3pm Sat (book
in advance for groups of 5 or more).
♿ Caters for children.
ⓦ **dar.org/museum**

Founded in 1890 as a non-profit
organization, the Daughters
of the American Revolution
(DAR) is dedicated to historic
preservation and promoting
education and patriotism. In
order to become a member,
you must be a woman with
blood relations to any person,
male or female, who fought in
or aided the Revolution. There
are currently over 160,000
members in 3,000 regional
branches throughout the USA
and in nine other countries.

The DAR Museum is located
in the Memorial Continental
Hall, designed for the
organization by Edward Pearce
Casey and completed in 1910.

The 13 columns in the south
portico symbolize the 13 original
states of the Union. Entrance to
the museum is through the
gallery, which displays an
eclectic range of pieces from
quilts to glassware and china.

The 33 period rooms that
form the State Rooms in the
museum house a collection of
over 50,000 items, from silver to
porcelain, ceramics, stoneware,
and furniture. Each room is
decorated in a unique style
particular to an American state
from different periods during
the 18th and 19th centuries.
An attic room filled with 18th-
and 19th-century toys will
delight children. Also, there is
a huge genealogical library,
consisting of approximately
125,000 publications.

DAR Museum banners proclaiming
Preservation, Patriotism, Education

Fountain in the courtyard of the OAS building

⑩ Organization of American States

17th St & Constitution Ave, NW. **Map** 2 F4 & 3 A4. **Tel** (202) 458-3000. **Open** 9am–5:30pm Mon–Fri. **Closed** Sat & Sun, Federal hols. Art Museum of the Americas: 201 18th St, NW. **Tel** (202) 458-6016. **Open** 10am–5pm Tue–Sun. **Closed** Good Friday, Federal hols. Ⓜ Farragut West. ☎ Call (202) 458-6016. Ⓦ **museum.oas.org**

Dating back to the First International Conference of the American States, held from October 1889 to April 1890 in Washington, the Organization of American States (OAS) is the oldest alliance of nations dedicated to reinforcing the peace and security of the continent, and maintaining democracy. The Charter of the OAS was signed in Bogotá, Colombia, in 1948 by the US and 20 Latin American republics. Today there are 35 members. The building houses the Columbus Memorial Library and the **Art Museum of the Americas**, which exhibits 20th-century Latin American and Caribbean art.

⑪ Department of the Interior Building

19th St, between C St & E St, NW. **Map** 2 F4 & 3 A3. **Tel** (202) 208-3100. Ⓜ Farragut West. **Closed** for renovations; phone for opening times. ♿ 📷 Ⓦ **doi.gov/interiormuseum**

Designed by architect Waddy Butler Wood and built in 1935, this huge limestone building is the headquarters of the Department of the Interior. The building has a long central section, with six wings that extend off each side. In total it covers more than 16 acres of floor space, and has 2 miles (3 km) of corridors.

The Department of the Interior was originally formed of only the Departments of Agriculture, Labor, Education, and Energy, but it expanded to oversee all federally owned land across the United States. Visible inside, but only when taking the official guided tour, are 36 murals painted by Native American artists in the 1930s, including one of the singer Marian Anderson performing at the Lincoln Memorial in 1939 *(see pp86–7)*.

Displays in the small **Department of the Interior Museum**, located on the first floor, include an overview of the Department's history, and some intricate dioramas of American wildlife and important historical events, such as the 1929 Kinloch Mine explosion. Also on view are paintings by 19th-century surveyors, and crafts by Native Americans, including a great collection of basketry.

The south façade of the immense Department of the Interior Building

Portrait, in crayon, by Saint Memin of Colonel John Tayloe III

The Tayloe Family

John Tayloe III (1771–1828), a colonel in the War of 1812, was responsible for the construction of the unusual Octagon building. He and his wife Ann, the daughter of Benjamin Ogle (the governor of Maryland), had their primary residence at Mount Airy, an estate and tobacco plantation in Richmond County, Virginia. The Tayloes decided they wanted to build a second house where they could spend the inclement winter seasons. President George Washington, a close friend of Tayloe and his father, was at the time overseeing the building of the US Capitol and was eager for people to move into the new city. The president encouraged Tayloe and his family to choose a plot in Washington rather than in the more popular Philadelphia. The family heeded his advice and the triangular-shaped corner plot for the Octagon was chosen. Tayloe's vast wealth enabled him to employ the services of William Thornton, the original designer of the US Capitol building, and spend a total of $35,000 on the construction of the house.

⓬ Federal Reserve Building

Constitution Ave & 20th St NW.
Map 2 E4 & 3 A4. **Tel** (202) 452-3778
for art exhibitions. Ⓜ Foggy Bottom.
Open by appointment.
Closed Federal hols. ♿
Ⓦ **federalreserve.gov**

Known to most people as "the
Fed," this building is home to the
Federal Reserve System. This is
the US banking system under
which 12 Federal Reserve banks
in 12 districts across the country
regulate and hold reserves for
member banks in their districts.
Dollar bills are not printed
here, however, but at the
Bureau of Engraving and
Printing *(see p81)*.

The four-story, white
marble edifice opened
in 1937 and was
designed by Paul
Philippe Cret, architect
for the OAS building
(see p117) and the Folger
Shakespeare Library *(see p50)*.
Small art exhibitions are held
in the building throughout
the year.

Marble eagle above the entrance to "the Fed"

⓭ National Academy of Sciences

2101 Constitution Ave, NW. **Map** 2 E4.
Tel (202) 334-2000. Ⓜ Foggy Bottom.
Closed for restoration until 2014. ♿
Ⓦ **nationalacademies.org**

Established in 1863, the National
Academy of Sciences is a non-
profit organization that
conducts over 200 studies
a year on subjects such
as health, science, and
technology, and edu-
cates the nation by
providing news

The gleaming, white marble exterior of the Federal Reserve Building

of scientific discoveries. Among
the past and present Members
of the Academy are nearly
200 Nobel Prize winners, most
notably Albert Einstein.
To be elected as a
member is considered
a great honor for
a scientist.

The three-story
white marble
building, designed by
Bertram Grosvenor
Goodhue, was completed in
1924. Inside is a gold dome
adorned with portraits of Greek
philosophers and panels
illustrating various scientists. A
700-seat auditorium hosts a
series of free chamber recitals
throughout the year. On the
building's upper floors are the
offices of the National Research
Council, the National Academy
of Sciences, and the National
Academy of Engineering.

Nestled among the trees in
front of the Academy is the
much-admired bronze statue
of Albert Einstein, sculpted by
Robert Berks. The same artist
created the bust of President
John F. Kennedy, which can
be seen in the Grand Foyer
of the Kennedy Center
(see pp120–21). The huge

statue of Albert Einstein reaches
12 ft (4 m) in height and weighs
7,000 pounds (4 tons). It was
erected in 1979.

⓮ State Department

23rd St & C St, NW. **Map** 2 E4 & 3 A3.
Tel (202) 647-4000. Ⓜ Foggy Bottom-
GWU. ⏰ daily by appointment; must
show photo ID; reserve up to 3
months in advance. **Closed** Federal
hols. ♿ Ⓦ **state.gov**

As the oldest executive
department of the United
States government, established
in 1781, the State Department
handles all foreign policy.

Covering an expanse of
2.5 million sq ft (232,250 sq m)
over four city blocks, the State
Department building rises eight
stories high. Workplace of the
Secretary of State, the State
Department, and the United
States Diplomatic Corps, the
building plays host to some
80,000 guests and 60,000
visitors every year. The State
Department's Diplomatic
Reception Rooms were lavishly
refurbished in the late 1960s,
and now contain antiques
worth over $90 million.

⓯ George Washington University

2121 I (Eye) St, NW. **Map** 2 E3.
Tel (202) 994-1000. Ⓜ Foggy Bottom-
GWU. Lisner and Betts Auditoriums:
Tel (202) 994-6800. Ⓦ **gwu.edu**

Founded in 1821, George
Washington University, known
as "GW" to many people, is

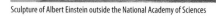

Sculpture of Albert Einstein outside the National Academy of Sciences named after the first president of the United States. George Washington is the largest university in Washington, DC. There are nine schools offering both undergraduate and graduate studies. Strong subjects on offer include International Affairs, Business Administration, Medicine, Law, and Political Science.

As a result of its location, the university has many famous alumni, including Colin Powell (US Secretary of State in George W. Bush's administration) and Jacqueline Bouvier (who married John Kennedy) as well as a number of children of past presidents, including Lynda Johnson, Margaret Truman, and D. Jeffrey Carter.

The on-campus Lisner, Morton and Betts auditoriums host a series of plays, dances, lectures, and concerts.

St. Mary's Episcopal Church, built for freed slaves

⓰ St. Mary's Episcopal Church

728 23rd St, NW. **Map** 2 E3. **Tel** (202) 333-3985. Ⓜ Foggy Bottom-GWU.
Open 9:30am–3pm Mon–Thu.
✝ 10am Sun, 12:10pm Wed. &
🆆 stmarysfoggybottom.org

Opened on January 20, 1887, the red-brick, Gothic St. Mary's Episcopal Church was the first church in Washington to be built specifically for freed slaves.

St. Mary's was designed by James Renwick, the architect of the Renwick Gallery (see p115), the Smithsonian Castle (see p74), and St. Patrick's Cathedral in New York City. The church was placed on the city's register of protected historic buildings in 1972.

⓱ Washington Circle

Map 2 E3. Ⓜ Foggy Bottom-GWU.

One of several circles and squares created by Pierre L'Enfant's original design of the city (see p21), Washington Circle lies at the northern edge of Foggy Bottom. It forms the point where Pennsylvania Avenue and New Hampshire Avenue meet K Street and 23rd Street. The circle boasts an imposing bronze statue of George Washington astride his horse, designed by artist Clark Mills and unveiled in 1860. The statue faces east, looking toward the White House and the US Capitol.

The distinctive curved walls of the infamous Watergate Complex

⓲ Watergate Complex

Virginia Ave between Rock Creek Parkway and New Hampshire Ave, NW. **Map** 2 D3. Ⓜ Foggy Bottom-GWU. &

Located next to the Kennedy Center (see pp120–21), on the bank of the Potomac River, the impressive, Italian-designed Watergate Complex was completed in 1971. The four rounded buildings that make up the complex were designed to contain shops, offices, apartments, hotels, and diplomatic missions.

In the summer of 1972 the complex found itself at the center of international news. Burglars, linked to President Nixon, broke into "the offices of the Democratic National Committee, sparking off the Watergate scandal that led to the president's resignation.

The Watergate Scandal

On June 17, 1972, during the US presidential campaign, five men were arrested for breaking into the Democratic Party headquarters in the Watergate Complex. The burglars were employed by the re-election organization of President Richard Nixon, a Republican.

Found guilty of burglary and attempting to bug telephones, the men were not initially linked to the White House. However, further investigation, led by Washington Post reporters Woodward and Bernstein, uncovered the extent of the President's involvement, including the possession of incriminating tapes and proven bribery. This led to an impeachment hearing, but before Nixon could be impeached, he resigned. Vice-President Gerald Ford succeeded him.

President Nixon addressing the nation while still in office

⑲ The Kennedy Center

In 1958, President Dwight D. Eisenhower signed an act to begin fund-raising for a national cultural center that would attract the world's best orchestras, opera, and dance companies to the US capital. President John F. Kennedy was an ardent supporter of the arts, taking the lead in fund-raising for it. He never saw the completion of the center, which was named in his honor. Designed by Edward Durrell Stone, it was opened on September 8, 1971. This vast complex houses several huge theaters; the Opera House, the Concert Hall, the Eisenhower Theater, and the Family Theater; on the roof are the Jazz Club, the Terrace Theater, and the Theater Lab.

Don Quixote Statue
This bronze and stone statue by Aurelio Teno was a gift to the center from Spain.

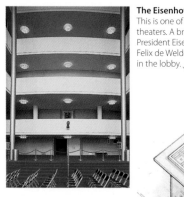

The Eisenhower Theater
This is one of the three main theaters. A bronze bust of President Eisenhower by Felix de Weldon hangs in the lobby.

Millennium Stage
The Millennium Stage provides free performances in the Grand Foyer every evening at 6pm.

KEY

① **East Roof Terrace**

② **The Hall of Nations** houses the flag of every country with which the US has diplomatic relations.

③ **The Concert Hall** is the largest auditorium, seating more than 2,400 people. It is the home of the National Symphony Orchestra.

The Hall of States
The flags of each of the 50 American states, the five US territories, and the District of Columbia hang here.

★ **The Opera House**
The Opera House seats over 2,300 people. The vast chandelier is made of Lobmeyr crystal and was a gift from Austria.

VISITORS' CHECKLIST

Practical Information
New Hampshire Ave & Rock Creek Parkway, NW. **Map** 2 D4.
Tel (202) 467-4600.
🌐 **kennedy-center.org**
Open 10am–9pm daily; 10am–9pm Mon–Sat, noon–9pm Sun and hols (box office).
⏰ 10am–5pm Mon–Fri, 10am–1pm Sat & Sun (call (202) 416-8340). ♿ 📷 🚫 🍴

Transport
Ⓜ Foggy Bottom. 🚌 80.

★ **Bust of JFK**
Created by sculptor Robert Berks, this bronze bust stands in the Grand Foyer.

The JFK Terrace
This stretches the length of the Center and overlooks the Potomac and has glorious views up and down the river. Quotes by John F. Kennedy are engraved into the marble walls.

★ **The Grand Foyer**
This enormous room stretches 630 ft (192 m) and provides an impressive entrance into the Opera House, the Concert Hall, and the Eisenhower Theater.

GEORGETOWN

Georgetown developed well before Washington, DC. Native Americans had a settlement here, and in 1703 a land grant was given to Ninian Beall, who named the area the Rock of Dumbarton. By the mid-18th century immigrants from Scotland had swelled the population, and in 1751 the town was renamed George Town. It grew rapidly into a wealthy tobacco and flour port and finally, in 1789, the city of Georgetown was formed. The harbor and the Chesapeake and Ohio Canal were built in 1828, and the streets were lined with townhouses. The birth of the railroad undercut Georgetown's economy, which by the mid-1800s was in decline. But by the 1950s the cobblestone streets and charming houses were attracting wealthy young couples, and restaurants and shops sprang up on Wisconsin Avenue and M Street. Today Georgetown retains its quiet distinction from the rest of the city, and is a pleasant area in which to stroll for a few hours (see pp150–51).

Sights at a Glance

See also Street Finder map 1–2

◄ Vine-covered walls of Dumbarton Oaks Summerhouse

For keys to symbols see back flap

Fountain at Washington Harbor

❶ Washington Harbor

3000-3020 K St, NW. **Map** 2 D3.

Washington is a city where few architectural risks have been taken. However, the approach used by architect Arthur Cotton Moore for Washington Harbor, which is a combination residential and commercial building on the Potomac River, is unusually audacious.

Moore's creation is a structure that hugs the waterfront and surrounds a semi-circular pedestrian plaza. The architect borrowed motifs from almost every type of design, such as turrets and flying buttresses. The harbor has a pleasant boardwalk, a huge fountain, and tall, columned lampposts. Under the ground are steel gates that can be raised to protect the building from floods. The top floors of the harbor are apartments. On the bottom floors are office complexes, restaurants, and shops. Sightseeing boats dock at the river's edge for trips to Mount Vernon and Alexandria. The spring of 2011 saw severe flooding to the harbor, which caused considerable damage. However, with new floodgates in place, Hurricane Sandy did not damage the waterfront in 2012.

❷ Wisconsin Avenue

Wisconsin Ave. **Map** 1 C2.
Ⓜ Foggy Bottom.

Wisconsin Avenue is one of two main business streets in Georgetown and is home to a wide variety of shops and restaurants. It is also one of the few streets in Washington that pre-dates L'Enfant's grid plan (see p69). It starts at the bank of the Potomac and runs north through Georgetown right to the city line, where it continues as Rockville Pike. On the

❹ The Chesapeake and Ohio Canal

When it was constructed in 1828, the C&O Canal featured an ingenious and revolutionary transportation system of locks, aqueducts, and tunnels that ran along its 184 miles (296 km) from Georgetown to Cumberland, Maryland. With the arrival of the railroad in the late 19th century, the canal fell out of use. It was only as a result of the efforts of Supreme Court Justice William Douglas that the Chesapeake and Ohio Canal was finally declared a protected national park in 1971. Today visitors come to enjoy its recreational facilities and also to study its fascinating transportation system. A 15-mile (20-km) walking and biking trail along the canal connects Georgetown with Great Falls Park (see p166).

Georgetown
The attractive federal houses of Georgetown line the banks of the canal for about 1.5 miles (2 km).

Great Falls 14 miles

Williamsport 75 miles

CANAL ROAD NW

Chesapeake and Ohio Canal

The Francis Scott Key Memorial Bridge was named after the the composer of the American national anthem, *The Star-Spangled Banner.*

Potoma

Canal Trips
The towpath trail runs north to Great Falls and historic Williamsport, where boat trips can be taken and costumed guides add colour to the waterside.

junction of Wisconsin Avenue and M Street is the landmark gold dome of PNC Bank (formerly the Riggs National Bank).

During the French and Indian Wars, George Washington marched his troops up the avenue on his way to Pittsburgh to engage the British.

The gold dome of PNC Bank

❸ Grace Church

1041 Wisconsin Ave, NW.
Map 1 C3. **Tel** (202) 333-7100.
Open call office in advance (office open 10am–6pm Mon, Tue, Fri). ♿
ⓦ **gracedc.org**

Built in 1866, Grace Church was designed to serve the religious needs of the boatmen who worked on the Chesapeake and Ohio Canal and the sailors of the port of Georgetown. Set on a tree-filled plot south of the canal and M Street, the Gothic Revival church, with its quaint exterior, is an oasis in Georgetown.

The building has undergone few extensive alterations over the years and has a certain timeless quality. The church's multi-ethnic congregation makes great efforts to reach out to the larger DC community and

Sign for Grace Church

works with soup kitchens and shelters for the homeless. The church also sponsors the "Thank God It's Friday" lunchtime discussion group, and holds a poetry coffee house on the third Tuesday of the month. Classical concerts, including chamber pieces, organ, and piano works, are held here regularly. There is also a popular annual festival devoted to the music of the German composer J.S. Bach.

Rowing on the Canal
Boating is popular on the C&O and is best between Georgetown and Violette's Lock – the first 22 miles (35 km) of the canal.

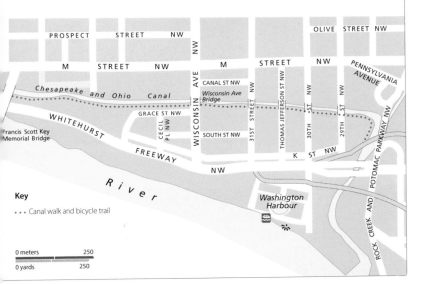

Key

••• Canal walk and bicycle trail

0 meters 250
0 yards 250

❺ Old Stone House

3051 M St, NW. **Map** 2 D2. **Tel** (202) 426-6851. **Open** noon–5pm daily. 🚌 30, 32, 34, 36, 38. 📞 call (202) 895-6070. ♿ limited
ⓦ nps.gov/olst

The Old Stone House may be the only building in Washington that pre-dates the American Revolution. It was built in 1765 by Christopher Layman, and the tiny two-story cottage has a large garden, which is a welcome respite from the shops of busy M Street.

There is a legend that still persists about the Old Stone House – that it was the Suter's Tavern where Washington and Pierre L'Enfant made their plans for the city. However, most historians today now believe that they met in a tavern located elsewhere in Georgetown.

Over the years, the building has housed a series of artisans, and in the 1950s it even served as offices for a used-car dealership. In 1960 the National Park Service restored it to its pre-Revolutionary War appearance. Today park rangers give talks (noon–5pm) about what Georgetown would have been like during the Colonial days. The Old Stone House is technically the oldest house in DC, although The Lindens, which is now in Kalorama, was built in the mid-1750s in Massachusetts and later moved to Washington.

The picturesque Old Stone House

❻ M Street

M St, NW. **Map** 1 C2. 🚌 30, 32, 34, 36, 38.

One of two main shopping streets in Georgetown, M Street is also home to some of the most historic spots in the city. On the northeast corner of 30th and M Streets, on the current site of a bank, stood Union Tavern. Built in 1796, the tavern played host to, among others, Presidents George Washington and John Adams, Napoleon's younger brother Jerome Bonaparte, author Washington Irving, and Francis Scott Key, the composer of the "Star Spangled Banner." During the Civil War, the inn was turned into a temporary hospital where Louisa May Alcott, the author of *Little Women,* nursed wounded soldiers. In the 1930s the tavern was torn down and replaced by a gas station. Dr. William Thornton, architect of the US Capitol and Tudor Place *(see p128)* lived at 3219 M Street.

On the south side of M Street is Market House, which has been the location of Georgetown's market since 1751. In 1796 a wood frame market house was constructed and later replaced by the current brick market in

❽ N Street

N St, NW. **Map** 1 C2. 🚌 30, 32, 34, 36.

N Street is a sampler of 18th-century American Federal architecture – a style favored by leaders of the new nation as being of a lighter and more refined design than the earlier Georgian houses.

At the corner of 30th and N Streets is the Laird-Dunlop House. Today it is owned by Benjamin Bradlee, the former editor of the *Washington Post.*

An excellent example of a Federal house is the Riggs-Riley House at 3038 N Street, most recently owned by Averill and Pamela Harriman. At 3041–3045 N Street is Wheatley Row. These houses were designed to provide not only maximum light from large windows but also maximum privacy as they were placed above street level.

Known as Wheatley Row, these three well-designed Victorian town homes were built in 1859.

Only the two end houses in this group of fine Federal homes (numbers 3327–3339) are still in their original state.

1865. In the 1930s the market became an auto supply store, and in the 1990s the New York gourmet food store Dean and Deluca opened a branch here.

Today M Street is home to a collection of fashionable stores and restaurants. Young buyers shop for alternative music at Smash and alternative clothing at Urban Outfitters. National chainstores such as Banana Republic, Pottery Barn, and Starbucks have branches along M Street. The fashionable Cady's Alley at 3318 M Street, is a haven of trendy boutiques, high end furnishing, and antique retailers.

Clyde's restaurant at number 3236 is a Georgetown institution, famous for its "happy hour."

The elegant façade of the Post Office in Georgetown

Attractive houses lining the bustling M Street

❼ Washington Post Office, Georgetown Branch

1215 31st St, NW. **Map** 2 D2. 🚌 30, 32, 34, 36. **Open** 9am–5pm Mon–Fri, 9am–2pm Sat.

Built in 1857 as a customhouse, the still-functioning Georgetown Branch of the Washington Post Office is interesting both historically and architecturally. A customhouse was a money-producing venture for the Federal government, and the US government's investment in such an expensive building provides evidence of Georgetown's

importance as a viable port for many years. Architect Ammi B. Young, who was also responsible for the design of the Vermont State Capitol building in 1832 and the Boston Custom House in 1837, was called to Washington in 1852. He designed several other Italianate buildings in the capital, but this post office is his finest work. The granite custom-house was converted to a post office when Georgetown's fortunes declined.

The building underwent a renovation in 1997 that increased its accessibility but retained the integrity of Young's simple, functional design.

The Thomas Beall House (number 3017) was built in 1794 by one of Georgetown's most prominent families. It has since been occupied by the Secretary of War during World War I, and by Jackie Kennedy, who lived here for a year after the death of JFK.

Number 3025–3027, with its raised mansard roof, shows the influence of the French during this period.

The Laird-Dunlop House (number 3014) was built by John Laird who owned many of Georgetown's tobacco warehouses. Laird modeled his home on those in his native Edinburgh. It was subsequently owned by President Lincoln's son, Robert.

Unusual flat roof

9 Georgetown University

37th St & O St, NW. **Map** 1 B2. **Tel** (202) 687-0100. **Open** varies, depending on university schedule. **W georgetown.edu**

Georgetown University was the first Catholic college to be established in America. Founded in 1789 by John Carroll, and affiliated with the Jesuit Order, the university now attracts students of all faiths from over 100 countries around the world.

The oldest building on the campus is the Old North Building, completed in 1872, but the most recognizable structure is the Healy Building, a Germanic design topped by a fanciful spiral. The university's most famous graduate is President Bill Clinton.

The Gothic-inspired Healy Building, Georgetown University

10 Tudor Place

1644 31st St, NW. **Map** 1 C2. **Tel** (202) 965-0400. **Open** 10am–4pm Tue–Sat, noon–4pm Sun. **Closed** Jan, Easter Sunday, Memorial Day, Jul 4, Labor Day, Thanksgiving, Dec 24, 25. **W tudorplace.org**

The manor house and large gardens of this Georgetown estate, designed by William Thornton, offer a unique glimpse into a bygone era.

Martha Washington, the First Lady, gave $8,000 to her granddaughter, Martha Custis Peter, and her granddaughter's husband. With the money, they purchased eight acres and commissioned Thornton, the

Stone dog in the garden of Tudor Place

architect of the Capitol (see pp52–3), to design a house. Generations of the Peters family lived here from 1805 to 1984. It is a mystery as to why this stuccoed, two-story Georgian structure with a "temple" porch is called Tudor Place, but it was perhaps illustrative of the family's English sympathies at the time.

The furniture, silver, china, and portraits provide a glimpse into American social and cultural history; some of the pieces on display come from Mount Vernon (see pp162–3).

11 Mt. Zion Church

1334 29th St, NW. **Map** 2 D2. **Tel** (202) 234-0148. 🕇 11am Sun.

This church is thought to have had the first black congregation in DC. The first church, at 27th and P Streets, was a "station" on the city's original Underground Railroad. It provided shelter for runaway slaves on their journey

Altar in Mt. Zion church

north to freedom. The present redbrick building was completed in 1884 after the first church burned down.

Mt. Zion Cemetery, the oldest black burial ground in Washington, is located a short distance away, in the middle of the 2500 block of Q Street.

12 Oak Hill Cemetery

3001 R St, NW. **Map** 2 D1. **Tel** (202) 337-2835. **Open** 9am–4:30pm Mon–Fri, 1–4pm Sun (weather permitting). **Closed** Federal hols. **W oakhillcemeterydc.org**

William Wilson Corcoran (see p115) bought the land and Congress then established Oak Hill Cemetery in 1849. Today, about 18,000 graves cover the 25-acre site, which is planted with huge oak trees.

Members of some of the city's most prominent families are buried here, their names featuring throughout the city's history, including Magruder, Thomas, Beall, and Marbury.

At the entrance to the cemetery is an Italianate gatehouse that is still used as the superintendent's lodge and office. Northeast of the gatehouse is the Spencer family monument, designed by Louis Comfort Tiffany. The granite low-relief of an angel is signed by Tiffany. Also notable is

The Founding of the United Nations

In 1944, a conference held at the Dumbarton Oaks estate laid the groundwork for establishing the United Nations. President Franklin Roosevelt and the British Prime Minister, Winston Churchill, wanted to create a "world government" that would supervise the peace at the end of World War II. Roosevelt proposed that a conference be held in Washington, but at the time the State Department did not have a room big enough to accommodate all the delegates. As a solution, Robert Woods Bliss offered the use of the music room in his former home, Dumbarton Oaks, for the event.

The structure of the United Nations was settled at the Dumbarton Oaks Conference and then refined at the San Francisco Conference a year later when the United Nations' charter was ratified. The UN Headquarters building, the permanent home of the organization, was built in New York on the East River site after John D. Rockefeller donated $8.5 million toward its construction.

The conference members in the music room of Dumbarton Oaks

---

the Gothic chapel designed by James Renwick. Nearby is the grave of John Howard Payne, composer of "Home, Sweet Home," who died in 1852. The bust that tops Payne's monument was originally sculpted with a full beard, but Corcoran requested a stonemason to "shave the statue" and so now it is clean shaven.

⓭ Dumbarton Oaks

1703 32nd St, NW. **Map** 2 D2. **Tel** (202) 339-6401 (call ahead to check times). **Open** House: 2–5pm Tue–Sun. Gardens: 2–6pm Tue–Sun (to 5pm Nov–Feb). **Closed** Federal hols. 🖼 gardens only. 🎟 for groups call (202) 339-6409. 📷 ♿ house only.
W doaks.org

In 1703, a Scottish colonist named Ninian Beall was granted around 800 acres of land in this area. In later years the land was sold off and in 1801, 22 acres were bought by Senator William Dorsey of Maryland, who proceeded to build a Federal-style brick home here. A year later, financial difficulties caused him to sell it, and over the next century the property changed hands many times.

By the time pharmaceutical heirs Robert and Mildred Woods Bliss bought the run-down estate in 1920, it was overgrown and neglected. The Blisses altered and expanded the house, with the architectural

advice of the prestigious firm McKim, Mead and White *(see p111)*, to meet 20th-century family needs. They engaged their friend, Beatrix Jones Farrand, one of the few female landscape architects at the time, to lay out the grounds. Farrand designed a series of terraces that progress from the formal gardens near the house to the more informal landscapes farther away from it.

Fountain in Dumbarton Oaks

In 1940 the Blisses moved to California and donated the whole estate to Harvard University. It was then converted into a library, research institution, and museum. Many of the 1,400 pieces of Byzantine Art on display were collected by the Blisses themselves. Examples of Greco-Roman coins, late Roman and early Byzantine bas-reliefs, Egyptian fabrics, and Roman glass and bronzeware are just some of the highlights. In 1962 Robert Woods Bliss donated his collection of pre-Columbian art. In order to house it, architect Philip Johnson designed a new wing, consisting of eight domes surrounding a circular garden. Although markedly different from the original house, a separate wing is well suited to the dramatic art collection it houses, which includes masks, stunning gold jewelry from Central America, and Aztec carvings.

Swimming pool in the grounds of Dumbarton Oaks

FARTHER AFIELD

North of the White House is Dupont Circle, a neighborhood of museums, galleries, and restaurants. The Embassy Row, Kalorama, Adams-Morgan, and Cleveland Park neighborhoods are a walker's paradise, especially for visitors interested in architecture. Arlington, Virginia, across the Potomac River, was one of DC's first suburbs. Arlington National Cemetery was founded in 1864 to honor those who died for the Union. The Pentagon was built 80 years later by Franklin D. Roosevelt and is the area's most famous landmark.

Sights at a Glance

Museums and Galleries

7 African American Civil War Memorial and Museum
10 National Geographic Museum
11 The Phillips Collection
12 Textile Museum
17 Mary McLeod Bethune Council House
18 Hillwood Estate Museum
29 Anacostia Museum

Historic Districts, Streets, and Buildings

2 The Pentagon
4 Southwest Waterfront
6 Heurich Mansion
9 Dupont Circle
13 Woodrow Wilson House
14 Embassy Row
15 Kalorama
16 Adams-Morgan
19 Lincoln Theatre

21 *Washington National Cathedral pp144–5*
27 Howard University
28 Frederick Douglass House

Monuments

3 Air Force Memorial
8 Iwo Jima Statue
24 Basilica of the National Shrine of the Immaculate Conception

Parks and Gardens

5 Theodore Roosevelt Island
20 *National Zoological Park pp140–41*
22 Cleveland Park
23 Rock Creek Park
25 National Arboretum
26 Kenilworth Park and Aquatic Gardens

Cemetery

1 *Arlington National Cemetery pp132–3*

Key

■ Central Washington
□ Greater Washington
--- Metro line
═ Freeway (motorway)
▬ Major road
═ Minor road
--- State Border

0 kilometers — 2.5
0 miles — 2.5

◄ Amphitheater, Arlington National Cemetery

For additional map symbols *see back flap*

❶ Arlington National Cemetery

For 30 years, Confederate General Robert E. Lee (1807–70) lived at Arlington House. In 1861 he left his home to lead Virginia's armed forces, and the Union confiscated the estate for a military cemetery. By the end of the Civil War in 1865, 16,000 soldiers were interred in the consecrated Arlington National Cemetery. Since then, around another 300,000 veterans have joined them. Simple headstones mark the graves of soldiers who died in every major conflict from the Revolution to the present. The focus of the cemetery is the Tomb of the Unknowns, which honors the thousands of unidentified soldiers who have died in battle.

Confederate Memorial
This bronze and granite monument hon the Confederate soldiers who died in the Civil War. It was dedicated in 1914.

Sea of Graves
More than 330,000 service members and their families are buried on the 624 acres of Arlington Cemetery.

0 meters 200
0 yards 200

★ Tomb of the Unknowns
This tomb contains four vaults – for World War I and II, Vietnam, and Korea. Each vault held one unidentified soldier until the Vietnam soldier was identified by DNA analysis and reburied in his home town.

Memorial Amphitheater
This marble amphitheater is the setting of the annual services on Memorial Day (see p38) when the nation's leaders pay tribute to the dead who served their country. It has also hosted many military ceremonies.

★ **Arlington House**
Once home to Robert E. Lee, this Georgian-Revival house is now a memorial to the general and his family. It is possible to tour the house during cemetery visiting hours.

Iwo Jima Statue (p136)

Main Entrance

SHERMAN DRIVE

RMAN DRIVE

SHERMAN DRIVE

SCHLEY DRIVE

SHERIDAN DRIVE

ROOSEVELT DRIVE

MEMORIAL DRIVE

Visitor Center

EISENHOWER DRIVE

MC CLELLAN DRIVE

DRIVE

EISENHOWER DRIVE

Seabees Memorial
This memorial is dedicated to the section of the US Navy that specializes in construction work.

★ **Grave of John F. Kennedy**
A flame lit by his wife, Jackie, on the day of his funeral in December 1963 burns here continually. Jackie is buried next to her husband.

Key to Tombs and Sites
1. Seabees Memorial
2. Grave of John F. Kennedy
3. Grave of Robert F. Kennedy
4. Tomb of Pierre L'Enfant
5. Arlington House
6. Lockerbie Memorial
7. Confederate Memorial
8. Rough Riders Memorial
9. Challenger and Columbia Shuttle Memorials
10. Memorial Amphitheater
11. Tomb of the Unknowns

Tomb of Pierre L'Enfant
The architect responsible for planning the city of Washington has a suitably grand burial site in the cemetery (see p69).

View of the Pentagon building's formidable concrete façade from the Potomac River

❷ The Pentagon

1000 Defense Pentagon, Hwy 1-395, Arlington, VA. **Tel** (703) 697-1776.
Ⓜ Pentagon. Tours by appointment for US citizens only. For information call the above number.
Ⓦ pentagon.afis.osd.mil

President Franklin Roosevelt decided in the early 1940s to consolidate the 17 buildings that comprised the Department of War (the original name for the Department of Defense) into one building. Designed by army engineers, and built of gravel dredged from the Potomac River and molded into concrete, the Pentagon was started on September 11, 1941 and completed on January 15, 1943, at a cost of $83 million. As the world's largest office building, it is almost a city in itself. Yet despite its size, the Pentagon's unique five-sided design is very efficient, and it takes only seven minutes to walk between any two points.

The Pentagon is the headquarters of the Department of Defense, a Cabinet-level organization consisting of three military departments, the Army, Navy, and Air Force, as well as 14 defense agencies. Leading personnel are the Secretary of Defense and the Chairman of the Joint Chiefs of Staff.

On September 11, 2001, the building was damaged in a terrorist attack. A memorial to the 184 people who died in the Pentagon and on Flight 77 was dedicated on September 11, 2008.

❸ Air Force Memorial

Off Columbia Pike. **Tel** (703) 979-0674.
Ⓜ Pentagon City & Pentagon.
Open Apr–Oct: 8am–11pm daily; Nov–Mar: 8am–9pm daily. 🎦 by appt.
Ⓦ airforcememorial.org

Located on a promontory overlooking the Pentagon, this memorial honors the service and sacrifices of the men and women of the United States Air Force and its predecessor organizations. Central to the bold, graceful design, intended to evoke flight, are three stainless steel spires which soar skyward, the highest reaching 270 ft (82 m). President George W. Bush accepted the Memorial on behalf of the American people in October 2006.

The elegant Air Force Memorial

❹ Southwest Waterfront

Ⓜ Waterfront. Fish Market:
Open 7:30am–8pm daily.
Ⓦ swdcwaterfront.com

In the 1960s, urban planners tested their new architectural theories on Washington's southwest waterfront along the Potomac River. Old neighborhoods were torn down, and apartment high-rises put up in their place. Eventually new restaurants developed along the waterfront, and

A stall at the waterfront's fish market

Arena Stage, a popular regional theater company, built an experimental theater here. The area enjoyed a regeneration, and today it is a relaxed place to eat or just take a stroll.

The fish market, a remnant of the old waterfront cultures located off Maine Avenue. Today it is still a thriving business, drawing customers from all over Washington and enjoying its reputation as one of the most vibrant spots in the area. Customers can buy lobster, crabs, oysters, and all kinds of fresh fish from the vendors selling from their barges on the river. There are also several good restaurants along the waterfront that specialize in freshly caught local fish and seafood. Arrive early during the summer months as this is a popular place to dine.

September 11

On September 11, 2001, one of four airplanes hijacked by terrorists was flown into the Pentagon, resulting in huge loss of life and causing the side of the building to collapse. Crews at the Pentagon worked tirelessly to rebuild the damaged 10 percent of the building (400,000 to 500,000 square feet). It was estimated that repairs would take three years to finish but they were completed in less than a year. The west wall has a dedication capsule and a single charred capstone. A memorial has been erected.

The damaged Pentagon after the September 11 attack

when it relocated to the City Museum in the Carnegie Library Building (see p98). The Heurich Mansion is a fine example of an upper-middle-class family house in Washington in the late 1800s.

The ornate carving in Heurich's Beer Hall

❺ Theodore Roosevelt Island

GW Memorial Pkwy, McLean, VA.
Map 1 C4. **Tel** (703) 289-2500.
Ⓜ Rosslyn. **Open** 6am–10pm daily.
🅿 by appt only. 🅦 **nps.gov/this**

A haven for naturalists, Theodore Roosevelt Island's 91 acres (37 ha) of marshlands and 2 miles (4 km) of nature trails are home to a variety of wildlife including red-tailed hawks, great owls, groundhogs, and wood ducks, as well as many species of trees and plants. President Theodore Roosevelt (1858–1919), a great naturalist himself, is honored with a 17-ft (5-m) tall memorial in bronze, and four granite tablets, each inscribed with quotes by the president.

The island is just one of several sites that form part of the George Washington Memorial Parkway. Enjoy a quiet stroll or visit one of the parkway's other historical sites. Remember to carry drinking water, especially during the summer months.

There is a carpark on the George Washington Memorial Parkway (northbound) from where you can access the footbridge leading to the island. Bicycles are not permitted on the island.

❻ Heurich Mansion

1307 New Hampshire Ave, NW.
Tel (202) 429-1894. Ⓜ Dupont Circle.
🕙 11:30am & 1pm Thu & Fri, 11:30am & 2pm Sat. Wed by appt.
Closed Federal hols. 🐾 donation.
♿ 🅦 **heurichhouse.org**

Brewer Christian Heurich built this wonderful Bavarian fantasy for his family just south of Dupont Circle in 1894. The turreted mansion built in the Romanesque Revival architectural style was home to the Historical Society of Washington, DC until 2003,

❼ African American Civil War Memorial and Museum

Museum: 1925 Vermont Ave, NW.
Memorial: 10th St and Vermont Ave, NW. **Tel** (202) 667-2667. Ⓜ U Street.
Open 10am–6:30pm Mon–Fri, 10am–4pm Sat (call for tours), noon–4pm Sun. 🅦 **afroamcivilwar.org**

Opened in January 1999, the African American Museum uses photographs, documents, and audiovisual equipment to explain the still largely unknown story of African Americans' long struggle for freedom. The Museum's permanent exhibition is entitled "Slavery to Freedom; Civil War to Civil Rights." Interactive kiosks bring together historic documents, photographs, and music in a powerful and evocative way. There is also a service for anyone interested in tracing relatives who may have served with United States Colored Troops during the Civil War. At the center of a paved plaza is situated the "Spirit of Freedom," a sculpture by Ed Hamilton, which was unveiled on July 18, 1998. It is the first major art piece by a black sculptor on federal land in the District of Columbia. It stands 10 ft (3 m) tall and features uniformed black soldiers and a sailor poised to leave home.

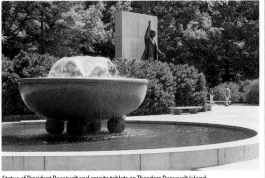
Statue of President Roosevelt and granite tablets on Theodore Roosevelt Island

The elaborate fountain at the heart of the Dupont Circle intersection

❽ Iwo Jima Statue (US Marine Corps Memorial)

Meade St, between Arlington National Cemetery & Arlington Blvd. **Map** 1 B5. Ⓜ Rosslyn. ♿

The horrific battle of Iwo Jima that took place during World War II was captured by photographer Joe Rosenthal. His Pulitzer Prize-winning picture of five Marines and a Navy Corpsman raising the American flag on the tiny Pacific island came to symbolize in the American psyche the heroic struggle of the American forces in the war against Japan.

This image was magnificently translated into bronze by sculptor Felix DeWeldon and paid for by private donations. The three surviving soldiers from Rosenthal's photograph actually posed for DeWeldon; the other three men, however, were killed in further fighting on the islands. The Iwo Jima Memorial is dedicated to all members of the Marine Corps who have died defending their country.

A poignant memorial to the men who died in the battle of Iwo Jima

❾ Dupont Circle

Map 2 F2 & 3 A1. Ⓜ Dupont Circle.

This area to the north of the White House gets its name from the fountain and is at the intersection of Massachusetts, Connecticut, and New Hampshire Avenues, and 19th Street, NW. At the heart of this traffic island is the Francis Dupont Memorial Fountain, named for the first naval hero of the Civil War, Admiral Samuel Francis Dupont. Built by his family, the original memorial was a bronze statue that was moved eventually to Wilmington, Delaware. The present marble fountain, which was constructed in 1921, has four figures (which represent the sea, the wind, the stars,

Playing chess in Dupont Circle

and the navigational arts) supporting a marble basin.

The park area around the fountain draws a cross section of the community – chess players engrossed in their games, cyclists pausing at the fountain, picnickers, and tourists taking a break from sightseeing. Do not stray into the Circle after dark as it may not be safe at night.

In the early 20th century the Dupont Circle area was a place of grand mansions. Its fortunes then declined until the 1970s, when Washingtonians began to buy the decaying mansions. The district is now filled with art galleries, bars, restaurants, and bookstores. The old Victorian buildings have been divided into apartments, restored as single family homes, or converted into small office buildings. Dupont Circle is also the center of Washington's gay community. The bars and clubs on the section of P Street between Dupont Circle and Rock Creek Park are the most popular area for gay men and women to meet.

❿ National Geographic Museum

1145 17th St at M St, NW. **Map** 3 B2. **Tel** (202) 857-7700. Ⓜ Farragut North, Farragut West. **Open** 10am–6pm daily. **Closed** Dec 25. ♿ 📷 Ⓦ nationalgeographic.com/museum

This small museum is located in the National Geographic Society's headquarters, designed by Edward Durrell Stone, the architect behind the Kennedy Center. A series of permanent and temporary exhibitions documents the richness of nature and the diversity of human culture all over the world. Past exhibitions include the Terra-Cotta Warriors and an exploration of the Golden Age of the pharaohs.

Auguste Renoir's masterpiece, *The Luncheon of the Boating Party* (1881)

⓫ The Phillips Collection

1600 21st St at Q St, NW. **Map** 2 E2 & 3 A1. **Tel** (202) 387-2151. Ⓜ Dupont Circle. **Open** 10am–5pm Tue–Sat (to 8:30pm Thu), 11am–6pm Sun. **Closed** Jan 1, Jul 4, Thanksgiving, Dec 25, Federal hols. 🎨 📷 11am Fri & Sat. ♿ 🖥 🏛
🌐 **phillipscollection.org**

This is one of the finest collections of Impressionist works in the world and the first museum devoted to modern art in the United States. Duncan and Marjorie Phillips, who founded the collection, lived in the older of the museum's two adjacent buildings. Following the death of his father and brother in 1917, Duncan Phillips decided to open two of the mansion's rooms as The Phillips Memorial Gallery.

The couple spent their time traveling and adding to their already extensive collection. During the 1920s they acquired some of the most important modern European paintings, including *The Luncheon of the Boating Party* (1881) by Renoir, for which they paid $125,000 (one of the highest prices ever paid at the time).

In 1930 the Phillips family moved to a new home on Foxhall Road in northwest Washington and converted the rest of their former 1897

Georgian Revival residence into a private gallery. The Phillips Gallery was then reopened to the public in 1960 and renamed The Phillips Collection. The museum currently has over 3,000 pieces of 19th-, 20th-, and 21st-century American and European art.

The elegant Georgian Revival building that was the Phillips' home makes for a more intimate and personal gallery than the big Smithsonian art museums. The Phillips Collection is best known for its wonderful selection of Impressionist and Post-Impressionist paintings; *Dancers at the Barre* by Degas, *Self-Portrait* by Cézanne and *Entrance to the Public Gardens in Arles* by Van Gogh are just three examples. The museum also has one of the largest collections in the world of pieces by French artist Pierre Bonnard, including *The Open Window* (1921).

Other great paintings to be seen in the collection include El Greco's *The Repentant Saint Peter* (1600), *The Blue Room* (1901) by Pablo Picasso, and the huge *Ochre and Red on Red* (1954) by Mark Rothko. In addition to the permanent exhibits,

Collector Duncan Phillips (1886–1966)

the museum supports traveling exhibitions, which start at The Phillips Collection before appearing in galleries around the country. The exhibitions often feature one artist (such as Georgia O'Keeffe) or one particular topic or period (such as the *Twentieth-Century Still-Life Paintings* exhibition).

The Phillips Collection encourages enthusiasts of modern art to visit the museum for a number of special events. On the first Thursday of each month the museum hosts "Phillips after 5." These evenings include gallery talks, live music, and light refreshments, and give people the opportunity to discuss the issues of the art world in a relaxed, social atmosphere. On Sunday afternoons from September through May, a series of concerts are staged in the gallery's Music Room. Running since 1941, these popular concerts are free to anyone who has purchased a ticket to the museum on that day. They range from piano recitals and string quartets to performances by established singers of world renown, such as the famous operatic soprano Jessye Norman.

The museum shop sells merchandise linked to permanent and temporary exhibitions. Books, posters, and prints can be found as well as ceramics, glassware, and other creations by contemporary artists. There are also hand-painted silks and artworks based on the major paintings in the collection.

Entrance to the Public Gardens in Arles (1888), by Vincent Van Gogh

18th-century Turkish embroidery on silk in the Textile Museum

⓬ Textile Museum

2320 S St, NW. **Map** 2 E1. **Tel** (202) 667-0441. Ⓜ Dupont Circle.
Open 10am–5pm Tue–Sat, 1–5pm Sun. **Closed** Dec 24 & 25, Federal hols. 🎨 donation. 🎫 "Highlights" tours 1:30pm Sat & Sun. Library: **Open** 11am–3pm Wed, noon–4pm Sat. 🏠 ♿ call in advance.
Ⓦ textilemuseum.org

George Hewitt Myers, the founder of the Textile Museum, began collecting oriental rugs while he was at college. In 1925 he opened a museum in his home to display his collection of 275 rugs and 60 textiles. It was a private museum, open only by appointment, until Myers' death in 1957.

Today the museum is still housed in Myers' home, which was designed by John Russell Pope, architect of the Jefferson Memorial (see p81). The collection is now in an adjacent building by Waddy B. Wood, architect of Woodrow Wilson's house.

There are around 17,000 objects in the collection from all over the world, including textiles from Peru, India, Indonesia, and Central America. Some pieces date from 3000 BC. The museum also hosts traveling exhibitions from other collections. During museum hours, the public can access the large formal gardens at the back of the building.

⓭ Woodrow Wilson House

2340 S St, NW. **Map** 2 E1. **Tel** (202) 387-4062. Ⓜ Dupont Circle.
Open 10am–4pm Tue–Sun.
Closed Federal hols. 🎨 🎫 ♿
Ⓦ woodrowwilsonhouse.org

Located in the Kalorama neighborhood, the former home of Woodrow Wilson (1856–1924), who served as president from 1913 to 1921, is the only presidential museum within the District of Columbia.

Wilson led the US through World War I and advocated the formation of the League of Nations, the precursor to the United Nations. Although exhausted by the war effort, Wilson campaigned tirelessly for the League.

In 1919 he collapsed from a stroke and became an invalid for the rest of his life. Many believe that Wilson's second wife, Edith Galt, assumed many of the presidential duties herself (she guided his hand when he signed documents). Unable to leave his sickbed, Wilson saw his dream, the League of Nations, defeated in the Senate. In 1920 he was awarded the Nobel Peace Prize – small consolation for the failure of the League.

Wilson and his wife moved to this townhouse, designed by Waddy B. Wood, at the end of his second term in 1921. Edith Galt Wilson arranged for the home to be bequeathed to the nation. Since then the building has been maintained as it was during the President's lifetime, containing artifacts from his life, such as his Rolls-Royce, and reflecting the style of an upper-middle-class home of the 1920s. The house today belongs to the National Trust for Historic Preservation.

⓮ Embassy Row

Massachusetts Avenue. **Map** 2 E1. Ⓜ Dupont Circle. See also pp148–9.

Embassy Row stretches along Massachusetts Avenue from Scott Circle toward Observatory Circle. It developed during the Depression when many of Washington's wealthy families were forced to sell their mansions to diplomats, who bought them for foreign missions. Since then, many new embassies have been built, often in the vernacular style of their native country, making Embassy Row architecturally fascinating.

At No. 2315 Massachusetts Avenue, the Embassy of Pakistan is an opulent mansion built in 1908, with a mansard roof (four steep sloping sides) and a rounded wall that hugs the corner.

Farther down the road, at No. 2349, is the Embassy of

Statue of Churchill, British Embassy

An elaborately decorated room in the Georgian Revival Woodrow Wilson House

the Republic of Cameroon, one of the Avenue's great early 20th-century Beaux Arts masterpieces. This romantic, Norwegian chateau-style building was commissioned in 1905 to be the home of Christian Hauge, first Norwegian ambassador to the United States, before passing to Cameroon.

Situated opposite the Irish Embassy stands a bronze statue of the hanged Irish revolutionary Robert Emmet (1778–1803). The statue was commissioned by Irish Americans to commemorate Irish independence.

At No. 2536 is the India Supply Mission. Two carved elephants stand outside as symbols of Indian culture and mythology. In the park in front of the Indian Embassy is an impressive bronze sculpture of Mahatma Gandhi.

The British Embassy, at No. 3100, was designed by Sir Edwin Lutyens in 1928. The English-style gardens were planted by the American wife of the then British ambassador, Sir Ronald Lindsay. Outside the embassy is an arresting statue of Sir Winston Churchill by William M. McVey.

Façade of the Croatian Embassy on Massachusetts Avenue

❾ Kalorama

Map 2 D1 & 2 E1.
Ⓜ Woodley Park or Duapont Circle.

The neighborhood of Kalorama, situated north of Dupont Circle, is an area of stately private homes and elegant apartment buildings. From its development at the turn of the 20th century as a suburb close to the city center, Kalorama (Greek for "beautiful view") has been home to the wealthy and upwardly mobile. Five presidents had homes here: Herbert Hoover,

The apartments at 2311 Connecticut Avenue, Kalorama

Franklin D. Roosevelt, Warren Harding, William Taft, and Woodrow Wilson. Only Wilson's home served as his permanent post-presidential residence.

Some of the most striking and ornate apartment buildings in Washington are found on Connecticut Avenue, south of the Taft Bridge that crosses Rock Creek Park. Most notable are the Georgian Revival-style Dresden apartments at No. 2126, the Beaux Arts-inspired Highlands building at number 1914, and the Spanish Colonial-style Woodward apartments at No. 2311 Connecticut Avenue. Also worth viewing is the Tudor-style building at No. 2221 Kalorama Road.

The best views of nearby Rock Creek Park (see p143) are from Kalorama Circle at the northern end of 24th Street.

❶❻ Adams-Morgan

North of Dupont Circle, east of Rock Creek Park, and south of Mt. Pleasant. **Map** 2 E1 & 2 F1. Ⓜ Dupont Circle or Woodley Park.

Adams-Morgan was one of the first racially and ethnically diverse neighborhoods in the city. It was given its name in the 1950s when the Supreme Court ruled that Washington must desegregate its educational system, and forced the combination of two schools in the area – Adams (for white children) and Morgan (an all-black school). Packed with

cafés, bookstores, clubs, and galleries, the district is a vibrant and eclectic mix of African, Hispanic, and Caribbean immigrants, as well as white urban pioneers, both gay and straight. People are attracted by the neighborhood's lively streets and its beautiful and relatively affordable, early 20th-century houses and apartments.

The area has a thriving music scene and, on any night, rap, reggae, salsa, and Washington's indigenous go-go can be heard in the clubs and bars. The cosmopolitan feel of Adams-Morgan is reflected in its wide variety of restaurants (see p189). Cajun, New Orleans, Ethiopian, French, Italian, Caribbean, Mexican, and Lebanese food can all be found along 18th Street and Columbia Road, the two main streets. Although the area is becoming increasingly modern and trendy, its 1950s Hispanic roots are still evident.

The area's cultural diversity is celebrated in September each year with food, music, and dance at the Adams-Morgan Day Festival (see p40).

It should be noted that this area can be dangerous after dark, so be wary if you are walking around at night. The area is not served by Metrorail and parking, especially on weekends, can be difficult.

Colorful mural on the wall of a parking lot in Adams-Morgan

⑳ National Zoological Park

Established in 1889 as the Smithsonian's Department of Living Animals and sited on the Mall, Washington's National Zoo moved to its present location in 1891. The park, which covers 163 acres, was designed by Frederick Law Olmsted, the landscape architect responsible for New York's Central Park. Today, the zoo is home to more than 2,000 animals, many of which are endangered. The zoo also runs a number of breeding programs, one of the most successful of which is the Sumatran tiger program.

Elephant Trails
This exhibit gives an innovative home with diverse habitats to a small herd of Asian elephants, and is part of a campaign to save this endangered species.

Rock Creek
(see p13.

Giant Panda Habitat
The National Zoo was the first zoo in the US to house pandas. Since 1972 these beloved bears have been the zoo's top attraction.

★ **Asia Trail**
This exhibit covers nearly 6 acres (2.4 hectares) and features seven Asian species, including sloth bears and red pandas.

Main
Entrance

Great Flight Exhibit
Endangered species such as the Guam rail and Bali Mynah can be seen here.

Bald Eagle
The only eagle unique to North America, the bald eagle is named for its white head, which appears to be "bald" against its dark body.

Key to Animal Enclosures

① Cheetah Conservation Station
② Zebras
③ Wallabies
④ Giant Panda Habitat
⑤ Elephants
⑥ Great Flight Exhibit
⑦ Bird House
⑧ Golden Lion Tamarins
⑨ American Trail
⑩ Bald Eagles
⑪ Seals and Sea Lions
⑫ Andean Bears
⑬ Amazonia
⑭ Gibbon Ridge
⑮ Great Ape House
⑯ Small Mammal House
⑰ Invertebrates
⑱ Reptile Discovery Center
⑲ Lemur Island
⑳ Think Tank
㉑ Sumatran Tigers
㉒ Great Cats
㉓ Kids Farm

| 0 meters | 100 |
| 0 yards | 100 |

Golden Lion Tamarins
These endangered mammals are protected by an international conservation program, which includes breeding and conservation education.

★ Great Ape House
Western Lowland Gorillas – whose males can weigh over 400 pounds (180 kg) – can be seen in the Great Ape House. Other occupants include tree-dwelling orangutans.

★ Komodo Dragons
These rare lizards can grow up to 10 ft (3 m) in length, and weigh up to 200 lbs (90 kg). They are the first to be born in captivity outside Indonesia.

Sumatran Tigers
Native to the Indonesian island of Sumatra, these are the smallest of all surviving tiger subspecies and are excellent swimmers.

Amazonia
This exhibit re-creates the Amazonian habitat. Visitors can see many creatures from poison-dart frogs to giant catfish.

⑰ Mary McLeod Bethune Council House National Historic Site

1318 Vermont Ave, NW. **Map** 3 B1. **Tel** (202) 673-2402. Ⓜ McPherson Square/U Street. **Open** 9am–5pm Mon–Sat. **Closed** Jan 1, Thanksgiving, Dec 25. 🎫 plus interactive tour for children. 📷 🖫 nps.gov/mamc

Born in 1875 to two former-slaves, Mary McLeod Bethune was an educator and civil and women's rights activist. In 1904 she founded a college for impoverished black women in Florida, the Daytona Educational and Industrial School for Negro Girls. Renamed the Bethune-Cookman College, it is still going strong.

In the 1930s, President Franklin D. Roosevelt asked her to be his special advisor on racial affairs, and she later became director of the Division of Negro Affairs in the National Youth Administration. As part of Roosevelt's cabinet, Bethune was the first black woman to obtain a high position in the US government.

Bethune went on to found the National Council of Negro Women, which gives voice to the concerns of black women. The Council grew to have a membership of 10,000, and this

Mary McLeod Bethune

house on Vermont Avenue was bought by Bethune and the Council as its headquarters.

It was not until November 1979, 24 years after Bethune's death, that the original Council House was opened to the public, with photographs, manuscripts, and other artifacts from her life on display. In 1982 the house was declared a National Historic Site and was bought by the National Park Service.

Entrance to the Mary McLeod Bethune Council House

⑱ Hillwood Estate Museum and Gardens

4155 Linnean Ave, NW. **Tel** (202) 686-5807. Ⓜ Van Ness/ UDC. **Open** 10am–5pm Tue–Sat, 1–5pm Sun. **Closed** Jan, Federal hols. 🎫 🏫 🎥 🖫 hillwoodmuseum.org

Hillwood was owned by Marjorie Merriweather Post, and it was opened to the public in 1977. The Museum contains the most comprehensive collection of 18th- and 19th-century Russian imperial art to be found outside of Russia, including Fabergé eggs and Russian Orthodox icons. It also has some renowned pieces of 18th-century French decorative art. The Gardens are set within a 25-acre estate, surrounded by woodlands in the heart of Washington, and have important collections of azaleas and orchids.

The stunning interior of the restored Lincoln Theatre

⑲ Lincoln Theatre

1215 U St, NW. **Map** 2 F1. **Tel** (202) 328-6000 (box office). Ⓜ U Street-Cardozo. **Open** 10am–6pm Mon–Fri. **Closed** Federal hols. 🎫 groups by appt. ♿ 🖫 thelincolntheatre.org

Built in 1922, the Lincoln Theatre was once the centerpiece of cultural life for Washington's downtown African American community. Like the Apollo Theater in New York, the Lincoln presented big-name entertainment, such as jazz singer and native Washingtonian Duke Ellington, Ella Fitzgerald, and Billie Holiday.

By the 1960s the area around the theater began to deteriorate; the 1968 riots turned U Street into a corridor of abandoned and burned-out buildings, and attendance at the theater dropped dramatically. By the 1970s the theater had closed down. Then, in the early 1980s fundraising began for the $10 million renovation. Even the original, highly elaborate plasterwork was carefully cleaned and repaired, and the theater reopened in 1994.

Today the Lincoln Theatre is a center for the performing arts, and one of the linchpins of U Street's renaissance. The magnificent auditorium hosts a program of concerts, stage shows, and events including the DC Film Festival (*see p204*).

⑳ National Zoological Park

See pp140–41.

㉑ Washington National Cathedral

See pp144–5.

㉒ Cleveland Park

Ⓜ Cleveland Park.

Cleveland Park is a beautiful residential neighborhood that resembles the picture on a postcard of small-town America. It was originally a summer community for those wanting to escape the less bucolic parts of the city. In 1885, President Grover Cleveland (1885–9) bought a stone farmhouse here as a summer home for his bride.

The town's Victorian summer houses are now much sought after by people wanting to be close to the city but live in a small-town environment. There are interesting shops and good restaurants, as well as a grand old Art Deco movie theater, called the Uptown.

㉓ Rock Creek Park

Ⓜ Cleveland Park. Rock Creek Park Nature Center: 5200 Glover Rd, NW. **Map** 2 D1–D3. **Tel** (202) 895-6070. Ⓜ Friendship Heights. 🚌 E2, E3, E4. **Open** 9am–5pm Wed–Sun. **Closed** Federal hols. ✉ by appt. 🆆 nps.gov/rocr

Named for the creek that flows through it, Rock Creek Park bisects the city of Washington.

Pierce Mill, the 19th-century gristmill in Rock Creek Park

The Shaw Neighborhood

This neighborhood is named for Union Colonel Robert Gould Shaw, the white commander of an all-black regiment from Massachusetts. He supported his men in their struggle to attain the same rights as white soldiers. Until the 1960s, U Street was the focus of black-dominated businesses and organizations. Thriving theaters, such as the Howard and the Lincoln, attracted top-name performers, and Howard University was the center of intellectual life for black students. The 1968 riots, sparked by the assassination of Dr. Martin Luther King, Jr., wiped out much of Shaw's business district, and many thought the area could never be revived. However, the restoration of the Lincoln Theatre, the renewal of the U Street business district, and an influx of homebuyers renovating historic houses, have all contributed to the rejuvenation. In the part of U Street closest to the U Street-Cardoza metro stop, many fashionable bars and clubs have opened.

Mural in the Shaw neighborhood depicting Duke Ellington

This 1,800-acre stretch of land runs from the Maryland border south to the Potomac River and constitutes nearly five percent of the city. Unlike the crowded lawns of Central Park, Rock Creek Park has a feeling of the wilderness. Although the elk, bison, and bears that used to roam the park have vanished, raccoons, foxes, and deer can still be found here in abundance.

The park was endowed in 1890 and is now run by the National Park Service. In addition to hiking and picnicking, the park has a riding stable and horse trails, tennis courts, and an 18-hole golf course. On Sundays, a portion of Beach Drive – one of the main roads running through the park – is closed to cars to allow cyclists and in-line skaters freedom of the road. The creek itself is inviting, with little eddies and waterfalls, but visitors are advised not to go into the water because it is polluted.

The **Rock Creek Park Nature Center** is a good place to begin an exploration of the park. It includes a small planetarium, and a 1-mile (1.6-km) nature trail, which is very manageable for children.

Pierce Mill near Tilden Street was an active gristmill, which was restored by the National Park Service in 1936. It was kept working as a visitor exhibit until 1993 when it was deemed unsafe to work any more. There is a barn next to the mill where works by local artists can be bought. The Carter Barron Amphitheater, near 16th Street and Colorado Avenue, stages free performances of Shakespeare's plays and summer jazz concerts.

㉑ Washington National Cathedral

The building of the Cathedral Church of Saint Peter and Saint Paul (its official name) began in 1907 and was completed in 1990. The world's sixth-largest cathedral, it dominates the city's skyline and measures 301 ft (94.8 m) from grade to the top of the central tower and 518 ft (158 m) in length – almost the length of two soccer fields. Built with Indiana limestone, the Washington National Cathedral boasts elements typical of Gothic religious architecture, such as soaring vaulting, stained glass windows, and intricate carvings. The exterior features fanciful gargoyles and dramatic sculpture. The cathedral has been the location of funeral and memorial services for several US presidents. Extensive renovations continue on some parts of the cathedral following an earthquake in 2011.

Exterior
A masterpiece of Gothic-style architecture, the towers of the cathedral dominate the skyline.

★ Ex Nihilo Above the center portal is *Ex Nihilo* by artist Frederick Hart. It depicts figures of men and women emerging from the swirling background.

Main Entrance
Three huge Gothic arches dominate the west façade, with pierced bronze gates depicting stories from the book of Genesis.

KEY

① **George Washington Bay**

② **Pilgrim Observation Gallery**

③ **The pinnacles** on the cathedral towers are decorated with leaf-shaped ornaments and topped by elaborately carved finials.

Space Window
Mankind's achievements in science and technology are commemorated in this window with the flight of Apollo 11 and a piece of moon rock.

High Altar
Carved on the high altar are 110 figures, surrounding the central statue of Christ. Encased in the floor in front of the altar is stone from Mt. Sinai.

VISITORS' CHECKLIST

Practical Information
3101 Wisconsin Ave and Massachusetts Ave, NW.
Tel (202) 537-6200; recorded information: (202) 364-6616.
W **nationalcathedral.org**
Open 10am–5:30pm daily.
$10 contribution requested.
every 30 mins.

Transport
M Tenleytown/AU, Red Line, or Cleveland Park (approximately 1 mile away).
32, 34, 36.

Children's Chapel
A statue of Jesus as a boy stands by this chapel built to the scale of a six-year-old. There are also motifs of baby and mythical animals.

Nave
From the West Portal to the High Altar, the iconography tells the story of humanity to redemption.

★ South Rose Window
The theme of this window by Joseph Reynolds and Wilbur Burnham is "The Church Triumphant."

㉔ Basilica of the National Shrine of the Immaculate Conception

400 Michigan at 4th St, NE. **Tel** (202) 526-8300. Ⓜ Brookland-CUA. **Open** Apr 1–Oct 31: 7am–7pm daily; Nov 1–Mar 31: 7am–6pm daily. 🚻 ⃞ ⃞ ⃞ ⃞ ⃞ **nationalshrine.com**

Completed in 1959, this enormous Catholic Church is dedicated to the Virgin Mary. The church was designed in the shape of a crucifix and has many stained-glass windows. The building can seat a congregation of 2,500 people or more.

In the early 1900s, Bishop Thomas Shahan, rector of the Catholic University of America, proposed building a national shrine in Washington. Shahan gained the Pope's support in 1913, and in 1920 the cornerstone was laid. The Great Upper Church was dedicated on November 20, 1959. An unusual and striking combination of Romanesque and Byzantine styles, the shrine boasts classical towers as well as minarets in its design. The basilica's large interior includes a number of chapels, each with a distinctive design of its own.

Visitors can also enjoy the peaceful and extensive Prayer Garden, which covers almost an acre (4,050 sq m).

View down the nave to the Basilica's altar

Entrance to the Chinese Pavilion at the National Arboretum

㉕ National Arboretum

3501 New York Ave or 24th St & R St off Bladensburg Rd, NE. **Tel** (202) 245-2726. Ⓜ Stadium Armory, then Metrobus B-2. **Open** 8am–5pm daily. Museum: **Open** 10am–4pm daily. **Closed** Federal hols. 📷 by appt only. 🏛 ⃞ limited. ⃞ **usna.usda.gov**

Tucked away in a corner of northeast Washington is the National Arboretum – a center for research, education, and the preservation of trees, shrubs, flowers, and other plants. The many collections here mean that the Arboretum is an ever-changing, year-round spectacle.

The Japanese Garden, which encompasses the National Bonsai and Penjing Museum, has bonsai that are from 20 to 380 years old. The herb garden has ten specialty gardens, where herbs are grouped according to use and historical significance. At the entrance to the garden is an elaborate 16th-century European-style "knot garden," with about 200 varieties of old roses. The National Grove of State Trees has trees representing every state.

㉖ Kenilworth Park and Aquatic Gardens

1550 Anacostia Ave, NE. **Tel** (202) 426-6905. Ⓜ Deanswood. **Open** 7am–4pm daily. **Closed** Jan 1, Thanksgiving, Dec 25. ⃞ **nps.gov/keaq/index.htm**

Opened in the late 1800s, this tranquil park offers 12 acres (5 ha) of natural wetland areas and historic ponds filled with beautiful water lilies and other aquatic plants from around the world. In late summer, the lotus pond is covered with pink blossoms. Abundant wildlife can also be seen, including otters, turtles, frogs, salamanders, and water birds.

㉗ Howard University

2400 Sixth St, NW. **Tel** (202) 806-6100. Ⓜ Shaw-Howard. ⃞ **howard.edu**

In 1866 the first Congregational Society of Washington considered establishing a seminary for the education of African-Americans – a school intended for "teachers and preachers." The concept expanded to include a multi-purpose university, and within two years the Colleges of Liberal Arts and Medicine of Howard University were founded, named for General Oliver O. Howard (1830–1909), an abolitionist and Civil War hero who later became a commissioner of the Freedman's Bureau. The impetus for establishing such a university was the arrival of newly-freed men from the South who were coming to the North seeking education to improve their lives. The university's charter was enacted by Congress and approved by President Andrew Jackson.

Famous graduates include Thurgood Marshall, who championed desegregation of public schools and was the first African-American Supreme Court Justice, Carter Woodson, Toni Morrison, Ralph Bunche, Stokely Carmichael, and Ossie Davis.

Frederick Douglass (1817–95)

Born a slave around 1818, Frederick Douglass became the leading voice in the abolitionist movement that fought to end slavery in the United States. Douglass was taught to read and write by his white owners. At the age of 20 he fled to Europe. British friends in the anti-slavery movement purchased him from his former masters, and he was at last a free man. For most of his career he lived in New York, where he worked as a spokesman for the abolitionist movement. A brilliant speaker, he was sent by the American Anti-Slavery Society on a lecture tour and won added fame with the publication of his autobiography in 1845. In 1847 he became editor of the anti-slavery newspaper *The North Star*, named after the constellation point followed by escaping slaves on their way to freedom. During the Civil War *(see p23)*, Douglass was an advisor to President Lincoln and fought for the constitutional amendments that guaranteed equal rights to freed blacks.

Frederick Douglass

㉘ Frederick Douglass House

1411 W St, SE. **Tel** (202) 426-5961.
Ⓜ Anacostia. **Open** mid-Oct–mid-Apr: 9am–4:30pm daily; mid-Apr–mid-Oct: 9am–5pm daily. **Closed** Jan 1, Thanksgiving, Dec 25. 🅿️ 📷
♿ call ahead. 🌐 nps.gov/frdo

The abolitionist leader Frederick Douglass lived in Washington only toward the end of his illustrious career. After the Civil War he moved first to a townhouse on Capitol Hill, and then to Anacostia. In 1877 he bought this white-framed house, named it Cedar Hill, and lived here, with his family, until his death in 1895.

Douglass's widow opened Cedar Hill for public tours in 1903, and in 1962 the house was donated to the National Park Service. Most of the furnishings are original to the Douglass family and include gifts to Douglass from

"The Growlery" in the garden of the Frederick Douglass House

President Lincoln and the writer Harriet Beecher Stowe, author of *Uncle Tom's Cabin* (1852).

In the garden is a small stone building that Douglass used as an alternative study, and which he nicknamed "The Growlery." From the front steps of the house there is a magnificent view across the Anacostia River.

㉙ Anacostia Museum

1901 Fort Place, SE. **Tel** (202) 633-4820.
Ⓜ Anacostia. **Open** 10am–5pm daily for tours. **Closed** Dec 25.
📷 by appointment only; call (202) 287-3369 or book online.
♿ 🌐 anacostia.si.edu

The full name of this museum is the Anacostia Museum and Center for African-American History and Culture. It is part of the Smithsonian Institution *(see p74)*, and is dedicated to increasing public understanding and awareness of the history and culture of people of African descent and heritage living in the Americas.

Basic needs such as housing, transportation, healthcare, and employment were long denied to members of the African-American community, and the Anacostia Museum sponsors exhibits addressing these concerns. Two of its major initiatives have been *Black Mosaic*, a research project on Washington's diverse Afro-Caribbean culture, and *Speak to MY Heart: African American Communities of Faith and Contemporary Life.*

The museum is as much a resource center as it is a space for art and history exhibitions; it has an extensive library and computers for visitors. Its collections include historical objects, documents, videos, and works of art. A nationally traveling exhibit, *Reflections in Black*, traces the history of African-American photography from 1840 to the present.

Façade of Cedar Hill, the Frederick Douglass House

Three Guided Walks

The best way to discover Washington's historic neighborhoods, diverse architecture, parks and gardens is on foot. The first walk takes you up and down Massachusetts Avenue, past many of the city's larger embassies and grand, imposing mansions into Kalorama, a pretty area that's home to many of the smaller embassies. Afterwards, you may wish to spend more time exploring. You'll find at least one hidden gem; the Embassy area also houses the Phillips Collection (see p137) and several art galleries. On the walks through Georgetown and Old Town Alexandria you'll notice that many of the historic buildings you pass are open to the public.

A Closer Look

In Georgetown you could tour Dumbarton Oaks, Tudor Place, or Georgetown University (see pp122–9). In Alexandria you might look inside the churches, the Lyceum (the local history museum), the Lee-Fendall House, Gadsby's Tavern Museum, or the Carlyle House (see pp160–61).

Dumbarton Oaks, Georgetown (see p131)

Embassy Row (see p149)

Georgetown (see pp150–51)

Carlyle House, a Georgian mansion on Fairfax Street, Alexandria (see p160)

Alexandria (see pp152–3)

Key

• • • Walk route

A Walk Around Embassy Row

For those fans of eclectic architecture this walk is a fascinating experience. Starting off west from Dupont Circle takes you along Massachusetts Avenue, past many of the larger embassies to the Italian Embassy and then back along Massachusetts Avenue to Kalorama, a quiet residential area where smaller embassies and museums are tucked away in its tree-lined streets.

⑦ Islamic Center's striking minaret

① Ornate Embassy of Indonesia

Walsh McLean (his daughter), who also owned the 44-carat Hope Diamond, which is at the Natural History Museum. Farther on, there's an Italianate palace, now home to the Society of Cincinnati ②, a charitable organization set up by officers who served George Washington. A statue of Civil War General Philip T. Sheridan on his horse greets you at Sheridan Circle ③. Walk around the circle to the left, passing the Irish and Romanian embassies. You'll see the former Turkish Embassy ④, an

garden behind the gate of the Japanese Embassy ⑤, a simple and graceful Georgian Revival building. After crossing the bridge over Rock Creek Park, you reach the Italian Embassy ⑥, a stunning contemporary structure that was designed by Piero Sartogo Architetti in Rome and Leo A. Daly in Washington. Its cantilevered copper eaves are reminiscent of a Renaissance palazzo. Cross Massachusetts Avenue and turn back toward Dupont Circle. Keep walking until you come to the the Islamic Center ⑦, a mosque with a 160-ft (48-m) minaret. Wander inside to see the exquisite tiles and carpets. (Head coverings for women are provided.) Turn left on California

At Dupont Circle Metro head northwest on the south side of Massachusetts Avenue. Look for the Indonesian Embassy ①. This Beaux Arts mansion was built at the turn of the century by an Irish immigrant from Tipperary who made his fortune in the gold mines. The house later became the property of Evalyn

ornate mansion that boasts a mixture of Romanesque and Turkish styles on the exterior, while inside there are Doric columns, marble floors, mosaic tiles, bronze statues, stained glass windows, and frescoes. It was built by Washington architect George Oakley Totten, who was inspired by palaces in Istanbul, for wealthy industrialist Edward Hamlin Everett. Known as the "bottle top king" (he obtained the patent for corrugated bottle tops), Everett staged elaborate musical evenings here. As you stroll along Massachusetts Avenue, take a look at the

Street, right onto 24th Street and left onto S Street past the Woodrow Wilson House ⑧ (the unpretentious home of the 28th president) and the Textile Museum ⑨. Go right onto 22nd Street, walking down the Spanish Steps to R Street. Turn left on R and right on 21st Street, passing the Phillips Collection ⑩, one of the country's most delightful modern art museums. Turn left on Q Street to make your way back to your start at the Dupont Circle Metro.

Tips for Walkers

Starting point: Dupont Circle Metro.

Length: 2.5 miles (4 km).

Stopping off points: Choose from one of several good restaurants near the Dupont Circle Metro stop.

Key

• • • Walk route

For additional map symbols *see back flap*

A 90-Minute Walk in Georgetown

Renowned for its beautiful and historic architecture, eclectic shops, and delightful restaurants, Georgetown has it all. Starting in upper Georgetown, this walk takes you along residential streets past grand homes and Federal-style rowhouses, past early churches and cemeteries, parks and river vistas, quiet lanes and crowded streets. The walk ends on M Street in the commercial heart of Georgetown at the oldest house built in the district. Details of many sights mentioned are in the section on Georgetown (see pp122–3).

and then left on 29th Street. Mt. Zion Church ⑧, on your right at 1334, was Washington's first African-American church, and has a tin ceiling that shows a West African influence (see p128).

At the corner, turn right on Dumbarton Street, left on 30th Street, and right on N Street, which is full of elegant

⑥ Dumbarton House, beautifully designed inside and out

Start at Wisconsin Avenue and S Street where you head east and then right on to 32nd Street. Dumbarton Oaks ① at 1703, a Federal-style mansion owned by Harvard University, contains a huge collection of pre-Columbian and Byzantine art, and may be worth returning to explore at length one afternoon (see p129).

Turn left on R Street and right onto 31st Street. Admire Tudor Place ②, designed by the Capitol architect William Thornton on the right (see p128). Turn left onto Avon Lane and left again on Avon Place. Walk across R Street to Montrose Park ③, which has a maze where you might like to meander for a bit, and then return to R Street. Head east and go into Oak Hill

Cemetery ④. James Renwick, architect of New York's St. Patrick's Cathedral, designed the chapel inside (see p128).

Back on R Street, head east to 28th Street. Turn right past Evermay ⑤, a private Georgian manor, built by Scotsman Samuel Davidson in 1792. Turn left on Q Street. On your left, the Federal-style Dumbarton House ⑥, is noted for its beautiful 18th- and 19th-century furnishings. Make a left at the corner on 27th Street. Facing you is the Mt. Zion cemetery ⑦ where African-Americans were buried before the Civil War.

Turning around, walk back on 27th Street until you come to O Street. Turn right on O Street

Tips for Walkers

Starting point: Wisconsin Ave & S Street. **Length:** 3 miles (5 km). **Getting there:** Metro Connection express bus from Foggy Bottom metro stop to Wisconsin Ave & R St, or Circulator bus from Union Station and points along K St NW.

⑪ Smith Row, American Federal-style architecture on N Street

③ Montrose Park, a tranquil space for city relaxation

18th-century architecture. On your right you pass 3017 N Street, the house where Jackie Kennedy once lived ⑨. At Wisconsin Avenue you can take a break at Martin's Tavern (est. 1933) or one of many cafés here. Turn right on Wisconsin and then left on O Street. Note the old streetcar tracks and St. John's Episcopal Church at 3240, once attended by Thomas Jefferson. Turn left on Potomac Street, then right.

Walk along N Street for several blocks. You'll pass Smith Row ⑪ with its brick Federal-style houses at 3255–63, John and Jackie Kennedy's home ⑫ from 1957 to 1961 at 3307, and Cox's Row ⑬ at 3327–39, built by Colonel Cox, a former merchant and mayor. Farther along N Street is Georgetown University ⑭ (see p128). Turn left on 36th Street to find The Tombs bar, a favorite haunt of students. On Prospect Street ⑮ next to the Car Barn (once used to house trolleys and now part of the university), go down three flights of steep steps (where a scene from The Exorcist was filmed) to M Street, the city's busiest and most colorful street, and the Potomac River.

Cross M Street and turn left, passing the Key Bridge and the Francis Scott Key Park ⑯, named for the author of "The Star-Spangled Banner". Still on M Street, look for the sign to Cady's Alley at 3316, make a right, and go down the steps. Turn left on Cady's Alley ⑰, browse in the high-end home furnishing shops, left again on 33rd Street to return to M Street. Turn right and you may want to stop at Dean & DeLuca ⑱, a lively café and gourmet market built in 1866. Stroll past the Victorian-style Georgetown Park ⑲, a former tobacco warehouse that now houses a variety of shops. Cross Wisconsin Avenue and go along M Street to 31st Street. Turn right then left onto the towpath by the C & O Canal ⑳ for a block, turning right on Thomas Jefferson Street and head toward Washington Harbor ㉑ (see pp124–5). Walk through this large complex of shops to the waterfront. After admiring the magnificent river view, retrace your steps to M Street and visit the Old Stone House ㉒, which dates from pre-Revolutionary days.

⑭ Georgetown University

Key

• • • Walk route

0 meters 300
0 yards 300

⑳ Passenger barge on the C & O Canal, a reminder of 19th-century shippers

For additional map symbols see back flap

A 90-Minute Walk in Alexandria

Stroll along cobblestone streets to see historic Alexandria, settled in the 18th century. This walk through the Old Town will take you by many historic homes, two of the oldest churches (George Washington attended both of them at one time or another), Gadsby's Tavern, and an old firehouse. The walk ends at the Torpedo Factory, now a thriving art center where over 200 artists exhibit their work. Afterward, go around to the back of the Torpedo Factory for a view of the Potomac River.

② Historic Farmer's Market in Market Square

Start at the Ramsay House Visitor Center ①, once the home of a Scottish merchant and city founder, William Ramsay. Built in 1724, it is the oldest house in Alexandria. Outside Ramsay House, you'll see Market Square ② where farmers have sold their produce for over 250 Years. At the corner of Fairfax and King Streets turn left onto South Fairfax Street. Walk past the Stabler-Leadbeater Apothecary Shop ③ *(see p160)*, built in 1792. This was formerly run by Edward Stabler who worked with the "Society for the Relief of People Illegally Held in Bondage" to free enslaved African Americans. Turn left on Prince Street to find

211, which was the former home of Dr. Elisha Cullen Dick, the doctor who attended George Washington on his deathbed. At the corner is the Athenaeum ④, a Greek Revival building dating from 1851, once the Bank of the Old Dominion. Cross Lee Street and continue walking on Prince Street. This block, dubbed Captain's Row ⑤, is still paved with cobblestones and was once home to sea captains and shipbuilders. Turn right on Union Street. You'll pass several art galleries and

catch a glimpse of the river on your left. Turn right on Duke Street to see the Federal-style homes and pretty gardens. Turn left on South Fairfax Street. The Old Presbyterian Meeting House ⑥ *(see p160)*, a brick church built by Scottish settlers in 1775 and rebuilt in 1837 after a fire, is on your right. On George Washington's death the bell of the Old Presbyterian tolled for four days. You'll find the Tomb of the Unknown Soldier of the American Revolution in the churchyard.

① Ramsay House, the oldest building in Alexandria

Go to the corner of South Fairfax Street and turn right onto Wolfe Street. This cuts through what was once a neighborhood called Hayti, home to many prominent African-American leaders in the early 1800s. Continue until you reach Royal Street. The house at 404 South Royal Street ⑦ is the home of George Seaton, a black

Tips for Walkers

Starting point: The Ramsay House Visitor's Center.
Length: 2.5 m (4 km).
Getting there: Take the Dash bus from the King Street Metro stop to the Ramsay House Visitor's Center.
Stopping Off Points: The Friendship Firehouse is open Fri–Sun. For lunch try Gadsby's Tavern or one of the restaurants on King Street.

master carpenter whose mother was freed by Martha Washington. Continue for three blocks. At 604 Wolfe Street is the Alexandria Academy ⑧, built with the support of George Washington and others. This free school was attended by white children before it became a school for African Americans in the first half of the 19th century.

Cross South Washington Street and turn right. After two blocks you'll come to the Lyceum ⑨, a building inspired by a Doric temple, which was originally a library, then a hospital for Union troops during the Civil War, and now a local history museum. A statue of a Confederate soldier, "Appomattox," stands in the center of the Prince and Washington Streets intersection, marking the spot where

⑯ Gadsby's Tavern, where President Jefferson's inaugural banquet was held

troops left Alexandria to join the Confederate army on May 24, 1861. Turn left on Prince Street and walk two blocks to South Alfred Street. Turn right to see the Friendship Firehouse ⑩ at 107. Turn right on King Street where you'll find colorful shops and restaurants. Turn left on Washington Street. Christ Church ⑪ will be on your left. Wander through the historic cemetery and into the church – this is where every year presidents have come to honor George Washington on his birthday. Continue on Washington Street past Lloyd House ⑫, a Georgian home built in 1796, once a station on the underground railroad. After two blocks turn right on Oronoco Street at the Lee-Fendall House ⑬ (see p161). The house, now a museum, was built by Philip Fendall who then married the sister of "Light Horse" Harry Lee (Robert E. Lee's father and a Revolutionary hero). Across the road at 607 Oronoco Street is Robert E. Lee's boyhood home ⑭ (see p160), which is now closed to the public. Alexandria loves

Portrait of Robert E. Lee ⑭

its dogs and they are all welcome at the Olde Towne School of Dogs on the corner of Oronoco and St. Asaph Streets. Turn right on St. Asaph and cross Princess Street with its cobblestones that were laid in the 1790s. Cross Cameron Street and turn left. A replica of the small house built by George Washington in 1769 is at 508 Cameron Steet ⑮.

Turning right on Royal Street, you'll find Gadsby's Tavern ⑯ (see p160), where Jefferson's inaugural banquet was held. Across the street is the City Hall ⑰. Continue on Cameron Street and cross Fairfax Street. The Bank of Alexandria, the city's oldest bank, established in 1792, stands on the corner. Next door is Carlyle House ⑱ (see p160), a Georgian mansion modeled after the Scottish estate Craigiehall. Go around to the rear to see the gardens. Back on Fairfax Street, continue on King Street and turn left. Enjoy the shop windows for two blocks to The Torpedo Factory on Union Street ⑲ (see p161), a dynamic arts center.

Key

• • • Walk route

0 meters   300
0 yards   300

⑲ The Torpedo Factory, with riverview studios, art galleries, and archaeology museum

Waterfalls at Great Falls Park, Virginia ▶

EXCURSIONS BEYOND WASHINGTON, DC

BEYOND WASHINGTON, DC

Within a half-day's drive of Washington lies enough history and natural beauty to satisfy the most insatiable sightseer. Alexandria and Williamsburg are a must for history buffs, while Chesapeake Bay and the islands of Chincoteague and Assateague offer a wealth of natural beauty. This area of Virginia and Maryland, along with parts of West Virginia and Pennsylvania, has been at the center of 400 years of turbulent American history.

Founded in 1623, Jamestown was the first permanent English settlement in America. In the 18th century, Williamsburg became the capital of Virginia and the first colony to declare independence from England. Today, Williamsburg is a living museum of the Colonial era.

The cultural influence of Europe is clearly seen in the architecture of this region. The two presidents largely responsible for crafting the character of the early republic lived in Virginia – George Washington at Mount Vernon, and Thomas Jefferson at Monticello. These homes reveal the lives their occupants led, at once imaginative, agrarian, inventive, comfortable – and, like many wealthy landowners, relying on slavery.

Cities and towns throughout the area have attractive historic districts that are a welcome contrast to the modern commercial strips on their outskirts.

Annapolis, for example, is a pleasant Colonial and naval port city. Baltimore also has a diverse charm, combining working-class neighborhoods and Old World character, and the town of Richmond blends the Old South's Victorian gentility with the luxuries of modern life.

Civil War battlefields are spread over the map as far as Gettysburg and tell the war's painful story with monuments, museums, cemeteries, and the very contours of the land itself.

The 105-mile (170-km) Skyline Drive through Shenandoah National Park, situated west of DC, makes the beautiful Blue Ridge Mountains accessible to hikers, cyclists, and drivers alike. To the east of the city, the Chesapeake Bay region attracts sailors and fishermen, as well as seafood lovers who can indulge in the delicious local specialty – blue crabs.

Mount Vernon Bike Trail

◄ Colorful clapboard house in Annapolis, Maryland

Exploring Beyond Washington, DC

Just minutes outside the bustling center of Washington is a striking and varied area of mountains, plains, and historic towns. To the west are Virginia's Blue Ridge Mountains, the setting for Shenandoah National Park. To the south is the Piedmont, an area of gently rolling hills that supports the vineyards of Virginia's burgeoning wine industry. To the east, the Chesapeake Bay divides Maryland almost in two, and to the south it travels the length of the Virginia coastline. To the north is the big port city of Baltimore, with its pleasant waterfront promenade, shops, museums, and stunning National Aquarium.

The Philadelphia Brigade Monument at Gettysburg

A re-created fort in Jamestown

Sights at a Glance

For additional map symbols see back flap

The dramatic Bearfence Mountain, part of Shenandoah National Park

Key

━━━ Freeway/Interstate highway

━━━ Major highway

━━━ Secondary route

━━━ Scenic route

╌╌╌ Main railroad

━━━ State boundary

Getting There

Four good interstate highways lace the area: I-95 runs south and north on the eastern side of Virginia; I-81 runs south and north in western Virginia; I-66 heads west from Washington; and I-270 goes toward Frederick. Trains depart from Union Station to most of the main towns, such as Baltimore, Alexandria, Richmond, Williamsburg, and Harpers Ferry, which is also served by the MARC (see pp214–15). Virginia Railway Express goes from Union Station to Alexandria and Fredericksburg. Greyhound buses also travel to most towns.

Boats moored in the Chesapeake Bay area

❶ Old Town Alexandria

Old Town Alexandria has kept a special historical flavor, dating back to its incorporation in 1749. It is still a busy seaport and offers many historic sights, as well as shops selling everything from antique hat racks to banana splits. Restaurants are abundant, art thrives here, and the socializing goes on day and night, in and around Market Square.

Exploring Alexandria

Alexandria's tree-lined streets are filled with elegant, historic buildings and make for a pleasant stroll (see pp152–3). Alternatively, a boat tour offers an attractive prospect as does a leisurely lunch on the patio overlooking the waterfront. Nearby Founder's Park is the perfect place to bask on the grass by the river.

Façade of the elegant Carlyle House

🏛 Carlyle House

121 N Fairfax St. **Tel** (703) 549-2997. **Open** 10am–4pm Tue–Sat, noon–4pm Sun; Last tour at 4pm. **Closed** Jan 1, Thanksgiving, Dec 25. 🅿 📷 ♿ (call in advance.) 📷
🆆 nvrpa.org/park/carlyle_house

This elegant Georgian Palladian mansion was built by wealthy Scottish merchant John Carlyle in 1753. The house fell into disrepair in the 19th century but was bought in 1970 by the Northern Virginia Regional Park Authority; it has since been beautifully restored. A guided tour provides fascinating details about 18th-century daily life. One room, known as the "architecture room," has been deliberately left unfinished to show the original construction of the house. The back garden is planted with 18th-century plant species.

🏛 Stabler-Leadbeater Apothecary Museum

105 S Fairfax St. **Tel** (703) 746-3852. **Open** Apr–Oct: 10am–5pm Tue–Sat, 1–5pm Mon, Sun; Nov–Mar: 11am–4pm Wed–Sat, 1–4pm Sun. **Closed** Jan 1, Thanksgiving, Dec 25. 🅿 📷 📷
🆆 apothecarymuseum.org

Established in 1792, this family apothecary was in business for 141 years, until 1933. It is now a museum, and the shop's mahogany drawers still contain the potions noted on their labels. Jars containing herbal remedies line the shelves. Huge mortars and pestles and a collection of glass baby bottles are among 8,000 original objects. George Washington was a patron, as was Robert E. Lee, who bought the paint for his Arlington house here.

🏛 Gadsby's Tavern Museum

134 N Royal St. **Tel** (703) 838-4242. **Open** Apr–Oct: 10am–5pm Tue–Sat, 1–5pm Sun, Mon; Nov–Mar: 11am–4pm Wed–Sat, 1–4pm Sun. **Closed** Federal hols. 🅿 📷 📷 📷
🆆 alexandriava.gov/gadsbystavern

Dating from 1770, this tavern and the adjoining hotel, owned by John Gadsby, were the Waldorf-Astoria of their day. Now completely restored, they evoke the atmosphere of a hostelry in this busy port.

You can see the dining room with buffet and gaming tables, the bedrooms where travelers reserved not the room but a space in a bed, and the private dining room for the wealthy. The hotel's ballroom, where George and Martha Washington were fêted on his last birthday in 1799, can be rented out. This is also a working restaurant.

Interior of the Old Presbyterian Meeting House

🏛 Old Presbyterian Meeting House

323 S Fairfax St. **Tel** (703) 549-6670. **Open** 8:15am–4:15pm Mon–Fri. 📷 ♿
🆆 opmh.org

Memorial services for George Washington were held in this meeting house, founded in 1772. In the churchyard are buried Dr. John Craig, a close friend of Washington, merchant John Carlyle, the Reverend Muir, who officiated at Washington's funeral, and the American Revolution's unknown soldier.

🏛 Boyhood Home of Robert E. Lee

607 Oronoco St.
Unfortunately, the boyhood home of Robert E. Lee is currently a private residence and not open to the public. General Lee lived in this 1795 Federal townhouse from the age of 11 until he went to West Point Military Academy. The drawing room was the setting for the marriage of Mary Lee Fitzhugh to Martha Washington's grandson, George Washington Parke Custis.

Bedroom of Robert E. Lee

🏛 Lee-Fendall House Museum

614 Oronoco St. **Tel** (703) 548-1789. **Open** 10am–3pm Wed–Sat, 1–3pm Sun. **Closed** Dec 25–Jan 31 (except 3rd Sun, Lee's birthday celebration). 🐾 once every hour, on the hour. ♿ 🌐 leefendallhouse.org

Philip Fendall built this stylish house in 1785, then married the sister of Revolutionary War hero "Light Horse" Harry Lee. Lee descendants lived here until 1904. The house is rich with artifacts from the Revolution to the 1930s Labor Movement.

Lee-Fendall House Museum

🏛 Torpedo Factory Art Center

105 N Union St. **Tel** (703) 838-4565. **Open** 10am–6pm daily (to 9pm Thu). **Closed** Jan 1, Easter, July 4, Thanksgiving, Dec 25. ♿ 🌐 torpedofactory.org

Originally a real torpedo factory during World War II, it was converted into an arts center by a partnership between the town and a group of local artists in 1974. Today there is gallery and studio space for over 150 artists to create and exhibit their work. Visitors can watch a potter at his wheel, sculptors, printmakers, and jewelry-makers.

🏛 Christ Church

Cameron & N Washington Sts. **Tel** (703) 549-1450. **Open** 9am–4pm Mon–Sat, 2–4:30pm Sun. **Closed** Jan 1, Thanksgiving, Dec 25. ♿ 🌐 historicchristchurch.org

The oldest church in continuous use in the town, this Georgian edifice was completed in 1773. George Washington's square pew is still preserved with his nameplate, as is that of Robert E. Lee.

On the other side of this Episcopalian church, a label

VISITORS' CHECKLIST

Practical Information
Alexandria. 🗺 143,000.
ℹ️ Ramsay House Visitor Center, 221 King St (703-746-3300).
🌐 visitalexandriava.com

Transport
🚉 Union Station, 110 Callahan St.
Ⓜ King Street.

reads "William E. Cazenove. Free pew for strangers." In the churchyard 18th-century gravestones wear away under the weather of the centuries.

🏛 Farmers Market

Market Square, King & Fairfax Sts. **Tel** (703) 746-3200. **Open** 5:30–11am Sat.

This market dates back to the city's incorporation in 1749. George Washington, a trustee of the market, regularly sent produce to be sold at the market from his farm at Mount Vernon (see pp162–3). A very pleasant aspect of the market square today is its central fountain. Shoppers can find fresh fruits and vegetables, cut flowers, herbs, baked goods, meats, and crafts.

Alexandria Old Town

Museums and Galleries
④ Gadsby's Tavern Museum
⑦ Stabler-Leadbeater Apothecary Museum

Historic Buildings
① Boyhood Home of Robert E. Lee
② Lee-Fendall House
⑥ Carlyle House

Churches
③ Christ Church
⑨ Old Presbyterian Meeting House

Markets
⑤ Farmers Market

Art Centers
⑧ Torpedo Factory Art Center

0 meters 200
0 yards 200

For keys to symbols see back flap

❷ George Washington's Mount Vernon Estate

This country estate on the Potomac River was George Washington's home for 45 years. Built as a farmhouse by his father, Augustine, Washington made many changes, including adding the cupola and curving colonnades. The house is furnished as it would have been during Washington's presidency (1789–97), and the 500-acre grounds still retain aspects of Washington's farm. The Ford Orientation Center and Donald W. Reynolds Museum offer exhibits about the life of the first US president, including his military and presidential career.

Kitchen
Set slightly apart from the main house, the kitchen has been completely restored.

★ Mansion Tour
Visitors can see the study and the large dining room, as well as Washington's bedroom and the bed in which he died.

Slave Quarters
Washington freed all his slaves in his will. Reconstructed quarters show their living conditions.

KEY

① **Overseer's House**

② **Coach House**

③ **Stable**

④ **The Lower Garden** was used for growing vegetables and berries. The boxwood bushes surrounding it were planted in Washington's time.

⑤ **The Bowling Green** was added to the estate by George Washington.

★ Upper Garden
The plants in this colorful flower garden are known to have grown here in Washington's time.

Wharf
Daytrip boats from central DC bring visitors to this wharf. Potomac cruise boats also stop off here.

VISITORS' CHECKLIST

Practical Information
South end of George Washington Memorial Parkway, Fairfax County, VA. **Tel** (703) 780-2000.
W **mountvernon.org**
Distillery State Route 235 South: **Open** Apr–Oct: daily.
first floor.

Transport
M Yellow line to Huntington Station. Fairfax Connector bus 101 to Mount Vernon: call (703) 780-2000. Boat cruises: Apr–Aug: 8am–5pm; Mar, Sep, Oct: 9am–5pm; Nov–Feb: 9am–4pm.

★ **Pioneer Farm**
This exhibit demonstrates farming techniques that were pioneered by George Washington. There is also a replica of his unique 16-sided treading barn, which was created using authentic tools.

Washington's Tomb
In his will, Washington requested that a new brick tomb be built for his family at Mount Vernon. Washington died in 1799 but the tomb was not completed until 1831.

❸ Gunston Hall

10709 Gunston Road, Mason Neck, VA. **Tel** (703) 550-9220. **Open** 9:30am–5pm daily. **Closed** Jan 1, Thanksgiving, Dec 25. 🦽 📷 ♿ 🏠
  W gunstonhall.org

This Georgian house, built in 1755, was the home of George Mason, author of the 1776 Virginia Declaration of Rights. Situated 20 miles (32 km) south of Washington, DC, it is an exquisite example of careful historic restoration.

Of particular interest is the finely carved woodwork in the entrance hall, the chinoiserie mantel and fireplace in the formal dining room, and the servants' staircase which was used by the slaves so that they wouldn't be seen by guests. Outside are the beautiful boxwood gardens.

❹ Annapolis

Anne Arundel County, MD.
🏔 36,000. ℹ️ Annapolis and Anne Arundel County Conference and Visitors Bureau, 26 West St. (410) 280-0445. **Open** 9am–5pm.
  W visitannapolis.org

The capital of Maryland, Annapolis is the jewel of Chesapeake Bay. It is defined by the nautical character that comes with 17 miles (27 km) of shoreline and the longtime presence of the US Naval Academy.

A walk down Main Street takes you past the 200-year-old Maryland Inn, and the shops and restaurants, to the City Dock lined with boats. It is then a short walk to the 150-year- old **US Naval Academy**. Inside the visitor center is the Freedom 7 space capsule that carried the first American, Alan Shepard, into space. The US Naval Academy Museum in Preble Hall is also worth visiting, especially to see the gallery of detailed ship models. The **Maryland State House** is the

The beautiful formal gardens of the William Paca House, in Annapolis

oldest state capitol in continuous use. Its Old Senate Chamber is where the Continental Congress (delegates from each of the American colonies) met when Annapolis was briefly the capital of the United States in 1783–4.

Annapolis teems with Colonial-era buildings, most still in everyday use. The **William Paca House**, home of Governor Paca, who signed the Declaration of Independence, is a fine Georgian house with an enchanting garden, both of which have been lovingly restored. The **Hammond Harwood House** has also been restored. This masterpiece of Georgian design was named after the Hammond and Harwood families, both prominent in the area. Cornhill and Duke of Gloucester streets are beautiful examples of the city's historic residential streets.

Many tours are offered in Annapolis, including

Tiffany window in the Naval Academy, Annapolis

walking, bus, and boat tours. It is particularly enjoyable to view the city from the water, be it by sightseeing boat, chartered schooner, or even by kayak.

🏛 US Naval Academy

52 King George St. **Tel** (410) 293-8687. **Open** 9am–5pm daily. Photo ID needed. **Closed** Jan 1, Thanksgiving, Dec 25.
  📷 **W** usna.edu

🏛 Maryland State House

State Circle. **Tel** (410) 974-3400. **Open** 9am–5pm (call ahead). Photo ID needed. **Closed** Jan 1, Dec 25. 📷 11am & 3pm. ♿ **W** msa.md.gov

🏛 William Paca House

186 Prince George St. **Tel** (410) 990-4543. **Open** 10am–5pm Mon–Sat, noon–5pm Sun (weekends only in winter). **Closed** Jan, Thanksgiving, Dec 24 & 25. 🦽 🎥 **W** annapolis.org

🏛 Hammond Harwood House

19 Maryland Ave at King George St. **Tel** (410) 263-4683. **Open** Apr–Oct: noon–5pm Tue–Sun; Nov–Dec: noon–4pm Tue–Sun. **Closed** Jan. 🦽
  W hammondharwoodhouse.org

❺ Baltimore

Chesapeake Bay, MD. 🏔 785,500. ℹ️ Inner Harbor West Wall (410) 837-4636. Visitor services (877) BALTIMORE. 🚆 🚌 **W** baltimore.org

There is much to do and see in this pleasant city. A good place to start is the Inner Harbor, the city's redeveloped waterfront, with the harborside complex of shops and restaurants. The centerpiece is the **National Aquarium**, which has many exhibits, including sharks, a seal pool, and a dolphin show. The Harbor is home to the **Maryland Science**

People walking along Baltimore's pleasant Inner Harbor promenade

Center, where "do touch" is the rule. The planetarium and an IMAX® theater thrill visitors with images of earth and space.

The **American Visionary Art Museum** has extraordinary works by self-taught artists whose materials range from matchsticks to faux pearls.

Uptown is the **Baltimore Museum of Art**, with its world-renowned collection of modern art, including works by Matisse, Picasso, Degas, and Van Gogh. There is also a large collection of Warhol pieces and two sculpture gardens featuring work by Rodin and Calder. Some galleries will be temporarily closed during a three-year renovation project.

The diversity of art at the **Walters Art Museum**, on Mount Vernon Square, includes pieces by Fabergé and Monet, among others; it is renowned for its ancient Egyptian art.

The Little Italy area is worth a visit for its knock-out Italian restaurants and also for the games of bocce ball (Italian lawn bowling) played around Pratt or Stiles Streets on warm evenings.

The eye-catching architecture of the National Aquarium, Baltimore

National Aquarium
501 E Pratt St, Pier 3, N side of Inner Harbor. **Tel** (410) 576-3800. **Open** Hours vary. Call ahead or check website for details. **Closed** Thanksgiving, Dec 25. aqua.org

Maryland Science Center
601 Light St. **Tel** (410) 685-5225. **Open** Hours vary. Call ahead or check website for details. **Closed** Thanksgiving, Dec 25. mdsci.org

American Visionary Art Museum
800 Key Highway at Inner Harbor. **Tel** (410) 244-1900. **Open** 10am–6pm Tue–Sun. **Closed** Mon, Thanksgiving, Dec 25. avam.org

Baltimore Museum of Art
N Charles St & 31st St. **Tel** (443) 573-1700. **Open** 10am–5pm Wed–Fri, 11am–6pm Sat & Sun. **Closed** Jan 1, Jul 4, Thanksgiving, Dec 25. artbma.org

Walters Art Museum
600 N Charles St. **Tel** (410) 547-9000. **Open** 10am–5pm Wed–Sun (8pm 1st Fri of month). **Closed** Jan 1, Memorial Day, Jul 4, Thanksgiving, Dec 24, 25. weekends. thewalters.org

❻ Gettysburg National Military Park

1195 Baltimore Pike, Gettysburg, Adams County, PA. **Tel** (717) 334-1124. Park: **Open** 6am–7pm daily (to 10pm Apr–Oct). Visitor Center: **Open** 8am–5pm daily (to 6pm Apr–Oct). **Closed** Jan 1, Thanksgiving, Dec 25. nps.gov/gett

This 6,000-acre park, south of the town of Gettysburg, Pennsylvania, marks the site of the three-

The Gettysburg Address

The main speaker at the dedication of the National Cemetery in Gettysburg on November 19, 1863 was the orator Edward Everett. President Lincoln had been asked to follow with "a few appropriate remarks." His two-minute, 272-word speech paid tribute to the fallen soldiers, restated his goals for the Civil War, and rephrased the meaning of democracy: "government of the people, by the people, for the people." The speech was inaudible to many, and Lincoln declared it a failure. However, once published, his speech revitalized the North's resolve to preserve the Union. Today it is known to every schoolchild in America.

Abraham Lincoln

day Civil War battle on July 1–3, 1863. It was the bloodiest event ever to take place on American soil, with 51,000 fatalities. A two- or three-hour driving tour begins at the visitor center. The National Cemetery, where Abraham Lincoln gave his Gettysburg Address, is opposite. Other sights include the Eternal Light Peace Memorial.

❼ Frederick

Frederick County, MD. 59,000. 19 E Church St (800) 999-3613, (301) 600-4046. **Open** 9am–5pm daily. **Closed** Jan 1, Easter, Thanksgiving, Dec 25. fredericktourism.org

Dating back to the mid-18th century, Frederick's historic center was renovated in the 1970s.

This charming town is a major antique center and home to hundreds of antique dealers. Its shops, galleries, and eateries are all in 18th- and 19th-century settings. Francis Scott Key, author of "The Star Spangled Banner," is buried in Mt. Olivet Cemetery.

❽ Antietam National Battlefield

Route 65, 10 miles (16 km) S of Hagerstown, Washington County, MD. **Tel** (301) 432-5124. **Open** Jun–Aug: 8:30am–6pm daily; Sep–May: 8:30am–5pm. **Closed** Jan 1, Thanksgiving, Dec 25. 🖼 🔊 🛆 **W** nps.gov/anti

One of the worst battles of the Civil War was waged here on September 17, 1862. There were 23,000 casualties but no decisive victory.

An observation tower offers a panoramic view of the battlefield. Antietam Creek runs peacefully under the costly Burnside Bridge. General Lee's defeat at Antietam inspired President Lincoln to issue the Emancipation Proclamation. The Visitors' Center movie recreating the battle is excellent.

John Brown's Fort in Harpers Ferry National Historic Park

❾ Harpers Ferry

171 Shoreline Dr, off Rte 340, Harpers Ferry, Jefferson County, WV. **Tel** (304) 535-6029. **Open** 8am–5pm daily. **Closed** Jan 1, Thanksgiving, Dec 25. 🖼 📷 spring–fall. **W** nps.gov/hafe

Nestled at the confluence of the Shenandoah and Potomac rivers in the Blue Ridge Mountains is

Harpers Ferry National Historical Park. The town was named for Robert Harper, a builder from Philadelphia who established a ferry across the Potomac here in 1761. There are stunning views from Maryland Heights to the foot of Shenandoah Street, near abolitionist John Brown's fort. Brown's ill-fated raid in 1859 on the Federal arsenal, established by George Washington, became tinder in igniting the Civil War.

The great importance of the town led to the area being designated a national park in 1944. It has been restored by the National Park Service.

❿ Great Falls Park

Georgetown Pike, Great Falls, Fairfax County, VA. **Tel** (703) 285-2965. **Open** daily (closes at dusk). 🖼 📷 🛆 **W** nps.gov/gwmp/grfa

The first view of the falls, near the visitor center, is breathtaking. The waters of the Potomac roar through a gorge of jagged rock over a 76-ft (23-m) drop at the point that divides Virginia's undulating Piedmont from the coastal plain. Only experienced kayakers are permitted to take to the turbulent whitewater below, which varies with rainfall upstream.

The park is crisscrossed by 15 miles (24 km) of hiking trails, some showing evidence of the commerce from the early 19th-century Patowmack, America's first canal. Guided nature walks are offered.

Situated just across the river, in Maryland, is the C&O Canal National Historical Park, entry to which is free for visitors to Great Falls Park.

The Red Fox Inn in Middleburg

⓫ Middleburg

Route 50, Loudoun County, VA. 🖼 600. **ℹ** Visitors' Center, 12 N Madison St. **Tel** (540) 687-8888. **Open** 11am–3pm Mon–Fri, 11am–4pm Sat–Sun. **W** middleburgonline.com

Horse and fox are king in this little piece of England in the Virginia countryside. Middleburg's history began in 1728, with Joseph Chinn's fieldstone tavern on the Ashby's Gap Road, still operating today as the Red Fox Inn. Colonel John S. Mosby and General Jeb Stuart met here to plan Confederate strategy during the Civil War.

The exquisite countryside has thoroughbred horse farms, some opening during the Hunt Country Stable Tour in May.

Foxcroft Road, north of the town, winds past immaculate horse farms. East of Route 50 is **Chrysalis Vineyard and Winery**. On the Plains Road at the west end of town is **Piedmont Vineyards**, and a mile east of Middleburg is **Swedenburg Winery**. All three have tours and tastings.

🍷 **Chrysalis Vineyard**
23876 Champe Ford Rd. **Tel** (540) 687-8222. **Open** 10am–5:30pm daily. **Closed** Jan 1, Thanksgiving, Dec 25. **W** chrysaliswine.com

🍷 **Piedmont Vineyards**
Off Route 626. **Tel** (540) 687-5528. **Open** by appt Mon–Fri, 11am–5pm Sat, Sun. **Closed** Jan 1, Thanksgiving, Dec 24, 25, 31. **W** piedmontwines.com

🍷 **Swedenburg Winery**
23595 Winery Lane. **Tel** (540) 687-5219. **Open** by appt Mon–Thu, 11am–5pm Fri–Sun. **Closed** Jan 1, Thanksgiving, Dec 25. **W** swedenburgwines.com

The roaring waterfalls in Great Falls Park

⓬ Steven F. Udvar-Hazy Center

Near Dulles International Airport, intersection of Rtes 28 and 50, Chantilly, VA. **Tel** (703) 572-4118. 🚌 Bus from Dulles International Airport. **Open** 10am–5:30pm daily (to 6:30pm May 25–Sep 3). **Closed** Dec 25. 🖉 Ⓦ nasm.si.edu/udvarhazycenter

This is a must for anyone who would like to view the Space Shuttles "Enterprise" and "Discovery," or who wants to find out about rockets and satellites, or see a rare Boeing B-29 Stratoliner. Opened in 2003 to coincide with the 100th anniversary of the Wright brothers' first powered flight, and named in honor of its major donor, this museum was built to display and also preserve historic aviation and space artifacts. The vast building of over 760,000 sq ft (7,000 sq m)

houses exhibit hangars with more than 300 aircraft and spacecraft. Visitors can walk among exhibits and view hanging aircraft from elevated walkways. As well as an education center and Imax® theater, a Wall of Honor offers a permanent memorial to those men and women who contributed to America's space exploration and aviation heritage.

⓭ Skyline Drive

Skyline Drive runs along the backbone of the Shenandoah National Park's Blue Ridge Mountains. Originally farmland, the government designated the area a national park in 1926. Deer, wild turkey, bears, and bobcats inhabit the park, and wildflowers, azaleas, and mountain laurel are abundant. The park's many hiking trails and its 75 viewpoints offer stunning natural scenery.

North entrance station

① **Pinnacles Overlook**
The view of Old Rag Mountain with its outcroppings of granite is spectacular.

② **Whiteoak Canyon**
The Whiteoak Canyon Trail passes six waterfalls on its route.

④ **Camp Hoover**
At the end of Mill Prong Trail, this 160-acre resort was President Hoover's weekend retreat until 1933, when he donated it to the Park.

0 kilometers 10
0 miles 10

③ **Big Meadows**
Close to the Visitor Center, this meadow is kept in its centuries-old state. It was probably kept clear by fire from lightning or Indians. Deer can easily be seen here.

⑤ **Bearfence Mountain**
Although it is a bit of a climb up this mountain, partly on rock scramble, it is not too difficult, and the reward is a breathtaking 360-degree view of the surrounding landscape.

⑥ **Lewis Mountain**
This awe-inspiring view from Lewis Mountain shows Shenandoah Valley in spring, when the lush scenery is interspersed with beautiful wildflowers.

Tips for Drivers

Starting points: north at Front Royal, central at Thornton Gap, south at Rockfish Gap.
Length: 105 miles (168 km), duration of 3–8 hrs depending on how many stops are taken.
When to go: Fall leaf colors draw crowds in mid-October. Wildflowers bloom through spring and summer.
What it costs: $15 per car, valid for 7 days ($10 Nov–Feb).

Key

--- Walk route
▬▬ Road

For additional map symbols *see back flap*

⑭ Charlottesville

Virginia. 🏔 41,000. 🚂 🚌 ℹ Visitors Bureau, 610 E Main St; Monticello Visitors Center, Route 20 South. **Tel** (434) 293-6789, (877) 386-1103 (toll free). **W** charlottesville.org

Charlottesville was Thomas Jefferson's hometown. It is dominated by the University of Virginia, which he founded and designed, and also by his home, **Monticello**.

Jefferson was a Renaissance man: author of the Declaration of Independence, US president, farmer, architect, inventor, and vintner. It took him 40 years to complete Monticello, beginning in 1769. It is now one of the most celebrated houses in the country. The entrance hall doubled as a private museum, and the library held a collection of around 6,700 books.

The grounds include a large terraced vegetable garden where Jefferson grew and experimented with varieties.

The obelisk over Jefferson's grave in the family cemetery lauds him as "Father of the University of Virginia." Tours of the house are available year round.

Vineyards and wineries surround Charlottesville. Michie Tavern, joined to the Virginia Wine Museum, has been restored to its 18th-century appearance, and serves a buffet of typical Southern food.

Montpelier, on a 2,500 acre (1000 ha) site 25 miles (40 km) to the north, was the home of former US president James Madison.

🏛 Monticello

Route 53, 3 miles (5 km) SE of Charlottesville. **Tel** (434) 984-9822. **Open** Mar–Nov: 9am–6pm; Dec–Feb: 10am–4pm. **Closed** Dec 25. 🎨 📷 ♿ 📷 **W** monticello.org

⑮ Fredericksburg

Virginia. 🏔 22,600. 🚂 🚌 ℹ Fredericksburg Visitor Center, 706 Caroline St. **Tel** (800) 678-4748. **Open** 9am–5pm Mon–Sat (to 7pm May–Aug), 11am–5pm Sun. **Closed** Jan 1, Dec 25. **W** visitfred.com

Fredericksburg's attractions are its historic downtown district, and four Civil War battlefields, including The Wilderness. The Rising Sun Tavern and Hugh

The elegant dining room at Kenmore House

Mercer Apothecary Shop offer living history accounts of life in a town that began as a port on the Rappahannock River. **Kenmore Plantation**, home of George Washington's sister, is famous for its beautiful rooms.

The visitor center offers useful maps as well as horse-and-carriage or trolley tours.

🏛 Kenmore Plantation

1201 Washington Ave. **Tel** (540) 373-3381. **Open** Mar–Oct: 10am–5pm daily; Nov, Dec: 10am–4pm daily. **Closed** Jan, Feb, Thanksgiving, Dec 24, 25, 31. **W** kenmore.org

George Washington's Ferry Farm
268 Kings Hwy. **Tel** (540) 370-0732. **Open** as above.

Monticello, Charlottesville

Situated in the leafy foothills of the Blue Ridge Mountains, this Palladian masterpiece was built between 1769 and 1809 by Thomas Jefferson.

East portico

The greenhouse was used by Jefferson to cultivate a variety of plants.

North piazza

Jefferson's bed straddles his cabinet (office) and bed chamber.

The entrance hall, where guests and visitors were greeted, is also a museum.

⑯ Richmond

Virginia. 🚇 202,000. 🚉 🚌
ℹ️ Richmond Metropolitan
Convention and Visitors Bureau,
405 N Third St. **Tel** (804) 783-7450. Toll
free 888-RICHMOND. **Open** 9am–5pm
Mon–Fri. 🅦 visitrichmondva.com

Richmond, the old capital of
the Confederacy (see p21), still
retains an Old South aura.
Bronze images of Civil War
generals punctuate Monument
Avenue. Brownstones and
Victorian houses testify to
this area's postwar prosperity.

The **Museum of the
Confederacy** contains Civil War
artifacts, including Robert E.
Lee's coat and sword. Another
popular museum is the
fascinating **Science Museum
of Virginia**.

The Neo-Classical State
Capitol, inside which is the life-
sized Houdon sculpture of
George Washington,
was designed by
Charles Louis
Clérisseau.

The **Virginia
Museum of Fine Arts**
has a fine collection
of world art and hosts
acclaimed special
exhibitions.

**Statue of Robert E. Lee
in Richmond**

🏛️ **Museum of the Confederacy**
1201 E Clay St. **Tel** (804) 649-1861.
Open 10am–5pm daily.
Closed Jan 1, Thanksgiving, Dec 25.
♿ 📷 🅦 moc.org

🏛️ **Science Museum of Virginia**
2500 W Broad St. **Tel** (804) 864-1400.
Open 9:30am–5pm Tue–Sat,
11:30am–5pm Sun.
Closed Thanksgiving, Dec 24 & 25.
♿ 📷 🅦 smv.org

🏛️ **Virginia Museum of
Fine Arts**
200 N Boulevard. **Tel** (804) 340-1400.
Open 10am–5pm Sat–Wed, 10am–
9pm Thu & Fri. 🅦 vmfa.state.va.us

⑰ Chesapeake Bay

🅦 baydreaming.com
ℹ️ Tilghman Island: 🅦 tilghman
island.com

Known as "the land of pleasant
living," Chesapeake Bay offers
historic towns, fishing villages,
bed-and-breakfasts, seafood

restaurants, beaches, wildlife,
and farmland. The Chesapeake
Bay Maritime Museum, in the
town of St. Michael's, depicts
life on the bay, both past and
present. **Tilghman Island**, in
mid Chesapeake, has the last
commercial sailing fleet in
North America and hosts a
seafood festival every June.

⑱ Chincoteague
and Assateague

Chincoteague, Accomack County, VA.
🚇 4,000. Assateague, Accomack
County, VA and MD (unpopulated).
🅦 nps.gov/asis ℹ️ Chincoteague
Chamber of Commerce, 6733 Maddox
Blvd. (757) 336-6161.
🅦 chincoteaguechamber.com

These sister islands offer
a wealth of natural beauty.
Chincoteague is a town
situated on the
Delmarva
(Delaware,
Maryland and
Virginia) Peninsula.
Assateague is an
unspoiled strip of
nature with an ocean
beach and hiking trails
that wind through
woods and marshes. It is
famously populated by wild
ponies, thought to be
descended from animals grazed
on the island by 17th-century
farmers. The woodlands and salt
marshes of Assateague attract
over 300 species of birds, and in
fall peregrine falcons and snow
geese fly in. Monarch butterflies
migrate here in October. There
are several campgrounds in the
area, and the ocean beach is
ideal for swimming and surf

fishing. **Toms Cove Visitor
Center** and **Chincoteague
Wildlife Refuge Center** can
provide extra information.

ℹ️ **Toms Cove Visitor Center**
Tel (757) 336-6577.

ℹ️ **Chincoteague
Wildlife Refuge Center**
Tel (757) 336-6122.

⑲ Yorktown and
Jamestowne

York County, VA, and James City
County, VA. ℹ️ York County Public
Information Office (757) 890-3300.

Established in 1607, Jamestowne was the first permanent
English settlement in America.
It has 1,500 acres of marshland
and forest, threaded with tour
routes. There are ruins of the
original English settlement and
a museum. There is a
recreation of James Fort, full-
scale reproductions of the
ships that brought the first
colonists to America and a
traditional Indian village.

Yorktown was the site of the
decisive battle of the American
Revolution in 1781. **Colonial
National Historical Park**'s
battlefield tours and exhibits
explain the siege at Yorktown.

🏛️ **Historic Jamestowne**
Tel (757) 856-1200.
Open 8:30am–4:30pm daily.
Closed Jan 1, Dec 25. ♿ 📷
🅦 historicjamestowne.org

🌳 **Colonial National
Historical Park**
Tel (757) 898-2410. **Open** 9am–5pm
daily. **Closed** Jan 1, Thanksgiving,
Dec 25. ♿ 🅦 nps.gov/colo

Historic Jamestowne, a re-creation of Colonial James Fort

⑳ Colonial Williamsburg

As Virginia's capital from 1699 to 1780, Williamsburg was the hub of the loyal British colony. After 1780 the town went into decline. Then in 1926, John D. Rockefeller embarked on a massive restoration project. Today, in the midst of the modern-day city, the 18th-century city has been re-created. People in colonial dress reenact the lifestyle of the original townspeople; blacksmiths, silversmiths, and cabinet makers show off their skills while horsedrawn carriages pass through the streets, providing visitors with a fascinating insight into America's past.

★ **Governor's Palace**
Originally built in 1720 by Governor Alexander Spotswood, the palace has been reconstructed in its full pre-Revolution glory.

0 meters 200
0 yards 200

Courthouse
Built in 1770–71 this was the home of the county court for more than 150 years.

Key
— Suggested route

Nursery
Costumed living-history interpreters work the land in Colonial Williamsburg using replica tools and the same techniques as the original settlers.

Fifes and Drums Displa
Revolutionary field music is recreated in these colorful parades. Local school children begin learning these instruments aged ten.

Print Office
This store stocks authentic 18th-century foods, including wine, Virginia ham, and peanuts.

Milliner
Owned by Margaret Hunter, the milliner shop stocked a wide range of items. Imported clothes for women and children, jewelry, and toys could all be bought here.

Raleigh Tavern
The Raleigh was once an important center for social, political and commercial gatherings. The original burned in 1859, but this reproduction has its genuine flavor.

★ Capitol
The capitol is a 1945 reconstruction of the original 1705 building. The government resided in the West Wing, while the General Court was in the East Wing.

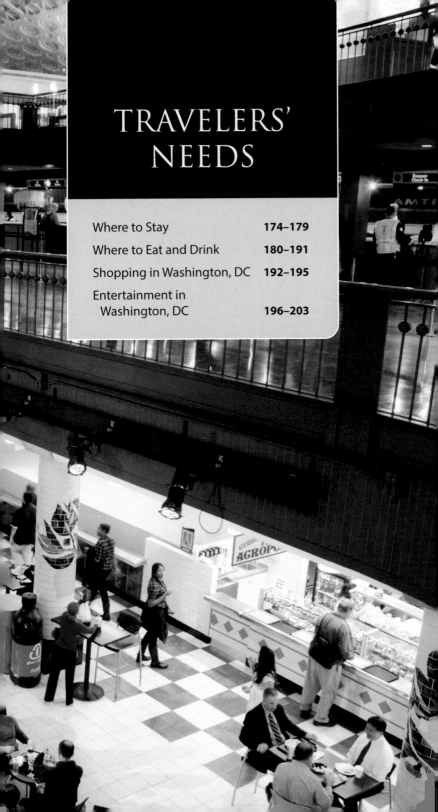

TRAVELERS' NEEDS

WHERE TO STAY

If you plan to be visiting the sights in Washington from dawn until midnight, you may simply need a roof over your head and a bed for your weary body. If you intend to take your time and relax, you may want to stay in a hotel with all the amenities: pool, health club, deluxe restaurant, and room service. Washington offers a wide range of accommodations. Generally, hotels that are closer to downtown and the Mall are more expensive, and those in the city suburbs are more affordable. Being a tourist destination as well as a business center, Washington's room rates are the second highest in the United States next to New York City. However, there are bargains to be had, especially during the off season and on weekends. A number of websites (see directory on p175) also offer special deals.

Lobby of the plush Capital Hilton *(see p178)*

How to Reserve

Many hotels have toll-free numbers for making reservations. It is also often possible to preview the accommodation options on the hotel's website. Weekend rates are often much cheaper than week-day rates.

Hotel Grading and Facilities

A five-star hotel will offer everything the visitor could wish for. Room service, health facilities, bathrooms with a Jacuzzi, valet parking, and 24-hour maid and butler service are just some of the luxury amenities provided, but at a price. At the opposite end of the spectrum, a one-star hotel will have a television and a telephone in the bedroom but may have shared bathrooms. Hotels of all price ranges are available in the city.

Discounts

Washington has different "seasons" from other cities. When the cherry blossoms around the Tidal Basin bloom in April, it is impossible to find a reasonably priced room in the city. Then in June the city is full of school groups taking end-of-the-year trips. Despite often broiling temperatures, families are lured to the capital in the summer. Labor Day in September is very big for tourists as is, of course, the Fourth of July.

However, you can find bargains during the winter months from November through March. Washington is a Monday-through-Friday convention town, so the best prices are on the weekend, often at a fraction of the vacation season, midweek rate.

Hidden Extras

Beware the hefty 14.5% tax levied on hotels in Washington. Also note that most establishments will invariably charge you extra for parking in the hotel's parking lot. There is no way to escape the tax, but you can shop around for a hotel with free parking. If you have to park your car in a garage, you may have to pay close to $40 per day.

Chains and Boutique Hotels

Staying at a **Hilton**, **Holiday Inn**, **Hyatt**, or **Marriott** hotel will guarantee a level of service and cleanliness mandated by the chain. An alternative to the large chain hotels are the increasingly popular boutique hotels. **Kimpton Hotels**, a national chain many of whose boutique hotels are housed in historic buildings, has several properties in Washington. These small, unique places all have their own character. The George Hotel on Capitol Hill *(see p176)*, for instance, is sleek and modern. It also houses Bistro Bis *(see p183)*, one of the city's most talked-about restaurants.

Other boutique hotels include the Henley Park *(see p177)*, which has the decor of a British aristocratic home and serves afternoon tea. The Morrison-Clark Inn *(see p177)* in Penn Quarter is a restored mansion filled with Victorian antiques. The Phoenix Park Hotel *(see p176)* on Capitol Hill has an Irish theme and staff – and a pub popular with Irish nationals and Irish-American politicians.

The George, a boutique hotel *(see p176)*

Business Travelers

Washington hotels accommodate the sophisticated communications needs of the business traveler. Wi-Fi is almost universally available in all rooms.

Bed-and-Breakfasts

Although bed-and-breakfast accommodations are not as popular in the United States as they are in Europe, both American and foreign travelers are increasingly seeking them out as an alternative to the more sterile and expensive hotels.

Bed-and-Breakfast Accommodations Ltd. matches visitors with the perfect room in a bed-and-breakfast, an apartment or small hotel, or even a private home. They have 85 properties in the city and suburbs, and charge a one-time booking fee of $10. The online booking service **airbnb.com** offers a wide selection of unfurnished apartments and rooms in private homes at reasonable rates.

Entrance to the Hay-Adams *(see p179)*

Budget Options

The best value accommodation option for young travelers in Washington is the welcoming **Hosteling International-Washington, DC**. It is located in the center of the city, in an area that is close to all major amenities and sights. Young travelers are advised to be cautious when returning after dark. The rate is around $40 per night for a bunk bed in a single-sex dormitory room.

Disabled Travelers

Nearly all the large, modern hotels are wheelchair accessible, but the independent hotels and bed-and-breakfasts may not be. Call in advance to ask about stairs, elevators, and door widths if you have special needs.

Children

Traveling with children may dictate your hotel reservations. There are many hotels, such as Sheraton Suites *(see p179)* and Georgetown Suites *(see p179)*, that have kitchens or kitchenettes and living rooms with sofabeds that provide space and privacy for parents. After walking around the Mall, children may crave a hotel with a pool or a game room. Consider a more expensive room in town rather than a less expensive room in the suburbs. The suburban rates may look appealing until you face a long drive to your hotel during Washington's rush hour.

Some hotels may ban children, but these are few and far between. More often than not hotels will be very accommodating toward young guests.

Recommended Hotels

Washington has a wide variety of accomodations for every type of traveler. The hotels listed on pages 176–9 are grouped under five categories: Bed-and-Breakfast, Boutique, Business, Family, and Luxury. For those with limited funds, bed-and-breakfast hotels might be a good choice. While there are relatively few within the city, many can be found farther from the Mall and the city center. Accommodations recommended for families may have special children's programs, games rooms, a pool, or suite arrangements that include a kitchen. Business hotels have a full range of amenities, although they are not in the luxury category. Luxury hotels have spas, concierge services, and large restaurants – at a price of more than $400 a night. Finally, boutique hotels are smaller and often have a theme, but perhaps without the splendor of the luxury options.

The historic Jefferson hotel *(see p178)*

Throughout the listings, notable accommodations from each category are highlighted as DK Choice. These hotels offer a special experience, because of their superb amenities, beautiful interiors, excellent restaurant, or a combination of these.

DIRECTORY

Special Deals

W hotels.com
W kayak.com
W priceline.com
W tripadvisor.com

Chain Hotels

Hilton
Tel (800) HILTONS.
W hilton.com

Holiday Inn
Tel (800) HOLIDAY.
W holidayinn.com

Hyatt
Tel (800) 233-1234.
W hyatt.com

Kimpton Hotels
Tel (800) 546-7866.
W kimptonhotels.com

Marriott
Tel (888) 236-2427.
W marriott.com

Bed-and-Breakfast

Bed-and-Breakfast Accommodations Ltd.
Tel (877) 893-3233 (toll free).
W bedandbreakfastdc.com

Budget Options

Hosteling International
1009 11th St, NW.
Tel (202) 737-2333.
W hiwashingtondc.org

Where to Stay

Bed-and-Breakfast

Capitol Hill

Maison Orleans $
414 5th St SE, 20003
Tel *544-3694*   **Map** 4 F5
Ⓦ bnblist.com
Housed in a beautiful 1902 Federal
row house, this hotel offers three
rooms furnished with antiques.

**The Carriage House on
Capitol Hill** $$
3rd and South Carolina Ave SE, 20003
Tel *(877) 893-3233*   **Map** 4 F5
Ⓦ bedandbreakfastdc.com
This hotel has four rooms with
private bathrooms. A continental
breakfast is served in the lovely
courtyard, weather permitting.

Penn Quarter

Hosteling International $
1009 11th St NW, 20001
Tel *737-2333*   **Map** 3 C2
Ⓦ hiwashingtondc.org
Over 200 dorm-style beds are
on offer at this lodging in a
gentrified neighborhood. Most
rooms have shared bathrooms.

Farther Afield

Adams Inn $
*1746 Lanier Place NW, Adams
Morgan, 20009*
Tel *745-3600*
Ⓦ adamsinn.com
Good budget choice in an
upmarket neighborhood. Not all
rooms have their own bathroom.

DK Choice

Kalorama Guest House $
*2700 Cathedral Ave NW,
Woodley Park, 20008*
Tel *588-8188*
Ⓦ kaloramaguesthouse.com

One of the best deals in the city,
this homey, comfortable B&B
has a choice of rooms with or
without a private bathroom. A
delicious breakfast is served,
and home-made chocolate
chip cookies are on offer later in
the day. The beds are very
comfortable, but there are no
TVs in the guest rooms.

The Swann House $$
*1808 New Hampshire Ave NW,
Dupont Circle, 20009*
Tel *265-4414*   **Map** 2 F1
Ⓦ swannhouse.com
The rooms in this stunning 19th-
century mansion all have private
bathrooms, some with a Jacuzzi,
and there is a swimming pool.

Beyond Washington

Atlantic Hotel $$
2 N Main St, Berlin, MD 21811
Tel *(410) 641-3589*
Ⓦ atlantichotel.com
A small, historic hotel offering
period charm, in a picture-
postcard town close to the
Maryland shore resorts. The
restaurant serves great seafood.

DK Choice

Colonial Houses $$
*136 East Francis St,
Williamsburg, VA 23187*
Tel *(800) 447-8679*
Ⓦ colonialwilliamsburg.com
These 18th-century houses,
right in the grounds of the
reconstructed colonial town
of Williamsburg, are furnished
with period reproductions.
Amenities include private
bathrooms and microwave
ovens, but do not expect the
spacious accommodations of a
modern hotel. Step out of the

front door to see people in
18th-century costume re-
enacting the former colonial
lifestyle on the unpaved streets.

Kenmore Inn $$
*1200 Princess Anne St,
Fredericksburg, VA 22401*
Tel *(540) 371-7622*
Ⓦ kenmoreinn.com
This nine-room establishment has
a gourmet restaurant that serves
an excellent Southern breakfast.

The Red Fox Inn $$$
*2 East Washington St,
Middleburg, VA 20117*
Tel *(540) 687-6301*
Ⓦ redfox.com
Antique furnishings, a hearty
breakfast, and a great restaurant
are on offer at this inn set in
Virginia hunt and wine country.

Boutique

Capitol Hill

Liaison $$
415 New Jersey Ave NW, 20001
Tel *638-1616*   **Map** 4 E3
Ⓦ affinia.com/laison
Part of the Affinia chain, Liaison
has an acclaimed restaurant,
rooftop pool, and attentive staff.

Phoenix Park Hotel $$
520 North Capitol St NW, 20001
Tel *(800) 824-5419*   **Map** 4 E3
Ⓦ phoenixparkhotel.com
A comfortable, historic hotel
with an Irish theme, above the
Dubliner restaurant *(see p183)*.

DK Choice

The George Hotel $$$
15 East St NW, 20001
Tel *347-4200*   **Map** 4 E3
Ⓦ hotelgeorge.com
This chic, modern Kimpton
hotel has state-of-the-art
rooms, an exemplary spa, the
excellent Bistro Bis restaurant,
and one of the city's best hotel
bars. With a hip political
theme, it is both eco-friendly
and pet-friendly, and hosts a
complimentary daily wine hour.

Luxurious bedroom in The Swann House, near Dupont Circle

Front entrance of the Hotel
Monaco in Alexandria

Penn Quarter

Henley Park Hotel $$
926 Massachusetts Ave NW, 20001
Tel *638-5200* **Map** 4 C2
Ⓦ henleypark.com
This English-style hotel serves an
elegant high tea in front of the
lobby fireplace.

Hotel Monaco $$$
700 F St NW, 20004
Tel *628-7277* **Map** 3 C3
Ⓦ monaco-dc.com
A National Historic Landmark
retrofitted into a colorful hotel
with a chic bar and restaurant.

DK Choice

Morrison-Clark Inn $$$
1015 L St NW, 20001
Tel *898-1200* **Map** 3 C2
Ⓦ morrisonclark.com
A well-appointed hotel, built in
1864 and filled with Victorian
antiques. Rooms vary from
standard doubles to two-room
parlor suites with marble
fireplaces and private balconies.
It has a lovely, wide veranda
and an excellent restaurant
serving Southern cuisine.

The White House and Foggy Bottom

Hotel Lombardy $$
2019 Pennsylvania Ave NW, 20002
Tel *828-2600* **Map** 2 E3
Ⓦ hotellombardy.com
A historic hotel with 1920s decor,
but modern amenities. Spacious
rooms and attentive service.

Georgetown

The Georgetown Inn $$
1310 Wisconsin Ave NW, 20007
Tel *333-8900* **Map** 1 C2
Ⓦ georgetowninn.com
An elegant hotel, but the rooms
overlooking the street can be
noisy. Good restaurant.

Farther Afield

The Churchill $$
*1914 Connecticut Ave NW,
Dupont Circle, 20009*
Tel *797-2000* **Map** 2 E1
Ⓦ thechurchillhotel.com
In a Beaux-Arts building, this cozy
hotel has full amenities, including
24-hour room service and a spa.

Palomar $$
2121 P St NW, Dupont Circle, 20037
Tel *448-1801* **Map** 2 E2
Ⓦ hotelpalomar.com
Large rooms and modern
decor feature here. Enjoy
outstanding dining and fine
drinks at Urbana restaurant.

Tabard Inn $$
1739 N St NW, Dupont Circle, 20036
Tel *331-8528* **Map** 2 F2
Ⓦ tabardinn.com
A quaint, romantic inn tucked
into a side street. Meals are served
by a fire. A favorite for brunch.

Topaz $$
1733 N St NW, Dupont Circle, 20036
Tel *(800) 775-1202* **Map** 2 F2
Ⓦ topazhotel.com
A Kimpton hotel with a wellness
theme, in-room spa treatments,
and a nightly wine reception.

Dupont Circle Hotel $$$
*1500 New Hampshire Ave, Dupont
Circle, 20009*
Tel *483-6000* **Map** 2 F2
Ⓦ doylecollection.com
This cosmopolitan hotel, part of
the Irish-owned Doyle Collection,
has a fitness center, attentive
service, and free Wi-Fi.

Hotel Rouge $$$
1315 16th St NW, Dupont Circle, 20036
Tel *(800) 738-1202* **Map** 3 B1
Ⓦ rougehotel.com
A hip, Kimpton retreat, decorated
in red. The fashionable Bar Rouge
hosts the Red Hot Happy Hour.

Beyond Washington

The Bavarian Inn $$
*164 Shepherd Grade Rd,
Shepherdstown, WV 25443*
Tel *(304) 876-2551*
Ⓦ bavarianinnwv.com
This romantic country chalet
overlooking the Potomac River has
gas fireplaces and whirlpool baths.

Boar's Head Inn $$
*200 Ednam Drive, Charlottesville,
VA 22903*
Tel *434-296-2181*
Ⓦ boarsheadinn.com
Owned by the University of
Virginia, this lovely inn in a
historic college town has a
golf course and a spa.

The Ashby Inn $$$
692 Federal St, Paris, VA 20130
Tel *540-592-3900*
Ⓦ ashbyinn.com
Every room is different at this
18th-century inn. It has a
Michelin-rated restaurant.

Hotel Monaco $$$
480 King St, Alexandria, VA 22314
Tel *703-549-6080*
Ⓦ monaco-alexandria.com
A signature Kimpton hotel, with
colorful, lavish decor, located on
historic King Street. Amenities
include a fitness center and a
good restaurant.

Lorien Hotel and Spa $$$
1600 King St, Alexandria, VA 22314
Tel *877-959-7436*
Ⓦ lorienhotelandspa.com
This luxury, eco-friendly hotel in
Old Town Alexandria has an
excellent spa.

Maryland Inn $$$
58 State Circle, Annapolis, MD 21401
Tel *410-263-2641*
Ⓦ historicinnsofmaryland.com
Three historic houses, full of
antiques, make up this hotel,
which offers 18th-century charm
amid 21st-century comfort.

Peabody Court Hotel $$$
612 Cathedral St, Baltimore, MD 21201
Tel *410-727-7101*
Ⓦ peabodycourthotel.com
Expect attentive service in this
old-world hotel. Good
promotional packages.

Business

Capitol Hill

Washington Court Hotel $$
525 New Jersey Ave NW, 20001
Tel *628-2100* **Map** 4 E3
Ⓦ washingtoncourthotel.com
This good-value hotel has
in-room Wi-Fi flatscreen TVs, a
restaurant, and offers special deals.

Hyatt Regency $$$
400 New Jersey Ave NW, 20001
Tel *737-1234* **Map** 4 E3
Ⓦ washingtonregency.hyatt.com
This 800-room hotel has full
amenities, including valet
parking and a large restaurant.

The Mall

L'Enfant Plaza Hotel $$$
480 L'Enfant Plaza SW, 20024
Tel *484-1000* **Map** 4 C4
Ⓦ lenfantplazahotel.com
This pet-friendly hotel has several
dining venues and a pool. Perfect
for visiting the Smithsonian.

For more information on types of hotels *see p175*

The comfortable, modern Four Seasons hotel in Georgetown

Mandarin Oriental $$$
1330 Maryland Ave SW, 20024
Tel *554-8588*   **Map** 4 C5
W mandarinoriental.com
Luxury and convenience at a price. The CityZen restaurant is one of the best in the city.

Penn Quarter

Grand Hyatt $$$
1000 H St NW, 20001
Tel *582-1234*   **Map** 3 C3
W grandwashington.hyatt.com
A huge convention hotel with an indoor pool, 32 meeting rooms, and a business center.

Loews Madison Hotel $$$
1177 15th St NW, 20005
Tel *862-1600*   **Map** 3 B2
W madisonhoteldc.com
This relatively small hotel offers a personal service. Each room has individual decor.

Renaissance Marriott $$$
999 9th St NW, 20001
Tel *289-0947*   **Map** 3 C2
W marriott.com
Popular for conferences, this hotel's amenities include a fitness center and several dining venues.

The Westin $$$
1400 M St NW, 20005
Tel *429-1700*   **Map** 3 B2
W westinwashingtondccitycenter.com
A large hotel with great weekend special deals, two full-service restaurants, plus a Starbucks.

The White House and Foggy Bottom

Capital Hilton $$$
1001 16th St NW, 20036
Tel *(885) 271-3621*   **Map** 2 B2
W hilton.com
A stylish hotel with a health club and spa services.

The Fairmont $$$
2401 M St NW, 20037
Tel *429-2400*   **Map** 2 E2
W fairmont.com
Amenities at The Fairmount include a state-of-the-art fitness center with an indoor pool and two restaurants.

Renaissance Mayflower $$$
1127 Connecticut Ave NW, 20036
Tel *347-3000*   **Map** 2 F3
W marriotthotels.com
Oozing historic charm, this hotel is a Washington landmark. Formal afternoon tea is served.

The Westin $$$
2350 M St NW, 20037
Tel *429-0100*   **Map** 2 E2
W westin.com
This hotel features modern decor and a full-service restaurant.

Georgetown

DK Choice

Four Seasons $$$
2800 Pennsylvania Ave NW, 20007
Tel *342-0444*   **Map** 2 D3
W fourseasons.com
A highly acclaimed hotel overlooking parkland and the Potomac River, the Four Seasons offers large rooms, a great bar, three fitness centers and world-class restaurants, and impeccable service. The modern decor includes over 1,500 artworks scattered across the hotel.

Farther Afield

Marriott Wardman Park $$
2660 Woodley Rd NW, Woodley Park, 20008
Tel *328-2000*
W marriott.com
A grand hotel with four dining venues, a pool, and a fitness center. Special packages on offer.

Omni Shoreham $$
2500 Calvert St NW, Woodley Park, 20008
Tel *234-0700*
W omnihotels.com
A luxurious hotel with 836 rooms, three dining venues, and a pool.

Beyond Washington

Hyatt Arlington $$
1325 Wilson Blvd, Arlington, VA 22209
Tel *703-525-1234*
W arlington.hyatt.com
This comfortable hotel offers hypoallergenic rooms on request.

The Jefferson $$
101 West Franklin St, Richmond, VA 23220
Tel *804-649-4750*
W jeffersonhotel.com
This elegant historic hotel offers excellent Southern hospitality and modern amenities.

Renaissance Harborplace $$$
202 East Pratt St, Baltimore, MD 21202
Tel *410-547-1200*
W marriott.com
A luxurious hotel offering large rooms and great views of Baltimore harbor. There is an extra fee for parking and Wi-Fi.

Ritz Carlton $$$
1250 South Hayes St, Pentagon City, VA 22202
Tel *703-415-5000*
W ritzcarlton.com
Plush and convenient, this hotel is minutes from downtown DC and the National Airport, with covered access to the Fashion City mall.

Family

Capitol Hill

Capitol Hill Hotel $$
200 C St NW, 20003
Tel *543-6000*   **Map** 4 F5
W capitolhillhotel.com
This all-suite hotel is pet-friendly and has kitchenettes. Good for long stays.

Courtyard Marriott $$
140 L St SE, 20002
Tel *479-0027*   **Map** 4 D2
W marriott.com
A stylish hotel, housed in a former bank, with comfortable rooms and an indoor pool. Check the website for special deals.

The Mall

Holiday Inn $$
550 C St SW, 20024
Tel *877-859-5095*   **Map** 4 D5
W holidayinn.com
Although a little worn, the Holiday Inn is in a good location and has a full restaurant service. All major attractions can be reached by foot.

Penn Quarter

Hotel Harrington $
436 11th St NW, 20004
Tel *628-8140*   **Map** 3 C3
W hotel-harrington.com
This funky hotel offers simple, family rooms at a reasonable price. It has both a full-service and a fast-food restaurant.

The White House and Foggy Bottom

One Washington Circle $$
1 Washington Circle NW, 20037
Tel 872-1680   **Map** 2 E3
w thecirclehotel.com
A modern hotel offering good-sized rooms with kitchenettes.

Georgetown

Holiday Inn $$
2101 Wisconsin Ave NW, 20007
Tel 338-4600   **Map** 1 C1
w holidayinn.com
This standard Holiday Inn has a complimentary shuttle service to the Metro and an outdoor pool.

Georgetown Suites $$$
1111 30th St NW, 20007
Tel 298-7800   **Map** 2 D2
w georgetownsuites.com
A hotel with spacious, modern suites and fully equipped kitchens.

Farther Afield

Days Inn $
4400 Connecticut Ave NW, Van Ness, 20008
Tel 244-5600
w daysinn.com
A basic motel with few amenities, but offering a good price.

Beyond Washington

Cacapon Resort State Park $
818 Cacapon Lodge Dr, Berkeley Springs, WV 25411
Tel 304-258-1022
w cacaponresort.com
Cabins, cottages, and bungalows in a state park with nature trails, horseback riding, and swimming.

Refuge Inn $
7058 Maddox Blvd, Chincoteague, VA 23336
Tel 757-336-5511
w refugeinn.com
A resort near the Chincoteague Wildlife Refuge, with a pool, fitness center, plus rental bikes to explore the wild seashore.

Wayside Inn $
7783 Main St, Middletown, VA 22645
Tel 540-869-1797
w alongthewayside.com
A basic inn with a full-service restaurant nestled in a village in the Shenandoah Valley.

Hyatt Regency Bethesda $$
7400 Wisconsin Ave, Bethesda, MD 20814
Tel 301-657-01234
w bethesda.hyatt.com
This hotel has a restaurant, a pool, and hypoallergenic rooms.

Sheraton Suites $$
801 North Saint Asaph St, Alexandria, VA 22314
Tel 1-703-836-4700
w starwoodhotels.com
An all-suite hotel with sofa beds, refrigerators, and microwaves.

Williamsburg Inn $$
136 East Francis St, Wiliamsburg, VA 23187
Tel 757-229-1000
w colonialwilliamsburg.com
Comfortable, spacious rooms with Regency-style furnishings are on offer at this country inn.

Luxury

Penn Quarter

Willard InterContinental $$$
1401 Pennsylvania Ave NW, 20004
Tel 628-9100   **Map** 3 B2
w washington.intercontinental.com
This historic hotel has hosted almost every US president.

The White House and Foggy Bottom

> **DK Choice**
>
> ### Hay-Adams $$$
> *800 16th St NW, 20006*
> **Tel** 638-6600   **Map** 3 B2
> **w** hayadams.com
> A neighbor of the White House, this historic 1920s hotel is elegant and well appointed. The 145 rooms include 21 luxury suites, some with a view of the Washington Monument.

The Jefferson $$$
1200 16th St NW, 20036
Tel 448-2300   **Map** 2 F2
w jeffersondc.com
This hotel has a quiet, refined ambience and 96 elegantly appointed rooms.

St. Regis $$$
923 16th St and K St NW, 20006
Tel 638-2626   **Map** 3 B2
w starwoodhotels.com
Founded in 1926, this supremely elegant hotel has a sophisticated bar and restaurant.

W Hotel $$$
515 15th St NW, 20004
Tel 661-2400   **Map** 3 B3
w wwashingtondc.com
A hip hotel that attracts dance crowds on the weekends. The rooftop bar has stunning views.

Georgetown

The Graham Hotel $$$
1075 Thomas Jefferson St NW, 20007
Tel 202-337-0900   **Map** 2 D3
w thegrahamgeorgetown.com
Luxury in the heart of Georgetown, with spacious, tranquil suites and a roof deck bar.

Farther Afield

The Fairfax $$$
2100 Massachusetts Ave NW, Embassy Row, 20008
Tel 293-2100   **Map** 2 E2
w fairfaxhoteldc.come
This splendid hotel is a favorite among the city's political elite.

Mansion on O Street $$$
2020 O St NW, Dupont Circle, 20036
Tel 496-2020   **Map** 2 E2
w omansion.com
A 19th-century mansion with quirky decor. Features hidden rooms and secret passages.

Beyond Washington

Inn at Little Washington $$
Middle St and Main St, Little Washington, VA 22747
Tel 540-675-3800
w theinnatlittlewashington.com
A sumptuous inn with extravagant decor, impeccable service, and a Michelin-starred restaurant.

The elegant dining room in The Jefferson hotel on 1200 16th St NW

For more information on types of hotels *see p175*

WHERE TO EAT AND DRINK

Joseph Alsop, a renowned Washington host of the early 1960s, routinely gave lavish dinner parties in his Georgetown home. When asked why he gave so many parties, Alsop replied that it was because Washington had no good restaurants. Today the capital rivals New York, offering restaurants of every cuisine and price range.

Washington's cosmopolitan population enjoys a wide array of cuisines, from Ethiopian to Vietnamese, with many new styles of "fusion food" in between. The seafood is also superb, freshly caught from the nearby waters of Chesapeake Bay. Crab and shellfish feature regularly on menus, especially in coastal areas outside the city.

Graffiato restaurant *(see p185)*

Places to Eat

Washington's restaurants are a reflection of its neighborhoods. Adams-Morgan has a mix of ethnic establishments, especially Salvadoran and Ethiopian, and cutting-edge cuisine. Perry's and Cashion's Eat Place *(see p190)* offer inventive fusion food with Asian and French influences, and the crowd is young and hip. An easy walk from the Mall, Washington's compact Chinatown in the Penn Quarter district has both expensive and moderately priced restaurants, such as the Spanish Jaleo *(see p184)*, Italian Graffiato, and Mexican Rosa Mexicana *(see p185)*. Few Asian restaurants have survived the gentrification of this area. Closer to the White House, a few of the old-guard stalwarts remain, including the historic Old Ebbitt Grill *(see p185)*, which specializes in superb regional seafood, and Georgia Brown's *(see p186)*, whose menu features Southern cuisine. Georgetown has a mix of expensive and inexpensive establishments. Good value can be found at Indian and

Vietnamese restaurants. More reasonable places, again mostly ethnic restaurants, are found closer to the Circle. The vortex of 14th Street and U Street has restaurants for a young crowd, including Eatonville, Busboys and Poets, and Marvin *(see p189)*.

All restaurants in Washington are air conditioned and most (except for a few located in historic buildings) are wheelchair accessible.

Reservations

Reservations may be necessary for popular restaurants; the most fashionable can get booked up weeks in advance. Call ahead if there is somewhere you really want to go. However, walk-in diners are expected in most places. You may be placed on a waiting list and expected to return at the appointed time or wait in the adjacent bar.

Prices and Paying

Restaurant prices range from the very cheap to the very expensive in Washington. Prices vary according to location, cuisine, and decor. All restaurants take major credit

cards, although street vendors and fast food places may only accept cash. Waiters rely on earnings from tips and a 15–20 percent tip is expected for good service in restaurants. The tip is not automatically added to the bill except in the case of large parties, which may incur an automatic 15 percent gratuity.

Unlike many European cities, the fixed-price meal is uncommon in Washington. Items are usually listed à la carte unless specified in the menu. Diners should expect to spend between $20 and $40 for dinner and a drink, including a tip, at a moderate restaurant. However, Indian, Ethiopian, Chinese, and Vietnamese restaurants are often considerably less expensive. You will generally be charged about 25 percent less for the same meal if you eat at lunchtime rather than in the evening, so visitors on a budget may choose to eat their main meal at lunchtime. Breakfasts are usually under $10 for bacon and eggs with coffee and juice, but some hotels include a free continental breakfast (rolls, coffee, and juice) in the cost of the room.

Chic interiors of Cashion's Eat Place in the Adams-Morgan neighborhood *(see p183)*

Mural on the side of Madam's Organ bar in Adams-Morgan *(see p189)*

Opening Hours

It is unusual for a restaurant to be open 24 hours, except for those in very large hotels. Restaurants also rarely serve food continuously throughout the day; they usually have a break of several hours after lunch. Most restaurants are open all year (except Thanksgiving and Christmas Day) but a few may be closed on Sunday or Monday. It is best to call in advance. Restaurants often open for dinner between 5pm and 6pm, with the busiest period usually between 7pm and 8pm. The last seating is often at 9pm, and the last customers usually leave by 11pm. Bars are open until 2am. Remember that Metrorail trains stop running at 2am on Friday and Saturday, and at midnight the rest of the week.

Alcohol

Restaurants are required by law to have a liquor license in order to sell alcohol, so you will notice that some do not offer it. Others may serve beer and wine only but not hard liquor or mixed drinks.

Bars rarely serve food other than perhaps some appetizers. Other restaurants may have a separate bar as well as a dining section. Patrons are not permitted to bring their own drinks to a restaurant. The drinking age in DC, in Maryland, and in Virginia is 21. Restaurateurs can and will ask for proof of age in the form of a driver's license or passport since the penalty for serving alcohol to underage drinkers is severe.

Smoking

In the Districts of Columbia and Maryland smoking is not permitted in restaurants or any public buildings. The Smoke-free Workplace law came into effect in 2006 and extended to restaurants in 2007. If caught smoking, you could be fined several hundred dollars.

In the District of Virginia smoking is prohibited in many public buildings although some restaurants allow smoking but must have a designated no-smoking area.

Dress Code

Dress varies from the very casual (shorts, t-shirt, and sneakers) to the very formal. In some restaurants men will not be admitted without a jacket and tie (the maître d' may have spares). But as a general guide, the more expensive the restaurant, the more formal the dress code will be. Some bars also have a very strict dress code, and customers may not be admitted in very casual dress. Respectable but casual attire is acceptable in the majority of establishments.

What to Eat

Washington's cuisine is immensely multicultural, and you will find French, Chinese, Ethiopian, and Vietnamese restaurants, among others. The hot dog vendors along the Mall offer an alternative to a sit-down meal. Like in many cities in the US, Washington has a proliferation of reasonably priced food trucks that assemble at various places throughout the day, including tourist areas (track them on foodtruckfiesta.com).

Children

The best indication as to whether children are welcome in a restaurant is the presence of a children's menu or the availability of high chairs. When dining in more formal places with children, it is best to reserve the earliest seating when the restaurant will not be too busy.

Wheelchair Access

Restaurants are not required to be wheelchair accessible. In general, restaurants in older neighborhoods like Dupont Circle and Adams-Morgan are less likely to accommodate wheelchairs than modern establishments on K Street. The Smithsonian Museum restaurants are all accessible for the disabled.

Recommended Restaurants

Washington has a broad spectrum of dining choices, ranging from food trucks to haute cuisine establishments. The restaurants listed on pages 183–91 include reasonably priced ethnic options, regional American cuisine, fine dining, and fast food establishments for busy families. From burgers and pizza to Ethiopian *wat* (stew), served on top of *injera* (flatbread), and Chesapeake Bay crab cakes, Washington has a plate for every palate.

Throughout the listings, DK Choice recommendations are highlighted in each area of the city. These offer the traveler a special experience and an insight into Washington, such as excellent local cuisine, dining in a historic building, superb ethnic food, a venue particularly popular with locals, or a fun and unusual setting such as a combination of restaurant, bookstore, and performance space.

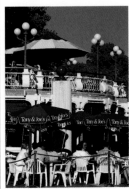

Tony and Joe's Seafood Place on the side of Washington harbor *(see p189)*

The Flavours of Washington, DC

Washington is a place where everyone has an opinion, and culinary preferences are no exception. For some it's a power dining town, where châteaubriand is the dish of choice and "two-martini lunches" are common. Others would point to nearby Chesapeake Bay, and its delectable seafood dishes that appear on many menus. Still others would see the city's vibrant ethnic communities as the key to current food trends. There's no disagreement, however, that DC's dining scene reflects the diversity of the city. As well as drawing on the bountiful harvest of the Atlantic, the city's chefs also make good use of seasonal, local produce from the farms of Maryland and Virginia.

Chef adding finishing touches to a dish at Founding Farmers (see p186)

Global Flavours

As the capital of the United States, Washington has long served as a gathering place for leaders and dignitaries from across the country and around the world, who have brought their own recipes and culinary traditions to the city. Refugees from places such as El Salvador, Ethiopia, and Cambodia have settled in Washington, introducing its well-traveled, globally-minded citizens to unusual flavors and dishes. In such ethnically diverse neighborhoods as Adams-Morgan or Mount Pleasant, it's not unusual to find African, Asian, and South American restaurants standing side by side.

Power Dining

True to its reputation, the city boasts an impressive collection of "power dining" restaurants, where lobbyists, pundits, and lawyers gather for steaks and cocktails. Slip into a cozy booth at one of these reputed steakhouses and you're likely to spot at least a few members of the United States Congress.

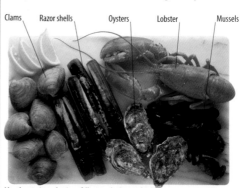

Clams — Razor shells — Oysters — Lobster — Mussels

Mouthwatering selection of Chesapeake Bay seafood

Washington's Signature Dishes

Maryland crab cakes

The unique nature of the capital makes it difficult to pin down its specialty dishes. The *Washington Post* has made a case for the "half-smoke," a mildly spicy hybrid of hot dog and smoked sausage, smothered in chili and cheese and often sold in sidewalk kiosks. Ben's Chili Bowl (see p189), is the best known purveyor, and a favorite of comedian Bill Cosby. Maryland Blue Crabs are also popular, often appearing as succulent crab cakes or tangy She-Crab Soup. The federal side of the city could be summed up with Senate Navy Bean Soup which has been served every day in the Senate Dining Room for more than 100 years. It's a humble, unassuming dish, and yet it is eaten on a regular basis by some of Washington's most influential residents.

Senate Navy Bean Soup uses navy (haricot) beans and ham hock to make a delicious, simple yet hearty soup fit for Senators.

Where to Eat and Drink

Capitol Hill

Banana Café $
Cuban **Map** 4 F5
500 8th St SE, 20003
Tel 543-5906
Enjoy a taste of the Carribean at reasonable prices. Occasional live music.

Five Guys $
American **Map** 4 E5
1100 New Jersey Ave SE, 20003
Tel 863-0570
This national chain started in Virginia. The burgers are often voted as the best in the country.

Market Lunch $
American **Map** F F4
Eastern Market, 225 7th St SE (at C St), 20003
Tel 547-8444
Crab cakes, local seafood, and excellent pancakes are served in a no-nonsense setting. Expect lines on weekends.

Bullfeathers $$
American **Map** F E5
410 1st St SE, 20003
Tel 488-2701
This restaurant-bar popular with local workers is known for its burgers and Trivia Night.

Cava Mezze $$
Mediterranean **Map** 4 F5
527 8th St SE, 20003
Tel 543-9090 **Closed** *Mon*
Incredible small plates and outstanding gyros are on offer here. The place is always packed.

Dubliner $$
Irish **Map** 4 E3
520 North Capitol St NW, 20001
Tel 737-3773
A favorite of Washington's Irish community, Dubliner serves generous helpings of pub food.

Ethiopic $$
Ethiopian **Map** 4 F3
401 H St NE, 20002
Tel 675-2066
A fresh, friendly addition to the city's Ethiopian culinary scene, with a pleasant dining room that overlooks the buzzing H Street.

Good Stuff Eatery $$
American **Map** 4 F5
303 Pennsylvania Ave SE, 20003
Tel 543-8222 **Closed** *Sun*
Great burgers and fries, including the Obama Burger. First Lady Michelle Obama is a patron.

Sonoma $$
Italian **Map** 4 F3
223 Pennsylvania Ave SE, 20003
Tel 544-8088
Great for sharing a big meal of locally sourced products. Elegant seating downstairs and casual dining upstairs.

Tortilla Coast $$
Mexican **Map** 4 F5
329 Pennsylvania Ave SE, 20003
Tel 542-6768
A friendly atmosphere and Tex-Mex food are the draw here. Kids will enjoy the burritos, and adults, the frozen margaritas.

DK Choice

Tunnicliff's $$
American **Map** 4 F5
222 7th St SE, 20003
Tel 544-5680
Next to the Eastern Market, Tunnicliff's is a Washington institution – a popular, historic tavern that serves "stick-to-your-ribs" dishes, such as boar stew, and other hearty fare including burgers, *quesadillas*, and pizzas, as well as many beers on tap. Outdoor dining in summer and cozy indoor seating in winter.

Price Guide

Prices are based on a three-course meal per person, including tax, service, and half a bottle of house wine.

$	up to $20
$$	$20–$40
$$$	over $40

We, the Pizza $$
Italian **Map** 4 F5
305 Pennsylvania Ave SE, 20003
Tel 544-4008 **Closed** *Sun*
Known for their pizzas cooked in cast-iron pans, which some say are the best in the city. Also serves pasta, salads, and ice-cream.

Acqua Al 2 $$$
Italian **Map** 4 F5
212 7th St, 20003
Tel 525-4375 **Closed** *Mon*
A duplicate of the flagship Acqua Al 2 in Florence, Italy. Pricey and crowded, but offers authentic fare.

Belga Café $$$
Belgian **Map** 4 F5
514 8th St SE, 20003
Tel 544-0100
A rare Belgian restaurant with a great selection of beer and, of course, mussels.

Bistro Bis $$$
French **Map** 4 E3
15 E St NW, 20001
Tel 661-2700
Upscale dining in the classy Hotel George Bistro Bis. Excellent duck and lamb dishes, and cream puffs.

The Monocle $$$
American **Map** 4 E3
107 D St NE, 20002
Tel 546-4488
A solid seafood and steak establishment near the Capitol. It gets crowded when Congress is in session.

Montmartre $$$
French **Map** 4 F5
327 7 St, SE 20003
Tel 544-1244 **Closed** *Mon*
A casual neighborhood restaurant right across from Eastern Market, Montmartre is a favorite for brunch.

Toscana Café $$$
Italian **Map** 4 F3
601 2nd St NE, 20002
Tel 525-2693
This is a small, hole-in-the wall eatery behind Union Station, but it serves authentic Tuscan cuisine. Reservations are needed as seating is limited in the tiny dining room.

Outdoor dining at the Bullfeathers restaurant-bar

For more information on types of restaurants *see p181*

The Mall

Atrium Café $
American   **Map** 3 C4
400 Virginia Ave SW, 20560
Tel 863-7590
Tucked away in L'Enfant Plaza, this tiny deli offers big, inexpensive sandwiches.

Cascade Café $$
American   **Map** 4 D4
4th St & Constitution Ave NW, 20565
Tel 712-7458
High-class cafeteria food in a stunning setting within the National Gallery of Art.

DK Choice

Mitsitam Café $$
American   **Map** 4 D4
4th St & Independence Ave SW, 20565
Tel 866-868-7774
Probably the most unusual, and one of the best restaurants in DC. Located in the National Museum of the American Indian, this café serves Native American cuisine from many tribes. The menu changes seasonally, but always includes bison and salmon. The Value Meal is a five-tribe sampler that is enough for two to share.

Pavilion Café $$
American   **Map** 4 D4
4th St & Constitution Ave NW, 20565
Tel 289-3360
Enjoy sandwiches and salads in the National Gallery's Sculpture Garden. Wine is available too.

CityZen $$$
American   **Map** 3 C5
1330 Maryland Ave SW, 20024
Tel 787-6006   **Closed** *Sun & Mon*
The 3-hour, 6-course tasting menu includes fish, lamb, and vegetarian options.

Penn Quarter

Chipotle $
Mexican   **Map** 3 C3
601 F St NW, 20005
Tel 347-4701
One of the few Mexican chains in the city. Stop here for fresh and cheap giant burritos.

District of Pi $
Italian   **Map** 3 C3
901 F St NW, 20004
Tel 393-5484
Choose between the thick-crust "Chicago" or the thin-crust

Entrance of the popular Carmines on 7th Street NW

St. Louis pizza. District of Pi is big, noisy, and popular with families.

Full Kee $
Chinese   **Map** 4 D3
509 H St NW, 20001
Tel 371-2233
Inexpensive, authentic Hong Kong-style food at one of the last Chinese restaurants in the area.

Luke's Lobster $
Seafood   **Map** 3 C3
624 E St NW, 20004
Tel 347-3355
A tiny, shack-like restaurant serving unmatched lobster rolls.

Merzi $
Indian   **Map** 3 C3
415 7th St NW, 20004
Tel 656-3794
Healthy Indian food that is ideal for a fast lunch or a reasonably priced dinner.

Paul Bakery $
French   **Map** 3 C3
801 Pennsylvania Ave NW, 20004
Tel 524-4500
The DC branch of a famous French bakery offers takeouts as

well as sit-down brunches. Try the ham and cheese crepe.

Austin Grill $$
Mexican   **Map** 3 C3
750 E St NW, 20004
Tel 393-3776
Better than a chain, but not as good, or as expensive, as some of its Penn Quarter competitors. Great for children.

Carmines $$
Italian   **Map** 3 C3
425 7th St NW, 20004
Tel 737-7770
The DC branch of the Manhattan classic. Huge, family-style place serving large portions.

District Chophouse & Brewery $$
American   **Map** 3 C3
509 7th St 20002
Tel 347-3434
Burgers, giant salads, and huge plates of seafood and beef are served here with handcrafted ales.

DK Choice

Jaleo $$
Spanish   **Map** 3 C3
480 7th St, NW 20004
Tel 628-7949
Owned by chef José Andrés, this restaurant offers some of the best tapas and sangria in the city. The menu changes often, keeping Jaleo fresh and witty, while retaining the old favorites such as spinach with pine nuts and chorizo.

Oyamel $$
Mexican   **Map** 3 C3
401 7th St NW, 20004
Tel 628-1005
Enjoy a creative and modern menu at this popular Mexican

Eye-catching exterior of the Pavilion Café at the National Gallery joint. The guacamole is made fresh to your taste. Great margaritas.

Proof
American $$
775 G St NW, 20001
Tel *737-7663*   Map 3 C3
Chic, contemporary cuisine and an impressive wine list. The entrées are excellent.

Rasika
Indian $$
633 D St NW, 20004   Map 4 D3
Tel *637-1222*   **Closed** *Sun*
High-end Indian cuisine served in a modern setting. Regional dishes plus traditional *tandoori* (cooked in a clay oven) and *sigri* (open barbecue).

Rosa Mexicana
Mexican $$
575 7th St NW, 20004   Map 3 C3
Tel *783-5522*
Fresh Mexican food served outdoors. Very popular, so expect a wait without a reservation.

Teaism
Japanese $$
400 8th St NW, 20004   Map 3 C3
Tel *638-6010*
Choose one of the many varieties of tea as an accompaniment to your delicate Japanese Bento box. The salty oat cookies are a winner.

Zaytinya
Mediterranean $$
701 9th St NW, 20001   Map 3 C3
Tel *638-0800*
Another restaurant by renowned chef José Andrés. Stop here for Mediterranean tapas in a glamorous setting.

Acadiana
American $$$
901 New York Ave NW, 20004   Map 3 C2
Tel *408-8848*
A classy evocation of New Orleans serving amazing gumbo, turtle soup, and oysters. The brunch is excellent.

Brasserie Beck
Belgian $$$
1101 K St NW, 20005   Map 3 C2
Tel *408-1717*
Owned by local star chef, Robert Wiedmaier, Brasserie Beck serves *moules frites* and around 100 types of Belgian beer.

Fogo de Chao
Brazilian $$$
1101 Pennsylvania Ave NW, 20004   Map 3 C3
Tel *347-4668*
This all-you-can-eat Brazilian eatery is a meat lover's dream. Just signal the attending

Elegant dining room at Acadiana

waiter to receive an unlimited supply of pork or beef.

Graffiato
Italian $$$
707 6th St NW, 20004   Map 3 C3
Tel *289-3600*
Top chef Mike Isabella serves his Italian-American grandmother's recipes. Great pizza and pasta. Patrons rave about the pepperoni sauce.

Oceanaire
Seafood $$$
1201 F St NW, 20004   Map 3 C3
Tel *347-2277*
This is a branch of the upscale national chain that specializes in excellent seafood including lobster and crab cakes.

Old Ebbitt Grill
American $$$
675 15th St NW, 20005   Map 3 B3
Tel *347-4800*
Stop at Washington DC's oldest saloon for traditional American fare. Old Ebbitt Grill specializes in seafood, including outstanding crab cakes, and steak.

Diners in the Mediterranean-style Zaytinya restaurant

Poste
French $$$
555 8th St NW, 20004   Map 3 C3
Tel *783-6060*
Enjoy great cocktails complemented by small plates such as sliders and fries at this bar in the stylish Hotel Monaco.

The Source
Asian $$$
575 Pennsylvania Ave NW, 20001   Map 3 D4
Tel *637-6100*
Wolfgang Puck's pricey Asian fusion restaurant is located on the first floor of the Newseum.

The White House and Foggy Bottom

City Bites
American $
1800 G St NW, 20006   Map 2 E3
Tel *289-1820*
This tiny deli whips up delicious sandwiches and salads. Open for breakfast and lunch only.

Cone E. Island
American $
2000 Pennsylvania Ave NW, 20006   Map 2 E3
Tel *822-8460*
A loud, tiny ice-cream shop on the campus of George Washington University.

Johnny Rockets
American $
2000 Pennsylvania Ave NW, 2006   Map 2 E3
Tel *822-1260*
A franchise of great burger, fries, and shake joints that echo the 1950s.

Potbelly Sandwich Shop
American $
1701 Pennsylvania Ave, 20004   Map 2 F4
Tel *775-1450*
Huge sandwiches, and a "skinny" menu with 30 percent fewer calories for the diet-conscious.

For more information on types of restaurants *see p181*

Façade of the sprawling Founding Farmers restaurant on Pennsylvania Avenue

Aroma $$
Indian   Map 3 E3
1919 I St NW, 20037
Tel *833-4700*   **Closed** *Sun*
Tandoori, *biryani* (a rice-based
dish), and *vindaloo* (a spicy curried
dish) feature on the menu in this
traditional Indian restaurant.

Bayou $$
American   Map 2 D3
2519 Pennsylvania Ave NW, 20037
Tel *223-6941*
A casual New Orleans restaurant
with an easy vibe, live music,
and Southern fare.

Firefly $$
American   Map 3 A1
1310 New Hampshire Ave NW, 20036
Tel *861-1310*
Comfort food such as *matzoh*
(dumplings) soup and pot
roast can be enjoyed here.
Great brunch.

McFadden's $$
Irish   Map 2 D3
2401 Pennsylvania Ave NW, 20037
Tel *223-2338*
One of a chain of Irish-themed
bars that cater to the college
crowd, serving beer and burgers.

Helpful waiting staff at Firefly, a restaurant
serving American comfort food

One Fish, Two Fish $$
Asian   Map 2 D3
2423 Pennsylvania Ave NW, 20037
Tel *882-0977*
Reliably good sushi and other
Asian standards such as curries
and pan-fried noodles.

The Public Bar $$
American   Map 3 F2
1214 18th St, 20036
Tel *223-2200*
A popular sports bar serving
wings, chips, and burgers. Large
crowds come to watch games.

Ancora $$$
Italian   Map 2 D3
600 New Hampshire Ave NW, 20037
Tel *333-1600*
Tucked into the Watergate,
Ancora is chef Robert Kinkead's
take on contemporary Italian
cuisine. Pair it with a night at the
nearby Kennedy Center.

Blue Duck Tavern $$$
American   Map 2 E3
1201 24th St NW, 20037
Tel *419-6755*
Consistently rated as one of the
best restaurants in DC, this trendy
spot has a wood-burning oven.
The duck, of course, is a specialty.

The Bombay Club $$$
Indian   Map 2 F3
815 Connecticut Ave NW, 20006
Tel *659-3727*
Refined Indian cuisine by the
Rasika group. Fancy setting close
to the White House; one of Bill
Clinton's favorite eateries.

DK Choice

Founding Farmers $$$
American   Map 2 F3
1924 Pennsylvania Ave NW, 20006
Tel *822-8783*
Everything at Founding Farmers
is organic, sustainable, and
made from scratch. The
ingredients are high quality,
seasonal, and locally sourced.
The resolutely American menu
includes Yankee pot roast,
shrimp and grits, and chicken
pot pie. Vegetarians are well-
catered to as well. The delicous
apple pie and red velvet cake
are universal favorites.

Georgia Brown's $$$
American   Map 3 B3
950 15th St NW, 20005
Tel *393-4499*
Located near the White House,
serving Lowcountry cuisine to a
clientele that includes high-
powered politicians.

Marcel's $$$
Belgian   Map 2 D3
2401 Pennsylvania Ave NW, 20037
Tel *296-1166*
This restaurant has impeccable
service and a great menu. It
offers a free shuttle service to
the Kennedy Center for the
pre-theater crowd.

Rasika West End $$$
Indian   Map 2 E3
1190 New Hampshire Ave NW, 20037
Tel *466-2500*
Modern Indian cuisine. The
highly rated menu is rivaled by
the dining room's elegant decor.

Roof Terrace Restaurant $$$
American   Map 2 D3
2700 F St NW, 20037
Tel *416-8555*   **Closed** *Mon*
A casual eatery on the roof of the
Kennedy Center with skyline
views. Popular with theatergoers.

Vidalia $$$
American   Map 3 A2
1990 M St NW, 20036
Tel *659-1990*
A high-end restaurant with
Southern roots. Sweetbreads,
shrimp and grits, duck, and the
Pie Plate are specialties.

Westend Bistro $$$
American Map 2 E3
1150 22nd St NW, 20037
Tel *974-4900*
A popular restaurant located in the chic Ritz-Carlton hotel. The deceptively simple but sophisticated menu includes *tuna carpaccio* and flat iron steaks.

Georgetown

Booeymonger $
American Map 1 C2
3265 Prospect St NW, 20007
Tel *333-4810*
Consistently rated as the best in "cheap eats." Offers great sandwiches, sides, and soups.

Café Divan $
Turkish Map 1 C2
1834 Wisconsin Ave NW, 20007
Tel *338-1747*
Well-priced Turkish food served in a stylish dining room, or as a takeout. Excellent doner kebabs and meze platter.

Five Guys $
American Map 1 C2
1335 Wisconsin Ave, 20007
Tel *337-0400*
A franchise of the family-favorite burger chain. Unlimited peanuts, and excellent burgers and fries.

Johnny Rockets $
American Map 2 D2
3131 M St NW, 20007
Tel *333-7994*
Part of a kitschy 1950s-themed chain that whips up great burgers, fries, and milkshakes.

ShopHouse Southeast Asian Kitchen $
Pan-Asian Map 2 D2
2805 M St NW, 20007
Tel *627-1958*
Build yourself a satisfying budget meal from rice or noodles, meat or tofu, vegetables, and toppings.

Sweetgreen $
American Map 1 C2
3333 M St, 20007
Tel *337-9339*
One of a small local chain that serves custom-made salads and superb frozen yogurt.

Café Bonaparte $$
French Map 1 C2
1522 Wisconsin Ave NW, 20007
Tel *333-8830*
A tiny bistro-bar serving crepes, *croques monsieur* (grilled ham and cheese sandwiches), and classic coffees. Ample choice for brunch or dessert.

Café La Ruche $$
French Map 2 D3
1039 31st St NW, 20007
Tel *965-2684*
A venerable café with classic bistro cuisine and delectable pastries. Sit on the patio with a coffee.

Chadwick's $$
American Map 1 C3
3025 K St NW, 20007
Tel *333-2565*
Away from the tourist crowd, this homey restaurant-sports bar has burgers, beers, and sides such as artichoke dip and potato skins.

Das Ethiopian Cuisine $$
Ethiopian Map 2 D2
1201 28th St NW, 20007
Tel *333-4710*
A range of meat, seafood, and vegetable entrées are on the menu here. Samplers are available for the uninitiated.

El Centro D.F. $$
Mexican Map 2 D2
1218 Wisconsin Ave NW, 20007
Tel *333-4100*
Outstanding tacos, *carnitas*, and margaritas at the Georgetown branch of this Mexican favorite.

Kafe Leopold $$
Austrian Map 1 C3
3315 M St NW, 20007
Tel *965-6005*
A beautiful café in a stunning setting near the canal. Artfully prepared small entrées, stellar desserts, and coffee.

DK Choice

Martin's Tavern $$
American Map 1 C2
1264 Wisconsin Ave NW, 20007
Tel *333-7370*
This Washington institution has been in the Martin family for four generations. Stop here for comfort food, including oyster stew, welsh rarebit, and burgers. For an

Colorful interior of the Italian restaurant Paolo's

intimate dinner sit in the "dugout" – a cozy space at the rear of the bar. This is where famous politicians have been known to eat and drink, and where JFK proposed to Jackie. Great atmosphere.

Le Pain Quotidien $$
French Map 2 D2
2815 M St NW, 20007
Tel *315-5420*
A *boulangerie* (bakery) chain that has both takeout and dine-in at communal tables. Great brunch.

Paolo's $$
Italian Map 1 C2
1303 Wisconsin Ave NW, 20007
Tel *333-7353*
Italian fare made California style. Great for people-watching, especially in the outdoor café.

Patisserie Poupon $$
French Map 1 C2
1645 Wisconsin Ave NW, 20007
Tel *342-3248* **Closed** Mon
A classic bistro-bakery with light fare including sandwiches, salads, and irresistible desserts. Possibly the best croissants outside of Paris.

Alfresco dining at Kafe Leopold, Georgetown

For more information on types of restaurants *see p181*

Patrons enjoying a meal on the patio of Café Milano, Georgetown

Paul $$
French   Map 1 C2
1078 Wisconsin Ave NW, 20007
Tel *524-4630*
An outstanding bakery with a small café serving croissants, sandwiches, and quiches.

Pizzeria Paradiso $$
Italian   Map 1 C2
3282 M St NW, 20007
Tel *337-1245*
Known for its artful thin-crust pizza and plethora of toppings, this pizzeria also has a large beer menu. Always crowded.

Puro $$
American   Map 1 C2
1529 Wisconsin Ave NW, 20007
Tel *787-1937*   **Closed** *Mon*
Nestled among the boutiques in Georgetown, Puro serves salads and tapas, plus Moroccan tea and special coffees.

Serendipity 3 $$
American   Map 1 C2
3150 M St NW, 20007
Tel *333-5193*
The DC branch of the venerable New York Serendipity, known for comfort food in huge portions and generous ice-cream sundaes.

The elegant Middleburg Room at 1789, roofed with New England barn siding

Key to prices *see p183*

The Tombs $$
American   Map 1 C2
1226 36th St NW, 20007
Tel *337-6668*
A hang-out for Georgetown University students, with a menu of sandwiches and salads.

1789 $$$
American   Map 1 B2
1226 36th St NW, 20007
Tel *965-1789*
Traditional fine American food and impeccable service. A special-occasion restaurant with prices to match.

Bandolero $$$
Mexican   Map 1 C2
3241 M St NW, 20007
Tel *625-4488*
Chef Mike Isabella whips up modern Mexican cuisine and artisanal cocktails at this big, casual, and fun restaurant.

Café Milano $$$
Italian   Map 1 C2
3251 Prospect St NW, 20007
Tel *333-6183*
One of the best places for celebrity-watching. Fine Italian food as well as lighter fare, such as pizza.

La Chaumiere $$$
French   Map 2 D2
2813 M St NW, 20007
Tel *338-1784*
A charming eatery with a quaint atmosphere; great for a date. Duck, mussels, *escargot*, and rabbit are the specialties.

Clyde's $$$
American   Map 1 C2
3236 M St NW, 20007
Tel *333-9180*
A big, raucous pub with an excellent bar menu including ribs and crab cakes. Brunch lovers rave about the *challah* (yeast-leavened) French toast.

Filomena $$$
Italian   Map 1 C3
1063 Wisconsin Ave NW, 20007
Tel *338-8800*
This family-run restaurant serves food from Abruzzi, central Italy. Its dining room is decorated like a holiday fantasy during Christmas.

Peacock Café $$$
American   Map 1 C2
3251 Prospect St NW, 20007
Tel *625-2740*
A great place for brunch on the patio, especially on a sunny day. The menu includes gluten-free items and there's a juice bar.

Sea Catch $$$
American   Map 2 D2
1054 31st St NW, 20007
Tel *337-8855*   **Closed** *Sun*
Stop here for simple and tasty dishes of fresh, locally caught seafood, including huge lobsters and oysters.

Sequoia $$$
American   Map 2 D3
3000 K St NW, 20007
Tel *944-4200*   **Closed** *Mon*
The best restaurant on the riverfront and a favorite for brunch ($35 fixed price). It boasts a huge patio.

Tony and Joe's Seafood Place $$$
American   Map 2 D3
3000 K St NW, 20007
Tel *944-4545*
Enjoy seafood and salads on the riverfront patio here. Live jazz during the Sunday brunch.

Unum $$$
American   Map 2 D2
2917 M St NW, 20007
Tel *621-6959*
This highly rated restaurant has been dubbed a "small wonder" for its craft beers and seasonal menu of American fare with international influences.

Farther Afield

Ben's Chili Bowl $
American
1213 U St NW, 20009
Tel *667-0909*
Everyone, including Bill Cosby and President Obama, eats at Ben's. Famous for its renowned chili dog and half-smoke.

BGR The Burger Joint $
American   Map 2 E1
1514 Connecticut Ave NW, Dupont Circle, 20036
Tel *387-9338*
Sample fresh, seasonal burgers; the Greek burger with lamb is a favorite. The sweet potato fries are a must.

Cactus Cantina $
Mexican
3300 Wisconsin Ave NW, Cleveland Park, 20016
Tel *686-7222*
Huge plates of Tex-Mex food make Cactus Cantina ideal for families. It has a big dining room and a large patio for eating alfresco.

District 2 $
American
3238 Wisconsin Ave NW, Cleveland Park, 20016
Tel *362-0362*
A sports bar with great burgers and a half dozen TVs. There's an outdoor patio for alfresco beer.

Madam's Organ $
American
2461 18th St NW, Adams Morgan, 20009
Tel *667-5370*
Live music every night, beer, and pub food. This mother-of-all dive bars is in Adams-Morgan – hence the pun.

Tony and Joe's Seafood Place, on the bank of the Potomac

Pizza Mart $
Italian
2445 18th St NW, Adams Morgan, 20009
Tel *234-9700*
Known locally as "the big slice" for its mammoth, inexpensive pizza slices. Not the best pizza in town, but reasonable and quick.

Sweetgreen $
American   Map 2 E1
1512 Connecticut Ave NW, Dupont Circle, 20036
Tel *387-9338*
The Dupont Circle branch of a local chain that makes healthy salads. It has both standard and custom dishes for less than $10.

2Amys $$
Italian
3715 Macomb St NW, Cleveland Park, 20016
Tel *885-5700*
Stop here for genuine Italian pizza or unmatched small plates, including deviled eggs, *burrata* (Italian cheese), eggplant confit, and olives.

Bistro La Bonne $$
French   Map 3 B1
1340 U St NW, 20009
Tel *758-3413*
French staples include *steak-frites*, *escargot*, and lots of mussel choices. The bar on the third floor often has happy hour specials.

DK Choice

Busboys and Poets $$
American
2021 14th St, 20009
Tel *387-6138*
A restaurant, bookstore, and performance space that hosts poetry readings, author talks, and improv theater, frequented by a cross-section of locals. The food is excellent too. Popular for brunch, but get here before noon to avoid a packed house.

Café Deluxe $$
American
3228 Wisconsin Ave NW, Cleveland Park, 20008
Tel *686-2233*
A bustling tavern and bistro serving comfort food. The service is attentive.

Café Saint Ex $$
American   Map 3 B1
1847 14th St NW, 20009
Tel *265-7839*
Named for the author of *The Little Prince*, this cozy aviation-themed bar/restaurant has impressive bar food and a good brunch menu.

The iconic Ben's Chili Bowl, a Washington institution

Dino $$
Italian
3435 Connecticut Ave NW, Cleveland Park, 20008
Tel *686-2966*
Italian *enoteca* (wine shop) with a big heart. Owner Dean Gold makes trips to Italy to add recipes to his repertoire. Excellent wine list.

Le Diplomate $$
French   Map 3 B1
1601 14th St NW, 20009
Tel *332-3333*
A hotspot for the hip, with a retro Parisian decor and feel. Book ahead for dinner.

Eatonville $$
American
2121 14th St NW, 20009
Tel *332-9672*
Southern food served with style and wit. The menu features catfish, fried green tomatoes, and po'boys (traditional Louisiana sandwiches). Ice tea is served out of a jar.

Marvin $$
American
2007 14th St NW, 20009
Tel *797-7171*
Named after singer and songwriter Marvin Gaye, a DC native, this bistro has a rooftop beer garden and a casual vibe.

Medium Rare $$
American
3500 Connecticut Ave NW, Cleveland Park, 20008
Tel *237-1432*
A great place for steak lovers, with a good-value fixed-price menu of steak, fries, salad, and bread. Amazing desserts.

For more information on types of restaurants *see p181*

Outdoor seating at Cashion's Eat Place in Adams Morgan

One Lounge $$
American   **Map** 3 A1
1606 20th St NW, 20009
Tel *299-0909*
A club-cum-restaurant with music and a happy hour. Serves pizza, tapas and small plates until 1am.

Perry's Restaurant $$
American
1811 Columbia Rd NW, Adams Morgan, 20009
Tel *234-6218*
The top-floor roof garden at this restaurant offers a fantastic view of Washington. It offers an eclectic menu, but is best known for its Sunday brunch.

St. Arnold's Mussel Bar $$
Belgian
3433 Connecticut Ave NW, Cleveland Park, 20008
Tel *621-6434*
Mussels of every description, as well as a great choice of Belgian beer, can be found at this bar. Reasonably priced happy hour.

Ardeo + Bardeo $$$
American
3311 Connecticut Ave NW, Cleveland Park, 20008
Tel *244-6750*
Two side-by-side eateries knocked into one, serving delicious modern American cuisine with Asian and Mediterranean influences. Dine on the romantic rooftop terrace in warm weather.

BlackSalt $$$
American
4883 MacArthur Blvd NW, Palisades, 20007
Tel *342-9101*
A restaurant specializing in inventive seafood; the corn-encrusted oysters and mussels are particular highlights of the menu.

Cashion's Eat Place $$$
American
1819 Columbia Rd NW, Adams Morgan, 20009
Tel *797-1819*
Seasonal American cuisine with Mediterranean influences. The menu changes daily and always includes a vegetarian entrée.

Makoto $$$
Japanese
4822 MacArthur Blvd NW, Palisades, 20016
Tel *298-6866*   **Closed** *Mon*
The best Japanese restaurant in DC, with a delicious fixed-price chef's menu. Take off your shoes at the threshold and enter Japan.

Obelisk $$$
Italian   **Map** 3 A1
2029 P St NW, 20036
Tel *872-1180*   **Closed** *Sun & Mon*
The fixed-price menu includes 10 courses served in a tiny dining room. High-end Italian cuisine.

Palena $$$
American
3529 Connecticut Ave NW, Cleveland Park, 20008
Tel *537-9250*
This award-winning restaurant serves fancy food, but the

cheeseburger with vegetable *frites* is a hands-down favorite.

Pearl Dive Oyster Palace $$$
Seafood   **Map** 3 B1
1612 14th St NW, 20009
Tel *986-8778*
The waiters here explain the provenance of the oysters, most of which are served raw. Be sure to try the bourbon pecan pie. Trendy and expensive.

Pulpo $$$
Spanish
3407 Connecticut Ave NW, Cleveland Park, 20008
Tel *450-6870*
A new twist on tapas, including a mini burger trio and roasted squab. There's an all-you-can-eat-and-drink Sunday brunch.

Restaurant Nora $$$
American   **Map** 2 E1
2132 Florida Ave NW, Dupont Circle, 20008
Tel *462-5143*
America's first certified organic restaurant, supervised by organic food pioneer Nora Poullion. Seasonal dining at its best.

Ripple $$$
American
3417 Connecticut Ave NW, Cleveland Park, 20008
Tel *244-7995*
The intriguing menu here includes a charcuterie and grilled cheese bar, mushroom *agnolotti* (ravioli), and okra with ricotta.

Beyond Washington

The Crab Claw $
American
304 Burns St, St. Michaels, MD 21663
Tel *(410) 745-2900*
A popular crab eatery since 1965. The decor is simple, but the fresh seafood and cold beer are superb.

The cozy and inviting Restaurant Nora, America's original organic restaurant

Michie Tavern, set amid sprawling gardens

Michie Tavern $
American
683 Thomas Jefferson Pkwy,
Charlottesville, VA 22902
Tel *(434) 977-1234*
The Michie Tavern has been serving traditional American fare for over 200 years. Delicious fried chicken is the speciality.

Yellow Brick Bank $
American
201 East German St,
Shepherdstown, WV 25443
Tel *(304) 876-2208* **Closed** *Sun & Mon*
Set in a former bank building, Yellow Brick Bank serves locally sourced food and rich desserts.

Christiana Campbells $$
American
101 South Waller St,
Williamsburg, VA 23187
Tel *(757) 229-2141* **Closed** *Sun & Mon*
A colonial tavern that has been serving traditional cuisine since George Washington's time.

Gadsby's $$
American
134 North Royal St,
Alexandria, VA 22314
Tel *(703) 746-4242*
Food from the Revolution era served in a genuine 18th-century tavern. Martha Washington's apple pie is a winner.

Mama's on the Half Shell $$
Seafood
2901 O'Donnell St,
Baltimore, MD 21224
Tel *(410) 276-3160*
A neighborhood restaurant with excellent regional seafood. Oysters, crabs, and crab cakes are served in huge portions.

Mon Ami Gabi $$
French
7239 Woodmont Ave,
Bethesda, MD 20814
Tel *(301) 654-1234*
A French bistro in suburban Maryland with traditional

specialties: *steak-frites, bouillabaisse,* and crepes.

Le Refuge $$
French
127 North Washington St,
Alexandria, VA 22314
Tel *(703) 548-4661* **Closed** *Sun*
Sample the superb dover sole, frog legs, beef Wellington, and crème brulée at this family-run French restaurant.

Vermilion $$
American
1120 King St, Alexandria, VA 22314
Tel *(703) 684-9669*
This restaurant is committed to supporting local farmers and regionally grown produce. Fixed-price "farm table" nights offer a chance to dine with chef Tony Chittum.

DK Choice

Inn at Little Washington $$$
American
309 Middle St,
Little Washington, VA 22747
Tel *(540) 675-3800*
One of America's most famous restaurants. Chef Patrick O'Connell's culinary jewel offers flawless service, and has a refined, seasonal menu. The herbs come from O'Connell's kitchen garden. Do not miss the decadent chocolate Seven Deadly Sins dessert. Dining at this Michelin-starred organic restaurant is a once-in-a-lifetime experience.

Old Angler's Inn $$$
American
10801 MacArthur Blvd,
Potomac, MD 20854
Tel *(301) 365-2425* **Closed** *Wed*
This inn, dating from 1860, is next to the C&O Canal. Dine by the fire in winter and on the patio in summer. There's a formal menu for dinner and mussels or burgers for lunch.

Ray's the Steaks $$$
American
2300 Wilson Blvd,
Arlington, VA 22209
Tel *(703) 841-7297*
Enjoy giant, perfectly cooked steaks in a no-frills setting. Fans also recommend the crab bisque.

Restaurant Eve $$$
American
110 South Pitt St,
Alexandria, VA 22314
Tel *(703) 706-0450* **Closed** *Sun*
A culinary showcase for chef Cathal Armstrong. The fixed-price menus in the tasting room are expensive, but the bistro and lounge are more reasonably priced alternatives.

Willow $$$
American
4301 North Fairfax Dr,
Arlington, VA 22203
Tel *(703) 465-8800* **Closed** *Sun*
This restaurant serves New American cuisine, including steak, lobster, chicken, and ricotta-stuffed squash blossoms. The desserts are outstanding.

The sunny patio with bay views at The Crab Claw

For more information on types of restaurants *see p181*

SHOPPING IN WASHINGTON, DC

Washington's vast selection of stores makes shopping in the capital a pleasurable experience. Souvenirs can be found anywhere from fashion boutiques and specialist food stores to museum and gallery gift shops. The many museums on the Mall and around the city sell a wide variety of unusual gifts, reproduction prints, and replica artifacts selected from all over the world. Although the many smart shopping malls and department stores in the DC area can provide hours of shopping, Georgetown offers visitors a far more lively and authentic environment in which to browse. It is a neighborhood packed with fashionable clothing boutiques and endless interesting shops that sell everything from antiques to hair dye, from one-dollar bargains to priceless works of art.

East Hall of the Union Station shopping mall

Opening Hours

Most department stores, shopping malls, and other centers are open from 10am until 8 or 9pm, Monday through Saturday, and from noon until 6pm on Sunday. Smaller shops and boutiques are generally open from noon until 6pm on Sundays, and from 10 until 6 or 7pm on all other days. Convenience stores such as supermarkets and local grocery stores may open for longer hours.

Drugstores (pharmacies) are also often open for extended hours.

How to Pay

Goods may be paid for in cash, in traveler's checks (in US dollars), or by credit card. VISA and MasterCard are the most popular credit cards in the United States, while American Express is often, but not always, accepted. A tax of 5.75% is added to all purchases at the cash register.

Sales

Department stores, such as **Macy's** in the Penn Quarter area and **Nordstrom** farther out in Arlington, often hold sales during holiday weekends, including Memorial Day, the 4th of July, Labor Day, and Columbus Day. Check the newspapers for advertisements to find good prices on electronics, jewelry, kitchenwares, shoes, and clothing. White sales (towels and bedlinen) occur in January.

Museum Shops

All the museums on the Mall have a wide selection of products on sale in their shops. The **National Gallery of Art** sells artwork reproductions, books, art-related games and children's toys, and the **Museum of African Art** offers a range of African textiles, ceramics, basketry, musical instruments, and books. In Penn Quarter, the **Smithsonian American Art Museum** shop has decorative items, books, and original handmade craft pieces.

The **National Museum of American History** shop carries a range of souvenirs such as American crafts, reproductions, and T-shirts, including merchandise inspired by the Star-Spangled Banner, as well as a range of books on American history. They also sell recordings from the 1940s to the 1970s, including Doo Wop, Motown, and Disco, from the Smithsonian Recordings and Smithsonian Folkways labels. Products can be purchased online too.

Also well worth a visit, near the White House, is the shop at the **Decatur House Museum**, home of Stephen Decatur, a naval hero from the War of 1812. It has a collection of items for sale related to Washington's history, art, and architecture.

For a selection of interesting books on architecture, contemporary design, and historic preservation, as well as a range of toys, ties, frames, and gifts, pay a visit to the **National Building Museum** shop at Judiciary Square.

Stalls selling an eclectic range of goods at Eastern Market

People walk past an Urban Outfitters store on M Street, Georgetown

Malls and Department Stores

There are a few small-scale shopping malls in central Washington. **Union Station**, the beautifully renovated train station in the Capitol Hill area *(see p57)*, houses 130 shops and restaurants on three levels, in a very pleasant environment. There are name-brand stores as well as an extensive collection of specialty shops that sell clothing, gifts, jewelry, crafts, souvenirs, and more.

Two small shopping malls – **Mazza Gallerie** and **Chevy Chase Pavilion** – are located on upper Wisconsin Avenue in the Friendship Heights neighborhood. The metro is convenient, but there is also plenty of parking for cars. Visitors can shop at Bloomingdale's or Lord and Taylor department stores, or the specialty boutiques and name-brand stores.

The larger malls are located in the Maryland and Virginia suburbs. The **Fashion Center at Pentagon City** is easily reached by metro. Discount-hunters should head for the 230 outlets at **Potomac Mills**, situated 30 miles (48 km) south of the city on I-95.

Galleries, Arts, and Crafts

Visitors will discover a cornucopia of art galleries and crafts shops in three of Washington's neighborhoods – Georgetown, Dupont Circle, and Adams-Morgan. Here visitors can spend a few hours feasting their eyes on the delightful objects on display.

Work by several local artists is on sale in the **Addison/Ripley Fine Arts**, located in Georgetown. Some of the best pottery can be found in the **Appalachian Spring** shops in Georgetown and at Union Station. **Eastern Market** in Capitol Hill offers a vibrant mix of stalls from antiques to ethnic artifacts, and is best at weekends. Art lovers should browse along 7th Street, NW, between D Street and the Verizon Center. Among the highlights are pieces of sculpture and contemporary art at **Zenith Gallery** for sale from $50 to $50,000. Out of town, in Alexandria, the **Torpedo Factory Art Center** is excellent for lovers of all kinds of arts and crafts.

Torpedo Factory Art Center logo

Souvenirs

Collectors' items and DC memorabilia are abundant at Political Americana and Made in America, two shops in **Union Station**. The **Old Post Office Pavilion** near Metro Center, is also worth a visit for DC souvenirs. The gift shops in the **Kennedy Center** sell gifts and books about the performing arts and Washington in general. People looking for religious items or unusual souvenirs should try the **Washington National Cathedral** museum and book shop in the basement of the cathedral or the Herb Cottage, a renovated octagonal baptistry in the Cathedral grounds.

Clothes

Wisconsin Avenue and M Street in Georgetown are home to a wide range of clothing stores. National highstreet chains include **The Gap**, while those seeking something a little more out of the ordinary should visit **Urban Outfitters**, **Intermix**, and **Cusp. H & M**, the international discount store, sells clothing for men, women, and children at reasonable prices.

The space formerly known as Georgetown Park, situated on the intersection of Wisconsin Avenue and M Street, maintains street-facing modern shops while its Victorian-style interior is being redeveloped. There are high-end boutiques here as well as branded clothing stores. There is also a great variety of clothes shops to browse in the Friendship Heights neighborhood.

Food and Wine

On Capitol Hill, you can shop for snacks and fresh produce or sit down for lunch in the bustling food hall of the Eastern Market, which also hosts an open-air farmers' market on Tuesdays.

For something more unusual, tasty, or exotic in the culinary field, there are several delicatessens worth visiting in Washington. In particular, try **Dean & Deluca** in Georgetown, which stocks an excellent selection of gourmet foods and also offers a fine range of American and European wines. While you are there, take the opportunity to sample the food and drinks available in the pleasant on-site café.

The Old Post Office Pavilion

One of many antique centers in Frederick

Antiques

There are some wonderful hidden treasures to be discovered in the many antique stores scattered throughout Washington. Along Wisconsin Avenue, between P and S streets and also along M and O streets, there are around 20 antique shops. Some specialize in expensive antiques, others in prints, lamps, silverware, perfume bottles, or just interesting knick-knacks.

Random Harvest on Wisconsin Avenue carries both upholstered and wooden furniture from the ate 1800s through to the mid-20th century. It also stocks a carefully chosen selection of home accessories, including pillows, mirrors, and lamps.

Adams-Morgan and Dupont Circle are also good neighborhoods for antique hunting. **Brass Knob Architectural Antiques**, on 18th Street, is worth visiting for their range of salvaged curiosities, including clawfoot bathtubs and unusual antique light fixtures. Customers are bound to leave with just the perfect relic for their home, which could be anything from a chandelier to an iron gate.

There is also a number of centers for antiques outside central Washington. Kensington in Maryland and Old Town Alexandria in Virginia are areas rich in antiques. **Studio Antiques** in Alexandria sells all kinds of antiques, such as dolls, china, and silver, but specializes in books. In Frederick, Maryland, there is the enormous **Emporium Antiques**. This paradise for antiques lovers houses over 100 shops that sell everything from huge pieces of furniture through household wares to jewelry.

Books and Music

Book lovers are spoiled for choice in Washington and will enjoy spending time browsing in the myriad bookstores that can be found in the city.

There are several excellent independent and second-hand bookstores, especially in the Dupont Circle area. In **Kramerbooks & Afterwords Café**, customers can sit with their new purchase while drinking a coffee. There is also a full-service restaurant. **Second Story Books** is DC's biggest second-hand store, which also offers CDs and vinyl, vintage prints and photographs, and other framed ephemera.

Farther north, on Connecticut Avenue, is the **Politics & Prose Bookstore**, a favorite among Washingtonians for its combination of books and coffee. Customers can chat with the knowledgeable staff, browse, or attend a reading. (The Sunday book review section of the *Washington Post* lists readings.) **Busboys and Poets** on 5th Street is a community hub for writers, activists, and thinkers. It combines a bookstore with a restaurant, bar, and performance space where author readings and open-mic poetry nights are held.

Miscellaneous

The many department stores in and around Washington, such as **Macy's**, **Nordstrom**, and **Neiman-Marcus**, are well-stocked with good quality household wares from linens to cutlery and crockery. They are also prepared to order any out-of-stock items for their customers.

Wake Up Little Suzie sells unusual and unique gifts, such as handmade books, jewelry, and hanging mobiles. Similarly, **Chocolate Moose**, on L Street, is a treasure trove of the unusual and unconventional, including ceramics, chocolates, jewelry, and children's toys, among other things. **Tabletop DC** on 20th Street sells everything from utensils, toys, and jewelry, to placemats, picture frames, and calendars.

Everything in contemporary products for the home, from kitchenware to furniture, can be found at **Crate & Barrel** in Spring Valley. In Georgetown is **Restoration Hardware**, which offers everything from decorative door knobs through gardening supplies and lamps, to old-fashioned toys and the popular, heavy oak Mission furniture that originated in the Arts and Crafts Movement.

A bookstore and café are combined at Kramerbooks & Afterwords Café

DIRECTORY

Malls and Department Stores

Bloomingdale's
5300 Western Ave,
Chevy Chase DC.
Tel (202) 774-3700.

Chevy Chase Pavilion
5335 Wisconsin Ave, NW.
Tel (202) 686-5335.

Fashion Center at Pentagon City
1100 South Hayes St,
Arlington, Virginia.
Tel (703) 415-2400.

Lord & Taylor
5255 Western Ave,
Chevy Chase, MD.
Tel (202) 362-9600.

Macy's Department Store
12th & G St, NW.
Map 3 C3.
Tel (202) 628-6661.

Mazza Gallerie Mall
5300 Wisconsin Ave, NW.
Tel (202) 966-6114.

Neiman-Marcus
Mazza Gallerie. Map 1 B1.
Tel (202) 966-9700.

Nordstrom
Fashion Center at
Pentagon City.
Tel (703) 415-1121.

Potomac Mills
Woodbridge, VA.
Tel (703) 496-9330.

Union Station Shops
40 Massachusetts Ave,
NE. Map 4 E3.
Tel (202) 289-1908.

Galleries, Arts, and Craft

Addison/Ripley Fine Arts
1670 Wisconsin Ave, NW.
Map 1 C2.
Tel (202) 338-5180.

Appalachian Spring
1415 Wisconsin Ave, NW.
Map 1 C2.
Tel (202) 337-5780.

Eastern Market
225 7th St, SE.
Map 4 F4.
Tel (202) 698-5253.

Torpedo Factory Art Center
105 N. Union St,
Alexandria, VA.
Tel (703) 838-4565.

Antiques

Brass Knob Architectural Antiques
2311 18th St, NW.
Map 3 A1.
Tel (202) 332-3370.

Emporium Antiques
112 E. Patrick St, Frederick,
MD.
Tel (301) 662-7099.

Georgetown Flea Market
Wisconsin Ave, between
S & T Sts, NW.
Map 1 C3.

Random Harvest
1313 Wisconsin Ave, NW.
Map 1 C2.
Tel (202) 202-5569.

Studio Antiques
524 N. Washington St,
Alexandria, VA.
Tel (703) 548-5188.

Souvenirs

Kennedy Center
New Hampshire Ave &
Rock Creek Parkway, NW.
Map 2 D4.
Tel (202) 467-4600.

Old Post Office Pavilion
Pennsylvania Ave
& 12th St, NW.
Map 3 C3.
Tel (202) 289-4224.

Washington National Cathedral
Massachusetts &
Wisconsin Ave, NW.
Tel (202) 537-6200.

Books and Music

Busboys and Poets
1025 5th St, NW.
Map 4 D3.
Tel (202) 789-2227.

Kramerbooks & Afterwords Café
1517 Connecticut Ave,
NW. Map 2 E2.
Tel (202) 387-1462.

Politics & Prose Bookstore
5015 Connecticut Ave,
NW. Map 2 E2.
Tel (202) 364-1919.

Second Story Books
2000 P St, NW.
Map 1 B1.
Tel (202) 659-8884.

Museum Shops

Decatur House Museum
1610 H St, NW.
Map 3 A3.
Tel (202) 842-0915.

National Building Museum
401 F St, NW.
Map 4 D3.
Tel (202) 272-2448.

National Gallery of Art
Constitution Ave at
6th St, NW.
Map 4 D4.
Tel (202) 842-4215.

National Museum of African Art
950 Independence Ave,
SW. Map 3 C4.
Tel (202) 633-4600.

National Museum of American History
The Mall between
12th and 14th Sts, NW.
Map 3 B4.
Tel (202) 357-1528.

Clothes

The Gap
1120 Connecticut Ave,
NW. Map 3 A2.
Tel (202) 429-0691.

H & M
Georgetown Park
(Wisconsin Ave and
M St, NW).
Map 1 C2.
Tel (202) 298-6792.

Urban Outfitters
3111 M St, NW.
Map 1 C2.
Tel (202) 342-1012.

Food and Wine

Dean & Deluca
3276 M St, NW.
Map 1 C2.
Tel (202) 342-2500.

Miscellaneous

Chocolate Moose
1743 L St, NW.
Map 2 F2.
Tel (202) 463-0992.

Crate & Barrel
4820 Massachusetts Ave,
NW. Tel (202) 364-6100.

Restoration Hardware
1222 Wisconsin Ave, NW.
Map 1 C2.
Tel (202) 625-2771.

Tabletop DC
1608 20th St, NW.
Map 2 E2.
Tel (202) 387-7117.

Wake-Up Little Suzie
3409 Connecticut
Ave, NW.
Tel (202) 244-0700.

ENTERTAINMENT IN WASHINGTON, DC

Visitors to Washington will never be at a loss for entertainment, from flying a kite in the grounds of the Washington Monument to attending a concert at the Kennedy Center. The city's diverse, international community offers a rich array of choices. If you are looking for swing dancing you will find it; you will also hear different beats around town, including salsa, jazz, and rhythm and blues. Outdoor enthusiasts can choose from cycling on the Rock Creek bike path to canoeing on the Potomac River. If you are looking for something less active, take in a film at the Smithsonian. Theater-goers have a wide range of choices, from Shakespeare through highly respected repertory companies to Broadway musicals. No matter what your budget is, you will find something to do. There are more free activities in DC than in any other American city.

Information Sources

The best places to find information on plays, movies, and concerts are the *Washington City Paper* and the Weekend section of Friday's edition of the *Washington Post*. Internet users can check out *Style Live*, the entertainment guide on the *Washington Post* website.

The "Where & When" section in the monthly *Washingtonian* magazine also lists events.

Booking Tickets

Tickets may be bought in advance at box offices, or by phone and through the Internet. Tickets for all events at the **Kennedy Center** can be obtained through **Instant Charge**. Tickets for the Verizon Center, the Jiffy Lube Live, and the Warner Theater can be bought by phone through **Ticketmaster**. For Arena, Lisner Auditorium, Ford's Theatre, Merriweather Post Pavilion, and Woolly Mammoth tickets, contact www.tickets.com.

Auditorium of the Shakespeare Theatre on 7th Street

Façade of the John F. Kennedy Center for the Performing Arts

Discount Tickets

Most theaters give group discounts, and several offer student and senior discounts for same-day performances. Half-price tickets for seats on the day of the performance may be obtained in person at **Ticketplace**, at 407 7th St, NW, or on their website.

In addition, theaters offer their own special discounts: The Arena sells a limited number of "Hottix," half-price seats, 30 to 90 minutes before the show. The Shakespeare Theatre offers 20 percent off for senior citizens Sunday through Thursday, 50 percent one hour before curtain rise for students, and discounts for all previews. The Kennedy Center has a limited number of half-price tickets available to students, senior citizens, and anyone with permanent disabilities. These go on sale at noon on the day of the performance (some are available before the first performance). Standing-room tickets may be available if a show is sold out.

Free Events

The daily newspapers provide up-to-date listings of free lectures, concerts, gallery talks, films, book signings, poetry readings, and shows.

Local and international artists offer free performances on the Millennium Stage at the Kennedy Center every evening at 6pm.

The **National Symphony Orchestra** gives a free outdoor concert on the West Lawn of the Capitol on Labor Day and Memorial Day weekends, and on the Fourth of July. In summer, various military bands such as the **United States Marine Band**, the Navy, Air Force or the **US Army Band** give free concerts (contact them direct for details).

From October to June, the **National Gallery of Art** sponsors free Sunday evening concerts at

Courtyard concert in the National Gallery of Art

7pm in the West Garden Court, and also free summer jazz concerts on Friday evenings in the Sculpture Garden. Free lectures and gallery talks are held at the **Library of Congress** and at the National Gallery of Art.

Open-Air Entertainment

During the summer months at **Wolf Trap Farm Park for the Performing Arts** world-famous performers can be seen on any night. Check their calendar of events and find your favorite form of entertain-ment – opera, jazz, Broadway musical, ballet, folk, or country music. You can bring a picnic to enjoy on the lawn.

On Thursday evenings in summer, the **National Zoo** hosts concerts on Lion Tiger Hill. They start at 6:30pm.

If you are in Washington in June try to catch the **Shakespeare Theatre Free for All** held at the Sidney Harman Hall in Penn Quarter.

The *Washington Post* lists the local fairs and festivals, held every weekend in warm weather. On the first weekend in May, the **Washington National Cathedral** sponsors the Flowermart, a festival featuring an old-fashioned carousel, children's games, crafts, and good food. The **Smithsonian Folklife Festival**, a two-week extravaganza held on the Mall at the end of June and early July, brings together folk artists from around the world. For details of other annual events in the city, see Washington, DC Through The Year (*pp38–41*).

Facilities for the Disabled

All the major theaters in Washington are wheelchair accessible. The Kennedy Center publishes a list of its upcoming sign-interpreted, audio-described, and captioned performances. For details of these and information on the venue's other accessibility services, check its website.

Many theaters, including the Kennedy Center, Ford's Theatre, the Shakespeare Theatre, and Arena Stage, have audio enhancement devices, as well as a limited number of signed performances. For the hearing impaired, TTY phone numbers are listed in the Weekend section of the *Washington Post*.

The National Gallery of Art provides assisted listening devices for lectures. Sign-language interpretation is available with three weeks' notice, and a telecommunications device for the deaf (TDD) can be found near the Concourse Sales Shop. For those with limited sight, the theater Arena Stage offers audio description, touch tours of the set, and program books in large print and Braille.

DIRECTORY

Information Sources

Washington City Paper
w washingtoncitypaper.com

Washington Post
w washingtonpost.com

Washingtonian
w washingtonian.com

Booking Tickets

John F. Kennedy Center for the Performing Arts
New Hampshire Ave at Rock Creek Parkway, NW.
Map 2 D4.
Tickets booked via Instant Charge **Tel** (202) 467-4600 or (800) 444-1324.
w kennedy-center.org

Ticketmaster
Tel (202) 397-7328.
w ticketmaster.com

Tickets.com
Tel (800) 955-5566.
w tickets.com

Discount Tickets

Ticketplace
407 7th St, NW.
Map 3 D3.
w ticketplace.org

Free Events

Library of Congress
1st St & Independence Ave, SE. **Map** 4 F4.
Tel (202) 707-5503.
w loc.gov/concerts

National Gallery of Art
Constitution Ave at 6th St, NW. **Map** 4 D4.
Tel (202) 737-4215.
w nga.gov

National Symphony Orchestra
Tel (202) 467-4600.

US Army Band
Tel (703) 696-3399.
w usarmyband.com

US Marine Band
Tel (202) 433-4011.
w marineband.usmc.mil

Open-Air Entertainment

National Zoo
3001 Connecticut Ave, NW. **Tel** (202) 633-4800.
w nationalzoo.si.edu

Shakespeare Theatre Free for All
Sidney Harman Hall, 610 F St, NW. **Map** 4 D3.
w shakespearetheatre.org

Smithsonian Folklife Festival
Tel (202) 633-1000.
w festival.si.edu

Washington National Cathedral
Massachusetts and Wisconsin Aves, NW.
Tel (202) 537-6200.
w nationalcathedral.org

Wolf Trap Farm Park for the Performing Arts
1645 Trap Rd, Vienna, VA.
Tel (703) 255-1900 (info).
Tel (877) 965-3872 (tickets).
w wolftrap.org

Cultural Events

For an evening out, Washington has much to offer. A seafood dinner on the waterfront followed by a play at Arena Stage, Washington's oldest repertory company; dancing at one of the clubs on U Street; jazz in Georgetown; a late-night coffee bar in Dupont Circle; or opening night at the opera at the Kennedy Center and a nightcap in the West End. Or if you are staying downtown and do not want to venture far from your hotel, see a show at the Warner or the National Theater, where the best of Broadway finds a home.

Dancing to live music at the Kennedy Center

Sign on the façade of the Warner Theatre on 13th Street

Film and Theater

Independent and foreign-language films, as well as classic revivals, are screened at the state-of-the-art **Landmark's E Street Cinema**. Film festivals are held at the **Kennedy Center**. Museums such as **The National Gallery of Art** show films relating to current exhibitions. **The Library of Congress** offers a free film series of documentaries and films related to the exhibits in the museum, shown in the Mary Pickford Theater. The DC Film Festival is based at the Lincoln Theatre.

National touring theater companies bring shows to the **John F. Kennedy Center for the Performing Arts**, the **Warner**

Theatre, and the **National Theatre**. For a more intimate setting, try **Ford's Theatre**. **Arena Stage** has a well-established repertory company. **The Studio** and the **Woolly Mammoth Theatre** produce contemporary works.

The Shakespeare Theatre produces works in a modern, elegant setting. For plays performed in Spanish, seek out the **Gala Hispanic Theater**.

Opera and Classical Music

Based at the Kennedy Center, the **Washington National Opera Company** is often considered one of the capital's crown jewels. Although many performances do sell out, standing room tickets are sometimes available. **The National Symphony Orchestra** performs classical and contemporary works.

A rich variety of chamber ensembles and choral groups perform regularly around the city. **The Washington Performing Arts Society** brings internationally renowned performers to DC.

Dance

The Kennedy Center offers a magnificent ballet and dance season every year, with sell-out productions from the world's finest companies including the Bolshoi, the American Ballet Theater, the Royal Swedish Ballet, and the Dance Theater of Harlem.

Dance Place showcases its own professional modern dance companies, as well as international contemporary dance companies.

If you would prefer to take to the floor yourself, make your way to **Glen Echo Park** where people from ages 7 to 70 enjoy evenings of swing dancing, contra dancing (line dancing), Louisiana Cajun zydeco dancing, and waltzes. The Kennedy Center also occasionally has dancing to live bands.

Rock, Jazz, and Blues

To see the "biggest names and the hottest newcomers" in jazz, head for the KC Jazz Club at the Kennedy Center. Oscar Brown, Jr., Phil Woods, Ernie Watts, and many more are featured here. You can hear international jazz stars at **Blues Alley** in Georgetown, or visit **Madam's Organ** in Adams-Morgan, home to some of the best R&B in Washington.

If you want to hear big-name rock stars or jazz artists, head to the **Verizon Center** (see p104), the **Merriweather Post Pavilion** in Columbia, Maryland, or the **Jiffy Lube Live** in Manassas, Virginia.

Actors in a play at the highly respected Shakespeare Theatre

Clubs, Bars, and Cafes

For late night dancing and clubbing, try the U Street neighborhood. Most highly recommended is the **930 Night Club**.

For salsa try the **Rumba Café** in Adams-Morgan. If you fancy a cigar and a martini, then check out **Ozio Martini and Cigar Lounge** downtown. **Black Cat**, with its schedule of both local and international bands, is the place for live independent and alternative music. Billiard parlors are also popular, as are the city's many coffee bars. **Cosi Dupont North** in Dupont Circle serves coffees and cocktails.

Gay Clubs

Many of the gay bars in DC can be found in the Dupont Circle area. **JR's Bar and Grill** attracts young professionals. **The Fireplace** is popular and stays open late. If you're looking for a good meal, visit **Annie's Paramount Steak House** on 17th Street.

Interior of Rumba Café

DIRECTORY

Film and Theatre

Arena Stage
1101 6th St, SW.
Map 4 D5.
Tel (202) 554-9066.
W arenastage.org

Ford's Theatre
511 10th St, NW.
Map 3 C3.
Tel (202) 347-4833.
W fordstheatre.org

Gala Hispanic Theater
3333 14th St, NW.
Tel (202) 234-7174.

Kennedy Center
New Hampshire Ave &
Rock Creek Parkway, NW.
Map 2 D4.
Tel (202) 467-4600 or
(202) 467-4600.
W kennedy-center.org

**Landmark's
E Street Cinema**
Lincoln Square Building
at 555 11th St, NW.
Map 3 C3.
Tel (202) 783-9494.
W landmarktheatres.
com

Library of Congress
Mary Pickford Theater,
Madison Building,
101 Independence Ave, SE.
Map 4 E4.
Tel (202) 707-5677.
W loc.gov

**National
Gallery of Art**
Constitution Ave at
6th St, NW.
Map 4 D3.
Tel (202) 737-4215.
W nga.org

National Theatre
1321 Pennsylvania Ave,
NW. **Map** 3 B3.
Tel (202) 628-6161.
W nationaltheatre.org

Shakespeare Theatre
450 7th St, NW.
Map 3 C3.
Tel (202) 547-1122.
W shakespeare
theatre.org

Signature Theatre
4200 Campbell Ave,
Springfield, VA.
Tel (703) 820-9771.
W sig-online.com

The Studio Theatre
1501 14th St, NW.
Map 3 B1.
Tel (202) 332-3300.
W studiotheatre.org

Warner Theatre
13th St (between E and F
Sts), NW. **Map** 3 C3.
Tel (202) 783-4000.
W warnertheatre.com

**Woolly
Mammoth Theatre**
641 D St, NW.
Map 3 C3.
Tel (202) 393-3939.
W woollymammoth.net

Opera and
Classical Music

**National Symphony
Orchestra**
Tel (202) 467-4600.

**Washington
Performing
Arts Society**
Tel (202) 785-9727.
W wpas.org

Dance

Dance Place
3225 8th St, NE.
Tel (202) 269-1600.

Glen Echo Park
Spanish Ballroom,
7300 MacArthur Blvd,
Glen Echo, MD.
Tel (202) 634-2222.

Rock, Jazz,
and Blues

Blues Alley
1069 Wisconsin Ave, NW.
Map 1 C3.
Tel (202) 337-4141.

Jiffy Lube Live
7800 Cellar Door Drive,
Bristow, VA.
Tel (703) 754-6400.
W nissanpavilion
online.com

**Madam's
Organ**
2461 18th St, NW.
Map 2 F1.
Tel (202) 667-5370.

**Merriweather
Post Pavilion**
Columbia, MD.
Tel (410) 715-5550.
W merriweather
music.com

Clubs, Bars,
and Cafés

9:30 Night Club
815 V St, NW.
Tel (202) 265-0930.
W 930.com

Black Cat
1811 14th St, NW.
Map 3 B3.
Tel (202) 667-7960.

**Cosi Dupont
North**
1647 20th St, NW.
Map 3 A1.
Tel (202) 332-6364.

**Ozio Martini and
Cigar Lounge**
1813 M St, NW.
Map 3 A1.
Tel (202) 822-6000.

Rumba Café
2443 18th St, NW.
Tel (202) 588-5501.
W rumbacafe.com

Gay Clubs

**Annie's
Paramount
Steak House**
1609 17th St, NW.
Map 2 F2.
Tel (202) 232-0395.

The Fireplace
2161 P St, NW.
Map 2 E2.
Tel (202) 293-1293.

**JR's Bar
and Grill**
1519 17th St, NW.
Map 2 F2.
Tel (202) 328-0090.

Sports and Outdoor Activities

Washingtonians are known for putting in long hours – whether on the floor of the Senate, the office of a federal agency, or in a newsroom. They compensate, however, by taking their leisure hours very seriously by rooting for their favorite teams or spending as much time as possible outdoors. You can join in the fun at the Nationals Park Stadium or the Verizon Center, both of which attract hordes of fans. You can meet joggers, cyclists, and in-line skaters on the Mall and around the monuments.

Cyclists enjoying the fine weather outdoors in DC

Spectator Sports

Fans of the NHL Capitals (National Hockey League), the NBA Wizards (National Basketball Association), and the WNBA Mystics (Women's National Basketball Association) should purchase tickets at the **Verizon Center**, an impressive sports arena that opened in 1997 and has helped revitalize the downtown area.

Depending on the season, you might also see Disney on Ice, the Harlem Globetrotters, or the Ringling Brothers Circus. Visit the Verizon's National Sports Gallery, which houses sports memorabilia and interactive sports games. There is plenty to eat at the Verizon Center, but you may prefer to slip out to one of the restaurants in Chinatown, which surrounds the center.

If you are not a season-pass holder, it is very difficult to get a ticket to a Washington Redskins game at the **FedEx Field** stadium, but you can always watch the game from one of Washington's popular sports

Redskins team member

bars. The DC United soccer team plays at the **RFK Stadium**. College sports are also very popular in DC – you will find Washingtonians cheering either for the **Georgetown Hoyas** or the **Maryland Terrapins**. Baseball fans lend their support to the Washington Nationals at **Nationals Park Stadium** in the southeast of the city.

Fishing and Boating

From April to October, to fish or boat on the Potomac River, head to **Fletcher's Boat House** at Canal and Reservoir Roads. You will need to obtain a permit if you are between 16 and 64, which lasts for a year but does not cost much. You can fish from the riverbank or rent a rowboat, canoe or kayak, which are available by the hour or the day.

In Georgetown there are boats for rent at **Thompson's Boat Center** and **Jack's Boat House**. Fletcher's sells snacks; if you go to Thompson's or Jack's there are cafés and restaurants along the waterfront.

Cycling

Rock Creek Park is one of Washington's greatest treasures and offers amazing respite from busy city life. Closed to traffic on weekends, it is a great place for cycling. Another popular trail is the Capital Crescent, which starts on the C&O Canal towpath in Georgetown and runs to Maryland.

One of the more beautiful bike trails in the area will take you 16 miles (26 km) to Mount Vernon. Bikes can be rented at Fletcher's Boat House, Thompson's Boat Center, **Bike and Roll**, or **Big Wheels** in Georgetown. For maps or trail information call or write to the **Washington Area Bicyclist Association**, or consult one of the bike rental shops in the city.

Tennis, Golf, and Horseback Riding

Many neighborhood parks have outdoor tennis courts, available on a first-come, first-served basis. Two public clubs in the city accept reservations: **East Potomac Tennis Center** at Hains Point, and the **Washington Tennis Center**. Each has outdoor and indoor courts.

If you want to take in views of the monuments while walking the golf fairways, go to the **East Potomac Golf Course & Driving Range**. (There is an 18-hole miniature golf course here as well.) Two other courses are open to the public: **Langston Golf Course** on the Anacostia

RFK Stadium, a major sports and entertainment venue

River and **Rock Creek Golf Course**, tucked into Rock Creek Park. You will also find **Rock Creek Park Horse Center**, where you can make reservations for a guided trail ride.

Exploring Nature

For an amazing array of trees and plants, visit the **National Arboretum** (see p146), which covers 444 acres in northeast Washington. There is something interesting to see all year round in the arboretum. Special displays, such as the National Bonsai Collection of miniature plants, can be enjoyed at any time of year. To catch the best of the flowering shrubs, the beautiful camellias and magnolias flower in late March through early April, and the stunning, rich colors of the azaleas, rhododendron, and dogwood appear from late April through early May. There is a 1,600-ft (490-m) long "touch and see trail" at the garden for visually impaired visitors. An

The beautiful and tranquil grounds of the National Arboretum

alternative to the arboretum is **Kenilworth Park and Aquatic Gardens** (see p146), which has ponds with more than 100,000 water lilies, lotuses, and other plants. It is a good idea to plan a trip early in the day when the blooms are open and before the sun gets too hot. Frogs and turtles can be seen regularly along the footpaths around the ponds. Park naturalists conduct

nature walks around the gardens on summer weekends.

One of the most enjoyable ways to spend time outdoors is with a picnic in the park. Visit **Dumbarton Oaks Park** in Georgetown when the wildflowers are in bloom, or visit **Montrose Park**, right next door to Dumbarton Oaks, where you can enjoy the variety of birds and the boxwood maze.

DIRECTORY

Spectator Sports

FedEx Field
Arena Drive,
Landover, MD.
Tel (301) 276-6000.
w redskins.com

Georgetown Hoyas
Tel (202) 687-4692.
w guhoyas.com

Maryland Terrapins
Tel (800) 462-8377.
w umterps.com

Nationals Park Stadium
1500 South Capitol St, SE.
Tel (202) 675-6287.

RFK Stadium
2400 East Capitol St, SE.
Tel (202) 587-5000.

Verizon Center
601 F St, NW.
Map 4 D3.
Tel (202) 628-3200.

Fishing and Boating

Fletcher's Boat House
4940 Canal Rd, NW.
Map 1 A2.
Tel (202) 244-0461.

Jack's Boat House
3500 K St, NW.
Map 2 D2. **Tel** (202) 337-9642.

Thompson Boat Center
Rock Creek Parkway &
Virginia Ave, NW. **Map** 2
D3. **Tel** (202) 333-9543.
w thompsonboat center.com

Cycling

Big Wheel Bikes
1034 33rd St, NW. **Map** 1
C2. **Tel** (202) 337-0254.
w bigwheelbikes.com

Bike and Roll
1100 Pennsylvania Ave,
NW. **Map** 3 C3.
w bikethesites.com

Washington Area Bicyclist Association
2599 Ontario Rd, NW.
Tel (202) 518-0524.
w waba.org

Tennis, Golf, and Riding

East Potomac Golf Course
972 Ohio Drive, SW at
Hains Point. **Map** 3 A5.
Tel (202) 554-7660.

East Potomac Tennis Center
1090 Ohio Drive, SW
at Hains Point.
Map 3 A5.
Tel (202) 554-5962.
w eastpotomac tennis.com

Langston Golf Course
26th St & Benning Rd, NE.
Tel (202) 397-8638.

Rock Creek Golf Course
1600 Rittenhouse St, NW.
Tel (202) 882-7332.

Rock Creek Park Horse Center

Military & Glover Rds, NW.
Tel (202) 362-0117 (ext 0).
w rockcreekhorse center.com

Rock Creek Tennis Center
16th & Kennedy Sts, NW.
Tel (202) 722-5949.
w rockcreektennis.com

Exploring Nature

Dumbarton Oaks Park
Entrance on Lovers Lane,
off R & 31st Sts, NW.
Map 1 C1.

Kenilworth Park and Aquatic Gardens
1550 Anacostia Ave, NE.
Tel (202) 426-6905.

Montrose Park
R & 32nd Sts, NW.
Map 2 D1.

National Arboretum
24th & R Sts, NE.
Tel (202) 245-2726.

Children's Washington, DC

Visiting the city's monuments can be one of the favorite and most memorable activities for children in DC. Book online in advance to arrange a tour with a park ranger, during which you take a trip in the elevator to the top of the Washington Monument, then walk down the steps. Young children will like feeding the ducks at the Reflecting Pool or Constitution Gardens. You can view the Jefferson Memorial from a paddleboat on the Tidal Basin, and before you leave Washington be sure to see the monuments lit up against the night-time sky.

Children in front of the National Museum of Natural History

Practical Advice

A good source of information on specific events for children can be found in the "Going Out Guide" of *The Washington Post*. It also lists family-friendly museums and dining options. As you would expect in a major city, food is widely available in DC, whether it is hot dogs from a seller along the Mall or even strange space food (such as freeze-dried ice cream) from the **National Air and Space Museum** gift shop *(see pp64–7)*.

Sea lion at the National Zoo

Outdoor Fun

For a trip into the past, take a ride on a mule-drawn barge on the C&O Canal rom April to mid-October at Great Falls (contact the **C&O Canal Visitor Center** for details). Park Service rangers are dressed up in 19th-century costumes to add to the experience.

The beautiful wooded park of the **National Zoo** *(see pp140–41)* is a good place for a walk, and you can also enjoy watching elephant training, panda feeding, and sea lion demonstrations.

For a break from the Mall museums, take a ride on the **Carousel on the Mall** (open in summer only), in front of the Arts and Industries Building. Also worth a visit is the carousel in **Glen Echo Park** (open in summer only), built in 1921. From December to March, ice skaters can head for the **National Gallery of Art Sculpture Garden Ice Rink**. Skate rental equipment is available and visitors can also take part in group skating lessons.

Museums

The Discovery Center, a vast educational complex with an IMAX® theater, is housed in the **National Museum of Natural History** *(see pp72–3)*.

If you want to experience outer space, then see "To Fly!" and the Albert Einstein Planetarium at the **National Air and Space Museum**. A series of children's films and family programs are run by the **National Gallery of Art** *(see pp60–62)*. Children can discuss paintings and take part in a whole range of hands-on activities.

The **National Museum of the American Indian** *(see pp70–71)* has many events, workshops, films and demonstrations designed for the family. Similarly, the **National Museum of African Art** *(see p69)* hosts educative music and storytelling events.

Children are always fascinated by the **National Postal Museum** *(see p55)*, with its many intriguing hands-on activities.

Children's Theater

The Ripley Center of the Smithsonian houses the **Discovery Theater**, which stages puppet shows and plays. See a puppet show or fairytale production at the **Adventure Theatre** in Glen Echo Park. The theater company **Imagination Stage**, located north of Washington in Bethesda, Maryland, presents lively theater productions for children.

The **Kennedy Center** *(see pp120–21)* and **Wolf Trap Farm Park for the Performing Arts** also provide information on all sorts of children's events in the city.

Children's tour in Cedar Hill, the historic home of Frederick Douglass

A Little Bit of History

Children studying American history will be fascinated by a visit to Cedar Hill, once the home of Frederick Douglass, in Anacostia. The video in the visitors' center helps to tell the amazing story of this American hero.

You can take a tour of **Ford's Theatre** *(see p98)* where President Lincoln was shot and the house across the street where he died.

The **Washington National Cathedral** *(see pp144–5)* provides a free brochure to take children on a self-guided scavenger hunt seeking carvings, specific images in stained-glass windows, and gargoyles. The National Building

Museum *(see p105)* runs special programs for children on Saturdays.

Shopping

The **National Museum of Natural History** *(see pp72–3)* shops stock a wide variety of goods that will keep children enthralled. Favorites include books, natural history toys, games related to sea life, dinosaurs, and nature, as well as science kits which allow children to reproduce at home some of the wonders of the natural world on display in the museum.

Dinosaur Hall in the National Museum of Natural History

DIRECTORY

Practical Advice

National Air and Space Museum
6th St & Independence Ave, SW.
Map 4 D4.
Tel (202) 633-1000.

National Museum of American History
Constitution Ave between 12th & 14th Sts, NW. **Map** 3 B4.
Tel (202) 633-1000.

Outdoor Fun

C&O Canal Visitor Center
1057 Thomas Jefferson St, NW. **Map** 2 D3.
Tel (202) 653-5190.

Carousel on the Mall
Arts and Industries Blg, 900 Jefferson Drive, SW.
Map 3 B4.
Tel (202) 633-1000.

Glen Echo Park Carousel
7300 MacArthur Blvd, Glen Echo, MD.
Tel (301) 320-1400 or (301) 634-2222.
W glenechopark.org

National Gallery of Art Sculpture Garden Ice Rink
7th St & Constitution Ave, NW. **Map** 4 D4.
Tel (202) 737-4215.

National Zoo
3001 Connecticut Ave.
Tel (202) 633-4888.

Museums

National Air and Space Museum
6th St & Independence Ave, SW.
Map 4 D4.
Tel (202) 633-4629 (IMAX® film schedule).

National Gallery of Art
Constitution Ave between 3rd & 7th Sts, NW.
Map 4 D3.
Tel (202) 737-4215, (202) 789-3030 (children's film program).

National Museum of African Art
950 Independence Ave, SW.
Map 3 C4.
Tel (202) 633-4600.
W nmafa.si.edu

National Museum of American History
Constitution Ave between 12th & 14th Sts, NW.
Map 3 B4.
Tel (202) 633-1000.

National Museum of the American Indian
4th St & Independence Ave, SW. **Map** 4 D4.
Tel (202) 633-1000.
W americanindian.si.edu

National Museum of Natural History
10th St & Constitution Ave, NW. **Map** 3 C4.
Tel (202) 633-1000 (general information).
Tel (202) 633-4629 (IMAX® film schedule).

National Postal Museum
2 Massachusetts Ave, NE.
Map 4 E3.
Tel (202) 633-1000.

Children's Theatre

Adventure Theatre
7300 MacArthur Blvd, Glen Echo Park, Md.
Tel (301) 634-2270.

Discovery Theater
1100 Jefferson Drive, SW.
Map 3 C4.
Tel (202) 633-8700.
W discoverytheater.org

Imagination Stage
4908 Auburn Ave, Bethesda, MD.
Tel (301) 280-1660.
W imaginationstage.org

Wolf Trap Farm Park for the Performing Arts
1551 Trap Rd, Vienna, VA.
Tel (703) 255-1900.
W wolftrap.org

A Little Bit of History

Ford's Theatre
511 10th St, NW.
Map 3 C3.
Tel (202) 347-4833.
W fordstheatre.org

Frederick Douglass National Historic Site
1411 W St, SE.
Tel (202) 426-5960.

Washington National Cathedral
Massachusetts & Wisconsin Aves, NW.
Tel (202) 537-6200 (Gargoyle tour).
W cathedral.org

Shopping

National Museum of Natural History Shops
Constitution Ave between 12th and 14th Sts, NW.
Map 3 C4.
Tel (202) 633-2060.
W mnh.si.edu

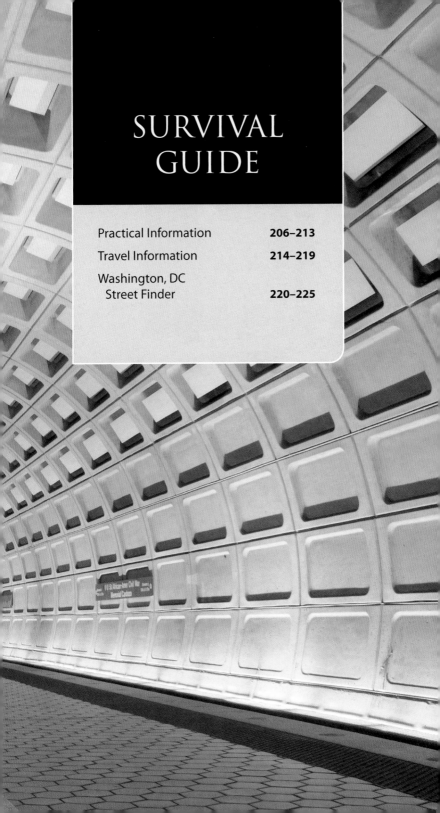

SURVIVAL GUIDE

PRACTICAL INFORMATION

Washington, DC is the heart of the American political world. It is a visitor-friendly place, especially for children and the disabled, since wheelchair accessibility is required almost everywhere, and most museums (including all under the Smithsonian umbrella *see pp100–103*) are free. The whole city shuts down on federal holidays, as well as anytime the government requires it to. With the US President and other world leaders coming and going, unexpected delays and closures can occur. Spring and fall are the best times to visit as the summers can be very hot and winters very cold.

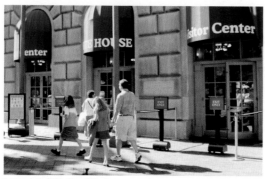

Entrance to the White House Visitor Center

Visas and Passports

Citizens of the UK, most western European countries, Canada, Japan, Australia, and New Zealand, need a valid passport and a return ticket to enter the US, and must register with the online Electronic System of Travel Authorization (ESTA) before departure. Visit https:// esta.cbp.dhs.gov to obtain the ESTA; there is a small charge but it is valid for two years. Citizens of all other countries require a valid passport and a tourist visa. Entry requirements may change. Be sure to check with the US embassy in your country before you travel. Be aware that anyone entering the US on a visa will be photographed and have their fingerprints checked.

All visitors should carry photo identification at all times. Your possessions will be checked before entering museums and some places, like the Library of Congress, have metal detectors.

Tourist Information

The Washington area is very welcoming to tourists. Visitor information desks at the airports will provide guides and maps, and staff will be able to answer questions. Major hotels usually have a knowledgeable guest services desk. Before you travel it may be worth contacting the **Destination DC** tourist office. The website provides information on special offers, local events, and free things to do.

Opening Hours

Most banks and offices in DC are open from 9am to 5pm, Monday through Friday. Some banks are also open on a Saturday morning *(see p210)*. Malls or department stores are open daily and have extended hours on a certain day of the week. Stores rarely close for federal holidays; in fact, many federal holidays are big shopping days with special sales.

All Smithsonian Museums are open on federal holidays. Some private museums, like the Phillips Collection, are closed on Mondays. Many gas stations, convenience stores and select pharmacies *(see p209)* stay open 24 hours.

Taxes and Tipping

Taxes will be added to hotel and restaurant charges, theater tickets, some grocery and store sales, and most other purchases. Be sure to ask whether the tax is included in the price displayed. Sales tax is 6 percent, hotel tax is 14.5 percent, with 10 percent tax on food and beverages.

Tipping is expected for most services: in restaurants tip 15–20 percent of the bill, give $2 per bag to airport and hotel porters, and $2 to valet parking attendants. Bartenders expect 50 cents to $1 per drink; if you visit a hair salon or barbershop, 15 to 20 percent of the bill should suffice.

Alcohol and Cigarettes

The legal minimum age for drinking alcohol in Washington is 21, and you will need photo identification (I.D.) as proof of your age in order to purchase alcohol and be allowed into bars. It is illegal to drink alcohol in public parks or to carry an open container of alcohol in your car, and penalties for driving under the influence of alcohol are severe. Cigarettes can be purchased by those over 18 years old; proof of age will be required.

Smoking is prohibited in all public buildings, bars, restaurants, and stores.

Electricity

Electricity flows at the standard US 110–120 volts, and a two-prong plug is required. For non-US appliances you will need a plug adapter and a voltage converter.

◀ Union Street Metrorail station

International Student Identity Card, accepted as I.D. in America

Student Travelers

While students from abroad should purchase an International Student Identity Card (**ISIC**) before traveling to Washington, they may not use it often as many sights have free entry. Paying museums such as the Phillips Collection give a $2 discount on their regular admission. The ISIC handbook lists places and services in the US that offer discounts to card holders, including accommodations, museums, and theaters. The **Student Advantage Card** is available to all American college undergraduates and offers a range of discounts.

Senior Travelers

Senior citizens are eligible for certain discounts with the appropriate proof of age. Amtrak gives a discount of 15 percent for persons over 62 on most trains (not valid for business or first class). Many movie theaters give reduced admission (usually $1 off the regular price) to those aged 60 or over. Most private museums offer a senior's discount similar to the student discount.

The **American Association of Retired Persons** is open to the over-50s. Members qualify for discounts of 5–30 percent on tours, hotels, and travel.

Disabled Travelers

Washington is a model of accessibility and almost all public buildings, including most hotels and restaurants, are required to be wheelchair accessible. Streets have curb cuts and there are elevators at all Metro stations. The exceptions are historic areas like Georgetown, where 18th-century buildings and cobblestone streets make using a wheelchair problematic. For general advice, contact the **Society for Accessible Travel and Hospitality**.

Gay and Lesbian Travelers

In 2009, Washington, DC passed a gay marriage act – one of the few places in the US to recognize same-sex union. The city's lively gay scene centers around Dupont Circle and the adjacent 17th, 14th, and P Streets. The **Human Rights Campaign**

Headquarters is home to the national organization for gay rights.

Responsible Tourism

Like many places in the US, Washington, DC is increasingly aware of environmental issues. Visitors can be assured that most public organizations and many restaurants recycle their trash and, in 2009, the city enacted a law charging 5 cents for every plastic and paper bag given at grocery stores.

Local and organic produce are widely available, especially at weekend markets such as the Eastern Market (7am–6pm Sat, 9am–5pm Sun) and the Dupont Circle Farmers' Market (8:30am–1pm; Jan–Mar: 10am–1pm). The mother of the organic food movement in eastern USA is Restaurant Nora (see p190).

Many hotel chains touting their green credentials have representatives in DC, including Fairmont Hotels (see p178), cited as the best hotel chain by treehugger.com.

Local produce on sale at the Eastern Market

DIRECTORY

Embassies

Australia
1601 Massachusetts Ave, NW. **Map** 2 F2.
Tel (202) 797-3000.
W usa.embassy.gov.au

Canada
501 Pennsylvania Ave, NW.
Map 4 D3.
Tel (202) 682-1740.
W canadainternational.gc.ca/washington

Ireland
2234 Massachusetts Ave, NW. **Map** 3 A1.
Tel (202) 462-3939.
W irelandemb.org

New Zealand
37 Observatory Circle, NW. **Tel** (202) 328-4800.
W nzembassy.com/usa

United Kingdom
3100 Massachusetts Ave, NW.
Tel (202) 588-6500.
W britainusa.com

Tourist Information

Destination DC
901 7th Street, NW.
Map 4 D2.
Tel (202) 289-7000.
W washington.org

Student Travelers

ISIC
W isic.org

Student Advantage Card
W student advantage.com

Senior Travelers

American Association for Retired Persons
601 E St, NW.
Map 4 D3.
Tel 888-687-2277.
W aarp.org

Disabled Travelers

Society for Accessible Travel and Hospitality
Tel (212) 447-7284.
W sath.org

Gay and Lesbian Travelers

Human Rights Campaign Headquarters
1640 Rhode Island Ave, NW.
Tel (202) 628-4160.
W hrc.org

Personal Security and Health

Although as in any major city there is crime, Washington has made great efforts in reducing problems and cleaning up its streets, and with success. If you stick to the tourist areas, avoid straying into outlying districts, and take common sense precautions as in any big city, you should not run into any trouble. The main sights are located in safe areas where there are many people, and serious crime is rare. When visiting sights off the beaten track, take a taxi to and from the destination. Most importantly, pay attention to your surroundings, especially after dark.

Law Enforcement

There are several different police forces in Washington, DC, including the Secret Service, the FBI (Federal Bureau of Investigation), and the more widespread M.P.D.C. (Metropolitan Police, Washington, DC) police. Many major sights also have their own police forces, such as the National Zoological Park Police and the United States Capitol Police.

At monuments, you will see green-uniformed Park Rangers. Their role is largely crowd control and as a source of information; many are trained historians.

Because the city is home to the President, whenever he travels, members of the law enforcement agencies follow. When foreign political leaders visit, the police are even more visible than usual: you will see them on horseback, on bicycles, in cars, and even on top of buildings.

As a visitor, should you encounter any trouble, approach any of the blue-uniformed M.P.D.C. officers that regularly patrol the city streets. All M.P.D.C officers carry weapons.

The DC police are well-known for their strict interpretation of the law. In other words: don't talk back, don't argue and never offer money in the form of a bribe; this could land you in jail.

What to be Aware of

Serious crime is rarely witnessed in the main sightseeing areas of Washington. However, avoid wandering into areas that you have no reason to visit, either during the day or at night. Pickpockets do operate in the city and will target anyone who looks like a tourist. Panhandlers (beggars) are also common, gathering near Metro stations and at shopping malls. It is best to keep walking, ignore their requests for money, and avoid engaging in conversation. Police officers regularly patrol the tourist areas, but it is still advisable to prepare the day's itinerary in advance, use common sense, and stay alert. Try not to advertise that you are a tourist; study your map before you set off, avoid wearing expensive jewellery, and carry your camera or camcorder securely. Carry small amounts of cash; credit cards are a more secure option. Keep these close to your body in a money belt or inside pocket. Before you leave home, make a photo-copy of important documents, including your passport and visa, and keep them with you, though separate from the originals. Also make a note of your credit card numbers, in case of theft or loss. Keep an eye on your belongings at all

M.P.D.C. officer

times. It is a good idea to put any valuables in the hotel safe – do not carry them around with you. Most hotels will not guarantee the security of any belongings that you leave in your room.

In an Emergency

Call 911 for police or fire assistance, or if you need an ambulance. If you are involved in a medical emergency, go to a hospital emergency room.

Lost and Stolen Property

Although the chances of retrieving lost or stolen property are slim, you should report all stolen items to the police. Call the **Police Non-Emergency Line** for guidance. Make sure you keep a copy of the police report, which you will need when making your insurance claim.

In case of loss, it is useful to have a list of serial numbers or a photocopy of all documents; keep these separate as proof of possession. If you can remember to do so, it is useful to make a mental note of the taxi company or bus route you use; it might make it easier to retrieve lost items.

If your passport is lost or stolen, get in touch with your country's embassy or consulate (see p207). If you lose your credit card, most card companies have toll-free numbers for reporting a loss or theft (see p210).

Hospital sign

Hospitals and Pharmacies

It is possible to visit a doctor or dentist without being registered with them, but you will be asked to pay in advance. Keep all receipts for medical costs to make a claim on your insurance later. Depending on the limitations of your insurance, it is better to avoid the overcrowded city-owned hospitals and opt instead for one of the private hospitals. If

Police car

Ambulance

Fire engine

taken by ambulance, however, drivers are required to take you to the nearest hospital. If you require a dentist you can call the **District of Columbia Dental Society**, which provides a free referral service.

Pharmacists are usually able to offer basic medical advice, and there are some pharmacies with clinics attached to treat common illnesses and small injuries. Patients are seen by nurse practitioners or physician assistants. One such clinic is the **CVS Minute Clinic**, which has three locations in DC, and several in the Virginia and Maryland suburbs.

If you need a prescription, there are plenty of pharmacies in and around the city, some staying open 24 hours. CVS is the most common chain.

Travel and Health Insurance

It is strongly recommended to obtain travel insurance before traveling to the United States. It is particularly important for visitors to have sufficient insurance for emergency medical and dental care, which can be very expensive in the States. Even with medical cover, you may have to pay for the services, then make a claim for reimbursement with your insurance company when you return home. Hospitals accept most credit cards, as do most doctors and dentists.

Should you go to a hospital or seek medical assistance, be sure to take proof of your insurance with you. If you usually take medication, it is a good idea to bring a back-up supply with you and to ask your doctor to provide a copy of the prescription in case of loss or the need for more.

It is advisable to make sure your personal property is insured and to obtain cover for lost or stolen baggage and travel documents, as well as trip cancellation fees, legal advice, and accidental death or injury. Your insurance company or travel agent should be able to recommend a suitable policy.

Legal Assistance

Non-US citizens requiring legal assistance should call their embassy (see p207). Embassies will not lend you money but can help with advice on legal matters in emergencies. Should you be arrested for any reason, it is advisable to be cooperative, but you have the right to remain silent.

Restrooms

Washington, DC does not have public restrooms. There are free bathrooms available in all visitor's centers, museums, and galleries, and all hotels and restaurants also have restrooms, but they may only be available to paying customers.

CVS/pharmacy®
for all the ways you care℠

Logo for CVS pharmacies, a common pharmacy chain in Washington, DC

Banking and Currency

Throughout Washington there are various places to access and exchange your money, from banks to cash machines to bureaux de change. The most important thing to remember is not to carry all your money and credit cards with you at once, and to be prepared to use ATM machines on Sunday when most banks and currency exchange offices are closed.

open weekdays from 9am to 5pm. Most exchange offices charge a fee or commission, so it is worth looking around to get the best value rates. Many major hotels can also change currency, but they often charge a higher rate of exchange or commission.

DIRECTORY

Main Banks

Bank of America
700 13th St, NW.
Map 3 B3. **Tel** (202) 624-4413.
w bankofamerica.com

Capital One Bank
701 Pennsylvania Ave, NW.
Map 3 C3. **Tel** (202) 737-4950.
w capitalone.com

Sun Trust Bank
1445 New York Ave, NW.
Map 3 B3. **Tel** (202) 879-6000.
Tel (888) 786 8787.
w suntrust.com

TD Bank
1753 Connecticut Ave, NW.
Tel 888-751-9000.
w tdbank.com

Foreign Exchange

American Express Travel Service
1501 K St, NW. **Map** 2 F2.
Tel (202) 457-1300.

Thomas Cook/Travelex
Tel 1-877-414-6359
(general information.)
w travelex.com
Branch at:
1800 K St, NW.
Map 3 A2.
Tel (202) 872-1428.

Lost or Stolen Cards

American Express
Tel 1-850-882-028.

MasterCard
Tel 1-800-627-8372.

Visa
Tel 800-847-2911.

Wiring Money

MoneyGram
w moneygram.com

Western Union
Tel 800-325-6000.
w westernunion.com

Banks and Foreign Exchange

Generally, most banks are open Monday through Friday from 9am to 3pm, although some may close later, and Saturday mornings from 9am to noon or 1pm. Most banks are closed on Sundays and federal holidays *(see p41)*. The exception is **TD Bank**, which has many branches with Sunday hours and is open on federal holidays.

Always ask if there are any special fees before you make your transaction. At most banks, traveler's checks in US dollars can be cashed with any photo identification, although passports are usually required to exchange foreign currency.

Foreign currency exchange is available at the main branches of large banks or at independent exchange offices. Among the best known are **American Express Travel Service** and **Thomas Cook/Travelex**, both of which have branches in and around DC. Exchange offices are generally

American Express credit cards

ATMs

Automated teller machines (ATMs) are found all over the Washington area, usually near the entrance to banks, or inside many convenience stores and supermarkets.

Widely accepted bank cards include Cirrus, Plus, Maestro, NYCE, and credit cards such as VISA or MasterCard. Note that a fee may be levied on your withdrawal (a pop-up screen should tell you the fee and ask if you want the transaction to continue). To minimize the risk of robbery, use ATMs in well-lit, populated areas only. Avoid withdrawing money at night or in isolated areas, and be aware of the people around you.

Credit and Debit Cards

American Express, VISA, MasterCard/Maestro, and most international debit cards are widely accepted almost everywhere in Washington,

Customers withdrawing cash from Bank of America ATMs

from theaters and hotels to restaurants and shops. Indeed, it is advisable to carry a credit card when visiting Washington as it may be required to reserve a hotel or rental car and to pay for gasoline (petrol), especially at self-service stations.

If your credit card is lost or stolen, contact your card company immediately.

Card Security

Because of the increasing problem of identity theft and card cloning, merchants may ask for photo identification when making a purchase.

If you are traveling overseas, alert your bank of your plans, or they may put a hold on your account if they see untoward charges.

Emergency Funds (Wiring Money)

MoneyGram and **Western Union** both offer immediate money transfer for a fee. Both sender and recipient will need to locate an agent to set up the transfer and collect the funds (Western Union also has an online facility for sending funds.)

Coins

American coins come in 1-dollar, 50-, 25-, 10-, 5-, and 1-cent pieces. There are also goldtone $1 coins in circulation and State quarters, which feature an historical scene on one side. Each coin has a popular name: 25-cent pieces are called quarters, 10-cent pieces are called dimes, 5-cent pieces are called nickels, and 1-cent pieces called pennies.

1-cent coin
(a penny)

5-cent coin
(a nickel)

10-cent coin
(a dime)

25-cent coin
(a quarter)

An American Eagle
on a $1 gold coin

Bills (Bank Notes)

The units of currency in the United States are dollars and cents. There are 100 cents to a dollar. Bank notes come in the following denominations: $1, $5, $10, $20, $50, and $100. Security features include subtle color hues and improved color-shifting ink in the lower right hand corner of the face of each note.

1-dollar bill ($1)

5-dollar bill ($5)

10-dollar bill ($10)

20-dollar bill ($20)

50-dollar bill ($50)

100-dollar bill ($100)

Communications and Media

The almost universal use of cell phones has caused the demise of coin-operated pay phones. It is now difficult to find a public pay phone in the street, although they are still available at main stations. Like most major cities, Washington, DC is thoroughly wired for Internet access. Free Wi-Fi is provided in many public places and there are several other ways to get online. Since Washington, DC is the political capital of the United States, news is readily available from newspapers, magazines, television, and radio.

Cell Phones

Cell phone service in Washington is generally excellent. If you are coming from overseas and want to guarantee that your cell phone will work, make sure you have a quad-band phone. Tri-band phones from outside the US are also usually compatible but, because the US uses two frequency bands itself, it is recommended to contact your service provider for clarification before you travel; you may also need to activate the "roaming" facility.

Other options include buying a prepaid cell phone in the US or a SIM chip for a US carrier. Many car rental companies also rent cell phones for customers (see p219).

Public Telephones

In the last decade, the number of public pay phones in the United States has decreased by half and Washington is no exception. However, public pay phones are still available at Union Station, the Smithsonian Museums, and some Metro stations, and occasionally on the street. The area code for Washington is 202. When dialing within the district, omit the code. When dialing outside the district from within DC, you will need to use the appropriate area code. The area code for the Maryland suburbs is 301 and for the Virginia suburbs, 703.

Credit card calls can be made by calling 1-800-CALL-ATT. Directory Assistance is 411 and calls are charged at the local rate. Phone cards of various values can be purchased from most supermarkets, 24-hour stores,

newspaper stands, and some branches of Western Union.

Telephone Charges

Local calls cost around 50 cents for 3 minutes from pay phones. Calls made from hotel rooms will cost much more, so it is a good idea to locate a pay phone or use your cell. Operator assistance can also be used to help you connect your call, but again, this will cost more.

Internet Access

Although Internet cafés are rare in Washington, many public places – such as bookstores, cafés, airports, and the Mall – have a free wireless service. Most hotels in the city have wireless Internet in their rooms, and many also have a dedicated business center (with computers) within the hotel. For those without their own laptops, computers (with Internet) are available for use in public libraries and in stores such as FedEx, DHL, and UPS.

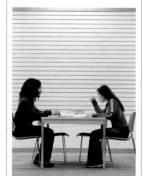

Using the Internet in the reading room of a Washington public library

Post Service

Post offices are open from 9am to 5pm, Mondays through Fridays, and have limited Saturday service, usually 9am to noon. Post offices are closed on all federal holidays. Stamps can also be bought from most major supermarkets, such as Giant and Safeway.

If the correct postage is affixed, you can send a letter by putting it in one of the blue mailboxes found on street corners all over Washington. Times of mail pickup are written inside the mailbox's lid; there are usually several collections a day. It is mandatory to use a five-digit zip code when sending mail. Be aware that small packages may not be posted in mailboxes for security reasons; they must be taken to a post office.

Depending on how far the mail needs to travel in the US, it can take from one to five days to

Useful Dialing Codes

- To make a direct-dial call outside the local area code, but within the US and Canada, dial 1 before the area code. Useful area codes for DC and the surrounding area include: Washington, DC 202; Baltimore 410; MD 301, 240; Delaware 302; Northern Virginia 703; West Virginia 304.
- For international calls, dial 011 followed by the appropriate country code. Then dial the area code, omitting the first 0, and t he local number.
- To make an international call via the operator, dial 00; note that the call will be charged at a higher rate.
- For international operator assistance, dial 01.
- For local operator assistance, dial 0.
- For international directory inquiries, dial 00.
- For local directory inquiries, dial 411.
- For emergency police, fire, or ambulance services, dial 911.
- 1-800 and 888 indicate a toll-free number.

arrive at its destination. The most economical way to send international mail is First Class International at less than $1 per ounce, depending on the destination. Express and Priority mail are also available at the post office for a faster, though more expensive, service. If you are a visitor to the city and you wish to receive mail, poste restante, you can have it sent to you by addressing it care of "General Delivery" at the **Main Post Office**, or any other main post office, quoting the city name. They will hold the mail for 30 days for you to collect.

It is worth noting that USPS refers to the United States Postal Service, while UPS is a private courier company.

Courier Services

Courier services are a popular, if more expensive, alternative to the postal service. Many hotels will arrange for your packages and letters to be shipped either by Federal Express (**FedEx**), **DHL**, a division of Deutsche Poste, or **UPS**. DHL only operates internationally while FedEx and UPS handle both national and international letters and packages. FedEx

US mailbox

services are available at Fedex Office Centers (easily recognizable by the FedEx arrow logo); DHL is offered at independent office storefront locations like Parcel Plus. FedEx and UPS also have self-service kiosks throughout the city for letters and flat packages. Registration for self-service packages is completed online, and a label downloaded to attach to the package.

Television and Radio

Televisions are everywhere in the United States, from bars and restaurants to hotels and stores. Most have cable hook-up, allowing access to more than 60 different channels. Some of the best to view are CBS, NBC, CNN, ABC, and Fox. For those interested in the political goings-on in the city, tune in to channels C-Span 1 and C-Span 2 to watch the proceedings in Congress as they are broadcast live. Radios can be found in most hotel rooms, as well as in rental cars, and offer a wide range of music, from country through classical and jazz to rock. Popular radio stations include National Public Radio (WAMU at 88.5), modern rock on WHFS (99.1), and soft rock on Easy 101 (101).

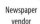
Newspaper vendor

Newspapers

The most widely read newspaper in the DC area is *The Washington Post*, which is also one of the best newspapers published in the country. The local *Washington Express* is widely available as are *USA Today*, *The Wall Street Journal*, and *The New York Times*. Newspapers can be bought from street dispensers (boxes on the sidewalk that dispense newspapers), newsstands, gas stations, convenience stores, hotel lobbies, and bookstores. They are also all available online. Newsstands and some bookstores carry newspapers from most large US cities and many foreign countries.

DIRECTORY

Postal Services

Georgetown Station
3050 K St, NW. **Map** 2 D2.

Main Post Office
Brentwood Station, 900 Brentwood Road, NE, Washington, DC 20066. **Tel** (202) 636-1581.

Martin Luther King Jr. Station
1400 L St, NW. **Map** 2 F3. National Capitol Station 2 Massachusetts Ave, NE. **Map** 4 E3.

Temple Heights Station
1921 Florida Ave, NW. **Map** 2 E1.

Courier Services

DHL
Branches all over the DC area. For customer services call: **Tel** (800) 225-5345.
Ⓦ dhl.com

FedEx
Branches all over the DC area. For customer services call: Tel (800) 463-3339.
Ⓦ fedex.com

UPS
Branches all over the DC area. For the nearest branch call: **Tel** (800) 275-8777.
Ⓦ ups.com

Washington Time

Washington is on Eastern Standard Time. Daylight Saving Time begins on the second Sunday in March, when clocks are set ahead 1 hour, and ends on the first Sunday in November, when clocks go back 1 hour.

City and Country	Hours + or − EST	City and Country	Hours + or − EST
Chicago (US)	−1	Moscow (Russia)	+8
Dublin (Ireland)	+5	Paris (France)	+6
London (UK)	+5	Sydney (Australia)	+15
Los Angeles (US)	−3	Tokyo (Japan)	+14
Madrid (Spain)	+6	Vancouver (Canada)	−3

TRAVEL INFORMATION

Washington is easy to get to via any mode of transportation. Three airports serve the DC area; they are used by most major airlines for domestic and international flights. Two major bus lines also operate to the city, as do Amtrak trains, which arrive at and depart from Union Station, right in the center of Washington. Visitors often tend to travel first to DC, base themselves in the city, and then arrange day or weekend trips into Maryland and Virginia.

Glass-walled interior of Reagan National Airport

Arriving by Air

There are three main airports in the Washington, DC area: **Dulles International Airport**, **Reagan National Airport**, and Baltimore-Washington International Thurgood Marshall Airport (known as **BWI**). Most of the major carriers, including American Airlines, British Airways, Air France, and United Airlines, fly to at least one of these airports. The majority of international and overseas flights land at Dulles International, 26 miles (42 km) west of Washington in Virginia. Dulles is not directly served by a Metro but there is a connecting shuttle service, the **Washington Flyer Coach Service**, to take new arrivals to West Falls Church

Metro. Between the coach service and the Metro, expect to spend up to an hour-and-a-half to reach the city center. Alternatively, the **SuperShuttle** share-ride bus service runs every hour and will drop passengers at their door. It is a cheaper option than a taxi but journey times depend on detours made to drop off the other passengers. Taxis are plentiful and are the quickest but most expensive option. Make sure the fare is negotiated before departure.

Located about 5 miles (8 km) outside the city in Arlington County, Virginia, the Reagan National Airport is the most convenient airport for central Washington. The city is easily accessible using the Metro, or by taking the SuperShuttle (every 30 minutes), or a taxi.

BWI Airport, which is situated 30 miles (48 km) northeast of DC, tends to be used by low-cost airlines. The Maryland Rail Commuter Service (**MARC**) is the cheapest way to get from the airport to the city, but it runs only on weekdays. Amtrak *(see p215)* offers the next-best train service for just a few dollars more. The SuperShuttle is also available

from BWI, but it is more costly and takes longer than a train ride. The taxi fare from BWI into central DC is rather expensive.

For security reasons, anyone arriving in the US on a visa is now photographed, and will have their fingerprints taken, before being allowed into the country *(see p206)*.

Air Fares

The busiest season for travel to the US is March through June and September through early November. Christmas and Thanksgiving are also busy. Flights will be at their most expensive during these periods. Fwlights in June and July are usually the most expensive but there are many discounted accommodations at this time. Weekend flights are usually less expensive than weekdays, while Apex tickets are often the best deal. Apex tickets must be booked at least one week in advance, and your visit must include a Saturday night. Cheap air fares can be obtained by shopping around, so it is worth checking with the airlines and websites such as **Expedia**, **Kayak**, and **Priceline**.

The Washington Flyer, shuttling from Dulles to West Falls Church Metro

Airport	Information	Distance/Time to Washington, DC	Taxi Fare	SuperShuttle
Dulles	(703) 572-2700	26 miles (42 km) 40 minutes	$50–5	$26–35
Reagan National	(703) 417-8000	5 miles (8 km) 15 minutes	$15–20	$13–23
BWI	(410) 859-7111	30 miles (48 km) 50 minutes	$62–5	$32–42

Main concourse at Union Station

Arriving by Train

Amtrak is one of the best ways to travel to the DC area. Trains from other cities arrive in Washington at Union Station. Trains are also available from Union Station to Baltimore, Philadelphia, Richmond, and Williamsburg. Amtrak offers a deluxe train service to New York City, called the Acela, which travels slightly faster and more comfortably than the regular train, but is more expensive. Trains (either the Acela or the slower Northeast Regional) to New York leave every hour. **MARC,** Maryland's commuter train, departs on weekdays to Baltimore.

Arriving by Car

The center of Washington, DC is surrounded by Interstates I-95 and I-495, which together form the congested Capital Beltway. Driving on the Beltway, especially during rush hour, can be intimidating for the inexperienced driver. Interstate I-66 connects Washington to West Virginia, and Interstate I-50 heads east from DC to Annapolis, Maryland, and the surrounding areas. Beyond the Beltway, Interstate I-95 goes north toward Baltimore, Philadelphia, and New York. Interstate I-270 heads north to Frederick, Maryland.

Arriving by Bus

Intercity buses are a great, economical way to get to Washington. As well as the traditional **Greyhound** buses, there are half a dozen bus companies serving DC, including **Megabus**, **Bolt Bus**, **Vamoose**, and the **Washington Deluxe**. Many are equipped with restrooms, free Wi-Fi, power outlets, and even DVD players. Tickets are sold on a scale – one-way to New York is generally about $25, but may be as little as $1 with advance purchase.

Greyhound buses depart from the bus terminal near Union Station, but many of the other bus companies leave from more central locations.

Greyhound bus, an inexpensive way to see the whole country

DIRECTORY

Arriving by Air

BWI Airport
Linthicam, MD.
Tel (410) 859-7111 or (800) I-FLY-BWI. Lost & Found
Tel (410) 859-7387.
w bwiairport.com

Dulles International Airport
Chantilly, VA.
Tel (703) 572-2700. Lost & Found **Tel** (703) 572-8479.
w metwashairports.com

Reagan National Airport
Arlington, VA.
Tel (703) 417-8000. Lost & Found **Tel** (703) 417-8560.
w metwashairports.com

SuperShuttle
Tel (800) 258-3826 or (800) BLUE-VAN.
w supershuttle.com

Washington Flyer Coach Service
Tel (888) 927-4359 or (888) WASH-FLY.
w washfly.com

Air Fares

Expedia
Tel 1-877-787-7186.
w Expedia.com

Kayak
w kayak.com

Priceline
Tel (800) 774-2354.
w priceline.com

Arriving by Train

Amtrak
Union Station, 50 Massachusetts Ave, NE.
Tel 1-800-872-7245.
w amtrak.com

MARC
Tel (410) 539-5000 or 1-866-743-3682.
w mtamaryland.com

Arriving by Bus

2000 New Century Travel
Tel (215) 627-2666 or (917) 577-6781.
w 2001bus.com

Bolt Bus
Tel 1-877-265-8287.
w boltbus.com

DC2NY
Tel (202) 332-2691.
w dc2ny.com

Greyhound Busline
Tel (800) 231-2222 or (800) 289-5160.
w greyhound.com

Megabus
Tel 1-877-462-6342.
w megabus.com

Vamoose
Tel (212) 695-6766 or (301) 718-0036.
w vamoosebus.com

Washington Deluxe
Tel 1-866-287-6932 or 1-718-387-7523.
w washny.com

Getting Around Washington, DC

Washington has a very comprehensive public transportation system. Visitors and locals alike find that it is easier to get around by public transportation than by car, especially as they do not then have the aggravation of finding a much-coveted parking space. All the major tourist attractions in the capital are accessible on foot, by Metrorail, by Metrobus, or by taxi.

Busy night-time traffic in central Washington, DC

Green Travel

With such an excellent public transportation system, it is easy to get around Washington, DC without causing undue harm to the environment. Almost every tourist sight is accessible via public transportation. Furthermore, Metrobus runs a fleet of buses powered by Compressed Natural Gas (CNG), a cleaner alternative to gasoline (petrol).

Cycling has become an increasingly popular way to travel in Washington, and there is an excellent network of cycle lanes throughout the center. Cycling has been further encouraged with the Capital Bikeshare self-hire scheme (see p217).

If it is necessary to use a taxi, visitors can encourage green practices by requesting a "hybrid" taxi, powered by a combination of battery and gasoline, although these cabs are not always available. If using a taxi in the Virginia suburbs, **Envirocab** runs an all-hybrid fleet. They are not licensed to operate in the District, however.

All car rental companies offer hybrid cars, but with limited availability. Book ahead to make sure your request is considered.

Getting your Bearings

It is important to know that the city is made up of four quadrants: northeast (NE), northwest (NW), southeast (SE), and southwest (SW), with the US Capitol at the central point. Every address in DC includes the quadrant code (NE, and so on) and, with building numbers running into the thousands on the same street in each quadrant, its use is necessary to distinguish the location.

A useful tip for when you are first trying to find your way around the city is to remember that most numbered streets run North and South, and most lettered streets run East and West. However, be aware that there is no "J," "X," "Y," or "Z" Street, and that "I" Street is often written as "Eye" Street.

Walking

Washington is a terrific city for walking, as long as you wear comfortable shoes and keep your wits about you. Many of the main sights are clustered around the Mall. In Georgetown, walking is the best way to soak up the atmosphere.

Metrorail

A map of the Metrorail (see back endpaper and City Map) is one of the most important pieces of information visitors will need when trying to get around DC. The system takes some getting used to, and the instructions are in English only, so allow plenty of time when first using the Metrorail (or "Metro," as it is also called).

The cost of the fare depends on the time and distance you wish to travel, and ranges from $1.35 to $3.90. Tickets, or "farecards," for single or multiple trips can be bought from vending machines. Coins and bills (but no bills over $20) can be used to pay the exact fare; or add more money if you wish to use the farecard again. Passengers need to swipe their farecards through the turnstile at the beginning and end of the trip. If there is any unused fare left at the final destination the ticket will be returned to you; if not, the ticket will be retained. You can top up tickets for further trips. Metrorail passes are on offer for one day ($15) and seven days' ($40.50) travel. These can be used to transfer from Metro to bus. For convenience, it may be worth purchasing a SmarTrip card. This is a plastic rechargeable farecard which can also be used on other modes of public transportation in DC.

Five Metrorail lines operate in downtown DC, with frequent services: the Orange Line; Blue Line; Red Line; Yellow Line; and Green Line. Trains run from 5:30am to midnight Monday through Thursday, from 5:30am to 3am on Friday and 7am to 3am on Saturday, and from 7am to midnight on Sunday. Trains run frequently (less than 10 minutes' wait) and, on board, stops are announced at every station. The entire system is accessible for wheelchairs. One warning: eating, drinking, smoking or littering on the Metro is grounds for arrest.

Metro sign

Washington, DC Metrobus

Metrobus

Metrobus is a fast, inexpensive way to get around. Fares can be paid either with exact change on boarding, with a SmarTrip card, or a Metrorail farecard pass (*see* Metrorail). The standard, off-peak fare is $1.45 (or $1.35 with SmarTrip). If paying with cash, there is a 25 cent charge for bus-to-bus transfers; if using SmarTrip, transfers are free within a 3-hour period. Up to two children under five can travel for free with a fare-paying passenger and there are discounts for disabled travelers and senior citizens. The **Circulator** bus links the main sights in the center and runs every 10 minutes. Fares are $1 for adults and 50 cents for kids.

Maps of all the bus routes are available in Metrorail stations, and maps of specific lines are posted at each bus stop.

Many Metrobuses are wheelchair accessible with a "kneeling" feature that lowers the bus for the disabled rider.

Taxis

Taxis can usually be hailed from the street corner of major arteries, but if you need to be somewhere at a specific time it is advisable to book. The **DC Taxi Cab Commission** will provide names of cab companies. Taxi fares in DC are operated using time and distance meters. Passengers should expect to pay a starting "drop" rate of $3, and then $2.16 for every mile after this. Luggage, rush hour travel, and gas prices can all incur surcharges from 50 cents to $2, and each extra passenger costs $1.50. Be aware that drivers do not always know the way to addresses beyond the tourist center.

Driving and Parking in the City

Driving in DC need not be stressful as long as you avoid the rush hour (between 6:30 and 9:30am, and 4 and 7pm on weekdays). During these times the direction of traffic flow can change, some roads become one way, and left turns may be forbidden to ease congestion. These changes are usually marked, but always pay close attention to the road. Curbside parking is hard to find at the more popular locations, and is illegal at rush hour in many areas. If using metered parking, it is important to keep within the

time limit; you could otherwise be fined, risk being clamped, or towed away. Parking restrictions on Sundays and public holidays are different from other days, so read the parking signs carefully.

Cycling

There is a great network of cycle paths in DC. Bike shops rent out bikes, and will be able to suggest routes. They can usually provide route maps. **Better Bikes** will deliver a rental bike to you for a cost of $25–50 per day. **Capital Bikeshare** is a 24-hour, self-service hire scheme where bikes can be rented from more than 110 stations around the city. **Bike the Sites** offers bike rentals, as well as organized tours of the city.

Road sign

Guided Tours

There are many city bus tours available in DC. **DC Tours** offers a hop-on-hop-off sightseeing service with numerous pick-up points. For something a bit different, **Old Town Trolley Tours** offers a ride around the main sites in an old-fashioned trolley bus. **DC Metro Food Tours** run culinary walking tours of several DC neighborhoods. **Bike and Roll** offers bike tours in and around the city, including a 1-hour Early Bird Fun Ride and a 10-mile (16-km) Capital Sites Ride. **DC Ducks** provides a tour of the city and a tour down the Potomac River.

DIRECTORY

Green Travel

Envirocab
Tel (703) 920-3333.
w envirotaxicab.com

Metrorail and Metrobus

Circulator
Tel (202) 962-1423.
w dccirculator.com

Metrorail and Metrobus
600 5th St, NW,
Washington, DC 20001.

Tel (202) 637-7000.
Tel (202) 638-3780 TTY.
w wmata.com

Taxis

DC Taxi Cab Commission
Tel (202) 645-6018.
w dctaxi.dc.gov

Diamond Cab
Tel (202) 387-6200.

Yellow Cab
Tel (202) 544-1212.

Cycling

Better Bikes
w betterbikesinc.com

Bike the Sites
w bikethesites.com

Capital Bikeshare
w capitalbikeshare.com

Guided Tours

Bike and Roll
Tel 866-736-8224.
w bikeandroll.com

DC Ducks
Tel 855-323-8257.
w dcducks.com

DC Metro Food Tours
Tel (202)-683-8847.
w dcmetrofoodtours.com

DC Tours
Tel 888-878-9870.
w dctours.us

Old Town Trolley Tours
Tel (202) 832-9800.
w trolleytours.com

Exploring Beyond Washington, DC

There is much to see beyond Washington's city limits, and traveling by car is easy with a good map. Many of the sights are reachable by public transportation, but it is generally easier and quicker to drive. Car rental is widely available but often expensive. Buses and trains are a cheaper alternative, but your choice of destinations may be more limited.

Driving along the scenic Skyline Drive *(see p167)*, Virginia

Car Rental

To rent a car in the US you must usually be at least 25 years old with a valid driving license and a clean driving record. All agencies require a major credit card. Damage and liability insurance is recommended just in case something unexpected should happen. It is advisable always to return the car with a full tank of gas; otherwise you will be required to pay the inflated fuel prices charged by the rental agencies. Check for any pre-existing damage to the car and note this on your contract.

It is often less expensive to rent a vehicle at an airport, as car rental taxes are $2 a day more in the city. Agencies with offices at the Washington airports include **Alamo**, **Avis**, **Budget**, and **Hertz**. You could also become a member of **Zip Car**, a car sharing scheme. These cars can be picked up from hundreds of locations across the city. Your car will come with fuel, insurance, and 180 miles (290 km) per day.

Road sign

Rules of the Road

The highway speed limit in the DC area is 55 mph (88 km/h) – much lower than in many European countries. In residential areas the speed limit ranges from 20 to 35 mph (32–48 km/h), and near schools it can be as low as 15 mph (24 km/h).

Roads are generally well-signed but it is still wise to plan your route ahead. It is important to obey the signs, especially "No U-turn" signs, or you risk getting a ticket. If you are pulled over by the police, be courteous or you risk facing an even greater fine.

In addition, all drivers are required to carry a valid drivers' license and be able to produce registration documents and insurance for their vehicle. Most foreign licenses are valid, but if your license is not in English, or does not have a photo ID, you must get an international driver's license. Many roads are surveyed by cameras that will issue a ticket even if you are going just a few miles per hour over the speed limit. This is not limited to major arteries.

Interstate highways are abbreviated on signs with a capital "I" followed by a number. Avoid the Capital Beltway (I-495) at rush hour.

Gasoline (Petrol)

Gas comes in three grades – regular, super, and premium. There is an extra charge if an attendant serves you, but patrons can fill their own tanks at self-service pumps without incurring an extra fee. Most stations are exclusively self-service and only accept credit cards. Gas is generally cheap in the US.

Breakdowns

In the unlucky event of a breakdown, the best course of action is to pull completely off the road and put on the hazard lights to alert other drivers that you are stationary. There are emergency phones along some of the major interstate highways, but in other situations breakdown services or even the police can be contacted from mobile phones. In case of breakdown, drivers of rental cars should contact their car rental company first.

Members of the American Automobile Association (AAA) can have their vehicle towed to the nearest service station to be fixed. For simple problems like a flat tire or a dead battery, the AAA will fix it or sell and install a new battery on site.

Parking

Most of the major sights that lie beyond Washington have adequate parking for visitors, but there may be a charge to use the facility. In general it is good practice to read all parking notices carefully to avoid fines, being clamped, or being towed away. Do not park beside a fire hydrant, or you risk the car being towed.

Parking sign

Tips and Safety Advice for Drivers

- Traffic drives on the right-hand side of the road.
- Seat belts are compulsory in front seats and suggested in the back; children under three must ride in a child seat in back.
- You can turn right at a red light as long as you first come to a complete stop, and if there are no signs that prohibit it. Be aware, however, that turning right on a red light is illegal in Virginia and will incur a fine.
- A flashing yellow light at an intersection means slow down, look for oncoming traffic, and proceed with caution.
- Passing (overtaking) is allowed on any multi-lane road, and you must pass on the left. On smaller roads safe passing places are indicated with a broken yellow line on your side of the double yellow line.
- Crossing a double-yellow line, either by U-turn or by passing the car in front, is illegal, and you will be charged a fine if caught.
- If a school bus stops, all traffic from both sides must stop completely and wait for the bus to drive off.

- Driving while intoxicated (DWI) is a punishable offense that incurs heavy fines or even a jail sentence. Do not drink if you plan to drive.
- Avoid driving at night if unfamiliar with the area. Washington's streets change from safe to dangerous in a single block, so it is better to take a taxi than your own car if you do not know where you are going.
- Single women should be especially careful driving in unfamiliar territory, day or night.
- Keep all doors locked when driving around.
- Do not stop in a rural area, or on an unlit block, if someone tries to get your attention. If a fellow driver points at your car, suggesting something is wrong, drive to the nearest gas station and get help. Do not get out of your car.
- Avoid sleeping in your car.
- Avoid short cuts and stay on well-traveled roads.
- Avoid looking at a map in a dark, unpopulated place. Drive to the nearest open store or gas station before pulling over.

Bus Tours

Although Greyhound buses (see p215) do serve some towns beyond DC (such as Charlottesville and Richmond, with serveral departures daily), the easiest and most enjoyable way to see the sights by bus is on a private tour. Several companies offer bus tours of DC's historic surroundings. **Gray Line** takes you on the Black Heritage tour, to Gettysburg, Colonial Williamsburg, or Monticello; Tourmobile's (see p217) destinations include Mount Vernon, the Frederick Douglass House, and Arlington Cemetery; DC Tours (see p217) organizes combination day trips covering Gettysburg, Mount Vernon, Arlington Cemetery, Alexandria Old Town, and Charlottesville. Most bus tours depart from Union Station.

Trains

Amtrak trains (see p215) travel from DC's central Union Station to New York City and most of the surrounding area, including Williamsburg, Richmond, and Baltimore. The MARC (see p215), Maryland's commuter rail, also runs from DC to Baltimore on weekdays for a few dollars less.

DIRECTORY

Car Rental

Alamo
Tel (877) 222-9075.
W alamo.com

Avis
Tel (800) 331-1212.
W avis.com

Budget
Tel (800) 527-0700.
W budget.com

Hertz
Tel (800) 654-3131.
W hertz.com

Zip Car
Tel (202) 737-4900.
W zipcar.com

Breakdowns

American Automobile Association (AAA)
701–15th St, NW, Washington, DC 20005. Tel (202) 481-6811.
General breakdown assistance for members:
Tel (800) 222-4357.
W aaa.com

Bus Tours

Gray Line
Union Station, 50 Massachusetts Ave, NW. Tel (202) 289-1999 or (202) 862-1400.
W graylinedc.com

Tourists line the street to get on a red double decker tour bus

Street Finder Index

Key to the Street Finder

Major sight	Tourist information office	Synagogue
Place of interest	Hospital with emergency room	Pedestrian street
Other building	Police station	Ferry terminal
Railroad station	Church	State boundary
Metrorail station	Mosque	DC quadrant boundary
Bus station		

Key to Abbreviations used in the Street Finder

Ave	Avenue	NE	Northeast	SE	Southeast
DC	District of Columbia	NW	Northwest	St	Street/Saint
		Pkwy	Parkway	SW	Southwest
Dr	Drive	Pl	Place	VA	Virginia

0 meters 300
0 yards 300
1:19,100

Index

Acknowledgments

Dorling Kindersley would like to thank the following people whose contributions and assistance have made the preparation of this book possible.

Main Contributors

Susan Burke lives in Virginia and works as an editor for the Air Line Pilots Association. She has taught creative writing for many years and has been a freelance editor of many books and journals primarily in the fields of sociology, economics, and politics.

Alice Powers is a freelance writer living in Washington, DC. She has written many articles for the Washington Post and other newspapers. She has also written several literary anthologies and teaches writing at the Corcoran College of Art and Design.

Jennifer Quasha lives in New York City but has a long association with Washington. She has written many articles on subjects ranging from travel to health, and has worked on other Dorling Kindersley books, including *Walking With Dinosaurs*.

Kem Sawyer has lived in Washington for over 20 years and has written children's books, feature articles and book reviews. She particularly enjoys writing about local history.

Design and Editorial

Managing Editor Louise Lang
Factchecker Litta W. Sanderson
Art Director Gillian Allan
Design and Editorial Assistance Sue Megginson, Johnny Pau, Hugh Thompson.
Proofreader Stewart Wild
Indexer Hilary Bird
Researcher Sarah Miers

Special Assistance

Particular thanks go to Kathleen Brooks at the National Air and Space Museum, Jessie Cohen and Leah Overstreet at the National Zoological Park, Julie Heizer at the Washington, DC Convention and Visitors' Association, Sarah Petty and Brennan Rash at the National Museum of American Art, Shannon Roberts at the National Gallery of Art and Morgan Zinsmeister at the National Museum of American Art. Thanks also to Dumbarton House, National Headquarters of The National Society of The Colonial Dames of America.

Additional Photography

Max Alexander, Frank Greenaway, Paul Franklin, Dave King courtesy of Natural History Museum, Tim Mann, Ian O'Leary, Rough Guides/Angus Osborn, Jon Sawyer, Kim Sayer, Giles Stokoe, Clive Streeter, Scott Suchman, Matthew Ward, Stephen Whitehorn.

Additional Illustration

Arun K. Pottirayil.

Additional Cartography

Uma Bhattacharya

Revisions Team

Louise Abbot, Namrata Adhwaryu, Ashwin Adimari, Emma Anacootee, Shruti Bahl, Tessa Bindloss, Vandana Bhagra, Subhashree Bharati, Divya Chowfin, Sherry Collins, Anne Coombes, Karen D'Souza, Anna Freiberger, Camilla Gersh, Lydia Halliday, Claudia Himmelreich, Sarah Holland, Rose Hudson, Bharti Karakoti, Zafar ul-Islam Khan, Esther Labi, Jude Ledger, Hayley Maher, Sam Merrell, Susan Millership, Rakesh Kumar Pal, Catherine Palmi, Sangita Patel, Pollyanna Poulter, Alice Powers, Khushboo Priya, Rada Radojicic, Pamposh

Raina, Melanie Renzulli, Litta W. Sanderson, Sands Publishing Solutions, Kem Sawyer, Azeem Siddiqui, Susana Smith, Avantika Sukhia, Alka Thakur, Lauren Thomas, Conrad Van Dyk, Ajay Verma, Deepika Verma, Ros Walford, Dora Whitaker, Hugo Wilkinson.

Additional Picture Research

Marta Bescos, Sumita Khatwani.

Photography Permissions

Dorling Kindersley would like to thank the following for their assistance and kind permission to photograph at their establishments, as well as at the cathedrals, churches, museums, restaurants, hotels, shops, galleries and other sights too numerous to thank individually.

Picture Credits

Key: a-above; b-below/bottom; c-centre; f-far; l-left; r-right; t-top.

Works of art have been reproduced with the permission of the following copyright holders:

©2006 Air Force Memorial Foundation 134bc; *John F. Kennedy Monument*, 1971 and *Albert Einstein Centennial Monument*, 1979 © Robert Berks Studios, Inc., All rights reserved – 33cra, 121cra, and 118bl respectively; United States Navy Memorial *Lone Sailor*, 1990 © Stanley Bleifeld 94bl; *Calder Mobile*, Alexander Calder © ARS, NY and DACS, London 2011 – 61bl; *Franklin D. Roosevelt and his dog Fala*, 1997 © Neil Estern 37br, 86tr; *Korean War Veterans Memorial* © KWVM Productions Inc., Memorial Designers: Cooper-Lecky Architects; Sculptor: Frank Gaylord 36tr and 85bl; *Hunger* George Segal © The George and Helen Segal Foundation/ DACS, London/VAGA, New York 2011 – 87tl; *Oscar S. Straus Memorial Fountain* © Adolph Alexander Weinman, 1947 – 95c; *Iwo Jima Memorial*, 1995 and *Seabees Memorial*, 1971 © Felix DeWeldon 36bl, 133cra; 1789 Restaurant: 188bl.

Acadiana/Simonsez.com: Chris Granger 185tl; Scott Suchman 5cra; **AFP:** Stephen Jaffe 27c; Joyce Naltchayan 38cr; Mario Tama 30br; **Alamy Images:** Jenny Andre 85c; David Coleman 68br; Rob Crandall 193tl; Ian Dagnall 218cla; John Foxx 11br; GhostWorx Images/Wm. Baker 84bl; William S. Kuta 84t; 134bc; LeighSmithImages 84cr; Dennis Macdonald 203tr; Nikreates 204-5; Kumar Sriskandan 172-3; Marmaduke St. John 13tr; Wiskerke 2-3; **Allsport:** Doug Pensinger 200c/b; **Associated Press** AP: Will Morris 135tl.

Dan Beigel: 121tc; **Bridgeman Art Library, London & New York:** Freer Gallery, Smithsonian Institution *Sheep and Goat* by Chao Meng Fu 58bc; National Gallery of Art, Washington D. C. *The Alba Madonna* (c. 1510) by Raphael (Raffaello Sanzio of Urbino, 1483–1520) 60cla; National Gallery of Art, Washington DC, East Building designed by I. M. Pei, 1978, suspended sculpture by Alexander Calder 61bl; The Phillips Collection, Washington DC *The Luncheon of the Boating Party* 1881 by Pierre Auguste Renoir (1841–1919) 137tl; The White House, Washington DC, *Portrait of Woodrow Wilson* by Sir William Orpen (1878–1931) 29tl; **Bullfeather's/2themoonmedia.com:**183bl.

Capitol Hilton Hotel: 174cl; **Cashion's Eat Place:** 180br, 190tl; **Colonial Williamsburg Foundation:** 170br; **Corbis:** 23clb, 24clb, 29cra, 30crb, 31tl/cr, 83tl; AFP: 27cb; Dave Bartruff: 33crb; Blend Images/Andersen Ross 212bc; Joseph Sohm; Chromosohm Inc. 37tr, 40br, 93bl; Corbis-Bettmann 25cb, 26tr, 26clb, 27tr, 29ca, 30clb, 31cla/cra/clb, 74br, 87c, 93cr, 98c, 153cl; James P. Blair 11t; Corcoran Gallery of Art 18; Philip James Corwin 85tr; EPA/ Michael Reynolds 210br; Hulton Deutsch Collection 25tl, 29br; Katherine Karnow 124br; Kelly-Mooney Photography 55t, 122, 148cl, 202bl; Brooks Kraft 12tl; Wally McNamee 119bc; David Muench 158br; Richard T. Nowitz 1, 40cla, 41cr, 151c; Mark Peterson, 5cra; Moshe Shai 31bc; Sipa 27bc; Lee Snider/Photo Images 150tcl, 151br; Paul A. Souders 191br; Bequest of Mrs. Benjamin Ogle Tayloe, Collection of the Corcoran Gallery of Art 28cla; Mark Thiessen 41bl; Underwood & Underwood 80cra; UPI 94br; Oscar White 29clb; **CVS/Pharmacy:** 209bl.

Danita Delimont (Agent): David R. Frazier Photolibrary/NASM 67c; Karen Huntt Mason 39br; Carol Pratt 198tr; Scott Suchman 139clb, 214cla; **Destination DC:** 206, 207crb, 215tl;

Philippe Limet Dewez: 199tr; Dreamstime.com: Jiawangkun 56; Kropic 106; Luckydoor 219bl; Mesutdogan 88; Orhancam 44; Rabbit75 32, 42-3; Raodahead 154-5; Rosepeterson 156; Vanessagifford 130.

Firefly Restaurant/Kimpton Hotels and Restaurants: Scott Suchman 186bl; Founding Farmers: Greg Powers 186t; Renee Comet 182cl; Four Seasons Hotel Washington, DC: Tom McCavera 178tl; Michael Freeman: 52bc, 53cb, 64clb/br, 65tl, 67br; Freer Gallery of Art, Smithsonian Institution, Washington DC: 75tl.

Getty Images: AFP/Stephen Jaffe 209cla; Pablo Martinez Monsivais-Pool 29crb; Hotel George: 5c, 174br; Graffiato/Know Public Realtions: Greg Powers 180cla; Granger Collection, New York: 8-9, 19b, 20tr/cb, 21tr/clb/br, 22t/bc, 23tr/bc, 24bl, 25br, 28ca/clb/ bl/ bc/br, 29cla/bl, 49cra, 93ca, 93cl, 147tr.

Image Bank: Archive Photos 99br; Andrea Pistolesi 52cla, 80bl.

The Jefferson Hotel: 175tr, 179br.

Kiplinger Washington Collection: 80cla; Kramerbooks & Afterwords Cafe & Grill: 194br; Library of Congress: Carol M. Highsmith 48bc.

Matisse Restaurant: 180cl; Michie Tavern: 191tl; Courtesy Mount Vernon Ladies' Association: 162cla.

National Air and Space Museum © Smithsonian Institution: SI Neg. No. 99-15240-7–33cla; National Gallery of Art, Washington, DC: Samuel H. Kress Collection, Photo: Philip A. Charles Bust of Lorenzo de' Medici 59tl; Ailsa Mellon Bruce Fund, Photo: Bob Grove Ginevra de' Benci c. 1474 by Leonardo da Vinci 60tr; Samuel H. Kress Collection A Young Man With His Tutor by Nicolas de Largilliere, 1685–61tc; Samuel H. Kress Collection Christ Cleansing the Temple (d), pre-1570, by El Greco 62tr, Samuel H. Kress Collection Madonna and Child, 1320–1330 by Giotto 62cl; Collection of Mr. and Mrs. Paul Mellon Woman with a Parasol, 1875, by Claude Monet 6oclb; Harris Whittemore Collection Mother of Pearl and Silver: The Andalusian 1888-1900, by James McNeill Whistler 61br; Timken Collection Diana and Endymion, c. 1753, by Jean-Honore Fragonard 62br; Chester Dale Collection Miss Mary Ellison, 1880, by Mary Cassatt 63c; John Russell Pope (architect) 197tl; National Museum of American Art/© Smithsonian Institution: 58cl; 100tr, Gift of Mr. and Mrs. Joseph Harrison Old Bear, a Medicine Man, 1832, by George Catlin 101bl; Achelous and Hercules, 1947, © T. H. Benton and R. P. Benton Testamentary Trusts/VAGA, New York/DACS, London 2011 – 100–1c; Bequest of Helen Huntington Hull, granddaughter of William Brown Dinsmore who acquired the painting in 1873 for "The Locusts," the family estate in Dutchess County, New York Among the Sierra Nevada, California 1868 by Albert Bierstadt 100bl; Gift of John Gellatly In the Garden (Celia Thaxter in Her Garden), 1892, by Childe Hassam 101bc; © Untitled Press, Inc/VAGA, New York and DACS, London 2011 Reservoir, 1961, by Robert Raus-Chenberg 102cr; Gift of Anonymous Donors The Throne of the Third Heaven of the Nations Millenium General Assembly, c. 1950–1954, by James Hampton 102bl; Gift of the Georgia O'Keeffe Foundation Manhattan 1932 by Georgia O'Keeffe 101br; National Museum of American history/© Smithsonian Institution: 76cl/clb, 77tl/cra, 78br, 79 all; National Museum of the American Indian: 70 -1 all; National Museum of Natural History/© Smithsonian Institution: 72bl, 73br; Dane Penland 73tl; National Park Service: J. Fenney 113t, 206cla; Richard Freer 167cla; Rick Latoff, courtesy www.Parkphotos. com 69br; Mary McLeod Bethune Council House NHS,

Washington D.C. 142c; National Portrait Gallery/© Smithsonian Institution: Gift of The Morris and Gwendolyn Cafritz Foundation and Smithsonian Institution Trust Fund Selfportrait, 1780–1784, by John Singleton Copley 101ca; Gift of Friends of President and Mrs. Reagan, Ronald Wilson Reagan, 1989, © Henry C. Casselli 103tr; Diana Ross and the Supremes, 1965, © Bruce Davidson/Magnum 103br; Transfer from the National Gallery of Art, Gift of Andrew W. Mellon, 1942, Pocahontas, Unidentified artist, English school, after the 1616 engraving by Simon van de Passe, after 1616 – 103c; Gift of the Morris and Gwendolyn Cafritz Foundation and the Regents' Major Acquisitions Fund, Smithsonian Institution Mary Cassatt, 1880–1884, by Edgar Degas 101tl; Courtesy National Portrait Gallery "Casey" Stengel, 1981 cast after 1965 plaster by © Rhoda Sherbell 101tr; National Postal Museum/© Smithsonian Institution: Jim O'Donnell 55c; National Zoological Park/© Smithsonian Institution: Jessie Cohen 140–1; Newseum: 95tl; Richard T. Nowitz: 64cla, 83crb; Abe Nowitz 39c.

Octagon Museum/American Architectural Foundation, Washington DC: 117bl.

Paolo's Ristorante/Capital Restaurant Concepts: 187tr; Phillips Collection: 137br/c; Popperfoto: Reuters 30cla/cr.

Restaurant Nora: 190br; Rex Features: 29tc; SIPA Press/Trippett 29cb.

Mae Scanlan: 33ca, 34tr, 38bl, 79t, 202tr; Shakespeare Theatre Company: 196cr, 198bl; Smithsonian National Air And Space Museum: 66br; Len Spoden Photography: 149tl/tr, 150br, 151tl, 153br/tr; Frank Spooner Pictures: Markel-Liaison 93br; Courtesy of The Spy Museum: 104tl/c; STA Travel Group: 207tl; SuperStock: age fotostock 12cr; Swann House Historic Dupont Inn: 176bl.

Textile Museum: Gift of Mrs. Charles Putnam 138tl; Topham Picturepoint: 127clb; TRH Pictures: National Air and Space Museum 65cr, 66cla.

University of Virginia: Library Special Collections Department, Manuscript Print Collection 129tl; United States Holocaust Memorial Museum: 83cr.

Courtesy of the Washington, DC Martin Luther King, Jr. National Memorial Project Foundation, Inc.: Gediyon Kifle 37tl; White House Collection, Courtesy White House Historical Association: 110cl/b, 111t/c/bl/br, 112bl, Peter Vitale 113bl; Bruce White 113cr. Zaytinya/Heather Freeman PR: Greg Powers and Audrey Crewe 185bc.

Front Endpaper: Corbis: Kelly-Mooney Photography Lclb; Dreamstime.com: Jiawangkun Rbc; Kropic Ltr; Mesutdogan Rtl; Orhancam Rtr; Rosepeterson Lbr; Vanessagifford Lbc.

Back Endpaper: © 2012 Washington Metropolitan Area Transit Authority.

Map Cover: Alamy Images: JLImages.

Jacket: Front Alamy Images: JLImages main; Spine: Alamy Images: JLImages t.

All other images © Dorling Kindersley. See www.dkimages.com for more information.

M System Map
metro

wmata.com
Customer Information Service: 202-637-7000
TTY Phone: 202-638-3780
Metro Transit Police: 202-962-2121

Legend

RD Red Line • Glenmont / Shady Grove
OR Orange Line • New Carrollton / Vienna
BL Blue Line • Franconia-Springfield / Largo Town Center
GR Green Line • Branch Ave / Greenbelt
YL Yellow Line • Huntington / Fort Totten
SV Silver Line • Wiehle-Reston East / Largo Town Center

Station Features

🚌→✈ Bus to Airport
P Parking
H Hospital
✈ Airport

Connecting Rail Systems

AMTRAK MARC VRE MARC

Transfer Station

Station in Service

Under Construction

Full-Time Service

Rush-Only Service: Monday-Friday
6:30am - 9:00am 3:30pm - 6:00pm

Stations

RD Glenmont P
Wheaton P
Forest Glen P H
Silver Spring P MARC
Takoma P
Fort Totten P

YL
GR Greenbelt P MARC 🚌→✈ P MARC
College Park-U of Md P
Prince George's Plaza P
West Hyattsville P
Brookland-CUA
Rhode Island Ave P Brentwood
NoMa-Gallaudet U

Shaw-Howard U
Mt Vernon Sq
7th St-Convention Center
U St
African-Amer Civil War Mem'l/Cardozo
Columbia Heights
Georgia Ave-Petworth

McPherson Sq

Van Ness-UDC
Tenleytown-AU
Cleveland Park
Woodley Park Zoo/Adams Morgan
Dupont Circle
Farragut North

RD Shady Grove P AMTRAK MARC
Rockville P
Twinbrook P
White Flint P
Grosvenor-Strathmore P
Medical Center
Bethesda
Friendship Heights

Wiehle-Reston East P
Spring Hill
SV

OR New Carrollton P
Rhode Island Ave P

Prince George's Co
District of Columbia

Montgomery Co
Prince George's Co

Montgomery Co
District of Columbia

Why
me,
GOD?

Randy Petersen

Publications International, Ltd.

Randy Petersen is the author of *A Time for Prayer* and coauthor of *Jesus: His Life and Times*. He earned a B.A. in ancient languages from Wheaton College before becoming executive editor of *Bible Newsletter* and other publications. Now a full-time freelance writer and editor, he has also contributed to more than 20 other books, such as *The Revell Bible Dictionary* and *The Christian Book of Lists*, and to a wide variety of magazines, such as *Christian History*.

Louis Weber, CEO
Publications International, Ltd.
7373 North Cicero Avenue
Lincolnwood, Illinois 60712

Permission is never granted for commercial purposes.

Manufactured in U.S.A.

8 7 6 5 4 3 2 1

ISBN: 1-4127-0432-4

Contents

Asking the Question

Why Me, God?

*T*hat question has been asked by a million hurting hearts and considered silently by millions more. Some bristle with pride, while others bow with shame. Some scream in anger, and others pretend there's nothing wrong. This question has caused some to abandon their faith and others to draw closer to God. It has sapped the energy of some who ask it, and it has helped others find strength they didn't know they had.

The circumstances vary.

A man sits in his doctor's office and receives a diagnosis: "The tests weren't good. We need to plan treatment options."

A mother gets a midnight call from the police: "A drunk driver ran a light. Your daughter was brought to the hospital."

A student reads the letter from the college he's pinned his hopes on: "We regret to inform you that, though your application was commendable, we cannot at this time accept it."

A teenage girl gazes into the eyes of the boy she planned to marry, only to hear: "This just isn't working out. We need to see other people."

Whatever the news, it's devastating. Your life is changed, perhaps forever. You wonder how you will go on living. You search frantically for someone to blame. Maybe you pin the blame on yourself. "If only I had done this differently. If only…" You replay the scene in your mind, over and over. Perhaps you replay your life.

Sometimes people will put the blame on God. This causes problems for religious people, who raise their voices with the congregation extolling God's goodness but now feel as if that goodness has been withheld. How can you scold God? And yet that's exactly what many believers try to do. This throws a big roadblock in the path of those who try to draw near to God in their time of need. It's hard to have a heart-to-heart talk with someone while you're holding a grudge against him. Maybe you know what that can be like.

Why me, God? You've picked up this book, presumably, because you're asking this question. Something has happened to change your life, maybe to shatter it. Or perhaps you are seeking to support a friend in such a situation. Unfortunately, this book will not make everything all right. And it won't answer all your questions, though it might answer a few.

What will it do? *Why Me, God?* will take your suffering seriously. You don't need anyone else telling you that it's always darkest before dawn, that when the going gets tough the tough get going, or that you can take the lemons life gives you and make a tasty lemonade. There's a germ of truth in each of those sayings, and we'll try to dig for that truth in these pages. But you're looking for more than just bumper stickers right now.

You will not find this book attempting to defend God; he can take care of himself. But you will encounter honesty in these pages, and this might inspire you to a new level of openness in your conversations with God. Moses, David, Jeremiah, and even Jesus all prayed the "Why Me" prayer. Why shouldn't you?

This book will share with you a new awareness of God as one whose love and power exceeds all our expectations. It is hoped that, after reading these chapters, you will have a stronger faith and a more faithful strength. Some people set up an either/or situation—either you're to blame for your troubles or God is. But that's not a good way to look at it. You're in this together with God, and he will stand by you as you put the pieces back together, whether you know he's there or not.

Why me, God? Good question. This book will help you ask this question, maybe find some answers, and get past your current situation. You're in pain now, but you can heal. It will take some time, but you can emerge with a deeper connection to God. This book can show you the first few steps on that path.

How Do You Feel?

Big Troubles Unleash Big Emotions, and That's Okay

Janice was blindsided by the news. After eight years of marriage, her husband was leaving her. Just like that. They hadn't been fighting—in fact, just a month earlier they had enjoyed a vacation in Florida. Tim had seemed a bit quiet recently, but he'd explained that work was piling up at the office and he was tired. Then one evening she came home to see his suitcases by the front door.

In the following weeks, Janice received support from friends and family. Her sister was on the phone with her every day, as Janice cried her eyes out. Her parents invited her to move back in with them, but Janice wanted to stay in her own home, the home she had shared with . . . well, she found it hard to utter her husband's name.

Soon there were lawyers and accountants involved. Janice steeled herself for each meeting, trying to appear healthy, and she succeeded in conveying that image. But inside, she felt like a vat of tapioca pudding—nothing solid anymore. One day a friend asked, "How do you feel?" Janice just stood there for two minutes, unable to articulate a reply. How *did* she feel? She was sad—no, more than sad, *devastated*. She was angry—no, *livid*. She was afraid—no, *terrified*. She was embarrassed—no, *ashamed*. And all of that in just the past half hour.

As a Christian, Janice attempted to turn her problems over to the Lord. Echoes of old Sunday school classes and TV preachers bounced through her mind. "Let go, and let God." "Turn your scars into stars." "There's no problem too big for the Lord." She began scolding herself for feeling so . . . well, so *emotional*. It had been two months since old what's-his-name walked out. Wasn't it time to stop crying and start trusting? If she were truly a Christian, wouldn't she be happy by now?

Well, she tried that. She began preparing for church as she would prepare for a meeting with her lawyer, putting on that strong face. "I am together. I am fine, now. I can handle this." Her friends at church were glad to see her recovering so well. Obviously their prayers for her had been answered.

But Janice would come home from church to her empty house, sink into the couch weeping, and stay there for the next 20 hours. She was an emotional wreck, and the more she tried to pretend otherwise, the worse her true feelings became. On top of the anger, sadness, and fear, she now felt guilt and shame for feeling those feelings. "No wonder he left me," she said at one point.

Why are you cast down, O my soul,
    and why are you disquieted within me?
Hope in God; for I shall again praise him,
    my help and my God.
—Psalm 42:11

✚   ✚   ✚

Why do you say …
"My way is hidden from the Lord,
and my right is disregarded by my God"?
Have you not known? Have you not heard?
The Lord is the everlasting God,
the Creator of the ends of the earth.
He does not faint or grow weary;
his understanding is unsearchable.
He gives power to the faint,
and strengthens the powerless.
Even youths will faint and be weary,
and the young will fall exhausted;
but those who wait for the Lord shall renew
their strength,
they shall mount up with wings like
eagles,
they shall run and not be weary,
they shall walk and not faint.
—Isaiah 40:27–31

✝   ✝   ✝

The Emotional Roller Coaster

Janice was experiencing a process that has been observed in thousands of people. A few decades ago, psychologists began to identify certain "stages of grief"—denial, anger, bargaining, depression, and finally acceptance. At first they applied these stages to bereavement. When a loved one passes away, you tend to feel this stream of emotions. Then these stages were seen in those diagnosed with terminal illness. In fact, a Broadway play, *The Shadow Box*, was written about this very situation: terminally ill patients going through these stages of grief. Over the last 20 years or so, researchers have observed these same stages in people going through any crisis.

The process goes something like this:
"This is not happening." (Denial)
"This isn't right." (Anger)
"Maybe I can undo this." (Bargaining)
"I'll never get over this." (Depression)
"I will get through this and start a new life." (Acceptance)

You might know about that process already. What you may not know is that people can bounce around the stages quite a bit. You could be angry all morning, slip back into denial after lunch, try a few bargaining points that evening, and then go to bed depressed. Yes, there is a general progression through the stages, but there's a lot of slippage. Denial is certainly dominant in the first few months after the bad news hits, and it tends to fade after that, but it doesn't disappear. Anger generally gives way to bargaining, as a person decides to stop stewing and *do something*, but it can come back with a vengeance.

That's why we call this an emotional roller coaster. Any personal crisis puts you on track to experience slow rises and sudden falls, loop-de-loops, twirls, and times when everything seems upside down. That's just normal. So let's look briefly at the different stages that make up this roller-coaster ride.

Denial. Our bodies are designed with a kind of denial: numbness. If you break your arm, it hurts like crazy, but then it goes numb. Your body shuts down the pain it can't deal with. Our brains do a similar thing. When an event occurs that seems too hard to accept, we naturally try to find a way to believe that it might not have happened at all. We've all seen soap-opera stories of hysterical amnesia—a character witnesses a murder and blocks it all out. Those are extreme cases of an ordinary process. People don't often lose their memories, but they do act as if the painful event never happened. Janice might find herself continuing to set the table for two, because she doesn't want the visual reminder that she's eating alone now. And sometimes people don't deny the event itself, just its severity. A ballplayer with a career-ending injury might say, "Give me some R & R and a good spring training, and I'll be right back out there."

Well-meaning friends might want to slap your face and bark, "Snap out of it! Get a grip on reality!" But the truth is that denial is perfectly normal and healthy... for a time. That time is about three to six months, but it can vary widely, depending on the shock involved. Since Janice was completely surprised by her husband's departure, it might take as long as a year for her to get past denial, and even then the roller coaster might swing her back to it.

Anger. Whether we're in a crisis or not, we all tend to feel angry when we think we're treated unfairly. We have an innate sense of justice, and we're hardwired to protest injustice, especially when we're on the receiving end. The problem is, we don't always analyze the situation correctly. We tend to overestimate what we deserve and underestimate what we owe. This is where the "count to ten" strategy works. Those ten seconds we count off can give us time to get different perspectives on a situation and plan an appropriate response.

Anger is a fire. Like fire, it can be destructive or it can be useful. Many people fear their tempers because they tend to rage out of control, and that's wise, but others have the mistaken idea that anger is always wrong.

When something bad has happened to you, something you don't deserve, it's natural for you to get angry about it, and that's not necessarily wrong. You might get angry with the person who has caused your misfortune, the world that allowed it to happen, yourself for not avoiding it, or God for not protecting you. Or maybe all of the above. Janice would certainly be upset at her husband for walking out, but she might also rail against her employer for making her work so much that she wasn't investing time in her marriage. She might turn some of her anger against herself, assuming that she did something to drive her husband away. And she might even blame God for allowing it to happen at all.

Church libraries have prayers for all sorts of occasions, but there are few if any for those times when you're angry—especially if you're angry with God. That's probably because it still seems somewhat wrong to launch your ire toward heaven—despite the fact that many people in the Bible did just that. Perhaps these verses and the prayer that follows them will give you a model for those heated times, so you can communicate with God honestly about your feelings without turning your back on him.

My God, my God, why have you forsaken
    me?
    Why are you so far from helping me, from
    the words of my groaning?
O my God, I cry by day, but you do not
    answer;
    and by night, but find no rest.
Yet you are holy,
    enthroned on the praises of Israel.
In you our ancestors trusted;
    they trusted, and you delivered them.
To you they cried, and were saved;
    in you they trusted, and were not put to
    shame.
—Psalm 22:1–5

A Prayer of Anger

Dear Lord, what do you think you're doing?

*I really don't mean any disrespect. I just feel so…
betrayed! How could you let this happen? How could
you let me suffer like this? Don't you care about me?*

*I believe that you do care, but this is an odd way of
showing it. Seriously, I still trust you, but trusting is
very hard these days. I don't understand what you're
up to. Maybe you need to teach me more about how
you operate. I'm willing to learn, but please—please!—
make it very clear to me, because right now I feel as if
you've forgotten all about me, and I'm very angry.*

*Still, I want to work this out. Help me get through
this. Help us both find a way to get along.*

Amen.

As with denial, people can get stuck in anger. They
become bitter, ready to explode with little provoca-
tion. But with some perspective and proper venting,
you can get through it.

Bargaining. This is the hardest stage to understand; even some professionals have trouble explaining it. But once you get it, you'll see lots of examples. Think of bargaining as an oasis between denial and acceptance. It's a healthy step forward from anger, because the person stops blaming and starts acting to make the situation better. But it's also a half step backward toward denial, because bargaining efforts usually deny the magnitude of the problem. Someone once called this "microwave solutions to Crock-Pot problems."

For instance, Janice might say: "Here's what I'll do. I'll call my husband and request a meeting to work out the financial details of our divorce. Then I'll arrive looking like a million bucks, and I'll make him want to come back to me." It's a plan. Not a good one, but it's something. Janice's plan does little to address the core problems, and it probably sets her up for major disappointment.

As with the other stages, bargaining is an important part of the process, and it's not necessarily a bad thing. In fact, you might improve your situation in small, slow ways during this stage, but don't get your hopes too high. Many people who have been diagnosed with terminal cancer get to this stage and start seeking alternative treatments—and sometimes this helps. Just be careful.

Depression. It's the dark before the dawn. You're well past denial, anger has only worsened things, and all your bargaining hasn't done a bit of good. Is there any hope for you? It doesn't seem like it. Depression saps your energy, drains your dreams, and does a clog dance on your self-esteem. You don't want to get up in the morning. You don't want to talk with people. You don't want to do anything. Your favorite foods have no taste. Comedians can't make you laugh. If you have any addictive tendencies, you are especially vulnerable to them right now, as you reach for anything to fill the yawning emptiness inside you. Alcohol, drugs, food, sex, gambling, shopping—none of them satisfy you, but what's the harm in trying?

This is the time when you need your closest friends around you. You will try to scare them off, but you need them to hang on. You are miserable, and you'll make them miserable, but if they are true friends they'll sit with you through the worst of it, guarding you from self-destruction and reminding you that the dawn will come.

Acceptance. This does not mean that everything is all better. You still feel some pain from your loss, and your life has changed, perhaps in major ways. But at this stage you accept those changes—you recognize that things are different now and that you need to get on with your life. You stop trying to go back to the way things used to be, and you start looking toward the future.

Many people report that they pass from depression to acceptance almost imperceptibly. They simply wake up one morning and smell the coffee (maybe literally). The joys of life that they had been missing are suddenly there again—aroma, music, color. It's as if a cloud has been blocking the sun, but once it passes everything looks brighter.

We can draw several conclusions from this. First, it's no use trying to stop being depressed; that will simply happen to you. And those friends who insist that you "cheer up"—well, it's nice of them to want you to be happy, but they just don't get it. Depression might have a purpose. It might be our way of saying a final good-bye to whatever we've lost: a loved one, our health, a way of life. We need to grieve over this loss for a certain amount of time, in order to give it proper honor. Once that is accomplished, we can accept the situation and move on.

✛ ✛ ✛

No Cheating

In fact, this might be true of all the stages: We need them. We need to deny things until it's safe to believe them. We need to be angry while we sort through the justice of our case. We need to seek bargain-basement deals if only to understand how expensive our loss really is. We need to sink into the depression of a final good-bye. And eventually, we need to wake up to a sunny new day.

If any of those stages gets cheated, you'll have to make it up later. So you might as well take your time the first time through. Let the roller coaster do its stuff. Don't rush it. Experts say it takes anywhere from one to five years to recover emotionally from a major loss.

Of course there are many other emotions that arise in times of crisis, and many variations on the emotions we've mentioned.

Some people feel *confused* by the swirl of feelings. Are these feelings normal or not?

Some feel *betrayed* by those who have hurt them.

Others feel *afraid* about the future. Will they get through this?

Some even feel *ashamed* of the problems they're going through.

And you might add a few more to this collection from your own experience. Big problems unleash big emotions. That's the way God made us.

All too often, Christians suggest that we ought to somehow rise above our emotions, as if our feelings are bad, or at least trivial. That approach adds a

needless helping of guilt to an already heaping plate.
You don't need to be shy about your emotional
responses. If you are crying your eyes out, sleeping
all day, or pounding on heaven's door, good!
Chances are, you're just employing the emotions
God gave you.

The Bible is stocked with emotional characters.
Moses got angry, Elijah got depressed, Mary got
worried, Martha got irked. In the Psalms, we have a
songbook from ancient Israel that overflows with
emotion: sadness, delight, and righteous indignation.
And don't neglect the shortest verse in the Bible:
"Jesus wept" (John 11:35, KJV). Scholars may debate
the reason for Jesus' tears, but the wonderful impact
of that verse is that our Lord and Savior openly
showed his feelings. This was no stoic statue, but a
God-man wired with the same emotions we have.

So the first prescription for your troubles is this: *Feel
your feelings*. Don't push them aside. They have a job
to do. They are instruments of God's grace and healing power. Let them work.

My soul is bereft of peace;
    I have forgotten what happiness is;
so I say, "Gone is my glory,
    and all that I had hoped for from the
    Lord."

.   .   .

My soul continually thinks of it
    and is bowed down within me.
But this I call to mind,
    and therefore I have hope:
The steadfast love of the Lord never ceases,
    his mercies never come to an end;
they are new every morning;
    great is your faithfulness.
"The Lord is my portion," says my soul,
    "therefore I will hope in him."
The Lord is good to those who wait for him,
    to the soul that seeks him.
It is good that one should wait quietly
    for the salvation of the Lord.
—Lamentations 3:17–18, 20–26

✢   ✢   ✢

Sit with Me

Sit with me in sadness, Lord.
Share with me my tears.
Draw my longings heavenward,
And soothe my restless fears.

I don't ask you to take away
The sorrow of my heart—
Not yet at least. The dawning day
Will surely chase the dark.

I'll languish here a little more
Until that dawn appears.
Just sit with me in sadness, Lord,
And share with me my tears.

Prescription

Experience your emotions. Don't buy the lie that your feelings are somehow "ungodly." God gave them to you! Allow yourself the normal ups and downs of this emotional roller coaster, and keep in touch with the Lord as you do.

It's Not Fair!

What to Do When God Seems to Be Breaking His Own Rules

*F*or 30 years Tony has served as president of a Christian ministry. Before that, he was a pastor and a professor. He had dedicated his whole life to the spiritual well-being of others. Now in his early 60s, he has just begun to think about retirement. Maybe, after all these years of loyal service, he could slow down a little and enjoy his golden years.

Then he noticed some chest pain. Probably just indigestion, he thought, but maybe he should get it checked out. Sure, he had put on a few pounds, but he was really quite fit. A swimmer all his life, he went to the gym regularly. Still, this new chest pain was worth a doctor's appointment, especially when he started having trouble breathing.

The doctor was concerned enough to send Tony for tests, and the tests showed a disturbing mass in his lung. More tests confirmed it: lung cancer. The condition has four stages, and Tony was already in stage three. Testing and treatment soon became a full-time job. As he waited in doctors' offices and hospitals, his new reality began to sink in. He needed to get his house in order, because he might not live long.

Tony is a mature believer. In his various ministries, he has coached many others through similar crises, but even he was not immune to that gut-wrenching question: "Why me, God?" His coworkers were stunned during one staff meeting when he broke down crying and left the room. They had looked to him for strength, but now he was struggling.

Sometimes life is just not fair. What did Tony ever do to be snatched away from his family like this, from his ministry, from his many friends? With lung cancer, you think about smoking, but Tony had never been a smoker, nor had others in his family. He'd lived a healthy lifestyle. Certainly he had not brought this on himself. And if anyone deserved to live a long and healthy life, it was this man. He had given himself in so many ways to so many others, he should get some credit for that, shouldn't he?

Well, shouldn't he?

Most of us believe in fairness. One good turn deserves another. You pick up the check today, and I'll pay next time. In many of our relationships we keep a kind of running tab. We repay kindness with kindness and snubs with snubs. In our human relationships, if a friend owes us a favor and refuses to come through, we feel betrayed. We believe we deserve better treatment.

We assume that God operates the same way. After all, doesn't our human sense of fairness derive from God's eternal justice? It would only make sense for God to honor those who honor him. Good people should get good things in return.

But when we look closely, we can see that the world has never worked like that. Even in the Psalms, we find people complaining that the wicked are prospering at the expense of the righteous. Just take a look at Psalms 10 and 73.

So here's the shocking truth: God isn't fair, at least not according to our common definitions of fairness. In its totality, the Bible does not promise the righteous person a life of ease, at least not on this earth. There are some mentions of the rewards of righteousness, but these rewards are paid off in many different ways and throughout all eternity. We are not assured that good people will automatically receive peace and prosperity in this lifetime. In fact, Jesus warned his followers, "In this world you will have trouble" (John 16:33, NIV).

> Do not fear, for I am with you,
> do not be afraid,
> for I am your God;
> I will strengthen you, I will help you,
> I will uphold you with my victorious right hand.
> —Isaiah 41:10

We find a disturbing parable in Matthew's gospel about a landowner who hired workers for his vineyard. First thing in the morning, the man went to the employment agency and found some day laborers. "I'll pay you a denarius for a day's work," he promised them. The denarius was a Roman coin usually paid for a full day of labor, so this was a fair wage. The workers agreed and began to pick grapes. As the day wore on, the owner needed more and more workers, so he returned to the agency at nine, noon, three, and five, offering to pay these new workers "whatever is right." Then at six o'clock, at the end of the day, all the workers lined up to get paid, beginning with the most recently hired. The owner paid them each a denarius—a full day's wage! *Whoa*, thought the workers at the end of the line. *If they get all that for just one hour, imagine what we'll get!*

But the owner continued down the line, paying each worker the same amount, even though they had worked different amounts of time. Those who had worked all day got the denarius they had been promised, but so did those who had only worked an hour. That's not fair, is it? Almost anybody would cry foul over such practices. We believe in equal pay for equal work, don't we? Work 12 times as long, and you should get 12 times the salary.

But when the workers complained, the owner reminded them that he had honored their contract. They had signed up for a full day of work for a denarius, and that's exactly what they got. The others didn't have such a contract. They trusted the landowner to figure out a proper amount, and he granted them a full day's pay. He didn't have to, but he did. "Am I not allowed to do what I choose with what belongs to me?" he asked them. "Or are you envious because I am generous?" (Matthew 20:15).

In Jesus' parables, a landowner or master is usually a figure of God. If that's true here, this story is saying several surprising things. For one thing, God doesn't always operate according to our principles of fairness. He does honor his promises, but he also shows grace, granting some people good things we might think they don't deserve.

The main sense of this parable is that grace is "unfair," at least on the scale we usually use. We like to know what things are worth. It used to be that you'd pick up a can of beans and see the tag on it, telling you exactly what it was worth. Then you could decide whether or not to spend 79 cents for that can of beans. Nowadays, with bar codes and scanners, you don't always know what something costs until you get to the checkout line.

In the same way, spiritually speaking, we want to see a price tag on righteousness. If we work for the Lord all day, we want to know we're getting that denarius at the end of the day. We want to count the blessings that accrue to those who honor God. We want to know what we're earning. If Tony spends his whole life in selfless service, we want him to get a few years at the end to play with his grandkids.

Ironically, in the parable, what bothers the full-day workers is the master's bigheartedness. They received their fair wage, but since he gave the same amount to everyone, they felt the other workers hadn't really earned it. If the first workers had slept in that morning, they would still have received the same pay. And they're right! The master's overwhelming grace violated all normal ideas of fairness.

That's something for us to keep in mind. We easily praise God for his great, giving spirit, but we don't always recognize how controversial his grace can be. "Love your enemies and pray for those who persecute you," Jesus once said, "so that you may be children of your Father in heaven; for he makes his sun rise on the evil and on the good, and sends rain on the righteous and on the unrighteous" (Matthew 5:44–45). In a farming culture, sun and rain are both blessings. "Enemies" don't deserve them, but God gives them the blessings anyway.

Let's consider the context in which Jesus told this story. He'd been getting grief from the Pharisees, religious leaders of his society, for hanging out with prostitutes and swindlers, offering them a place in God's kingdom. The Pharisees followed a rigid contract with God: Follow his law, and receive his blessing. They were clearly the all-day workers in Jesus' parable. And, like those workers, they objected when God's blessings were offered to others who hadn't worked so hard. But don't miss one important detail about the sinners Jesus was welcoming into the kingdom. They didn't claim any right to God's blessing. Like the late arrivals in the parable, they were happy with whatever they got. They trusted God to bless them however he wanted.

So let's pull this into the modern day, into our own lives. As we interact with God, we have two choices. We can sign a contract with God, or we can trust in his grace. Many of us try to do both. That is, even if

The Lord is my shepherd, I shall not want.
 He makes me lie down in green pastures;
 he leads me beside still waters;
 he restores my soul.
 He leads me in right paths
  for his name's sake.
Even though I walk through the darkest valley,
 I fear no evil;
for you are with me;
 your rod and your staff—
 they comfort me.
You prepare a table before me
 in the presence of my enemies;
you anoint my head with oil;
 my cup overflows.
Surely goodness and mercy shall follow me
 all the days of my life,
and I shall dwell in the house of the Lord
 my whole life long.
—Psalm 23

we understand that we are sinners, relying on Jesus' sacrifice to gain eternal life, we still think of ourselves as pretty good people, people who deserve God's blessings.

Have you flown on a plane lately? Before the common folk get on the flight, the first-class passengers and special "club members" are invited aboard first. They get special treatment because . . . well, they've paid a lot more money than the rest of us have. In the same way, we tend to expect that people such as Tony and other faithful servants of God should have a preferred status. And let's be honest—most of us would put ourselves in that club, too.

That's also why we're so upset when bad things happen to faithful believers. It seems as if God is reneging on the contract.

But let's look at the terms of that contract. We don't need to get overly theological here, but Paul spelled it out pretty simply in the Book of Romans. Chapter 1 criticizes all the sinners, the pagans who show no interest in following God. Certainly they deserve whatever disaster befalls them. But Chapter 2 turns to the "righteous" readers and says, essentially, "Guess what? You're sinners, too. You know what's right, but you don't always do it." Chapter 3 concludes that "all have sinned and fall short of the glory of God" (v. 23). We receive God's blessings only through faith in his goodness, not because a contract demands it. What payment do we deserve for our shortcomings? Death. "For the wages of sin is death, but the free gift of God is eternal life in Christ Jesus our Lord" (Romans 6:23).

According to this, then, we have violated our contract through sin. We don't deserve even a denarius; we deserve to be cut off from God forever. We might be "sort of good," but none of us is good enough to win God's blessings on our own. Paul himself had been a Pharisee, putting great importance on acts of righteousness, but as he later lists his accomplishments, he says, "I regard them as rubbish" (Philippians 3:8). By the way, he uses a rather vulgar term there, one we're too polite to translate correctly in these pages. It's similar to the comment in Isaiah that "all our righteous deeds are like a filthy cloth" (64:6), referring to the rags a leper might wear. Whatever goodness we might gather, it doesn't come close to meeting our contractual obligations with God. As the Lord says in Job, "Who has a claim against me that I must pay?" (41:11, NIV).

Not very encouraging, is it? Here you are, suffering from some tragic circumstances, questioning the very heart of your faith, and now you read that you really shouldn't expect any blessings from God in the first place, because you're just a filthy sinner. That's the last thing you need to be told right now!

Hang on. This is the bad news that precedes the good news of the gospel. It gets better, much better. If we insisted that God function according to the contract, we'd all be in trouble. We're fortunate God operates in a spirit of generosity, in which he gives us blessings we don't deserve. Put yourself in the sandals of the vineyard's late arrivals, who received full pay for an hour's labor. We are completely dependent on the master's grace.

So, where is this grace? When Tony is stricken with cancer, or when you face your tragedy, is God's grace absent? Has he turned his back?

No. The greatest grace of all is God's own presence. "I will never leave you or forsake you," he has vowed (Hebrews 13:5). As Jesus told his disciples, "Remember, I am with you always, to the end of the age" (Matthew 28:20). He doesn't promise us health or wealth or long life or peaceful families. But he does say he'll be there with us.

That's the simple truth that Tony hangs onto as he goes for treatment each day. It's not fun to fill your body with chemicals that *might* kill the cancer. On his darker days, he fears that God has cursed him, and he's tempted to curse God in return. But then he gains a new sense of the blessing of God's presence. This ordeal has slowed him down to the point where he can recognize more of the invisible ways God is working in and around him. Tony is certainly walking through the valley of the shadow of death, but he can pray, "thou art with me."

God has allowed things to happen in your life that don't seem fair. Maybe you understand all the Bible says about this and still feel cheated. But one great thing about God is that he understands our feelings. He's more than willing to enter into dialogue with us.

When the people of Israel, wandering in the Sinai, became angry that they didn't have enough meat to eat, they wasted no time in letting Moses know about it. In turn, he complained to God: "Why have you treated [me] so badly?" (Numbers 11:11). Likewise, Jeremiah, blaming God for putting him in a no-win situation, compared God to a streambed that dried up in the hot summer. "Truly, you are to me like a deceitful brook, like waters that fail" (Jeremiah 15:18). God never slammed the door on these people, or on others who present him with their honest frustrations. In fact, he continued to talk with them and work through them.

So bring your grievances before the Lord. Don't bottle them up or stew over them by yourself. Confront the situation. Open a dialogue. If life doesn't seem fair, say so. Present your case, and then listen for the Lord's response. He just might unveil the vastness of his grace, far exceeding any contract you could imagine.

Moses heard the people weeping throughout their families, all at the entrances of their
tents. Then the Lord became very angry, and
Moses was displeased. So Moses said to the
Lord, "Why have you treated your servant so
badly? Why have I not found favor in your
sight, that you lay the burden of all this people on me?... Where am I to get meat to give
to all this people? For they come weeping to
me and say, 'Give us meat to eat!' I am not
able to carry all this people alone, for they
are too heavy for me. If this is the way you
are going to treat me, put me to death at
once—if I have found favor in your sight—
and do not let me see my misery."
—Numbers 11:10–11, 13–15

*God heard Moses' protest and answered it in two
ways. First, he instructed Moses to select 70 elders
who would share the burden of leadership. Then he
sent a covey of quail to provide meat for the people.*

A Prayer of Protest

Dear Lord, I've tried to follow you faithfully. I've done a lot of things for you. And with this current crisis, well, I'm feeling kind of used and abused. I don't think I deserve this!

I look at people around me, people who don't know you, who don't want to know you, and they're doing great. They don't have a care in the world. Me, I'm in church at least three times a week, I give my money and time to causes that honor you, and this is what I get? It's not quite what I signed up for.

Lord, I'm not perfect. We both know that. And whatever goodness I have, it's nothing compared to yours. I'm not asking for any special treatment. I'm just wondering why you felt the need to dump this challenge in my life when I've been so loyal to you.

I'm not turning my back on you. I really want to draw closer to you through this whole ordeal. But I need to feel your presence in my life. I believe you're here with me, but it would be a lot easier if you made yourself a little more obvious. Be near me, Lord Jesus.

Amen.

You will be in the right, O Lord,
    when I lay charges against you;
    but let me put my case to you.
Why does the way of the guilty prosper?
    Why do all who are treacherous thrive?
You plant them, and they take root;
    they grow and bring forth fruit;
you are near in their mouths
    yet far from their hearts.
But you, O Lord, know me;
    You see me and test me—my heart is
    with you.
—Jeremiah 12:1–3

Fair Grounds

"It isn't fair," I grumbled as the crisis came to pass.
I've been a righteous person all my life.
Other than that cheating incident in history class,
I've really always done what's good and right.

I truly love all people, despite their creed or race.
I'm frequently performing thoughtful acts—
Except my next-door neighbor. That's a special case:
He kept me up nights, practicing his sax!

I've tried to treat folks fairly; I seek fairness in return.
That's just a principle I believe in.
One good turn earns another, but if ever I get burned,
I won't get mad—trust me—I'll get even.

So now I face a challenge. Yes, God has mysterious
ways.
I'm feeling pain I'm sure I don't deserve.
In the school of life it's obvious that I have earned
straight As,
At least if God is grading on a curve.

Why, O Lord, do you stand far off?
    Why do you hide yourself in times of
    trouble?
In arrogance the wicked persecute the
    poor—
    let them be caught in the schemes they
    have devised.

For the wicked boast of the desires of their
    heart,
    those greedy for gain curse and
    renounce the Lord.
In the pride of their countenance the wicked
    say, "God will not seek it out";
    all their thoughts are, "There is no God."

. . .

But you do see! Indeed you note trouble and
    grief,
    that you may take it into your hands;
the helpless commit themselves to you;
    you have been the helper of the orphan.

. . .

O Lord, you will hear the desire of the meek;
   you will strengthen their heart, you will
   incline your ear
to do justice for the orphan and the
   oppressed,
   so that those from earth may strike terror
   no more.
—**Psalm 10:1–4, 14, 17–18**

✟   ✟   ✟

Prescription

Make your case to God. Some people turn their backs on God when they feel mistreated by him. That doesn't do any good. If you think God is acting unfairly toward you, tell him so. You wouldn't be the first. Keep those lines of communication open. Listen for his response, and look for his gracious activity in your life.

✟   ✟   ✟

You Call This Love?

The Baffling Trio of Love, Power, and Suffering

When she was 17, Aisha decided to stop believing in God. It was not a personal tragedy that forced her decision, just something that happened in her neighborhood. A school bus had hit some of the children who had just been let off. Several of them were dead; others were badly injured. The whole community went into shock. How could this have possibly happened?

Aisha was not related to any of the children, but the incident struck her deeply. She had been brought up with a solid belief in God, but now it just seemed illogical. If there really was a God, why would he let children get hit by a bus? Certainly he would have the power to prevent such a tragedy. Why didn't he? Aisha had gone through life generally assuming that people deserved the bad things that happened to them, but these were innocents. She had seen them playing on their front stoops. How could they deserve this pain, suffering, and death?

Many others have gone the same route as Aisha, giving up the assumptions of their youth when they slam into some unexplainable tragedy. It's largely an intellectual issue, though it might involve some personal pain as well. People rethink what they've been taught about God because it no longer fits the world they see around them.

Scholars call this the "problem of evil," and they've been ruminating on it for centuries. The question has taken various forms, but we'll word it like this: *If God is love, and if he's all-powerful, then how can he allow suffering?*

Notice the three parts of this question.

God is love. This is as scriptural as you can get (1 John 4:8). Certainly a loving God would not want people to suffer. (Another version of this question focuses on God's righteousness: *Why is there evil if God is good?*)

God is all-powerful. This also comes from Scripture (Job 42:2; Isaiah 40:26). He's the Creator, after all. Surely he holds the whole world in his hands. "See, I am the Lord, the God of all flesh; is anything too hard for me?" (Jeremiah 32:27).

There is suffering (and evil) in the world. If you're paying attention at all, you can't deny this. Our world is rife with qualities that God doesn't like.

These three truths don't seem to fit together. Various attempts to explain the problem usually shortchange one of them.

Is there any way to combine all three truths into a logical explanation? Maybe not, but let's try.

Power Play

While it might be tempting to think that your problems are just illusions, and that you can rise above them by ignoring them—you know better. The pain and sorrow you feel are real. One of the great things about the Bible is its solid footing in real life. We have a flesh-and-blood faith. So we can't take the easy way out of denying our suffering. It's there; we have to deal with it.

So, as we move around this seeming contradiction, let's consider God's *power*. Maybe you've had an experience something like this: You walk into a business meeting and hear one executive going on and on about standards of excellence and how he's going to fire every employee who doesn't meet them. He's unveiling new proposals for the company that will take it in a new direction. Clearly this man is wielding some sort of corporate power, and you can see others nodding as he speaks. But they're also sneaking some peeks down to the other end of the table, where a woman sits quietly listening, sometimes nodding, sometimes frowning, sometimes tapping a pen on the table. Who has the real power in that room? It's probably that woman.

Often the people who show off their power don't have as much as they think. The truly powerful hold much of their power in reserve, waiting for the most effective time to use it. They know they have it, so they don't need to display it for everybody else.

We believe in an omnipotent God, one who created the universe out of nothing, one who overruled his own laws of nature on several biblical occasions, one who raised Jesus Christ from the dead. Surely he has the power to do anything he fancies. Presumably he could undo the tragedy that has befallen you; he could turn back the clock and restore all you've lost. You know he has such power, so why doesn't he give you a break?

Maybe he's waiting for the best time to act. Maybe he's holding some power in reserve, in order to achieve some much greater good in the future. Maybe he's saying no.

When Jesus was tempted, it was all about power. First the devil challenged him to use his wonder-working power to feed himself. Jesus had been fasting for 40 days, and the desert rocks probably looked tantalizingly like dinner rolls. "Turn these stones into bread," the tempter challenged. Jesus said no. Why? There's nothing wrong with eating bread! But there's more to life than a full stomach. By fasting, Jesus had been exercising an age-old ritual that brought people closer to God. It was more important to focus on God than to feed himself, as his response made clear: "It is written, 'One does not live by bread alone, but by every word that comes from the mouth of God' " (Matthew 4:4).

This provides a crucial commentary on the miracles he later performed. Yes, he met the physical needs of people, healing them and even mysteriously creating bread on at least two occasions, but this was not his purpose. These were "signs" designed to prove his divine authority; his main purpose was to bring people into God's kingdom. His own wholeness spilled over to the people he touched, but he was focusing on his task of connecting people with the God who loved them.

Once a paralyzed man was lowered through the roof of a house where Jesus was teaching. The man wanted to be healed. After probably brushing the dust out of his hair, Jesus said, "Son, your sins are forgiven." This caused a stir among the religious folk, who knew that only God could forgive sins. Then Jesus said, "Why do you raise such questions in your hearts? Which is easier, to say to the paralytic, 'Your sins are forgiven,' or to say, 'Stand up and take your mat and walk'?"

Which *is* easier? Well, it's more challenging to announce a healing, because people will immediately see whether you have any power or not. Forgiveness of sins is less verifiable. "But," Jesus continued, "so that you may know that the Son of Man has authority on earth to forgive sins," he asked the young man to get up and walk, which the young man did (Mark 2:1–12). This story shows that Jesus' spiritual power was the main event. Physical healing was just an extra feature.

In the second temptation of Jesus, at least as Matthew tells it, the devil took Jesus to the pinnacle of the temple and asked him to jump. Since the temple towered over Jerusalem, this wasn't an every-day request. And why did the devil think Jesus should do this? The answer came when he quoted Psalm 91:11–12, which promises protection to those who trust the Lord: "He will command his angels concerning you to guard you in all your ways. On their hands they will bear you up, so that you will not dash your foot against a stone." (It's interesting that the tempter didn't quote the next verse, which talks about trampling the serpent underfoot.)

Jesus responded by quoting another Scripture, "Do not put the Lord your God to the test." This quote, from Deuteronomy 6:16, refers to a time when the Israelites were wandering in the desert wilderness. They were getting thirsty, and they demanded that God provide them with water. "Is the Lord among us or not?" was their taunt (Exodus 17:1–7). In other words, *if you don't work a miracle now, Lord, we might as well stop believing in you.*

> For as the heavens are higher than the earth, so are my ways higher than your ways and my thoughts than your thoughts.
> **—Isaiah 55:9**

So the "testing" that's prohibited is a kind of black-mail. Do this, Lord, or else! We might translate this verse to say, "You must not force the Lord's hand." In Jesus' situation, he knew angels were ready to protect him (and others) in certain dangerous situations. But did he have the right to put himself in such a spot to demonstrate his angelic protection? No, that would be a misuse of power.

God uses his awesome power to achieve his purposes, but, as we see in these two temptations, he sometimes chooses not to use the power he has. That can be very frustrating when you want him to act in a specific situation. Why doesn't he step in and work a miracle to help you *right now?* Is he powerless to help you? No, of course he's not powerless. Instead, he's holding that power in reserve, waiting for the right moment. And we must wait with him, which isn't always easy. Many biblical writers have voiced this cry: "How long, O Lord, how long?" (Psalms 13:1–2, 35:17; Habakkuk 1:2).

There's a phrase that has become popular in business: "Keep the main thing the main thing." That is, figure out what the central activity of your business

How long, O Lord? Will you forget me
　　forever?
　　How long will you hide your face from
　　me?
How long must I bear pain in my soul,
　　and have sorrow in my heart all day long?
How long shall my enemy be exalted over
　　me?

Consider and answer me, O Lord my God!
　　Give light to my eyes, or I will sleep the
　　sleep of death,
and my enemy will say, "I have prevailed";
　　my foes will rejoice because I am shaken.

But I trusted in your steadfast love;
　　my heart shall rejoice in your salvation.
I will sing to the Lord,
　　because he has dealt bountifully with
　　me.
—Psalm 13

is, and make sure it stays central. That was essentially what Jesus was doing during his temptation, and we can apply this principle to all of God's activity. He is working to redeem the created order, to bring it all into a loving relationship with him. That's the main thing. In his time, in his way, God is working in that direction.

> O hope of Israel,
>> its savior in time of trouble,
> why should you be like a stranger in the
>> land,
>> like a traveler turning aside for the
>> night?
> Why should you be like someone confused,
>> like a mighty warrior who cannot
>> give help?
> Yet you, O Lord, are in the midst of us,
>> and we are called by your name;
>> do not forsake us!
> **—Jeremiah 14:8–9**

✦ ✦ ✦

"My child, do not regard lightly the discipline
    of the Lord,
  or lose heart when you are punished by
    him;
for the Lord disciplines those whom he
    loves,
  and chastises every child whom he
    accepts."

Endure trials for the sake of discipline. God is treating you as children; for what child is there whom a parent does not discipline? If you do not have that discipline in which all children share, then you are illegitimate and not his children. Moreover, we had human parents to discipline us, and we respected them. Should we not be even more willing to be subject to the Father of spirits and live? For they disciplined us for a short time as seemed best to them, but he disciplines us for our good, in order that we may share his holiness. Now, discipline always seems painful rather than pleasant at the time, but later it yields the peaceful fruit of

righteousness to those who have been
trained by it.

Therefore lift your drooping hands and
strengthen your weak knees, and make
straight paths for your feet, so that what is
lame may not be put out of joint, but rather
be healed.
—**Hebrews 12:5–13**

✠   ✠   ✠

He Loves Me,
He Loves Me Not

Let's talk about love. We have three parts to our
quandary, and we've already looked at two. That
means if our suffering is real, and if God is all-
powerful, the only question remaining is how much
he loves us. It is reasonable to think that love would
lead him to use his power to prevent our suffering.
Reasonable, yes. Practical, no.

If you have children, you already know this very well. Your heart aches for them. Every stubbed toe, every slivered finger somehow connects with your own nervous system. You feel their pain. There is a profound truth in that age-old parental dictum, usually said while administering punishment: "This hurts me more than it hurts you." When you heard that as a kid, you probably thought it was the dumbest comment ever. But when you say it as a parent, you realize how true it is.

Parents love their children, and yet they let them ride bicycles, which sometimes totter and crash. They let them play soccer, where they can collide with other children. They send them to school, where they can face the disappointment of receiving bad grades. If parents really loved their children, wouldn't they use their power to prevent these sufferings? No, not at all. Children need to play and grow and learn, and there is suffering in that process.

Imagine the parent who devotes all of life to preventing a child's suffering. "Stay in the house!" "Those toys have sharp edges!" "Here, let me do that homework for you!" "No, you may not borrow the car!" In fact, some parents *are* overprotective, and we recognize how unhealthy that is. *For the child's own benefit,* a parent must allow some freedom, and that freedom may lead to suffering. Consider this scenario.

"Dad! Why are you hanging onto my bike?"

"I don't want you to fall."

"I know, but I'm 14 now. You've been doing that for five years!"

Our loving God is the father who's helping us learn to ride. There have been times when he has offered protection, running alongside, holding us up. But then there are times he has let go, to let us ride freely and, perhaps, to let us crash.

Hebrews 12:6 says, "The Lord disciplines those whom he loves." Imagine that Jenny and two friends are whooping it up one wintry day by throwing snowballs at passing cars. Suddenly one car stops, and the driver gets out.

"Uh-oh," says Jenny. "I'm in trouble."

"We all are," says a friend.

"No, you don't understand," Jenny replies. "That's my mom. She has high standards for me."

That's absolutely right. The other kids might be sent home with a scolding, but Mom will ground Jenny for two weeks, disciplining her because she loves her.

Parenting experts have proposed a system they call "reality discipline," in which parents let the child face the consequences of his or her actions. Daria used this with her son, who had trouble getting ready in the morning. If he sometimes missed the bus, he'd ask his mom to drive him to school. One morning she said no. He was furious. How could she make him late to school? And she claimed to love him! But Daria knew her son would only get ready if he had to face being late, so she decided against using her automotive power to help him.

When we read about the Lord interacting with us, it's usually something like that. Occasionally he might send special challenges our way, but most often he's just allowing us to face the consequences of our own bad decisions. Is he turning his back on us? Not really. He's just taking his hands off the bike, so we can learn to ride through life.

Who will separate us from the love of Christ? Will hardship, or distress, or persecution, or famine, or nakedness, or peril, or sword? As it is written,
"For your sake we are being killed all day
     long;
we are accounted as sheep to be
     slaughtered."
No, in all these things we are more than conquerors through him who loved us. For I am convinced that neither death, nor life, nor angels, nor rulers, nor things present, nor things to come, nor powers, nor height, nor depth, nor anything else in all creation, will be able to separate us from the love of God in Christ Jesus our Lord.
—Romans 8:35–39

The Strange Equation

We have only begun to take a look at what seems to be a major contradiction—if God is loving and powerful, why do we suffer?—but maybe we've found a few footholds. Some, such as Aisha, have hit an intellectual roadblock here, but it's an emotional issue for many, many others. *You call this love? How can you love me and let me suffer like this?*

If God is loving and lacks the power to help us, sometimes we think we should go find someone else to trust in. And maybe we have turned to money, success, or various addictions. Perhaps those substitute saviors can ease the pain.

If God has power but doesn't care about us, then that's a huge blow. What kind of tyrant is he? Indeed, some have gone this direction, spouting the wrath of God while practicing a loveless legalism.

Try to understand both sides of this strange equation. God is both loving and powerful, though it's not always clear how those two qualities coexist. Perhaps we can take some comfort in this, though.

God is bigger than our ability to figure him out, and don't we want a God that size?

✛ ✛ ✛

And not only that, but we also boast in our sufferings, knowing that suffering produces endurance, and endurance produces character, and character produces hope, and hope does not disappoint us, because God's love has been poured into our hearts through the Holy Spirit that has been given to us.
—Romans 5:3–5

✛ ✛ ✛

God Moves in a Mysterious Way

God moves in a mysterious way
His wonders to perform
He plants his footsteps in the sea
And rides upon the storm.

Why Me, God?

Deep in unfathomable mines
Of never-failing skill
He treasures up his bright designs
And works his sovereign will.

Ye fearful saints, fresh courage take.
The clouds ye so much dread
Are big with mercy, and shall break
In blessings on your head.

Judge not the Lord by feeble sense,
But trust him for his grace;
Behind a frowning providence
He hides a smiling face.

Blind unbelief is sure to err,
And scan his work in vain;
God is his own interpreter,
And he will make it plain.

—William Cowper (1731–1800)

✛   ✛   ✛

A Prayer of Doubt

Dear Lord, sometimes I'm not even sure you're here. Maybe I'm launching my prayers up into the silence. But if you are there, please hear me, and please respond in some way.

I don't get you. Let's get that straight right away. People talk to me about your qualities, and it sounds as if they have you all figured out, but I don't. You are a complete mystery to me. For one thing, I'll never understand how you let the world get into such a mess. If you're really in charge, I'd expect you to make things better. But maybe I'm missing something.

I want you to be there. I want to love you and to know that you love me. I just have a lot of questions about you, about the world, and about myself. It's hard to put it all together. So, help me understand. I don't need to know everything, just a few things, just something that will start making sense.

You can reach me right here. I'll be listening. Amen.

When the angel of the Lord appeared to Gideon, he said, "The Lord is with you, mighty warrior."

"But sir," Gideon replied, "if the Lord is with us, why has all this happened to us? Where are all his wonders that our fathers told us about when they said, 'Did not the Lord bring us up out of Egypt?' But now the Lord has abandoned us."
—Judges 6:12–13, NIV

Prescription

Understand that there are things you don't understand. You might try to squeeze God into a box that fits your idea of what God should be, but he won't fit. His ways are too mysterious for that. Let him keep teaching you who he really is.

Wrong Answers

Friends Know When to Stay Mum

Rain had fallen all day, and dusk only dimmed an already dismal sky. Annie was driving home from work when she skidded through a stoplight on the wet pavement. Another car struck the driver's side, and she was killed. Instantly, they said.

Her husband Victor was devastated, crying a lot the first few days after the accident. But he seemed to get himself together for the funeral, and he actually comforted many of the friends who offered their condolences.

"She's in a better place now," he would say. "They tell me she didn't suffer at all."

"God will give you strength," people would promise. "All things work together for good. You'll see her again someday."

As a leader in his church, Victor forged ahead in his activities, despite his loss. Friends asked if he wanted to take some time off from teaching Sunday school. If he missed a board meeting, everyone would understand. But he insisted on continuing his church work as if nothing had happened. He appeared to be unscathed by the tragedy. In fact, the pastor even used Victor as an example of God's joy. Happiness, he suggested, is based on circumstances, but true joy abides forever, rising above even the worst of circumstances. It seemed obvious to everyone that Victor had true joy.

About a year later, Victor was watching television—an episode of *ER*—when he began to cry. The tears kept him awake that night, and he stayed home from work the next day. That Saturday he called his pastor. "I need some help," he pleaded.

For 12 months he had dammed up his grief, and now the dam was bursting. He had convinced himself that God was preventing him from feeling bad, and so the natural emotions of sadness, loneliness, or abandonment were kept behind that dam. But now he couldn't hold them back any longer. In his counseling session with the pastor, he spewed a torrent of feelings—grief and anger, doubt and fear. "I'm sorry," he whimpered, "I guess I don't have that joy you were talking about."

"Joy comes in the morning," the pastor wisely replied. "But there are some dark hours we need to get through yet."

As [Jesus] walked along, he saw a man blind from birth. His disciples asked him, "Rabbi, who sinned, this man or his parents, that he was born blind?" Jesus answered, "Neither this man nor his parents sinned; he was born blind so that God's works might be revealed in him."
—**John 9:1–3**

The Army of Good Intentions

When tragedies happen in your life, an army of well-meaning friends rushes in to encourage you. They say some wise and true things. But they can also say some things that are half-true, misleading, simplistic, or insensitive. You should love these people—they really do want you to feel better, and in most cases they don't know what to say, so they say something that sounded good when someone else said it to them. While appreciating their intentions, you need to sort through their comments. Take the words that are truly helpful, and let the rest roll off.

Job had friends with good intentions. Eliphaz, Bildad, and Zophar showed up to share his grief, and they sat with him in silence for a

> Job replied:
> "I have heard many things like these; miserable comforters are you all! Will your long-winded speeches never end? What ails you that you keep on arguing?"
> —**Job 16:1–3, NIV**

week. Then they started talking. They should have stayed with the silence. For about 30 chapters in the Book of Job, they offer their opinions on Job's problems, suggesting that he must have done something wrong. Why else would God be sending him such disasters? Again and again, Job protested his innocence, but his friends kept challenging him.

Maybe your friends do something similar, making you feel guilty for your suffering. This adds insult to injury. It's not bad enough that you have to deal with the pain of your tragedy, now you have to defend your reputation as well!

Friends try to cheer you up, but you may feel guilty for still being sad. They try to fix your problems with simple solutions, and you feel bad when those solutions don't solve anything. They try to answer your questions, but their answers don't always fit. They try to give you spiritual counsel, but sometimes it seems that they're ignoring the harsh realities of life.

Don't take this the wrong way. In times of trouble, friends can be a wonderful means of support. You need friends to listen to you, to coach you through your grief, and sometimes merely to sit with you. Some friends offer comments that can truly help you, assuring you of their love, giving perspective on your trials, or even challenging you to take the next step of recovery. But not all friends are so helpful.

Some are more interested in speaking than in listening. These friends fulfill some need in their lives by helping you. They want to say the perfect thing that will lift your spirits and heal your soul, so they don't always take the time to hear how you really feel. They assume they know what you're going through, and they dash off some advice that's appropriate for cases like yours. But the focus is on them and their ability to help you. They never really listen to your unique feelings. As a result, they can be insensitive, impersonal, and unhelpful.

Some want to force their feelings onto you. "I know exactly how you feel," they tell you. "When I faced a similar situation, I felt the same way." These friends may honestly be trying to empathize with you, but it doesn't make you feel any better to be pushed into an emotional corner. You are an individual, and your reaction, based on your own history and other complex factors, is unique to you. Even if your friends did confront the same event, they can't understand how you feel now.

Some look for a quick fix. People can be very impatient. "Shouldn't you be over this by now?" They want you to be healthy, but they don't understand how long the road to recovery can be. If you've lost someone, depending on the nature of that loss, the grieving process can last up to five years—or more. If you have an illness or disability, that can affect you even longer. Yet after a few weeks these friends are saying, "Enough already!"

Some underestimate the complexity of the problem. They're looking for that one phrase that will make everything all better. But you may have a jumble of emotions you haven't even begun to sort through. "Look on the bright side," they say, and that might distract you for a few hours, but it does nothing to dispel the darkness.

Some look only at the surface of things. "You look so depressed," they say. "Would it hurt you to smile once in a while?" And so you smile to get them off your back, but deep down you *are* depressed, and you have good reason to be. They don't seem to care about your inner issues, only about the symptoms. And so, like Victor, you learn to live a double life—happy on the outside but hurting within—and sometimes even fooling yourself.

Some see every problem as basically spiritual. Yes, there is a spiritual component to many of our difficulties, but the issues are also emotional and psychological. "Trust God more," these friends say, and that's certainly helpful in any situation, but it won't always take away the pain. The nasty underside of this over-spiritual approach is that it makes you feel that you're not spiritual enough.

Some use the Bible as a pharmacy. They dispense Scripture verses like aspirin. "Here, take one Romans 8:28 now and a 23rd Psalm in the morning, and you'll feel chipper again." Even this book, while demonstrating that the Bible has tremendous resources to help you through hard times, is no magic elixir. In the Bible, God reveals himself to you—it's this relationship that will restore your soul. Read the Bible avidly, and meet God there. But don't just sprinkle a few Scriptures on a situation and expect instant therapy.

Some seem to fear sadness. This was Victor's problem. He was so focused on showing "God's joy" that he never let himself feel the natural sadness of his loss. People feel uncomfortable when you cry around them. They will say practically anything to make you stop. But the Bible says, "Rejoice with those who rejoice, weep with those who weep" (Romans 12:15). Let the tears flow, if that's what you need to do. If others refuse to weep with you, that's their problem.

Some try to answer every question. The title of this book is a question—"Why me, God?" And we've already unpacked many other questions that arise in times of trouble. How could God let this happen? Does this mean God doesn't love me? What did I do wrong? Will life ever be the same again? These are important questions to ask, and as time goes by, you might find some answers. But such questions make some Christians uneasy. They worry that if you ask these questions, you're losing your faith, so they scurry in to shore up your beliefs. They could be right to worry, but that may not be the response you need right now. You don't need answers, you need peace. You don't always need explanations; sometimes you just need a hug.

Some put God in a box. Ever since the Ark of the Covenant, God's people have tried to contain him. The Israelites felt that if they carried the Ark into battle they couldn't lose. But they *did* lose, and the Ark was captured. In Jeremiah's day, the people of Jerusalem felt that the city would never fall because the Temple of the Lord was there. But Jerusalem *did* fall to the Babylonians, and the Temple was destroyed. The Pharisees felt that if Israel kept God's law in every detail God would have to bless them. Jesus shocked them by announcing that prostitutes and greedy tax collectors would enter God's kingdom first. In your time of questioning, some will tell you that they have God figured out. They know exactly what he will and will not do. Don't believe it. One of Jesus' regular preaching themes was that God keeps surprising us. God will work in your life in mysterious ways. Don't try to box him up.

O the depth of the riches and wisdom and knowledge of God! How unsearchable are his judgments and how inscrutable his ways! "For who has known the mind of the Lord? Or who has been his counselor?"
—**Romans 11:33–34**

✛　✛　✛

Friendship 101

After looking at all that, do you really want any friends at all? Forgive this book for making them seem like ogres. The truth is that it's difficult to be a good friend, and it's especially tough to know what to say when a friend is grieving. You have probably slipped into some of these errors when comforting others; almost everybody has. So don't be too hard on those who say the wrong things to you. They usually mean well.

But maybe you can teach your friends what to say. You could show them this chapter, for one thing. You could also talk about what comments are truly helpful. In good marriages, husbands and wives tell each other how they like to be treated. (In bad marriages, they assume that's common knowledge and feel offended when they don't get the right treatment.) Why not do the same thing in a friendship? "Thank you for wanting to help me in this tough time. I really appreciate it. Let me tell you the sort of support I need from you...."

Here are some things you might talk about.

Listening. You're going through a lot of crazy feelings right now. Sometimes you just need to talk them out. You don't need anyone to solve your problems or provide answers for your questions—you just need a listening ear. You need to know that someone can hear about what you're feeling and not run screaming from the room.

Permission. There are lots of psychobabble terms ' for this one. *Validation. Affirmation.* Basically you just need a listener to tell you that you're not losing your mind. You are communicating a strange mix of feelings right now, but considering what you are going through, that's understandable. It's okay to be sad. It's okay to be angry. That's all part of the recovery process. If you start plotting murders or rendezvous with alien starships, your friends can challenge you. But basically you just need permission to feel what you're feeling.

Prayer. Friends can pray for you, *and with you.* This is especially important if you are feeling distant from God. You might not feel much like praying. But if a friend leads the way, you can join in. It's helpful to keep those lines of communication open, even if you're not sure God is paying attention. The simple faith of a friend can be a blessing in a barren time. You don't need preaching or scolding, just an invitation to pray along.

Hope. You need some friends who speak in the future tense. Times are tough now, but they won't always be. Make some plans for a year or two from now, when you'll be better able to enjoy yourself. Your friends need to understand that it takes a while to deal with loss, and they shouldn't rush you through it. But they should remind you from time to time that there is a light at the end of this tunnel. That day will dawn.

Pathway. You are on the road to restoration, but it's a foggy one. You might need some help in seeing where to find the next step. Do you need to toss aside denial and claim your grief? Do you need to allow yourself some anger? Do you need to finally find acceptance? A sensitive friend can illuminate your path as you go.

Nudging. Be careful here, because nudging isn't far from pushing. You don't want pushy friends, but you might need some precious pals who know when to coax you forward. Grief will sap your energy, and it's good to have friends to provide some extra horse-power. This might be as simple as "We're going out tonight and having a good time, whether you like it or not!" If that happens at the right time, it can provide a very healing moment for you. At the wrong time, it's just pushy. You need friends who know the difference.

I consider that the sufferings of this present time are not worth comparing with the glory about to be revealed to us. For the creation waits with eager longing for the revealing of the children of God; for the creation was subjected to futility, not of its own will but by the will of the one who subjected it, in hope that the creation itself will be set free from its bondage to decay and will obtain the freedom of the glory of the children of God. We know that the whole creation has been groaning in labor pains until now; and not only the creation, but we ourselves, who have the first fruits of the Spirit, groan inwardly while we wait for adoption, the redemption of our bodies.
—Romans 8:18–23

Those Easy Answers

Let's flash back to the story of Victor and his rushed recovery. In the wake of the tragedy, friends offered him words of comfort, including the text of Romans 8:28: "All things work together for good."

This is a stunning biblical promise that is often dispensed too lightly. When some people quote this verse, it's as if they're saying, "Don't worry. Be happy. Everything will turn out all right." In that tone, it sounds like an out-and-out denial of the trouble you face. For that reason, some suffering souls have grown to hate Romans 8:28 for what they take as its oversimplification. It's escapist! It's the sort of thing people say when they don't want to wade through the muck with you.

But the actual meaning of this verse is much stronger than that.

Some medical experts are concerned these days because antibiotics have been overprescribed. So many people are taking these helpful drugs for sniffles and sore throats that bacteria have developed resistance to them. As a result, the powerful medicine has lost its effect.

Maybe it's the same thing with Romans 8:28. A powerful promise has been brandished so freely that people forget how powerful it really is. It becomes "that silly thing Christians say to forget about their problems." Some folks develop a resistance to it.

> Call to me and I will answer you, and will tell you great and hidden things that you have not known.
> **—Jeremiah 33:3**

Maybe right here we can begin to reclaim this verse and restore its true effectiveness.

Romans 8:28 sits within one of the Bible's greatest chapters. The apostle Paul has been setting forth his case for Christianity. We are sinners. We deserve eternal death. Jesus offers life, which we access through faith. Our righteous deeds can't save us, only the righteous deed of Jesus on the cross can. The law has done its job, showing us how much we need Jesus. Now we live by the power of the Spirit. But it can be a struggle.

The end of Romans 7 poignantly depicts that struggle. "I do not understand my own actions," the apostle writes. "For I do not do the good I want, but the evil I do not want is what I do" (vs. 15, 19). You might need to read that a few times to get the point, but then you'll recognize it as familiar territory. Even when we know what's right, it's hard to do it.

Then this fabulous Chapter 8 opens with a great assurance: "There is therefore now no condemnation for those who are in Christ Jesus. For the law of the Spirit of life in Christ Jesus has set you free from the law of sin and of death" (vs. 1–2). We have life! We are empowered by the same Spirit that raised Jesus from the dead (v. 11).

This doesn't mean that we will be able to avoid suffering. Just as Jesus suffered and was later glorified, so will we. Paul writes: "I consider that the sufferings of this present time are not worth comparing with the glory about to be revealed to us" (v. 18). At that time, the drumbeats of Roman persecution were just beginning. The Roman believers were starting to feel discrimination, and there was some violence from other Roman citizens. Perhaps Paul had a premoni-

tion of the furious persecution that would be
unleashed by Nero several years later, in which he
himself would be arrested and beheaded.

So, whatever our current circumstances, we are
"waiting for glory." In fact, Paul enlarges his scope to
include all of creation, which "waits with eager longing," "groaning in labor pains," anticipating the
fulfillment of God's purposes (vs. 19, 22). Earth-
quakes, plagues, wars, and addictions are all part of
the same package—a world in "bondage to decay,"
waiting for the glory of God (v. 21).

We also "groan inwardly," as we wait for our
redemption (v. 23). We are so spiritually bankrupt,
we don't even know how to pray. But the Spirit
translates our feeble cries into "sighs too deep for
words" (v. 26).

This is the grand context of Romans 8:28. "We
know that all things work together for good for
those who love God, who are called according to his
purpose." Sufferings and disasters are to be expected.
It's all part of the groaning, the waiting. Like the rest
of the world, we will have our share of sorrow. But

in this loving relationship with the God who understands our babbling, we know that he is up to something. He has a purpose. He is working toward an
ultimate good. He is scraping up the muck we're
wading through and sculpting a thing of beauty.

We are not told that all things *are* good. That's
where some of our well-wishers go wrong, when
they ask us to ignore the pain of our tragedies. No,
suffering hurts! Romans 8:28 never tells us otherwise. But these bad things work together to create an
ultimate good, which God is crafting.

A little boy was helping his mom bake brownies. The
brownie mix came with a special flavor packet, a plastic pouch of rich chocolate. The boy loved chocolate,
and this flavor packet seemed like the very essence of
life. All that chocolate flavor in one little pouch! So he
squeezed out a spoonful of that flavoring and eagerly
tasted it. It was horrendous. Without the sugar from
the mix, this pure cocoa taste was extremely bitter.
And the boy was left with a mystery. How could this
terrible taste make such delicious brownies?

Romans 8:28 shows us a God who is tossing ingredients into his mixing bowl and stirring them up into something delicious. That tragedy, that disaster, that disappointment, however distasteful at the time, all go into the mix. The resulting confection might come out of the oven next week, next year, or in heaven—we don't know. But we are assured that the result will be good, according to God's purpose.

✦ ✦ ✦

The Serenity Prayer

God grant me the serenity to accept the things I cannot change, courage to change the things I can, and wisdom to know the difference.

—Reinhold Neibuhr

✦ ✦ ✦

A great windstorm arose, and the waves beat into the boat, so that the boat was already being swamped. But [Jesus] was in the stern, asleep on the cushion; and they woke him up and said to him, "Teacher, do you not care that we are perishing?" He woke up and rebuked the wind, and said to the sea, "Peace! Be still!" Then the wind ceased, and there was a dead calm. He said to them, "Why are you afraid? Have you still no faith?" And they were filled with great awe and said to one another, "Who then is this, that even the wind and the sea obey him?"
—Mark 4:37–41

✛　✛　✛

A Prayer for Restoration and Comfort

You could certainly pray this for yourself, but it's also a prayer that others can pray for you, as you go through your difficulties. Insert specifics of the situation where appropriate.

Dear Lord, we remember today this good friend, who is having a hard time right now. We ask you to provide comfort and healing.

We don't understand why you allow these things to come into our lives, Lord. But we trust that you are working in all situations to bring about your good purposes. We ask that you would continue to work your will in the life of our suffering friend. Use us to provide support and nurture. Give us the wisdom we need to aid in the healing process. Help each of us know what to say and do.

You are a God who loves wholeness, Lord, and we have seen your healing in Scripture and in our own lives. So in this case we boldly ask you to provide healing and restoration of body, mind, and spirit. Bring this dear one back to wholeness, for your eternal glory. Amen.

Why? Why? Why? Why? Why?

The question fails philosophy
And it rings in awkward artists' ears
Until it dies in dull monotony.

Jesus is the reason.
Jesus makes the melody
That mollifies the questions
That gives our life its quality.

He's far more of an answer
Than anyone can prove
He's much more like a dancer
Who loves in how he moves.

—From "Jesus Stood"

✝   ✝   ✝

Prescription

See how God is working his good purposes in your bad situation. Maybe you won't see much right away, but keep looking. The stunning promise of Romans 8:28 will come true. We can expect God to mix up good results even from painful ingredients, in this life or the next.

Meanwhile, shrug off the well-meant but too-easy comments of unhelpful friends. Instead, grab onto those friends who understand what you're going through and take it seriously.

Freedom and the Suffering of God

Why God Lets People Make Bad Choices

*B*liss had reigned in Richard's life for six months or so, ever since he'd started dating Janet. She seemed perfect for him, intelligent and witty, creative and talented. She even laughed at his jokes. Richard had resisted commitment in several previous relationships with women who didn't meet his high standards, but Janet exceeded every expectation. She brought joy and meaning to his life. He found his personality changing for the better, from cynical to sociable. He dared to admit he loved her.

That's why it was so devastating when Janet broke up with him.

She did it sweetly, which almost made it worse. If she'd been nasty, he could have assumed she'd been abducted by aliens or something. But no, she liked him, she wanted to be friends, she just didn't think they had a future together, and it wouldn't be right to keep seeing each other romantically. In that one conversation, Richard's world fell apart.

He'd been a Christian since childhood, so he turned to God. His prayers flowed fast and furious. "How could you let this happen?" "Show me how to win her back." "Tell her to love me." "Reveal to her how much I love her." "Bring events into her life that make her change her mind."

None of those prayers worked. Janet never came back to Richard. He sank into a deep sadness for several months. During that time, he tried to maintain a habit of regular prayer and Bible reading, hoping that some Scripture would give him hope or peace. Day after day the words just seemed like splotches of ink on the page ... until he ran across the prophet Hosea.

God had guided Hosea into an unusual marriage, telling him to marry a prostitute named Gomer. It's likely that she was involved in the worship of a

Canaanite fertility god named Baal, a cult that involved certain sexual rites. Apparently Hosea got her out of this cultic prostitution, possibly even "buying" her as his wife. But Gomer couldn't stop straying. Despite all of Hosea's kindnesses, she continued to sneak back into her old ways. She bore two children, but Hosea wasn't sure they were his. At God's direction, he gave them Hebrew names meaning "Not Mine" and "Not Loved." Only later was he instructed to adopt them as his own, renaming them "Mine" and "Loved."

> For Christ also suffered for sins once for all, the righteous for the unrighteous, in order to bring you to God.
> **—1 Peter 3:18**

The details of Hosea's story are somewhat blurry, because it's not always clear whether the lush poetry in the Scripture is talking about the prophet or the Lord himself. But Hosea's turbulent marriage was an object lesson. As God saw it, Israel was a wayward wife. He had loved the Jewish people, provided for them, and delivered them from slavery, but they were ignoring him. He gave them sun and rain to grow their crops, but they imagined it was Baal who offered these blessings. He wanted them to be his people, specially loved by him, but they kept chasing after idols and adopting the ways of their pagan neighbors. God's heart was breaking.

"The more I called them, the more they went from me; they kept sacrificing to the Baals, and offering incense to idols."
—**Hosea 11:2**

Richard knew that feeling. Oh, there was nothing sinful about her breaking up with him. But he still felt a bit like the lovelorn prophet. She had looked him in the eye and said, "I'm sorry. I don't love you anymore." And there was nothing he could do. Try as he might, he could not undo her decision. She was free to choose to love him or not, and she chose not to. Richard felt this was the wrong choice. He knew that he and Janet were perfect together, and he had believed that God had brought them together with great plans for them. He scolded God for letting her make such a mistake.

But he learned something from the Book of Hosea. Whatever sorrow Richard felt over the loss of this relationship, God had felt more. The emotional kick in the head that Richard had experienced—God had gone through that too, and for much the same reason. God had been madly in love, but his beloved people of Israel turned their backs and said to him, "We don't love you anymore."

> For surely I know the plans I have for you, says the Lord, plans for your welfare and not for harm, to give you a future with hope. Then when you call upon me and come and pray to me, I will hear you. When you search for me, you will find me; if you seek me with all your heart, I will let you find me, says the Lord.
> **—Jeremiah 29:11–14**

✛   ✛   ✛

A Prayer of Connection in Suffering

Dear Lord, as bad as I'm feeling right now, I know you've felt the same way. You have experienced physical and emotional pain, and you continue to feel unrequited love toward those who reject you. Sometimes I feel very alone, but in this moment I know I'm not alone. You are suffering right along with me.

So please speak comfort to me. Lift my heart into yours. Help me to understand you in a way I never have before.

I ask you to show me how to get through this. Give me peace and assurance for now, hope and direction for the future. Shine your light in my life again.

Thank you. Amen.

> Now faith is the assurance of things hoped for, the conviction of things not seen.... And without faith it is impossible to please God, for whoever would approach him must believe that he exists and that he rewards those who seek him.
> **—Hebrews 11:1, 6**

✦ ✦ ✦

Planting the Tree

But why would God allow himself to suffer like that? It's one thing to wonder how a loving God could let *us* suffer, but God does not exempt *himself* from pain, either. Certainly an omnipotent deity could fix things so he didn't have to go through all that. If we had that power, we would certainly try to protect ourselves from suffering, but God doesn't do that. He gives people the power to choose him or refuse him. He won't even force his own chosen people to love him.

It started back in Eden. God made the first man and woman and placed them in a beautiful garden. In this paradise, they named the animals, ate all the food they wanted, and took a walk with God each day. It was perfect... except for one thing. God placed one tree in the garden that was off-limits. Adam and Eve could eat any other fruit they found, but not the fruit of this forbidden tree. God called it the tree of the knowledge of good and evil.

You know the story. Tempted by a serpent, the couple ate the forbidden fruit, and everything changed. When God came calling for their daily stroll, they hid from him. This beautiful relationship between humans and their Creator was damaged. The man blamed the woman, the woman blamed the serpent, and all of them received the curse of their sin.

But there's another party we might consider blaming—God. If he had not planted that tree in the garden, they would not have sinned. If he had created a paradise with no opportunity for disobedience, they could have stayed there forever. Why on earth did he give them that choice?

Because God loves human freedom.

Think about the alternative. Adam and Eve would go about their perfect lives loving God because, frankly, they would not be able to do anything else. They would be moral robots, programmed to do whatever God wanted. Where's the joy in that?

God wanted people who would choose to love him. When the Bible says we were made "in his image" (Genesis 1:27), it might very likely be referring to our ability to choose. Like God, we have power to make decisions. We have a will. God didn't want to force obedience on anyone. He longed to walk with friends who knew good and evil and chose good.

As Richard turned this around in his mind, he realized the futility of his prayers to "make Janet love me again." True love can only come from a free heart. God wouldn't force that issue with Janet any more than he did with his own love, Israel. Richard had to accept the fact that, in this world God created, sometimes people would make decisions he didn't like. But he also took comfort from the thought that God knew exactly how he was feeling.

Hard to Get

There was a recent stage presentation of C. S. Lewis's classic work *The Screwtape Letters*. In a black-box theater on a back street of the city, a brilliant actor named Tony Lawton brought this strange piece to life in a new way, even for people who had read the book more than once.

Lewis imagined a correspondence between a novice demon named Wormwood and his uncle, Screwtape, who functions as a kind of trainer for tempters. The genius of the work is that its moral universe is upside-down. To these demons, God is "the Enemy." They delight in war and sin and pride and gossip, and they run in terror from grace and love. In a series of instructional letters, Screwtape coaches his protégé in the tempting of a particular Christian, and we see the ups and downs of this believer's life. From this skewed perspective, we get a new angle on our own faith.

In the stage production, Lawton paced around a desk as Screwtape, dictating letter after letter to his nephew. He was glib, angry, fearful, impatient, proud. Occasionally he seemed downright demonic, his otherworldly passions bringing on ferocious growls and howls. Then he'd straighten up and be absolutely professorial.

At one point the demons spoke of the spiritual valley the subject of their temptations had been experiencing. Wormwood was enjoying the fact that this Christian felt far from God at the moment, but Uncle Screwtape was cautioning against premature glee. He reminded his pupil that some of God's favorites had gone through lengthy valleys in their relationship with him. It's just the way God works.

Demons don't understand this, he said, because they are focused on dominating and consuming. They want to bend a subject's will to their own. But God has different methods. All that talk about God's love, says Screwtape, is "an appalling truth." God wants people to freely conform their will to his. For this reason, he refuses to use "the Irresistible and the Indisputable."

The actor showed the demon's puzzlement and distaste over the strange ways of God, and the audience gained a new insight. Certainly God could dazzle us so that we had no choice but to follow him, but our choice is exactly what he wants to preserve. Perhaps he intentionally seems far away from us because he wants us to seek after him. Maybe God plays hard to get.

On stage, the actor was ranting on and on about the strange love of God. "Merely to override a human will . . . would be for him useless. He cannot ravish. He can only woo."

That is the premium God places on human freedom. He will not override our will. He wants us to love him because we want to. And so he'll woo us, but he won't overwhelm us. He not only gives us a choice, but he guards our freedom to choose.

As servants of God, live as free people, yet do not use your freedom as a pretext for evil.
—1 Peter 2:16

You know what it's like, dear Lord,
To give and give and be ignored.
You know what it means to woo
The very ones who turn from you,
To hear harangue from hateful voices,
To suffer harm from foolish choices,
And ache from acts of angry hearts.
So when my world falls apart,
When I'm neglected or abused
By sinful ways that people choose,
When my heart hurts and my mind reels,
I know you know just how it feels.

I thought
    how I would set you among my children,
and give you a pleasant land,
    the most beautiful heritage of all the
    nations.
And I thought you would call me, My Father,
    and would not turn from following me.
Instead, as a faithless wife leaves her
    husband,

so you have been faithless to me, O house of
    Israel,
        says the Lord.

A voice on the bare heights is heard,
    the plaintive weeping of Israel's children,
because they have perverted their way,
    they have forgotten the Lord their God:
Return, O faithless children,
    I will heal your faithlessness.
—Jeremiah 3:19–22

✢ ✢ ✢

The Princely Pauper

In the last few years, television has featured a lot of
what people call "reality shows." One of these programs presented a situation exactly the opposite of
what we're talking about. The producers set up a
low-wage construction worker in a millionaire's
mansion and brought in a number of single women
who tried to win his heart. It was a cruel joke, all
sizzle and no substance. The women might not have
looked twice at this guy if he hit on them at a party,

but they were dazzled by his "wealth," which turned out to be fictional.

What would happen in the opposite scenario? Take a genuine millionaire, dress him in a T-shirt and tattered jeans, and see if he can find a date. That's sort of what God does with us. He is the prince who dresses as a pauper.

Of course you'll recognize this idea as the story of Jesus, who did not cling to his equality with God, but took the form of a servant. For most of his earthly life, the Prince of Peace was a carpenter. As a wandering rabbi, he antagonized rulers and embraced lepers. He walked away from the king-makers and headed straight for the cross.

God still uses that strategy in his dealings with us. It would be so much easier if he made it all clear, if he ripped the heavens open and revealed his full glory. Faith would be no problem if he instantly punished sin and rewarded righteousness. Getting zapped by lightning would surely prevent crime. And if all believers experienced a supernatural bliss every moment of their lives, churches would be packed.

But that's not the way God chooses to run this world. He refuses to overwhelm us with the irresistible and indisputable. Instead, he quietly woos us, and sometimes he plays hard to get. He wants to make sure we have the opportunity to choose to love him—or not.

Maybe you are suffering because of what other people have done. Your husband has left you, your daughter has run away, your boss is making work miserable, or your neighbor is stealing your mail. You wish those people would make better choices. So does God.

You might blame God for the actions of those people. Why didn't he stop them from hurting you? Because human freedom is so important to him. If you want to be freely loved, you run the risk of being freely disobeyed. God aches as you ache over the sinful choices of these people.

And this might be small consolation, but your current suffering gives you a unique opportunity. Through this crisis, you now know how God feels. You can curl up in the heart of God.

Maybe God seems far away from you right now. The tragedies of your life make you think that God does not care. You feel as if he's gone on vacation and left the world to fend for itself.

Those feelings are understandable. Don't beat yourself up over them. But consider the idea that God is still loving you at a distance. Maybe he wants to make it harder for you to love him in order to see if that love will grow. And if that's the case, you need to step up to that challenge. Seek his face. Double your prayers. Draw near to him during this troubling time, and he will draw near to you.

Sow for yourselves righteousness;
    reap steadfast love;
    break up your fallow ground;
for it is time to seek the Lord,
    that he may come and rain righteousness
    upon you.
—Hosea 10:12

Prescription

Use this experience to understand God in a new way.
Instead of fleeing from your emotions, *share* them
with God—and really share. Cry with him. Seek to
understand his sorrow, his frustration, his pain. As
one Christian leader has prayed, "Let my heart be
broken by the things that break the heart of God."

Sorting It Out

How Much of This Is Our Own Fault?

*T*alk about midlife crisis! Malcolm had it bad. He'd grown up in a generation that was told not to trust anyone over 30, so when he turned 40 he was desperate to reassert his youth. What did he do? He took up surfing.

It started innocently enough, on a family vacation with his wife and teenage daughters. But soon surfing was his passion. On any given Saturday, if the waves were good, he'd drive two hours to Malibu. Even though he was an elder in his church, he started surfing some Sundays as well. Though he had a corporate job, he began leaving early on Fridays to beat the weekend traffic and calling in sick on Mondays to stay a bit longer. His family didn't see much of him.

But the problem wasn't just surfing. That was merely the crowbar that pried open a cache of adolescent choices Malcolm began to make. After a day of hanging ten, he would down a few at a seaside pub. That's where Malcolm met Starr, a woman 15 years his junior. She seemed fascinated by his story, she applauded his exploits, and she didn't care that he was married. Apparently neither did he.

His wife was nagging him to see a counselor, his pastor was leaving messages on his answering machine, and his boss was complaining about Malcolm's frequent absences and hangovers. "You're never here, and when you are here you're not really here!" That was pretty much what everybody was saying. Except for Starr, who accepted Malcolm for what he was, an overgrown beach bum trying to squeeze a little more living out of life.

Everyone was stunned when Malcolm announced he had been fired from his job and was leaving his family to move in with Starr in Malibu.

Fast-forward three years. Starr had left to manage a rock band in Portland. Malcolm's wife had divorced him and was about to get remarried. His kids were embarrassed by him and wouldn't take his calls. He'd run out of money, and the meager amounts he earned from odd jobs were quickly spent on booze. Even surfing wasn't much fun anymore. Malcolm looked at his life and cried.

Fortunately, his old pastor hunted him down and wanted to talk. Though for years Malcolm had failed to return his pastor's phone calls, at this point Malcolm was ready. He sat across from his pastor at a burger joint and bluntly asked him, "How could God do this to me?"

"Excuse me?" Reverend Spahn replied.

"My life is a mess. I'm just wondering how God could let this happen."

The pastor shook his head in some disbelief. "Look, I love you, but somebody's gotta tell you. I don't see anything that has happened to you that you didn't do to yourself. You left your wife and kids, ignored your job, took up with another woman, and drank away your life savings. Blame God if you want to, but I don't think you have a case."

It was as if Malcolm awoke from a dream. He suddenly saw it all in the light of day. It wasn't his wife's fault or his boss's fault or Starr's fault. It wasn't weak waves or bad karma or turning 40 too soon. It was his own choices that had brought him to ruin. And if he didn't start making better choices, he began to realize things would only get worse.

That day was the beginning of a turnaround for Malcolm. He reconnected with God and stepped out on a pathway of repentance and rebuilding. He made friends with his children again and even talked with his ex-wife. He ventured out to Alcoholics Anonymous meetings and became a regular at church once again. He still bore scars from his bad choices, but he was climbing toward health through the sturdy grace of God.

If we say that we have no sin, we deceive ourselves, and the truth is not in us. If we confess our sins, he who is faithful and just will forgive us our sins and cleanse us from all unrighteousness.

—1 John 1:8–9

Bad Choices

"Why me, God?" you ask.

And sometimes, just sometimes, he could answer, "Because you've made some very dumb decisions."

Please don't get the wrong idea. Misfortune is not always your fault. Job's friends assumed that it was, and they were wrong. Perhaps you've gathered enough from this book so far to understand that we don't always deserve the tragedies we face. So you shouldn't automatically feel guilty when things go wrong. And don't go picking on others when they are in trouble.

But *sometimes* we do bring the pain on ourselves. Like Malcolm, we can make bad choices that lead us away from healthy ways of life and propel us toward self-destruction. We rationalize, excuse ourselves, and pooh-pooh the problems—sometimes so much that we blind ourselves to our own complicity. We feel victimized, and we are so self-righteous we fail to see that we have victimized ourselves. Sometimes.

Two ideas apply here that weave together through the Bible. We hit one of them head-on in the Book of Deuteronomy: "If you heed these ordinances, by diligently observing them, the Lord your God will maintain with you the covenant loyalty that he swore to your ancestors; he will love you, bless you, and multiply you.... The Lord will turn away from your every illness" (7:12–13, 15).

Live God's way and things will go well for you. That's the message. And the opposite is stated, too. Deuteronomy 28 describes this vividly, first listing all the types of blessings that befall those who obey God's law, and then turning to the downside: "But if you will not obey the Lord your God by diligently observing all his commandments and decrees, which

I am commanding you today, then all these curses shall come upon you" (v. 15). And the corresponding curses are spelled out.

This pattern was borne out in the history of Israel. We see a regular cycle in the Book of Judges and later in the Books of Chronicles. The nation is oppressed by enemies. God provides a leader who trusts God for deliverance—and the nation is restored to independence, power, or economic bounty. Things go well for a while, but then the nation drifts away from God. The people forget that he is the source of their blessings. They worship false gods. They sink into sin. The rich oppress the poor. And so God allows a new enemy to threaten them. In desperation, the people cry out to the Lord again, and the cycle repeats. Trouble–trust–deliverance–peace–complacency–sin–trouble.

Have you ever seen that cycle in your life? Many have. Most of us admit that we turn to God most passionately in times of need. After he restores our fortune, we often forget about him.

Is tragedy something that God sends to force us to turn to him? You might see it like that, but the underlying scriptural message is quite different. Throughout Scripture we see that sin carries its own penalty. When we live according to the guidelines set forth by our Creator, life goes well. We are functioning according to the manufacturer's specifications, so to speak. But when we violate those guidelines, things go wrong.

Malcolm, for instance, walked out on his relationship commitments and then—surprise—he suffered from the lack of committed relationships. He failed to give his employer the effort he was being paid for, and suddenly he wasn't getting paid anymore. He partied all night and felt tired all day. For the most part, the troubles he faced could be directly attributed to the choices he made. No need for God to zap him for being bad; he was getting zapped by the natural results of his behavior.

There was a sixth-grade teacher who seemed to know only one Bible verse. At least it was the only one he seemed to quote: "Be sure your sin will find you out"(Numbers 32:23). He used it as a scare tactic in those many cases where some kid had pulled a prank, but he didn't know who. With this favorite verse he tried to strike the fear of God in his students' hearts. Some of the students, in turn, had images of heavenly detectives sorting through clues to uncover all their sins.

A better interpretation is that it's the sin itself that "finds you out." Sin grows, and eventually it becomes too big to hide. Sin captivates you and controls you. Certainly Malcolm had that experience.

> If I sin, what do I do to you, you watcher of
>   humanity?
> Why have you made me your target?
> Why have I become a burden to you?
> Why do you not pardon my transgression
>   and take away my iniquity?
> **—Job 7:20–21**

Trust in the Lord with all your heart,
and do not rely on your own insight.
In all your ways acknowledge him,
and he will make straight your paths.
Do not be wise in your own eyes;
fear the Lord, and turn away from evil.
—Proverbs 3:5–7

A Prayer of Confession

A reminder: This prayer might not be necessary in your case. Sure, we all have sins to confess, but it's very possible that your current suffering has not resulted from anything you have done. Sort through it, and if this is an issue for you, a prayer like this might help get things squared away with God.

Dear Lord,

Now that I think about it, I have made some mistakes. I've opted for some selfish choices, and I've had some out-of-control moments. Maybe the trouble I face now stems, in part, from those sins. I don't understand it

all, but maybe that's part of it. And if so, then I confess those sins before you. I need to confess my sins
anyway, but I guess I need to face up to them, to take
responsibility for at least some of the problems I'm
facing as well. I am sorry for these actions that have
displeased you. Please forgive me, and give me the
strength to avoid those same sins in the future.

So what do we do now? I trust in your forgiveness,
and I trust in the power of your Spirit. Help me to
rebuild my life, based on this trust. I don't know if you
will choose to take away my trouble, but at least give
me strength to get through it, for your glory.

Amen.

Accepting Blame

I spend my time looking for someone to blame.
My heart can no longer ignore it.
Someone must answer for my senseless pain;
Someone's responsible for it.

I rage in the night at invisible foes,
But when the day dawns I can see.
A lot of my problems, as far as I know,
Come back to the culprit. That's me.

I still wonder how things went dreadfully bad,
And whether I've earned all this trouble.
But now that I see all the choices I've had,
It's no big surprise that I've struggled.

I now bow before you, my Lord and my King,
Confessing the errors I've made.
Forgive me, I beg you, for each evil thing,
And show me the ways that I've strayed.

I need your redeeming. Please pay off my debt.
Restore me to your kind of life.
Lord, could you perhaps just forgive and forget
By applying your Son's sacrifice?

✝ ✝ ✝

Manufacturer's Instructions

One year as a Christmas gift, Charlie received a coffee grinder. For several months he used it to grind coffee beans, and he enjoyed the fresh-tasting coffee. Then he thought that maybe it could grind other things—say, broccoli. Yes, that's right, he tried it. It wasn't pretty. In fact, it was downright disgusting. He had to work at least a week to get the broccoli goop out of the grinder. And even then, the morning blend had a subtle hint of vegetables.

Charlie was using a product in a way the manufacturer had not intended. The grinder was made for coffee, not broccoli. In the same way, we were created to live a certain way. "We are what he has made us, created in Christ Jesus for good works, which God prepared beforehand to be our way of life" (Ephesians 2:10). When we violate those intentions, we create a mess.

You might recall the commandment that says, "Honor your father and your mother"—but there is more: "so that your days may be long in the land that the Lord your God is giving you" (Exodus

20:12). In other words, do what your parents say, and you'll live longer. Is that some magical blessing God drops upon us? Not necessarily. You could probably list a dozen bits of advice your parents gave you that, in very practical ways, have lengthened your life—or kept you from shortening it. Everything from "Don't smoke" to "Look both ways before you cross the street." Most children derive clear benefits from obeying their parents. You can see how that might help you live longer.

And we find the same sort of childlike simplicity in the Book of Proverbs:

> The Lord's curse is on the house of the
> wicked,
> but he blesses the abode of the righteous.
> Toward the scorners he is scornful,
> but to the humble he shows favor.
> **—Proverbs 3:33–34**

Here are the manufacturer's guidelines: Your life works best when you follow these instructions. If Proverbs were the only book of the Bible, we would expect a world in which obedience always brought practical blessings. The righteous would prosper, and the wicked would fall. But we know it doesn't always work like that. Go forward or backward in the Bible, and you find the hard truth of the matter. The psalmist complains:

> For I was envious of the arrogant;
>   I saw the prosperity of the wicked.
> For they have no pain;
>   their bodies are sound and sleek.
> They are not in trouble as others are;
>   they are not plagued like other people.
> **—Psalm 73:3–5**

Is this a contradiction? Hardly. When we understand the Book of Proverbs for what it is, the inconsistency begins to make sense. It's a textbook, an ABC of moral instruction. The book is addressed to "my child," and it presumably was used to train young-sters. Even today, children are taught in black and white. This is good; that's bad. A few generations ago, *Romper Room* taught children how to behave with the "Do Bee" and "Don't Bee." Kids are quick to distinguish between good and bad. Gray areas are harder to grasp.

So you say to your children, "Do your homework, and you'll get good grades." Generally that's true, but there are exceptions. You teach your youngsters that "cheaters never prosper," and in the long run that's certainly true. But somewhere along the line the world gets more complicated. A student will study all night and still fail the test. Another student will cheat and get a better grade. It's not always as easy as Proverbs makes it sound.

Why should any who draw breath complain
    about the punishment of their sins?
Let us test and examine our ways,
    and return to the Lord.
Let us lift up our hearts as well as our hands
    to God in heaven.
We have transgressed and rebelled,
    and you have not forgiven.
—Lamentations 3:39–42

The Beginning of Wisdom

"The fear of the Lord is the beginning of wisdom" (Proverbs 9:10). That's the theme sentence of Proverbs. Everything else in the book basically describes the "wisdom" of the one who fears the Lord. Fearing the Lord means knowing that God sees our behavior and cares about it, enough to punish or reward us for it when appropriate. That is indeed the beginning of wisdom—but just the beginning. It can start us off, but we need much more than that to live our lives wisely.

Proverbs is one of five books commonly known as the "Wisdom Literature" of the Bible. The others are Job, Psalms, Ecclesiastes, and Song of Songs. As we've seen, the Book of Job involves an upright man who suffered precisely *because* he feared the Lord. Several of the psalms decry the success of the wicked. And Ecclesiastes is downright cynical. The author, obviously jaded, questions the value of everything, including hard work and religious devotion.

Apparently wisdom begins with the God-fearing behavior described in Proverbs, but wisdom grows as we recognize the trials the righteous, such as Job, often face. It grows as we learn to put our hope in God, despite the temporary success of those who flout his commands. God sets those people in "slippery places" (Psalm 73:18). For the moment they are standing tall, but it's only a matter of time before they fall. Wisdom continues to grow as we understand (from Ecclesiastes) that every human pursuit will fail to give ultimate meaning. Such meaning is only found in a relationship with the Creator. "Remember your creator in the days of your youth" (Ecclesiastes 12:1).

And there's one more wisdom book: Song of Songs. This is a beautiful love poem describing the relationship between a king and a beloved slave girl. At one level, it is a celebration of the love between a man and a woman. But people have always interpreted Song of Songs at another level too, as an allegory of God's love for his people. This too is a kind of wisdom: a loving relationship with God, a relationship in which we give and receive forgiveness, in which we don't always understand the other, but we remain committed.

Earlier, we said there were two strands of teaching interwoven through Scripture. The first is the basic arrangement that righteousness brings blessing and evil leads to ruin. Within that arrangement, we do right because we're afraid of the consequences of doing wrong. This "fear of the Lord" is the beginning of wisdom, as Proverbs tells us, but the rest of Scripture challenges us to take further steps, to get past the beginner level and into a committed, complex love. This is the second strand, the overwhelming power of a loving relationship with God. As John says, "Perfect love casts out fear" (1 John 4:18). When we fear the Lord, we know that God sees what we do and cares about it. When we *love* the Lord, all of that is still true, but now *we* care how he feels about our behavior—not because we're afraid of getting punished, but because we want to make him happy. "Fear has to do with punishment," John goes on to say, "and whoever fears has not reached perfection in love. We love [him] because he first loved us" (1 John 4:18–19).

"O my dove, in the clefts of the rock,
      in the covert of the cliff,
let me see your face,
      let me hear your voice;
for your voice is sweet,
      and your face is lovely.
Catch us the foxes,
      the little foxes,
that ruin the vineyards—
      for our vineyards are in blossom."

My beloved is mine and I am his;
      he pastures his flock among the lilies.
—Song of Songs 2:14–16

✛　✛　✛

Sorting Through Fear and Love

So let's apply all of this wisdom literature to the current crisis. We begin with the fear of the Lord, as in Proverbs. Understanding that bad behavior brings bad results, you might want to sort through your recent behavior. Have you brought any part of your troubles upon yourself through unwise, ungodly actions? This is a tricky question to answer, since personal tragedies can create a lot of false guilt. If you get beaten down enough, you'll confess to anything. This step really requires a careful sorting. It is quite possible that you, like Job, are innocent, that you have *not* brought your sufferings on yourself. But if you *can* identify bad actions that have resulted in bad consequences, that might just be the first step toward restoration.

Suppose you find some way in which you are responsible for your own troubles.

What can you do about that? Feel guilty?

Well, yes. For about an hour. Feelings of guilt have a purpose: to make us aware of our own misbehavior. But once we're aware, they've done their job. There's no need to wallow in guilt once you've taken proper responsibility. The fear of the Lord might induce feelings of guilt, but the love of the Lord inspires us to bring our guilt to him. *Whatever sin you've committed, Jesus died for it.* God longs to forgive your sin, if you'll let him.

So let your feelings of guilt drive you to your knees, begging forgiveness from your heavenly Father. And then let go of those feelings, because God lets go of your sin. "As far as the east is from the west, so far he removes our transgressions from us" (Psalm 103:12).

As you sort through your situation and claim some responsibility, you might find that you have wronged someone else. Try to make things right with that person. Apologize, seek forgiveness, and see if there's any way to undo the damage. Accept the fact that this relationship might be forever changed, but do what you can to make peace.

Malcolm, for instance, realized he had wronged his wife, and in his efforts at restoration, he told her so. They would never be a couple again, and it would be difficult to be friends in any active sense, but at least they could coexist at their daughters' graduations, weddings, and other family occasions.

You might also be facing ongoing consequences of your behavior in your own life. Excessive drinking might have left you with liver disease. A gambling addiction might have wiped out your life savings.

And maybe you'll just have to accept those consequences. But the Lord promises that his mercies are
"new every morning" (Lamentations 3:23). Sometimes he chooses to reveal his grace by undoing the
natural results of our sin. You can pray for that, but
you should also look for ways that you can grow,
troubles and all, into a vibrant new relationship with
your loving Lord.

> Set me as a seal upon your heart,
>   as a seal upon your arm;
> for love is strong as death,
>   passion fierce as the grave.
> Its flashes are flashes of fire,
>   a raging flame.
> Many waters cannot quench love,
>   neither can floods drown it.
> If one offered for love
>   all the wealth of one's house,
>   it would be utterly scorned.
> **—Song of Songs 8:6–7**

✢   ✢   ✢

To every thing there is a season, and a time
    to every purpose under the heaven:
A time to be born, and a time to die; a time
    to plant, and a time to pluck up that
    which is planted;
A time to kill, and a time to heal; a time to
    break down, and a time to build up;
A time to weep, and a time to laugh; a time
    to mourn, and a time to dance;
A time to cast away stones, and a time to
    gather stones together; a time to
    embrace, and a time to refrain from
    embracing;
A time to get, and a time to lose; a time to
    keep, and a time to cast away;
A time to rend, and a time to sew; a time to
    keep silence, and a time to speak;
A time to love, and a time to hate; a time of
    war, and a time of peace.
—Ecclesiastes 3:1–8, KJV

Prescription

Consider the possibility that you are suffering, at least in part, from your own sin. Maybe not, but if you are, confess that sin to God, and claim his forgiveness. Look for any ways your sin has hurt others, and try to make things right with them. Then work with God to rebuild your life.

Passing the Test

Are You Prepared to Make the Grade?

*D*ave was the youngest son of a well-to-do rancher, which meant he had to do all the dirty work—and it got real dirty. While his older brothers were learning how to run the ranch they would someday inherit, young Dave was stuck tending sheep. That gave him some time to think, to pray, and to sing, but he sure didn't seem to have much of a future to dream about. Sometimes he wondered why God would let him waste his talents on these woolly wanderers.

One day, a bear stepped out of the woods and made a run at some of his sheep. Dave was there in an instant, guiding his sheep to safety. It wasn't that he cared so much for the lambs' well-being—they'd be in someone's stew next spring—but he didn't want to be responsible for losing his father's investment. When you leave with 100 sheep, you'd better come back with 100 or more. His dad could be a real bear about that, so to speak.

And there was the actual bear, still lumbering toward Dave. He heard a chorus of bleating from the flock as he searched for available ammo. Picking up five rocks, he fired them at the beast, felling it.

Later that night, over bear stew, he pondered the events of the day. Not only had God seemed to forget him, leaving him out in the fields alone, but now God was actively threatening him, sending a wild creature to battle with him. What was going on? How could he ever sleep under the stars again, knowing that the night was full of terrors and the day just as dangerous?

> O Lord of hosts, you test the righteous,
> you see the heart and the mind.
> —**Jeremiah 20:12**

Suddenly he had a revelation. What if the Lord was acting as a shepherd, protecting Dave along with his sheep? What if God had given Dave the power to fend off the bear? Wasn't it true that God had always provided for him? And whenever Dave got too depressed about his dead-end job, God had granted him some insight, some image, some shred of a song, and that would somehow restore his soul.

Perhaps Dave had needed some excitement at this point in life—and God had provided it by means of a bear. What if Dave needed some confidence? What if he needed to learn that the Lord would always provide available ammo? Could this trying situation have been a testing experience? If that was the case, it wasn't evidence that God had forsaken Dave. On the contrary, it was testimony to God's continuing presence. He would be with Dave, helping the young shepherd do what had to be done.

Dave wrote a song about this. Perhaps you've heard it: "The Lord is my shepherd, I shall not want."

A Prayer for Times of Testing

O Lord, I'm not sure what I'm supposed to be learning through all this, but I'll try to be a willing student. I feel as if I'm failing this test. My faith isn't strong enough. My hope isn't great enough. And it's been a long time since I've seen any joy. But I'm hoping this test is more about your ability to help me than my ability to pass it.

Give me clarity of vision to see what's going on.

Give me an alert mind to understand your ways.

Give me a heart big enough to embrace both pain and encouragement.

And please keep teaching me, because right now I'm feeling pretty dumb.

I rest in your grace. I trust in your power. I long for your wisdom.

Amen.

✢   ✢   ✢

I also know that you are enduring patiently and bearing up for the sake of my name, and that you have not grown weary. But I have this against you, that you have abandoned the love you had at first. Remember then from what you have fallen; repent, and do the works you did at first.
—**Revelation 2:3–5**

A Giant Challenge

Years later, David's dad summoned him in from the fields: Somebody had to take sandwiches over to David's older brothers, who were serving in the army. This mundane task was an insult. While his brothers sought glory on the battlefield, David was forced to stay home and mind the ranch. That was bad enough, but now he had to play delivery boy. Why would God prepare him if he'd never have a chance to act?

But when he reached the camp, David saw a familiar sight. There was a bear of a man standing in the valley, snarling up at the troops, who were cowering on the ridge. "Who will come and fight me?" the warrior was saying. He was easily nine feet tall.

David's brothers, so full of bravado at home, gave no answer to the giant. Everyone looked for someone else to respond to the challenge. Maybe this was David's big chance. He volunteered to fight the foul-mouthed Philistine.

You know the story. The king tried to put his armor on the shepherd boy, but it didn't fit. Nevertheless, David said, "The Lord, who saved me from the paw of the lion and from the paw of the bear, will save me from the hand of this Philistine" (1 Samuel 17:37). Then he stepped into the valley, picked up five smooth stones for his slingshot, and sent one into the giant's skull.

He was now a champion, God's champion, and a celebrity. After all those lonely nights of wondering what God was up to, he now knew he'd been tested, smelted, prepared for greatness. This was his moment. Or was it?

Even though a secret ceremony had anointed David as the next king, the current king was still in power, and he was none too happy about David's new fame. One day David was in the king's parlor, playing soothing music on his lyre, when a spear came whizzing past his head. Apparently the music wasn't soothing enough. The king had tried to kill him.

So David set off through the crags and canyons of the Judean Desert and on the run from the murderous King Saul. For years he traipsed through this difficult terrain, pursued by all the king's men, never knowing whether this day would be his last.

Why, God, why? Why fame and fortune followed by fury and flight? "Even now they lie in wait for my life," David wrote. "The mighty stir up strife against me. For no transgression or sin of mine, O Lord, for no fault of mine, they run and make ready. Rouse yourself, come to my help and see!" (Psalm 59:3–4).

Funny thing, though. Those desert canyons weren't far from his hometown of Bethlehem. David might have played there as a boy. Perhaps he had searched through those caves himself for an errant sheep.

Maybe God had been preparing David even then for this challenge.

One day, David sensed the king's soldiers close behind him. He doubled back and waited for them to encamp for the night. Creeping into the cave where the king slept, David stood over the man who was making his life miserable. Should he kill him and take the throne for himself? David had been taking a major test, and this was the essay question. Should David take matters into his own hands or trust God and continue the struggle? No one would blame him if he plunged his sword into his snoring tormentor.

But no, Saul was still God's anointed king. David's time would come. God had led him this far—God could be trusted to keep leading him. David cut off the corner of the king's robe as a souvenir and stole out of the cave.

David was tested, and he passed.

Years later, after Saul was slain in battle with the Philistines, David took the throne. He united the tribes of Israel, established Jerusalem as the capital, and further made the city the central place of worship. David wasn't perfect, but God had prepared him well to lead this flock.

Of course, that didn't mean that everything ran smoothly in David's life. Many years later, when David had become the old king, his troubled son Absalom launched a rebellion against him. Now David was watching a younger, more popular prince stake a claim to the throne. Perhaps he could have chased his son through the desert canyons, but no. As Absalom's forces approached, King David packed up and left his capital city. He knew he could trust God, even in this trying time. "If I find favor in the eyes of the Lord," he said, "he will bring me back" (2 Samuel 15:25).

As it happened, the well-coiffed Absalom got his hair caught in a tree, which led to his death. David wept for his rebellious son, but he retook the throne. Throughout his life, David faced many troubles such as this, and in most cases he maintained his trust in God. It was never easy, and the many psalms he wrote leave us a record of his inner struggles. It is evident that God was testing him, refining him, shaping him into the kind of king he wanted on Israel's throne.

✛   ✛   ✛

And I will...refine them as one refines silver,
and test them as gold is tested.
They will call on my name,
and I will answer them.
I will say, "They are my people";
and they will say, "The Lord is our God."
—Zechariah 13:9

✛   ✛   ✛

Multiple Choice

In the same way, your troubles might be tests. In the previous chapter, we considered the notion that your own sins might have caused your problems, but it doesn't always work like that. The Bible shows us the examples of Job, Joseph, Ruth, David, and others who suffered tragedy through no special fault of their own. They weren't perfect, but it was clear that their struggles weren't of their own making.

That may be the case with you. If you've sorted through your situation and still find that your troubles seem undeserved, consider a new possibility. Maybe God is testing you, refining you, or preparing you.

A history teacher in high school announced that there would be a test next week, and, of course, the class groaned. The teacher said, "Maybe I shouldn't call it a test. No, it's a 'learning experience.'" But he could not fool his students. The change in terminology made it sound better, but they still had to study for that learning experience. That became the class joke for the rest of the year.

"How did you do on that history test?"

"No, you mean the learning experience."

"Whatever. I still bombed it."

But that teacher had a point. Tests are difficult, yet they can also be good for you—if you learn from them. The same is true of the life tests we go through. They can be learning experiences, helping us grow and preparing us for something greater.

You might say these are multiple-choice tests. What are your options?

Well, your first possibility when faced with difficulties is to take the advice of Job's wife. She had seen her family carried off, her wealth lost, and her husband contract an embarrassing disease. As she walked out the door, she suggested, "Curse God, and die" (Job 2:9).

No one said it was *good* advice, but it's one option that many take. They curse God by turning away from him, by quitting church, by holding a grudge. And there is something redundant about this advice because cursing God is itself a kind of death. To reject that life-giving relationship with God is to put oneself in a spiritual coma.

The response of Job's wife is very similar to that of Naomi. The Book of Ruth gives us a story of bereavement in a time of great need. During a famine, Naomi moved with her husband and two sons from Bethlehem to the neighboring land of Moab. There her sons married local women, but soon all three of the men died, leaving Naomi and her daughters-in-law with no means of support. Naomi thought it best to return to Bethlehem, where her extended family might take her in. To her surprise, one daughter-in-law, Ruth, joined her.

What was Naomi's response to her situation? She told her old friends in Bethlehem, "Call me Mara [which means *bitter*], for the Almighty has dealt bitterly with me" (Ruth 1:20).

Many people today go Naomi's way. Not only do they mourn their losses—

> Search me, O God,
>   and know my
>   heart;
> test me and
>   know my
>   thoughts.
> See if there is any
>   wicked way in
>   me,
>   and lead me in
>   the way
>   everlasting.
> **—Psalm 139:23–24**

nothing wrong with that—but they redefine themselves in the process. That's what bitterness is, a new way of understanding oneself and the world by squeezing out all hope. There's no future in it. Things are bad, and they always will be. That's when they just give up.

But things weren't all bad for Naomi. There was one ray of hope she was ignoring: her daughter-in-law. Ruth had left her own extended family in Moab to be with Naomi, and she would eventually turn Naomi's fortunes around.

When you choose the Naomi response to your test, renaming yourself as a bitter person, you can overlook the tiny blessings God still provides.

Ruth went through virtually the same crisis. Like Naomi, she was a widow, but instead of making complaints, she made a commitment. She didn't dwell on her loss; she devoted herself to love. In a way, she redefined herself, too—except she was taking the name of Naomi's daughter, an adopted Israelite, a follower of God.

This has little to do with "looking on the bright side." This wasn't the power of positive thinking. Ruth wasn't denying her grief. She just saw that her future lay not in self-pity but in self-sacrifice; not in loss but in love.

My brothers and sisters, whenever you face trials of any kind, consider it nothing but joy, because you know that the testing of your faith produces endurance; and let endurance have its full effect, so that you may be mature and complete, lacking in nothing.

If any of you is lacking in wisdom, ask God, who gives to all generously and ungrudgingly, and it will be given you.
—James 1:2–5

All the way my Savior leads me—
cheers each winding path I tread,
Gives me grace for ev'ry trial,
feeds me with the living bread.
Though my weary steps may falter
and my soul athirst may be,
gushing from the rock before me,
lo! A spring of joy I see.

—FANNY CROSBY

✦ ✦ ✦

Garden Groans

There are probably many more possible answers on this multiple-choice test, but let's look at just one more: Jesus' answer. As he approached Jerusalem in the last spring of his ministry, he knew exactly what he was walking into. He told his disciples, "See, we are going up to Jerusalem, and the Son of Man will be handed over to the chief priests and scribes, and they will condemn him to death" (Matthew 20:18). He rode a donkey into the city, where he was met by adoring crowds. After a few days of teaching in the Temple, fielding questions, and facing his foes, he celebrated a quiet Passover with his disciples. Then he went to the Garden of Gethsemane to pray.

Jesus wasn't just facing death—he was facing the full force of death that had enslaved all humanity. It wasn't just pain, but the weight of the world's sin. The Gospels tell us "his sweat became like great drops of blood" (Luke 22:44). He had previously talked about the "cup of suffering" and asked his disciples if they were ready to drink it. Now it was held up for him to drink. In this time of agonizing decision, he prayed, "Father, if you are willing, remove this cup from me; yet, not my will but yours be done" (Luke 22:42).

Not my will but yours be done. We will never know the full extent of Jesus' suffering, but we know he came to this testing point. He refused to give the answer of Job's wife, "Curse God, and die." Nor did he take Naomi's option, "Call me Bitter." But don't overlook the fact that he didn't want to suffer. He ached to have this cup taken away. We don't need to feel guilty in asking God to remove our suffering, to make our lives better. Jesus did exactly that, but he didn't stop there. He set the priorities straight. *Not my will but yours be done.* He ultimately trusted his father's plan.

So, what answer are you giving on this multiple-choice test?

a. Curse God, and die. (Job's wife)
b. Call me Bitter. (Naomi)
c. I commit myself to love. (Ruth)
d. Your will be done. (Jesus)

Obviously *c* is great, and *d* is even better. Get past your anger and bitterness. Respond to loss with love. Turn self-pity into willing self-sacrifice. If you can do all that, you can pass this test . . . er, rather, this learning experience.

Beloved, do not be surprised at the fiery ordeal that is taking place among you to test you, as though something strange were happening to you. But rejoice insofar as you are sharing Christ's sufferings, so that you may also be glad and shout for joy when his glory is revealed.
—1 Peter 4:12–13

Prescription

• Avoid the tendency to "curse God and die," holding a grudge against God that shuts him out of your life. You need him now more than ever.

• Do not let circumstances redefine you as a bitter person. Circumstances might be bitter, but you must remain open to hope.

• Open your heart to others and to God, as Ruth did. Commit yourself to love, even in the midst of this trying time.

• You can ask God to make life easier, but be aware that he might say no. Pray with Jesus, "Not my will, but yours be done."

Wounded Healers

God Can Use Our Hurts to Help Others

Nadia's mother passed away too soon. In her early 50s, she had always brimmed with energy, but then cancer appeared, and within a year she was gone. Nadia took it hard, especially that first Christmas. The family got together as usual, but their mom's absence put a damper on the whole holiday.

By the following autumn, Nadia had gotten through the worst of her grieving. Of course, she missed her mother terribly, but she was getting on with her life. Then she began talking with her pastor about starting a special service during the Christmas season, a service of grieving and remembrance for all those who had recently lost loved ones.

"Fine," said the pastor, who was already planning a dozen other Christmas events. "If you plan it, you can do it." So Nadia took on the task of planning this general memorial service: songs of comfort; lit candles; a brief talk by a church staff member who had recently lost her own father; and a chance for anyone present to offer words of remembrance. It was a beautiful time, and many people were helped—perhaps none more than Nadia herself, who had turned the pain of her mother's passing into a positive ministry to others.

This story could be retold in many ways about many people. Tamara was devastated by a divorce, but emerged years later to speak at divorce recovery seminars, helping others to endure what she had gone through. After a traffic accident, it took Bob years to relearn the simplest actions. He decided to become a physical therapist.

There are any number of more famous examples. After her husband was killed by terrorists on September 11, 2001, Lisa Beamer began writing and speaking to inspire others. A group of grieving mothers started Mothers Against Drunk Driving. You might know the speaker/singer/writer/artist Joni Eareckson Tada. Paralyzed in a diving accident, she devotes her life to helping others.

This is not just "turning lemons into lemonade." That's far too sweet a metaphor. These people, and many others like them, have suffered greatly, but somehow that suffering has empowered them to reach out. In each of these cases, a good thing has come from a bad thing. That doesn't make the bad things any less bad. It doesn't erase the pain. But it does accept the negative situation and transform it.

Bear one another's burdens, and in this way you will fulfill the law of Christ. For if those who are nothing think they are something, they deceive themselves.
—**Galatians 6:2–3**

Lord God,

I need your comfort. I need to feel your strong arms embracing me.

I don't need wise words or brilliant truth—just be there for me now.

Remind me of your love for me. Tell me every- thing's going to be all right.

Assure me again that you know what I'm going through, because you've been there.

You have felt my pain, and now you can share it.

Thank you for sitting with me through this crisis. I praise you for your awesome love.

Amen.

No Ordinary Joe

We also find this happening in the biblical story of Joseph. The second youngest of twelve sons of the patriarch Jacob, he was his daddy's favorite. In the blended family typical of that era, all of Joseph's older brothers were born to Jacob's first wife, Leah, or one of Jacob's concubines. Joseph was the first son of Jacob's most beloved wife, Rachel, who died during childbirth with Joseph's baby brother, Benjamin. Follow all that? In any case, Joseph was clearly favored over his older brothers, and they resented it.

He didn't help matters by telling them about the dreams he had in which his whole family bowed down to him. If you had to hear that sort of thing all the time, you might throw your brother into a pit, too. Yes, that's what the brothers did one day. They thought about killing him outright, but they ultimately decided to sell Joseph to a passing caravan as a slave. To cover themselves, the brothers told their father that Joseph had been killed by a wild animal.

That was just the beginning of Joseph's misfortunes. He was bought by an Egyptian householder named

Potiphar, who recognized a level of responsibility in Joseph and appointed him head of the servants. But Potiphar's wife lusted after Joseph. When he rebuffed her advances, she falsely accused him of attacking her. That landed him in jail.

Perhaps you've seen the Broadway musical based on this story, *Joseph and the Amazing Technicolor Dreamcoat*. In that show, the jailed Joseph sings a plaintive song—"Close Every Door"—bemoaning the injustice that has held him back, but also reaffirming his faith in God.

> This is the word of the Lord...: Not by might, nor by power, but by my spirit, says the Lord of hosts.
> **—Zechariah 4:6**

It's not hard to imagine Joseph feeling that way, but the Bible is strangely mum about his emotional state. All we know is that even prison couldn't keep this good man down. Rising to be an assistant to the warden, he became known as an interpreter of dreams, and he accurately predicted the release and restoration of the Pharaoh's cupbearer. Years later, when the Pharaoh himself had a disturbing dream, the cupbearer remembered Joseph. After brilliantly interpreting the dream, Joseph was given a position second in command in Egypt, overseeing a massive food collection and distribution program.

Later, Joseph's brothers came to Egypt seeking food. Joseph toyed with them at first, possibly enjoying their discomfort, but he eventually identified himself and reunited with his father. Then, to finish the whole story, he finally talked about his misfortunes. "Even though you intended to do harm to me, God intended it for good" (Genesis 50:20).

Don't get too wrapped up in the details of this verse. You could get into a dandy discussion over whether God *causes* bad things to happen, *allows* them to happen, or just *knows they will* happen. This book has tried to sidestep pronouncements along those lines, because we can't know. But in this verse Joseph wasn't talking about the bad things that *had* happened as much as the good things that resulted. He knew that his brothers acted out of awful motives, but he also saw God working in his life after every disaster—restoring, strengthening, massaging the situation. Good things can come out of bad things.

That's fine, you might say, as long as you're a spiritual giant. It takes a certain level of faith to be a Joseph or a Joni. To get through a life tragedy and use the experience to serve others—well, that's saint stuff, beyond the capability of ordinary Christians like us. Right?

Wrong.

✝   ✝   ✝

A Prayer for Wounded Healers

Lord, you know exactly what I have to offer, and it's not much. I've been struggling with the circumstances of my life, and sometimes that struggle has led me into some pretty dark moments. I've questioned you, I've doubted you, I've complained to you, I've scolded you. I'm amazed you still want to be friends, but I know you do.

I'm getting the feeling that you want me to serve you in some way, and that's just crazy. There are so many

others who can do much more for you—what could I
possibly do? I'm wounded. I'm spiritually limping.
How can I show anyone else how to run this race?

I'm willing to try. But it will have to be your power
working, not mine.

Amen.

✛   ✛   ✛

Not to us, O Lord, not to us, but to your name
   give glory,
for the sake of your steadfast love and your
   faithfulness.
—Psalm 115:1

✛   ✛   ✛

I cannot hope to help
Anyone else
When I need so much help
Myself.

Why Me, God?

My energies are sapped
In struggle
With my own mishaps
And troubles.

So do not look to me, my sister,
Go away, brother.
There's no way I can fix up
Another.

But now that you mention
Your condition
It makes me question
My position.

I'm certainly no healer
Absolutely, no.
But what you're feeling
I know.

The trial you're facing
I've gotten through,
And by God's grace
You can, too.

Bless the Lord, O my soul,
    and all that is within me,
    bless his holy name.
Bless the Lord, O my soul,
    and do not forget all his benefits—
who forgives all your iniquity,
    who heals all your diseases,
who redeems your life from the Pit,
    who crowns you with steadfast love and
        mercy,
who satisfies you with good as long as you
    live
    so that your youth is renewed like the
        eagle's.

.   .   .

He does not deal with us according to our
        sins,
    nor repay us according to our iniquities.
For as the heavens are high above the earth,
    so great is his steadfast love toward
        those who fear him;
as far as the east is from the west,
    so far he removes our transgressions
        from us.

As a father has compassion for his children,
    so the Lord has compassion for those
        who fear him.
For he knows how we were made;
    he remembers that we are dust.
—Psalm 103:1–5, 10–14

✛   ✛   ✛

A Thorny Problem

The apostle Paul had a problem. We're not sure exactly what it was. He called it his "thorn in the flesh," which makes us think it might have been a physical ailment of some kind. Some suggest he was going blind; others say he had epileptic fits. Whatever the case, Paul hated it. Calling it a "messenger of Satan," he prayed for its removal.

Three times he prayed to be free from this "thorn," and finally God answered him. But the answer was no. "My grace is sufficient for you," the Lord told him. "[My] power is made perfect in weakness" (2 Corinthians 12:9).

Let's try that again. "My power is made perfect in weakness." The word *perfect* refers to completion, fullness. That's a stunning idea. Wouldn't God's power be perfect already? Yet here he says that his own strength finds its completion in our weakness.

Have you ever used Christmas lights that operated on a serial circuit? You may remember the process of testing the strings of lights you put on your Christmas tree. If one bulb was out, the whole string was out. But if the bad bulb was replaced with a good one, the circuit would be completed, and the power would flow through.

That's the sense of God's statement to Paul. His power could flow through Paul's world only if Paul completed the circuit. The same is true in our world. If you're looking for God to act in your surroundings, you've got to let his power flow through you. And what is the qualification you need? What enables you to be the conduit of divine energy?

Weakness.

What is a lightbulb after all? It's a vacuum, an empty space with a path for the power to go through.

✝ ✝ ✝

Strong Words

Jesus came into a culture with two well-defined groups. One group studied the Scriptures and tried to follow them. They made it their job to be as righteous as possible. The other group knew they were in a losing battle. They could never be good enough for God.

Which of these two groups did the Son of God identify with, and which did he thoroughly criticize? Surprise! You might expect him to pat the "righteous" folks on the back and shun the "sinners," but, as a matter of fact, he did quite the opposite. Becoming known as a "friend of sinners," he railed against the religious leaders.

Why? He attacked their pride, their arrogance, their refusal to see how blind they were. They expected that they could take the kingdom of God by force, the sheer force of their holiness. But it's weakness that God rewards, it's humility, it's the awareness of God's grace. Where did we ever get the idea that God wants us to be more religious? No, he wants us to be more *reliant*. He's not looking for "strong Christians" to work with. He wants Christians who know how weak they are.

So if you feel wounded, scarred, and unable to do much for God—he has you exactly where he wants you. Seriously! His strength is completed in your weakness. You are the vacuum tube, the empty bulb showing forth the radiance of his power. He can use you precisely because of your weakness. When you accomplish great things for him, you will know (and everyone else will, too) that it's not through your power, but his.

There are all sorts of aptitude tests that people use to figure out what to do in life. They generally survey your strengths and direct you to a field that suits these abilities. But if we take Paul's thorn in the flesh seriously, we'll take a much different approach. What are your weaknesses? Where are your wounds? What are your struggles? When have you had to rely

most on God? This is your aptitude. This is how
God can use you.

Consider your own call, brothers and sisters:
not many of you were wise by human standards, not many were powerful, not many
were of noble birth. But God chose what is
foolish in the world to shame the wise; God
chose what is weak in the world to shame
the strong; God chose what is low and
despised in the world, things that are not, to
reduce to nothing things that are, so that no
one might boast in the presence of God. He
is the source of your life in Christ Jesus, who
became for us wisdom from God, and righteousness and sanctification and redemption, in order that, as it is written, "Let the one
who boasts, boast in the Lord."
—1 Corinthians 1:26–31

Chief of Staff

Think of Moses, the Israelite baby brought up in Pharaoh's court, the Prince of Egypt, who had to flee the country after defending an Israelite slave. After that he made his living as a nomadic shepherd. What a comedown! One day he's playing shuffle-board in the royal palace, and the next he's searching the Sinai Desert for adequate pasture.

But then he saw a strange phenomenon: a bush that was burning but wasn't consumed by the fire. The voice of God spoke to him from the shrubbery, calling him to set his people free. Of course, Moses had all sorts of excuses. He protested that he lacked the skills to do what God asked.

Then God asked, "What is that in your hand?"

It was a shepherd's staff, the tool of his distasteful new profession.

"Throw it on the ground," the Lord said. He wanted Moses to offer it before him. In modern slang, to "throw down" means to present what you've got, to lay your cards (or your weapons) on the table. That's what the Lord had in mind here. "Throw it down," God was saying, and Moses had to be hoping God would drop the subject. This staff was the symbol of everything that was wrong with his life.

Throw it down? he might have thought. *I want to throw it away, hide it, burn it. I wish I never saw it.*

Throw it down! Moses did, and God turned the staff into a snake. In Egyptian culture (which Moses knew well), the snake was a symbol of power. God turned Moses' weakness into something strong!

God is saying the same thing to you. Are you embarrassed by your struggle? Are you weary of your pain? Do you feel unqualified to be an active member of God's community? Are you held back by the trouble you have been facing?

Throw it down. Present it before God, and see how he will transform it.

You'll remember that Moses' story goes on after the burning bush. He confronted Pharaoh, requesting the release of his people. Pharaoh refused. Moses tried the staff-into-snake trick, but no one seemed very impressed. Nevertheless, he kept bugging Pharaoh (with real bugs), until God's final Passover miracle won the deliverance of Moses' people.

Moses led them out of Egypt, but Pharaoh changed his mind and sent the cavalry after them. The Red Sea lay before them, with Pharaoh's army behind. What could they do? Moses stretched out his arm over the sea and the waters parted, providing their passage to freedom. And what was in Moses' hand?

A staff.

The symbol of his weakness became the instrument for one of God's greatest miracles.

May I never boast of anything except the cross of our Lord Jesus Christ, by which the world has been crucified to me, and I to the world.
—Galatians 6:14

Prescription

Stop playing from your strengths, and start offering God your weakness. Whatever your struggle has been, see how God can use that for his purposes. He specializes in transforming bad situations into glorious ones. Throw down your troubles before him, and see what he makes of them.

Life Starts Now

It's a Matter of Quality,
Not Just Quantity

Maria had always tried to live the right way, but things kept falling apart for her. As a girl she went to church faithfully, and as a mother she took her kids to Sunday school each week. In one part of her mind she felt that God should recognize her strong morality and reward her for it. But in another part of her thinking, she was aware that she often fell short of God's standards.

When her marriage began to crumble, she was a mess. One day she'd be asking, "What did I do to deserve this?" The next day she'd be scolding *herself.* "Can't I do anything right?"

It was a painful breakup with fault on both sides, and it left Maria feeling unloved, unwanted, and very worried about her two kids. She tried to avoid bitterness, especially when the children went off to visit their father and his new love interest, but it was tough. Why couldn't he have had the same moral standards she had?

For a while there, Maria stopped going to church. What was the use of taking the children to Sunday school when they were spending every other weekend with their father? And at this point, sermons just made her feel guilty. She was already preaching to herself all day and all night—she didn't need any more of that. But after her dry spell, she was invited to visit a friend's church, one that offered forgiveness and hope. Jesus wanted a relationship with her, this church was saying. He didn't want to condemn her for her sins, but to forgive them.

> Christ in you, the hope of glory.
> —**Colossians 1:27**

Maria had a spiritual awakening. She grabbed the forgiveness that Jesus offered, began working on the process of forgiving herself, and even came to forgive her ex-husband. There was a new quality in her life. Energy. Awareness. Enthusiasm. The best word she had for it was *joy*. Over the next few years, she became more involved in the church, and she learned more about Jesus. She worked at parenting her children well, even teaming with their father to do so. She hit a crisis point when she lost her job, but she kept praying with her friends, and eventually she found a new career. She also met a man at church who was just as joyful as she was. They got married.

Just as she was delighting in this storybook solution to her personal crisis, she got the diagnosis. She had cancer. It was serious. She would need to go through an aggressive treatment of chemotherapy and radiation. Even then, she might not live.

> You show me the
> path of life.
> In your presence
> there is fullness
> of joy;
> in your right hand
> are pleasures
> forevermore.
> **—Psalm 16:11**

As you might expect, Maria was devastated by this news. Some of her old struggles came back—the questioning, the guilt. Had she done something to bring her illness on? Was she being punished? If not, why would God allow this, just when things were going so well?

Her body bore the physical battering of chemo and radiation, making her very weak. Maria was in and out of the hospital, and she often had to use a wheelchair. Her husband and kids rallied around her, but it was tough for them to see this woman they loved being ravaged by the disease and treatment.

But then the joy resurfaced. It was never really gone—there had just been a lot of things crowding in on it. Yet now, amid the pain and the sorrow of this possibly terminal illness, Maria began to smile and sing and share the certainty of her relationship with Christ. People around her began to notice her attitude, and they were drawn to this strangely joy-filled woman. When she started a Bible study group for people dealing with crisis, many people came.

As Maria saw it, everybody has a terminal illness: It's called humanity. Everyone will die, sooner or later. But Jesus gives us life, not just in the sweet by-and-by, but *now*. She could handle the pain of the cancer treatment because she knew she was already walking hand in hand with her Savior. If this was the road she would continue to walk, so be it. That gave her peace and satisfaction in a very trying time.

Be Still My Soul

Be still my soul: the Lord is on your side!
Bear patiently the cross of grief or pain;
leave to your God to order and provide—
in every change he faithful will remain.

Be still my soul; your best, your heavenly friend
through thorny ways leads to a joyful end.

Be still my soul: your God will undertake
to guide the future as he has the past;
your hope, your confidence let nothing shake—
all now mysterious shall be bright at last.

Be still my soul: the waves and winds still know
his voice who ruled them while he dwelt below.

—Katharina Amalia Dorothea von Schlegel
—(Translated by Jane Laurie Borthwick)

Quality and Quantity

You see, Maria no longer saw eternity as just a quantity of time. No, she saw it as a quality of life on earth. Jesus said, "I came that [we] may have life, and have it abundantly" (John 10:10). Abundantly! It's a picture of a cup overflowing with the waters of life. Our lives should be full right now, not just in heaven. And Maria caught sight of that.

She knew that life is not necessarily full of happiness. Suffering is a part of our lives, too. But rather than focusing on that suffering, we should be full of the awareness of God, the experience of God, the love of God. Even in times of pain and difficulty, we can be fully alive—feeling our feelings, storming the gates of heaven through prayer, keeping the dialogue going with God, getting refined, growing, helping others. "The glory of God," said second-century bishop Irenaeus, "is a person fully alive."

Irenaeus was no stranger to suffering himself. He lived in a time when Christians were being arrested and killed merely for being Christians. Many went to their martyrdom. These were not empty words for him or his fellow believers.

We know that God's kingdom is a future destination, but it is also a present reality. Jesus prayed, "Thy kingdom come," but he also told his followers, "The kingdom of God is among you" (Matthew 6:10; Luke 17:21).

✝ ✝ ✝

An Angel, Unaware

Greta had been depressed. Temporarily jobless, she was feeling worthless. Then things got worse. Someone plowed into her car at an intersection. Greta thanked God that she was unhurt, but she wasn't exactly pleased about this extra trauma, not to mention the hassle of dealing with insurance and car repair. *Sometimes you could do a better job of protecting me,* she silently accused God.

But an odd thing happened when she got out of the car. The driver who hit her was an elderly man on his way back from the doctor's office. Apologizing profusely, he explained to Greta that he must not have been concentrating because he had just received a terrible diagnosis. He was very ill.

Suddenly Greta's anger turned to concern. "I'm so sorry!" And there beside their damaged cars, with radiator steam rising to heaven, she told him, "I'll pray for you."

The man seemed genuinely touched. From the look on his face, Greta suspected that he might not have anyone else in his life who could comfort him with the power of prayer. She wasn't sure why, but somehow she felt better about this whole mess. She'd still be without wheels for a few days, but that was a small matter compared to the role she had just played. Greta had never really thought about herself this way, but she had been God's angel, delivering a message of comfort to a needy gentleman.

"What if God had given you a choice that morning?" a friend asked Greta later. "What if he said, 'Today you can give a man hope in his darkest hour, but in order to do that, you need to let him hit your car.' Would you have agreed to make that trade?"

It was a crazy question, and Greta wasn't quite sure how to answer. She didn't exactly want to put herself into harm's way, but she could see the good that came out of it. She began to recognize that instead of turning his back on her, God had been working for a greater good. The truth is that most of us would willingly endure some suffering if we knew there was a higher purpose to it. And God assures us that there is. He assures us that we are "called according to his purpose" (Romans 8:28). He employed Greta to show his love to a dying man, and he calls us to use our suffering for his glory—even though that might happen in some strange ways.

When we see our lives, in all their joys and sorrows, as part of our whole relationship with God, we bring eternal perspective and eternal priorities to each day. We begin to see God's hand working behind the scenes in both good and bad events. So when bad things happen and we're feeling the pain, we must keep looking for ways to honor God. Perhaps there is some way this struggle can help us grow, or inspire another struggler, or draw us closer to the heart of our Savior. Perhaps God's strength will be perfected in our weakness.

Suffering stinks; there's no way around it. As you deal with the harsh circumstances of your life, it's natural to cry out, "Why, God! Why me?" It doesn't seem fair; it doesn't seem right. And all your well-meaning friends who offer silver linings—they just don't get it. You are sitting alone on the trash heap, wondering how you got there. You're asking why God has turned down your prayers.

It may not always seem like it, but now is the time to see what God is going to do with you. Paul offered this prayer for the church in Ephesus.

> I pray that, according to the riches of his glory, he may grant that you may be strengthened in your inner being with power through his Spirit, and that Christ may dwell in your hearts through faith, as you are being rooted and grounded in love. I pray that you may have the power to comprehend, with all the saints, what is the breadth and length and height and depth, and to know the love of Christ that surpasses knowledge, so that you may be filled with all the fullness of God.

Now to him who by the power at work within us is able to accomplish abundantly far more than all we can ask or imagine, to him be glory in the church and in Christ Jesus to all generations, forever and ever. Amen.
—Ephesians 3:16–21

Is this prayer, written almost two thousand years ago, meant for you? Perhaps. God may be filling you with all of the necessary elements that lead you to the love of Christ and acceptance of the situation you face. The conditions of your life may improve, or they may not. But God is able to "accomplish abundantly far more than all we can ask or imagine," and that includes opening our hearts and minds to accepting his plan for our present circumstances. And, like Maria, whose struggle with cancer served as an example to her Bible study group, opening our hearts and minds to experiencing joy.

And this is my prayer, that your love may overflow more and more with knowledge and full insight to help you to determine what is best, so that in the day of Christ you may be pure and blameless, having produced the harvest of righteousness that comes through Jesus Christ for the glory and praise of God.
—Philippians 1:9–11

A Prayer to Live By

Dear Lord,

You know me, inside and out. You know how I'm dealing with this difficulty. You know what I'm doing right and wrong. You know my doubts and questions. You know the extent of my fragile faith.

When I cry myself to sleep, I know you hear me. When I lash out at others because of my own pain, I know you're there, too. And when I kneel before you in repentance and humility, I know you welcome me.

You promised life eternal, overflowing. That's what I want. Is there some way to bring me through these troubles in a way that brims with living? I must admit that sometimes I feel half-dead, but I need your energy flowing through me, your Spirit awakening my spirit. Let me radiate your presence to those around me. Let them see you living in me.

This I pray, in my struggling trust, clinging to the name of Jesus. Amen.

On the last day of the festival, the great day, while Jesus was standing there, he cried out, "Let anyone who is thirsty come to me, and let the one who believes in me drink. As the scripture has said, 'Out of the believer's heart shall flow rivers of living water.'"
—John 7:37–38

Prescription

As we go about living this life God has given us, let's review the prescriptions that have been offered throughout this book.

1. *Feel your feelings.* Allow yourself the normal ups and downs of this emotional roller coaster, but keep in touch with the Lord as you do.

2. *Make your case to God.* Keep the lines of communication open with God, even if you're angry. Listen for his response to you, and look for his gracious activity in your life.

3. *Understand that there are things you don't understand.* Let God keep teaching you who he really is.

4. *See how God is working his good purposes in your bad situation.* We can expect God to mix up good results even from the most painful ingredients, in this life or the next.

5. *Use this experience to understand God in a new way.* Let your heart be broken by the things that break the heart of God.

6. *Consider the possibility that you are suffering, at least in part, from your own sin.* You may not be, but if you are, confess that sin to God, and claim his forgiveness.

7. *Pass the test.* Avoid the tendency to "curse God and die" by refusing to redefine yourself as a bitter person, by opening your heart to others and to God, and by praying, "Not my will, but yours be done."

And finally...

8. *Stop playing from your strengths, and start offering God your weakness.* Whatever your struggle has been, see how God can use that for his purposes.